Volume 1

Written and Created by

Neil Gibson

Art by

Atula Siriwardane, Caspar Wijngaard,
Heru Prasetyo Djalal, Jan Wijngaard,
Ant Mercer, Dan West

Cover art by

Caspar Wijngaard

Lettering by
Jim Campbell

Layouts by
Eric Irving

T
PUB

Published in English in 2011 By T Pub
Copyright © T Pub. All rights reserved.
tpub.co.uk

ISBN (Print) 978-0-9569434-4-6
ISBN (Digital) 978-0-9569434-7-7

T Pub

CEO / Creative Director: Neil Gibson
Art Director: Caspar Wijingaard
Head of Operations: Ryan O'Sullivan
Marketing Manager: Will O'Mullane
Distribution (Print): Rafael Mondragón
Distribution (Digital): Dan Watters

To Louisa, for everything

This is a book by Neil Gibson, **not** Mel Gibson.
In any case of confusion here's how to tell the difference:

Mel Gibson

Neil Gibson

Mel Gibson is an actor.

Mel Gibson is good-looking.

Mel Gibson produced Passion of
the Christ and **made a fortune**.

Mel Gibson successfully broke into
his passion: acting.

Neil Gibson is a writer.

Neil Gibson is much better-look-
ing.

Neil Gibson financed this book on
his own and it **cost him a fortune**

Neil gibson successfully broke into
his passion: comics.

But, Neil needs your help. If you like Twisted Dark please pass it along
to others to read, and send Neil feedback, good or bad,

He promises that he will create characters in your honor if you help
him get better at making what we all love: **good** comics.

Foreword

The journey begins...

Firstly, thank you for reading this book. Comics are a huge passion of mine and whenever I see people reading one out in public, I have to stop myself from grinning like a kid. I usually fail.

At T Pub, we're lucky to get quite a lot of fan mail, which we LOVE receiving. It's great to know that we are pleasing people, and we like hearing what they want more of. However, people often refer to the Twisted Dark volumes as anthologies. I can see why they think that – it is a collection of short stories after all, but it concerns me a little because there's a bit more to it.

I really enjoy short stories. They're perfect for a commute or a short reading break. But I also like stories with involved longer arcs where you get to know the characters and see how they evolve. Twisted Dark is both of these. It is made up of self-contained short stories, however, right from the start I planned for the stories to connect, and some characters to develop through the volumes. Characters you may think are minor will appear again in the least expected of places.

Most people see about three connections in this first volume. You may see more, you may see less, but by the time you get to volume 3, the connections start becoming a lot more apparent. Indeed, someone in the studio finished volume 4 and went straight back to volume 2 to see if he was right about a connection. I heard a delighted 'Aha!' when he was proved right about spotting one. Again, I tried not to, but I grinned like a kid.

I hope that you enjoy the series and have fun spotting the links, because it is the connections that really make the journey more fun.

- Neil

Contents

Suicide...

Online chat rooms allow anonymity...

Complete anonymity.

You can tell strangers things you'd never reveal to your friends and family, releasing years of guilt, experiencing the catharsis of confession.

Or...

You can just talk about how you really feel.

Writer/Creator
Neil Gibson

Illustrator
Atula Siriwardane

www.tpub.co.uk

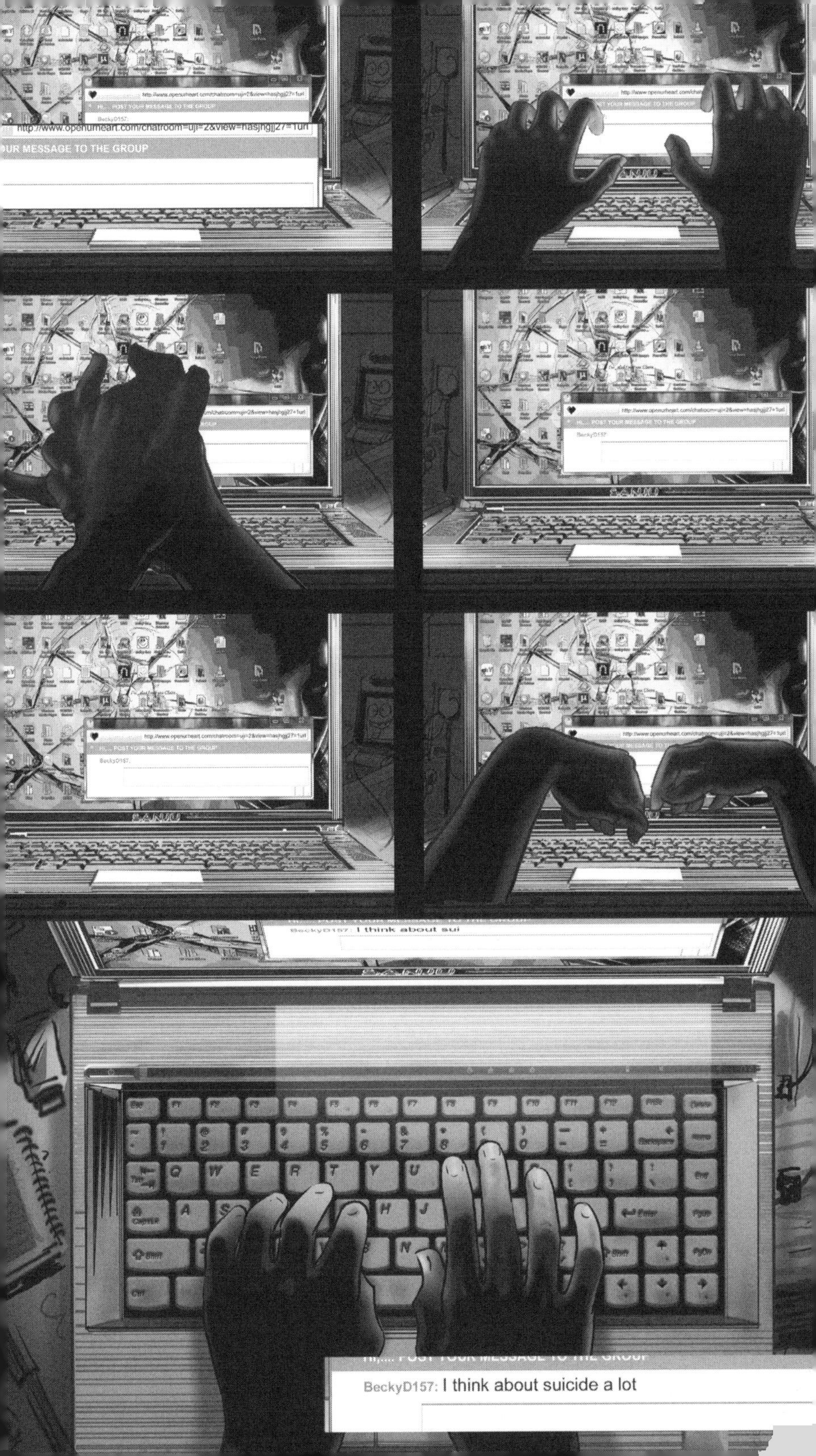
OUR MESSAGE TO THE GROUP
BeckyD157:
BeckyD157: I think about sui
BeckyD157: I think about suicide a lot

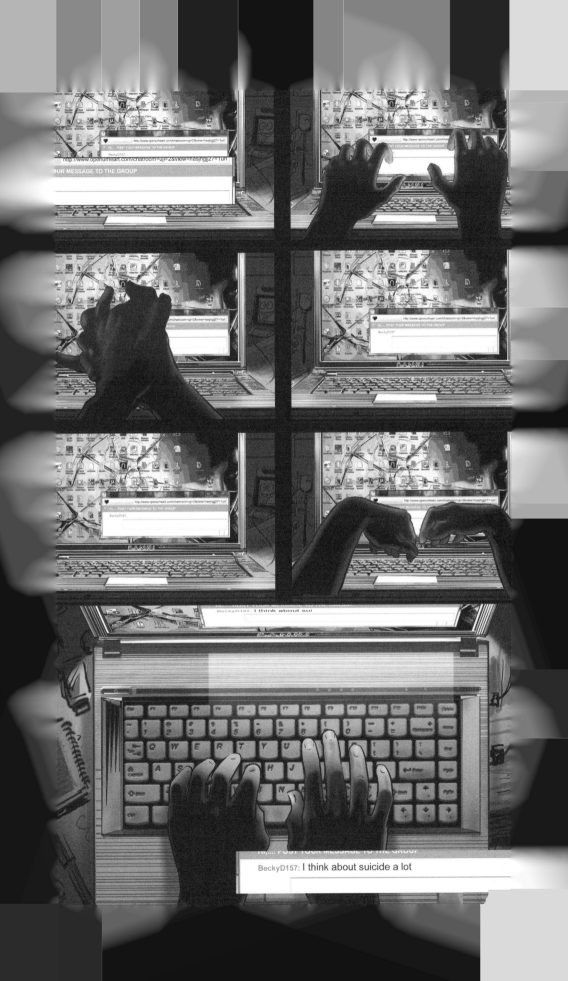

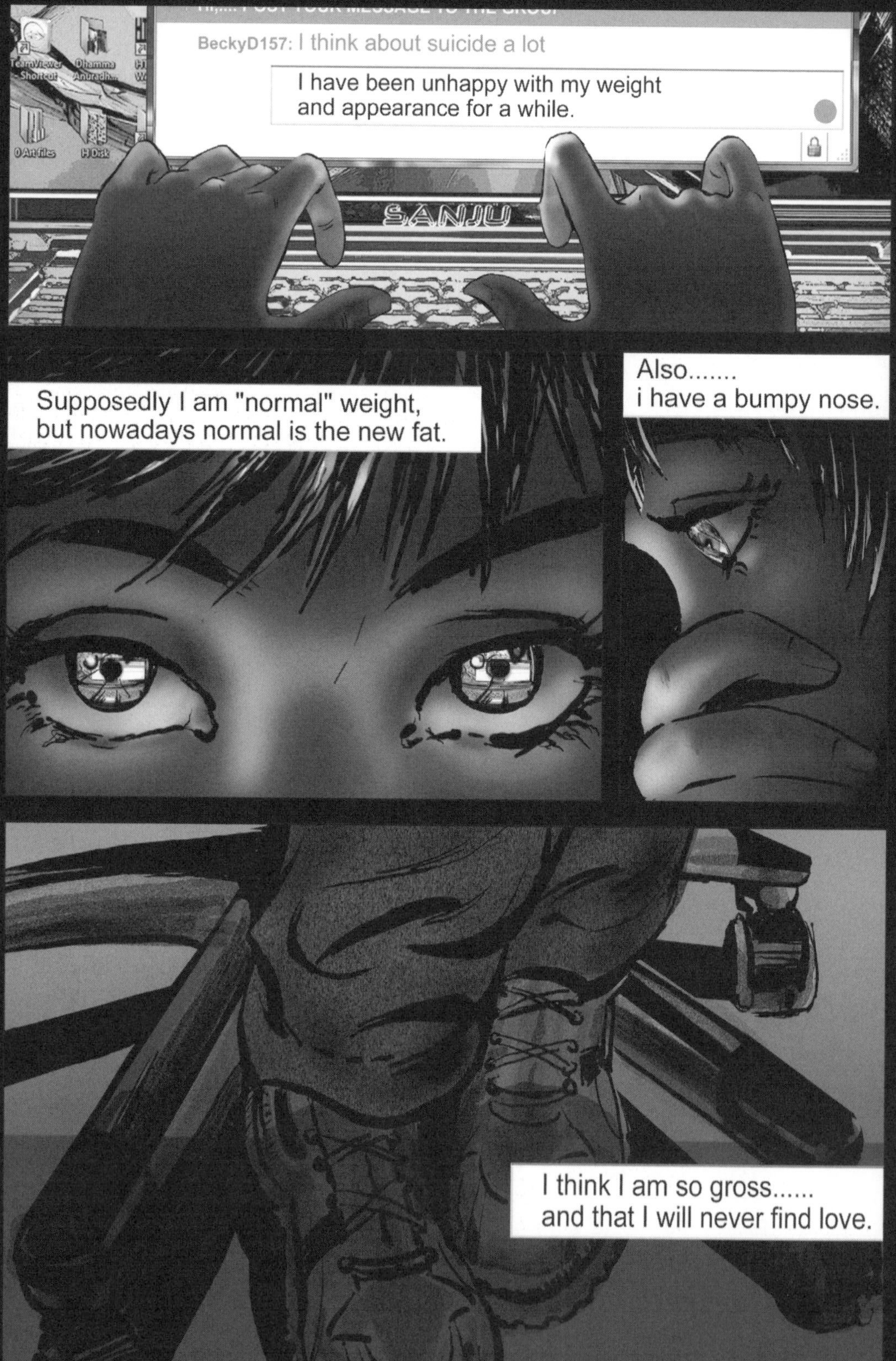
BeckyD157: I think about suicide a lot
I have been unhappy with my weight and appearance for a while.
SANJU
Supposedly I am "normal" weight, but nowadays normal is the new fat.
Also....... i have a bumpy nose.
I think I am so gross...... and that I will never find love.

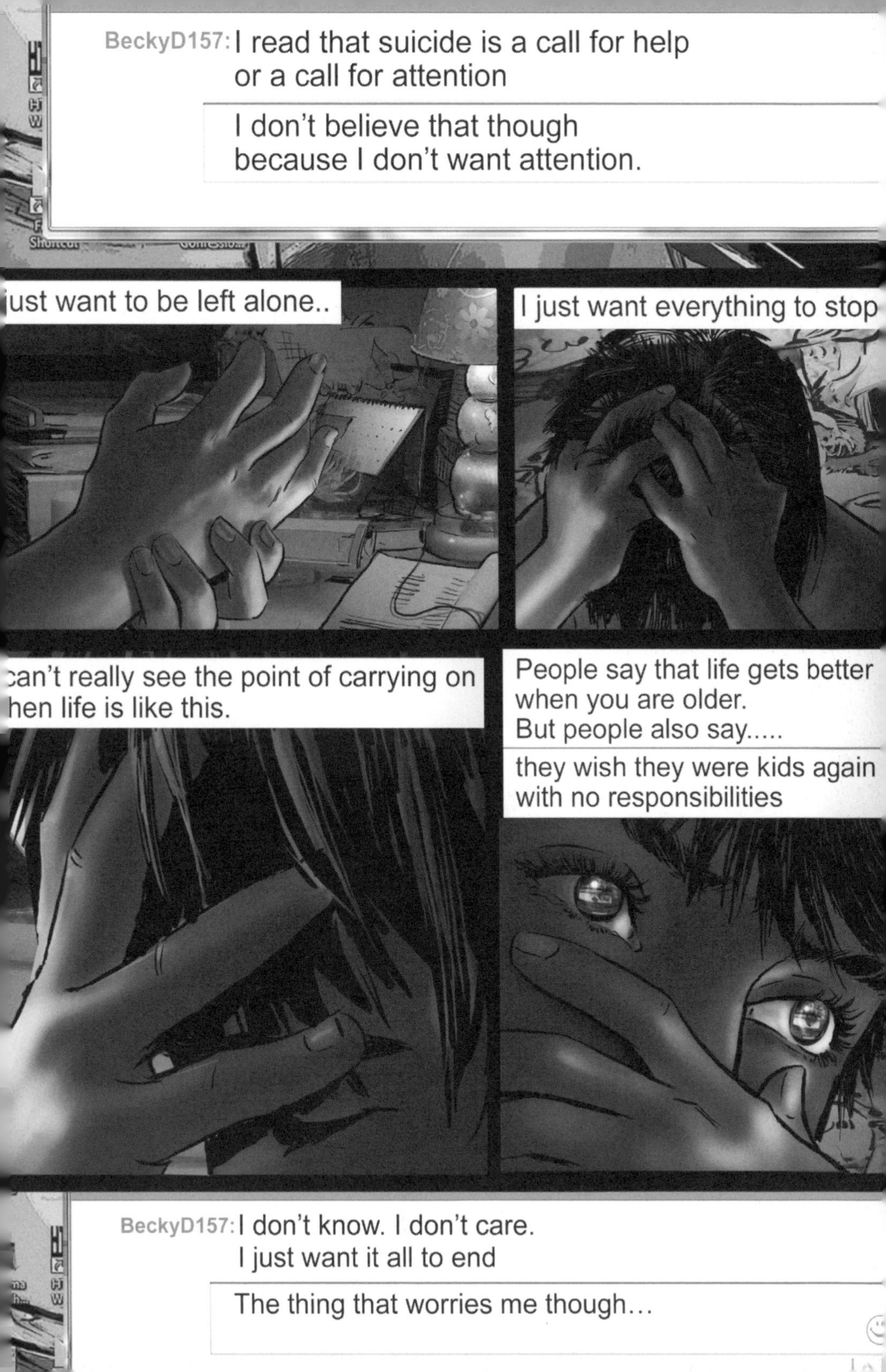
BeckyD157: I read that suicide is a call for help
or a call for attention
I don't believe that though
because I don't want attention.
ust want to be left alone..
I just want everything to stop
can't really see the point of carrying on
hen life is like this.
People say that life gets better
when you are older.
But people also say.....
they wish they were kids again
with no responsibilities
BeckyD157: I don't know. I don't care.
I just want it all to end
The thing that worries me though…

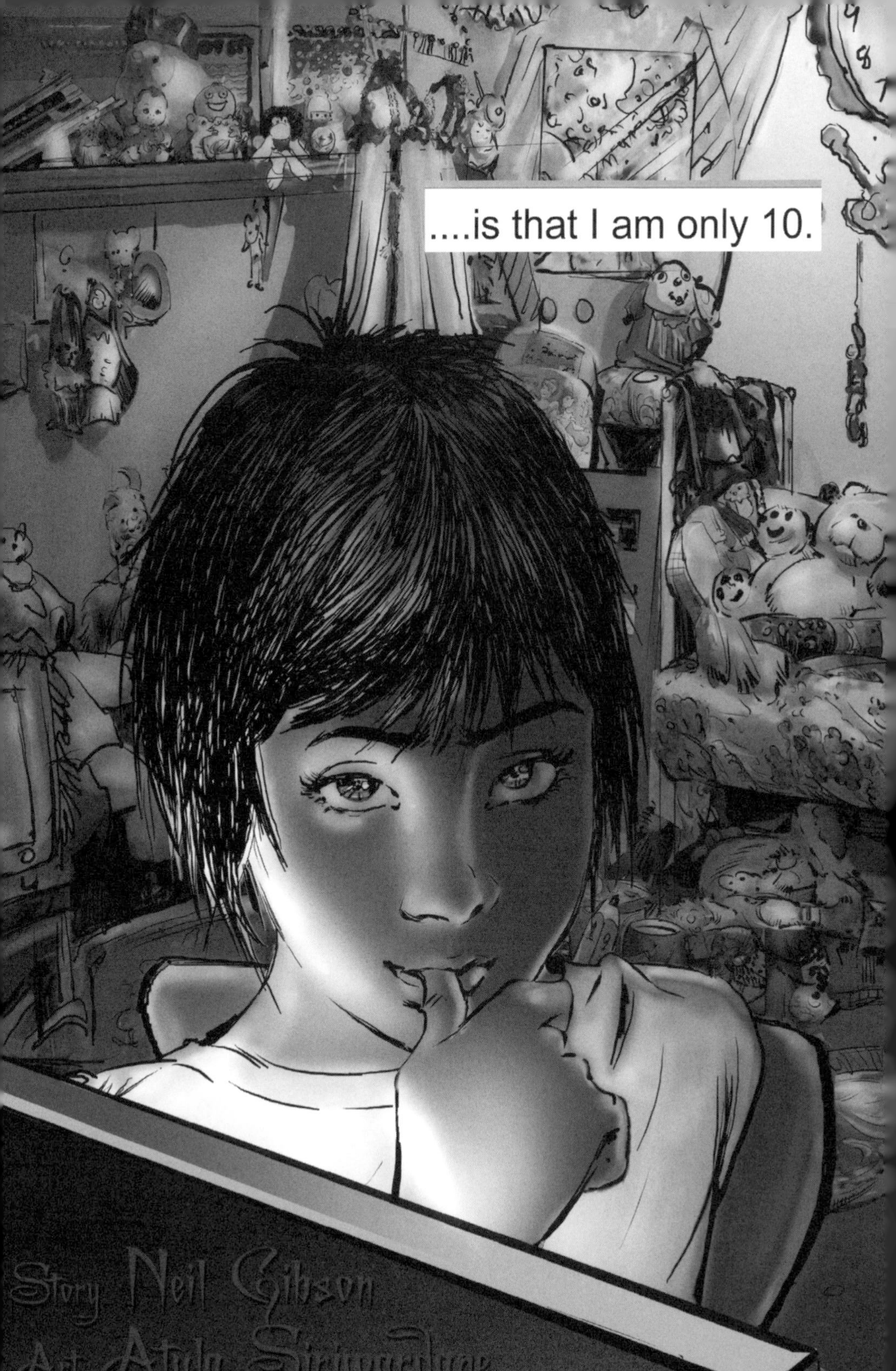
....is that I am only 10.
Story Neil Gibson
Art Atula Siriwardane

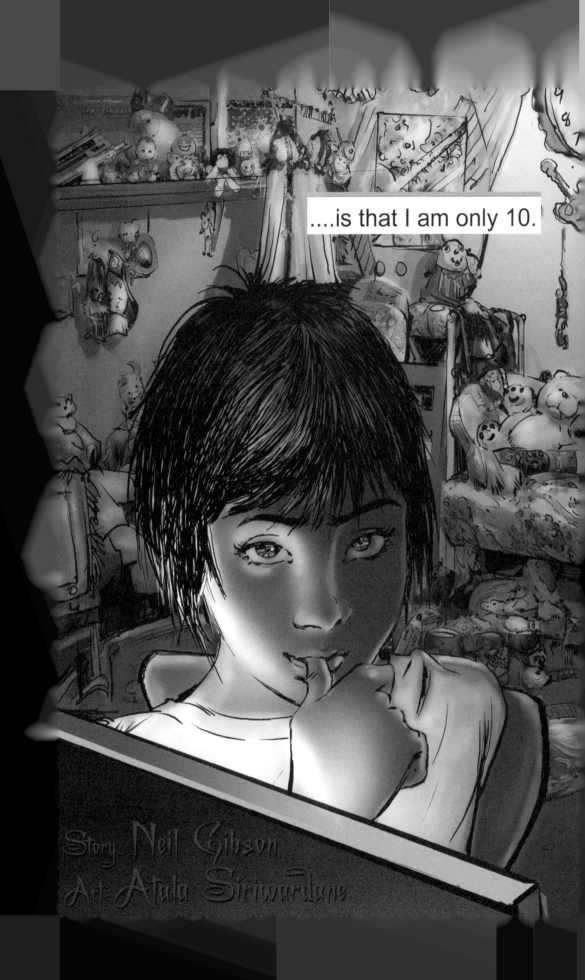

Routine...

"As long as habit and routine dictate the pattern of living, new dimensions of the soul will not emerge."

-Henry Van Dyke

Writer/Creator
Neil Gibson

Illustrator
Caspar Wijngaard

www.tpub.co.uk

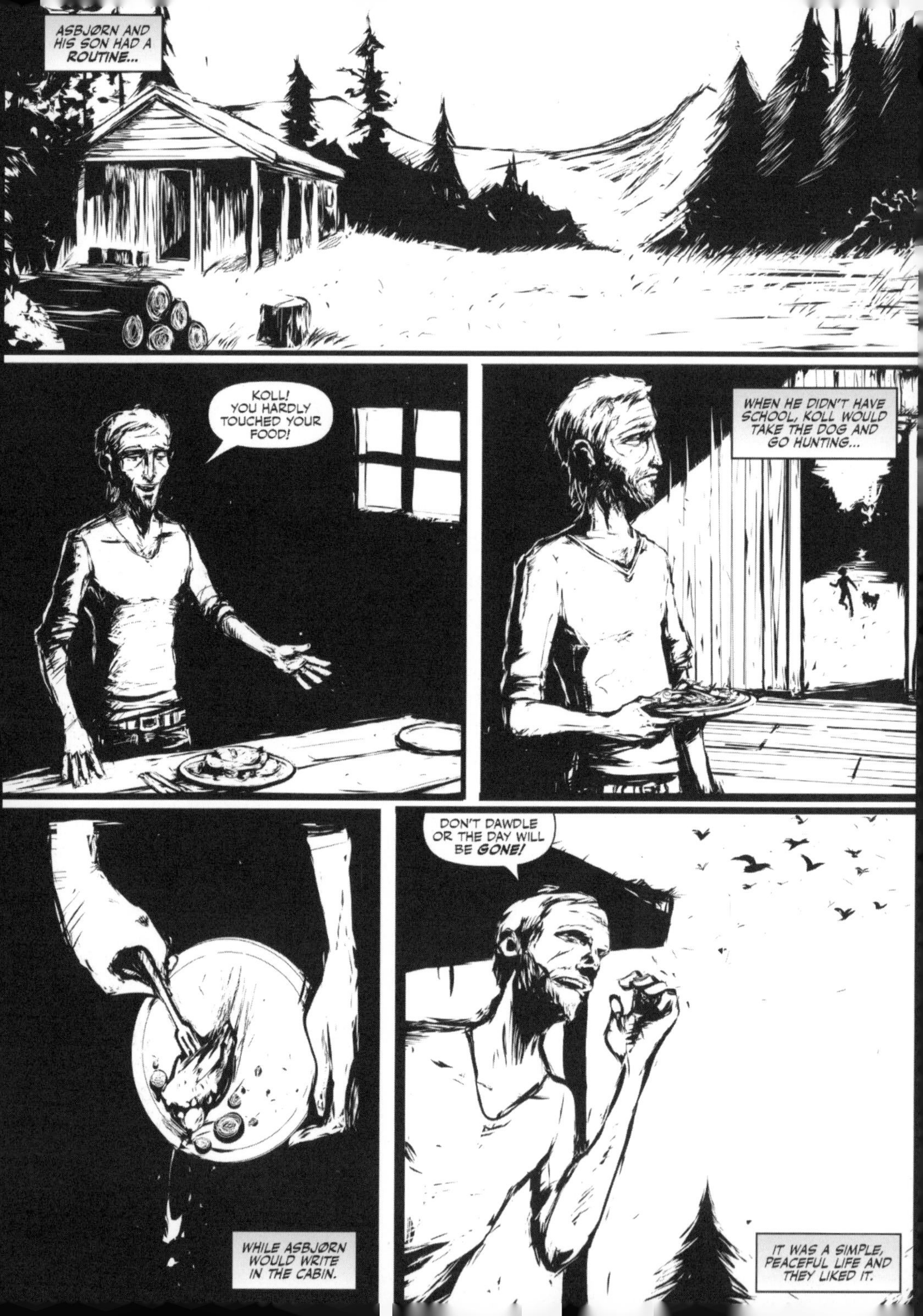
ASBJØRN AND HIS SON HAD A ROUTINE...
KOLL! YOU HARDLY TOUCHED YOUR FOOD!
WHEN HE DIDN'T HAVE SCHOOL, KOLL WOULD TAKE THE DOG AND GO HUNTING...
WHILE ASBJØRN WOULD WRITE IN THE CABIN.
DON'T DAWDLE OR THE DAY WILL BE GONE!
IT WAS A SIMPLE, PEACEFUL LIFE AND THEY LIKED IT.

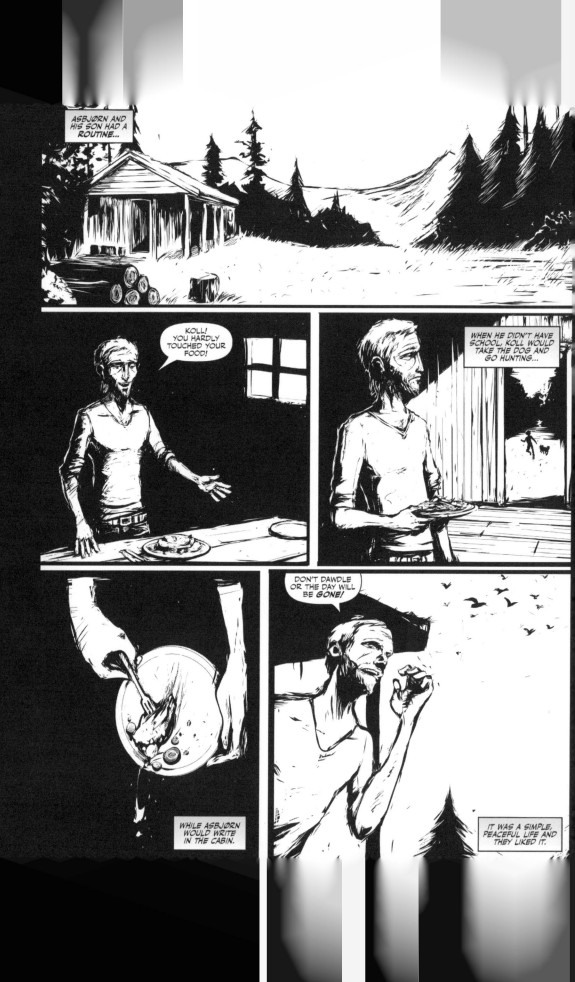

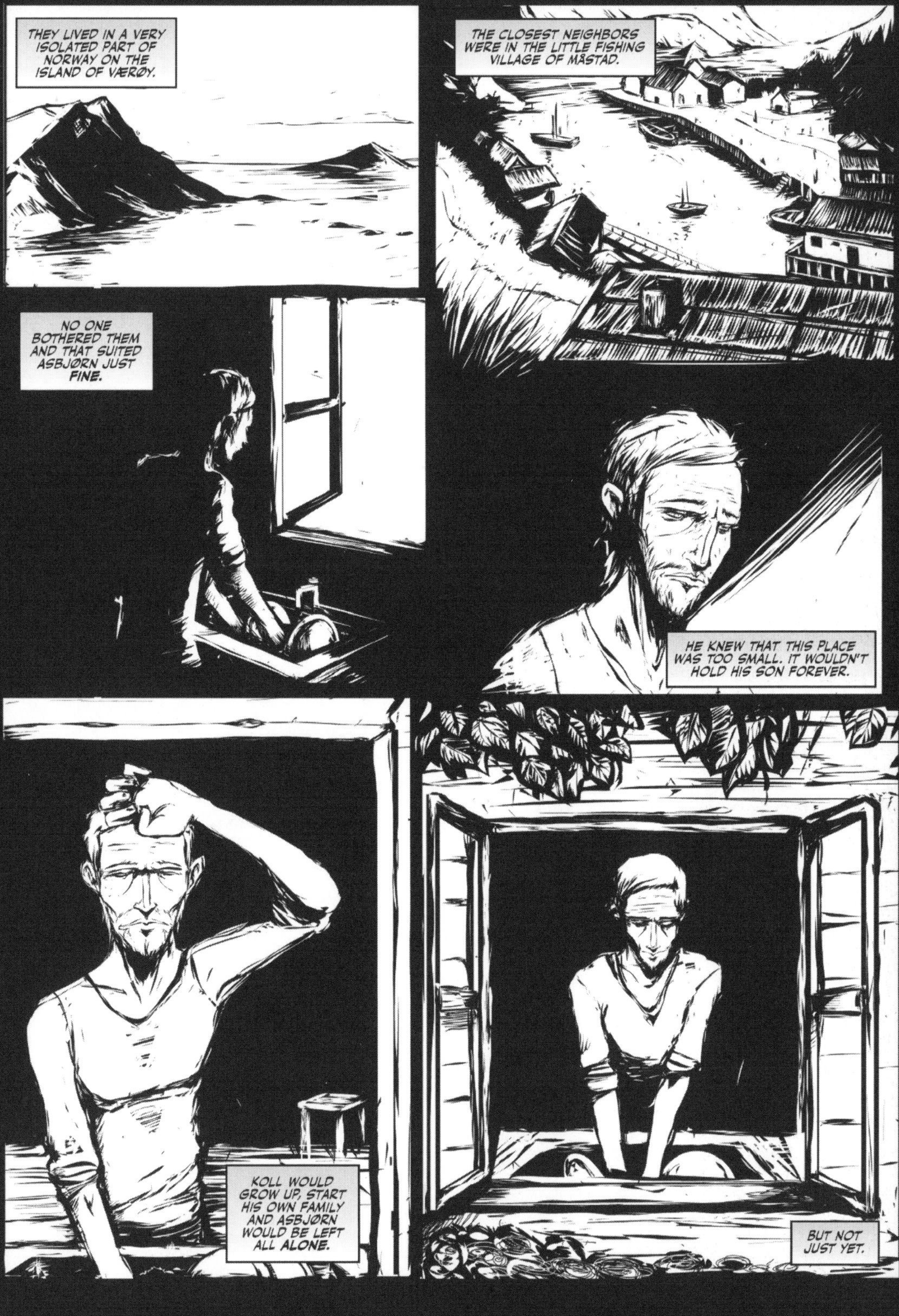
THEY LIVED IN A VERY ISOLATED PART OF NORWAY ON THE ISLAND OF VÆRØY.
THE CLOSEST NEIGHBORS WERE IN THE LITTLE FISHING VILLAGE OF MÅSTAD.
NO ONE BOTHERED THEM AND THAT SUITED ASBJØRN JUST **FINE.**
HE KNEW THAT THIS PLACE WAS TOO SMALL. IT WOULDN'T HOLD HIS SON FOREVER.
KOLL WOULD GROW UP, START HIS OWN FAMILY AND ASBJØRN WOULD BE LEFT ALL **ALONE.**
BUT NOT JUST YET.

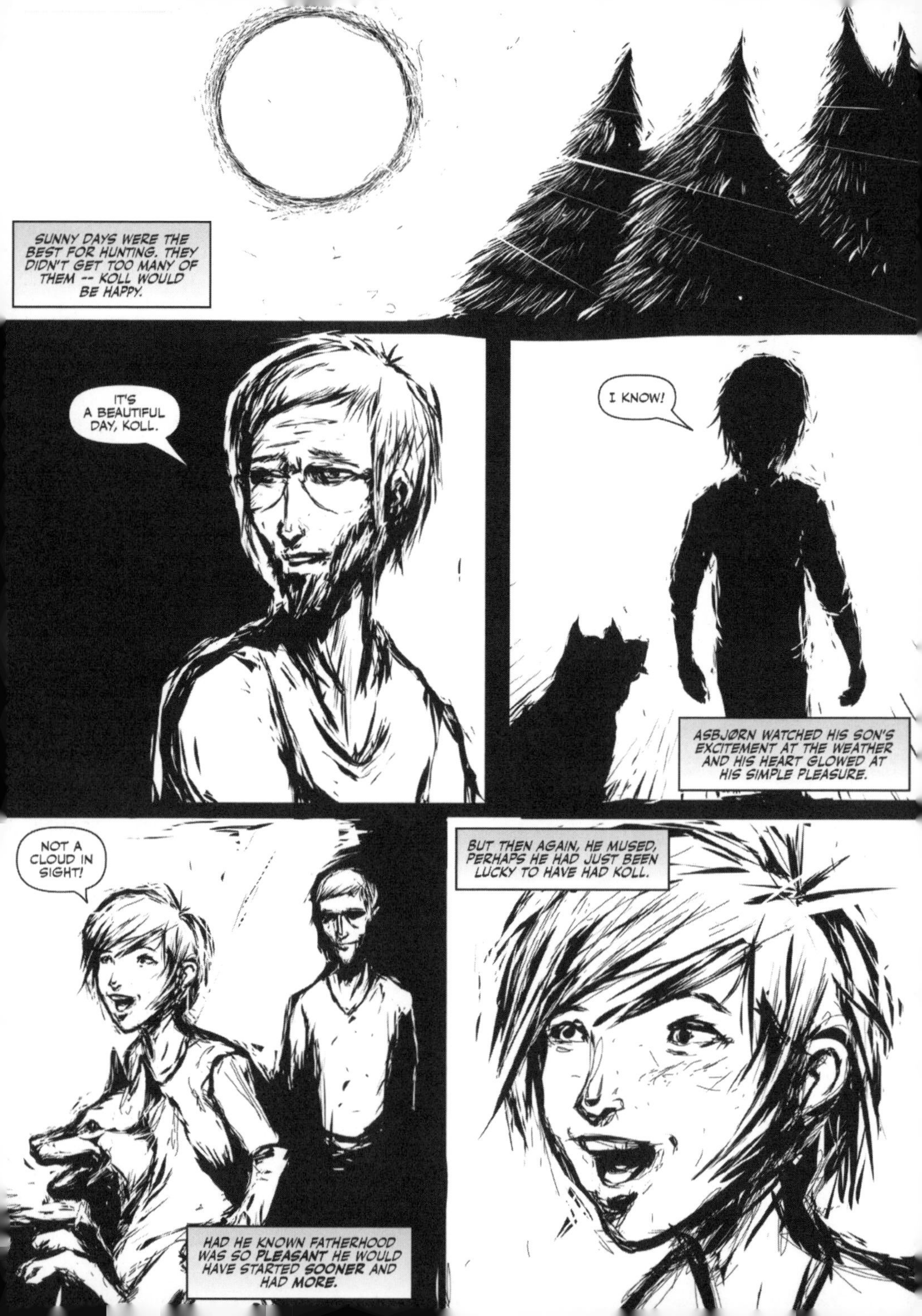
SUNNY DAYS WERE THE BEST FOR HUNTING. THEY DIDN'T GET TOO MANY OF THEM -- KOLL WOULD BE HAPPY.
IT'S A BEAUTIFUL DAY, KOLL.
I KNOW!
ASBJØRN WATCHED HIS SON'S EXCITEMENT AT THE WEATHER AND HIS HEART GLOWED AT HIS SIMPLE PLEASURE.
NOT A CLOUD IN SIGHT!
HAD HE KNOWN FATHERHOOD WAS SO PLEASANT HE WOULD HAVE STARTED SOONER AND HAD MORE.
BUT THEN AGAIN, HE MUSED, PERHAPS HE HAD JUST BEEN LUCKY TO HAVE HAD KOLL.

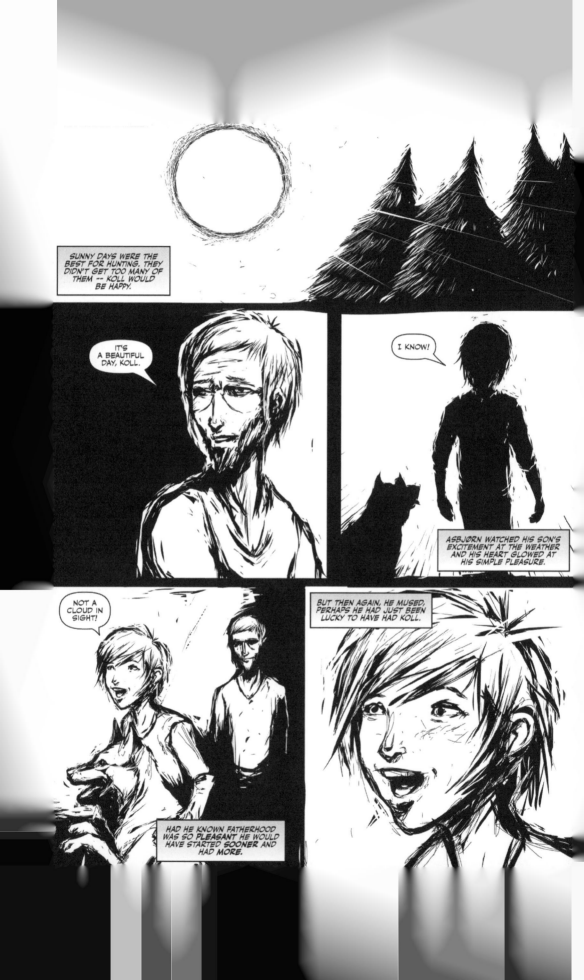

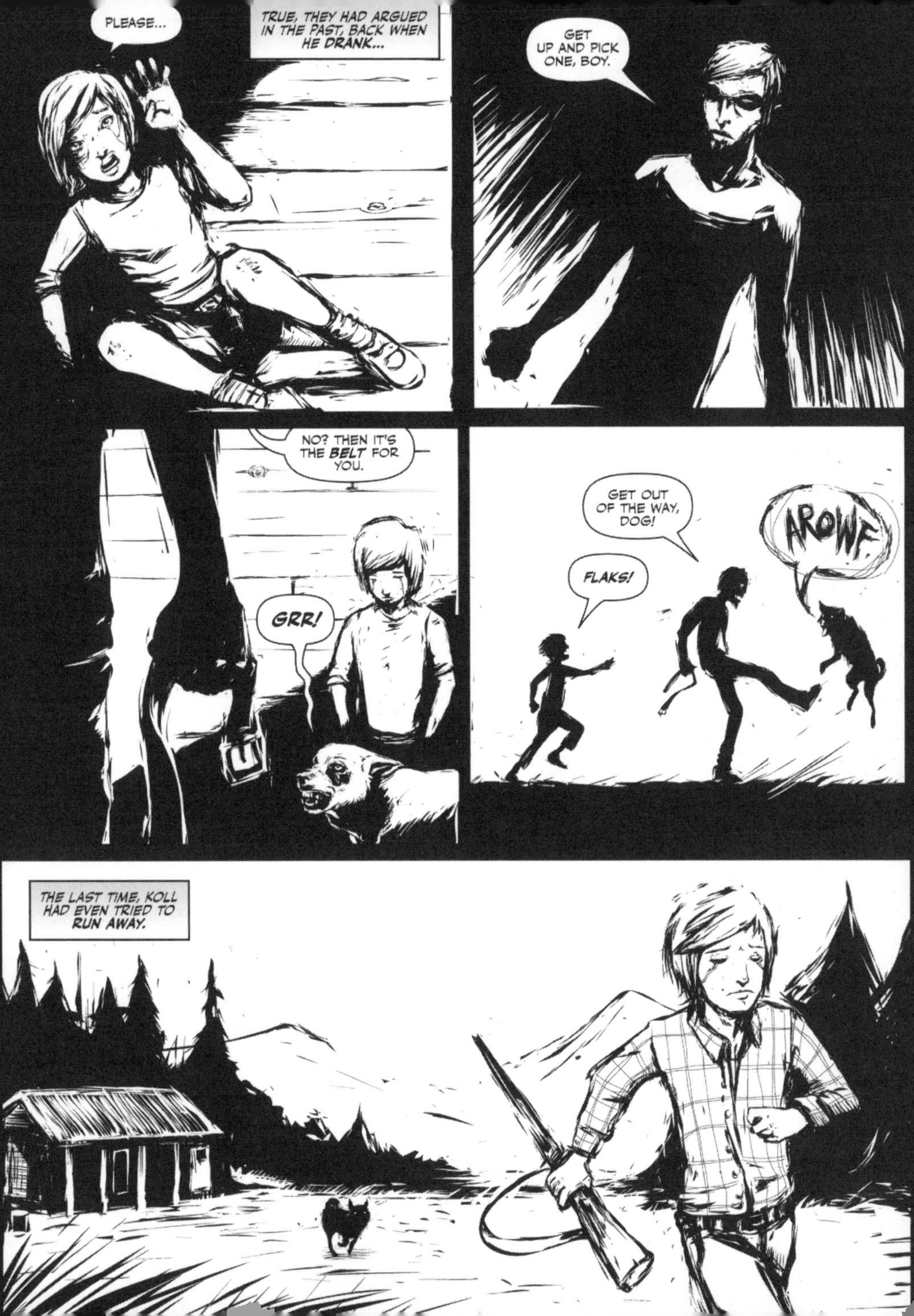

PLEASE...
TRUE, THEY HAD ARGUED IN THE PAST, BACK WHEN HE DRANK...
GET UP AND PICK ONE, BOY.
NO? THEN IT'S THE BELT FOR YOU.
GRR!
GET OUT OF THE WAY, DOG!
FLAKS!
AROWF
THE LAST TIME, KOLL HAD EVEN TRIED TO RUN AWAY.

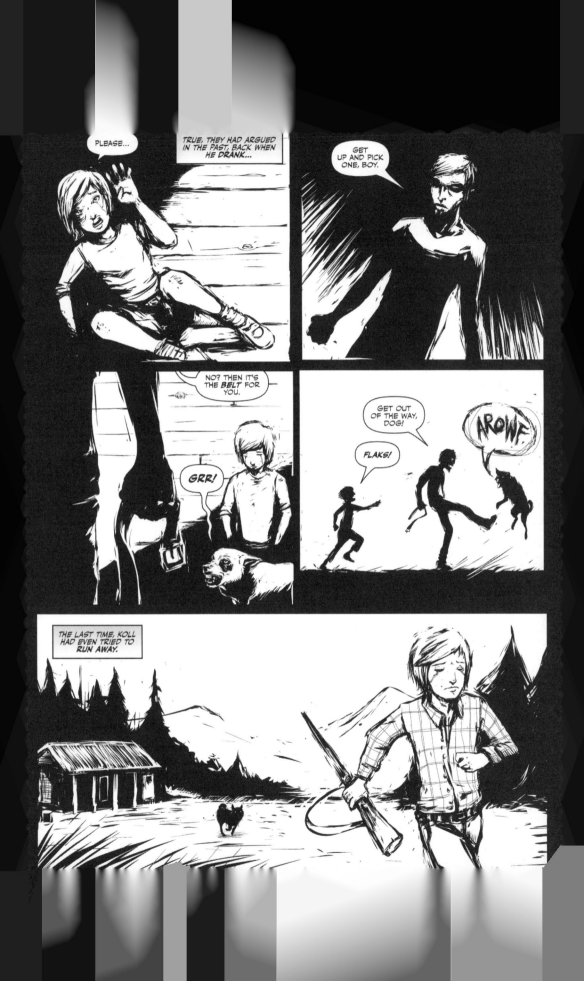

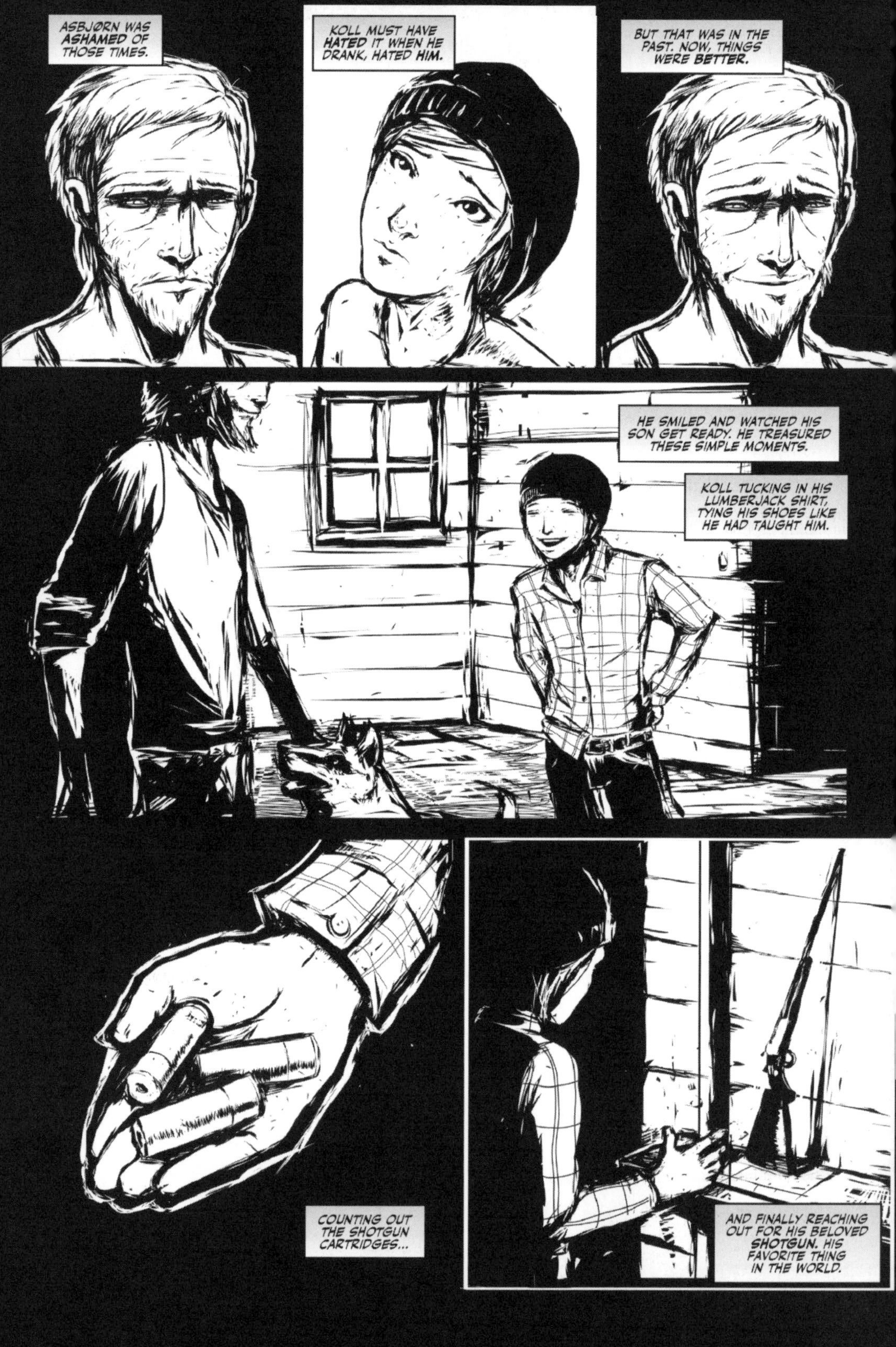

ASBJØRN WAS ASHAMED OF THOSE TIMES.
KOLL MUST HAVE HATED IT WHEN HE DRANK, HATED HIM.
BUT THAT WAS IN THE PAST. NOW, THINGS WERE BETTER.
HE SMILED AND WATCHED HIS SON GET READY. HE TREASURED THESE SIMPLE MOMENTS.
KOLL TUCKING IN HIS LUMBERJACK SHIRT, TYING HIS SHOES LIKE HE HAD TAUGHT HIM.
COUNTING OUT THE SHOTGUN CARTRIDGES...
AND FINALLY REACHING OUT FOR HIS BELOVED SHOTGUN. HIS FAVORITE THING IN THE WORLD.

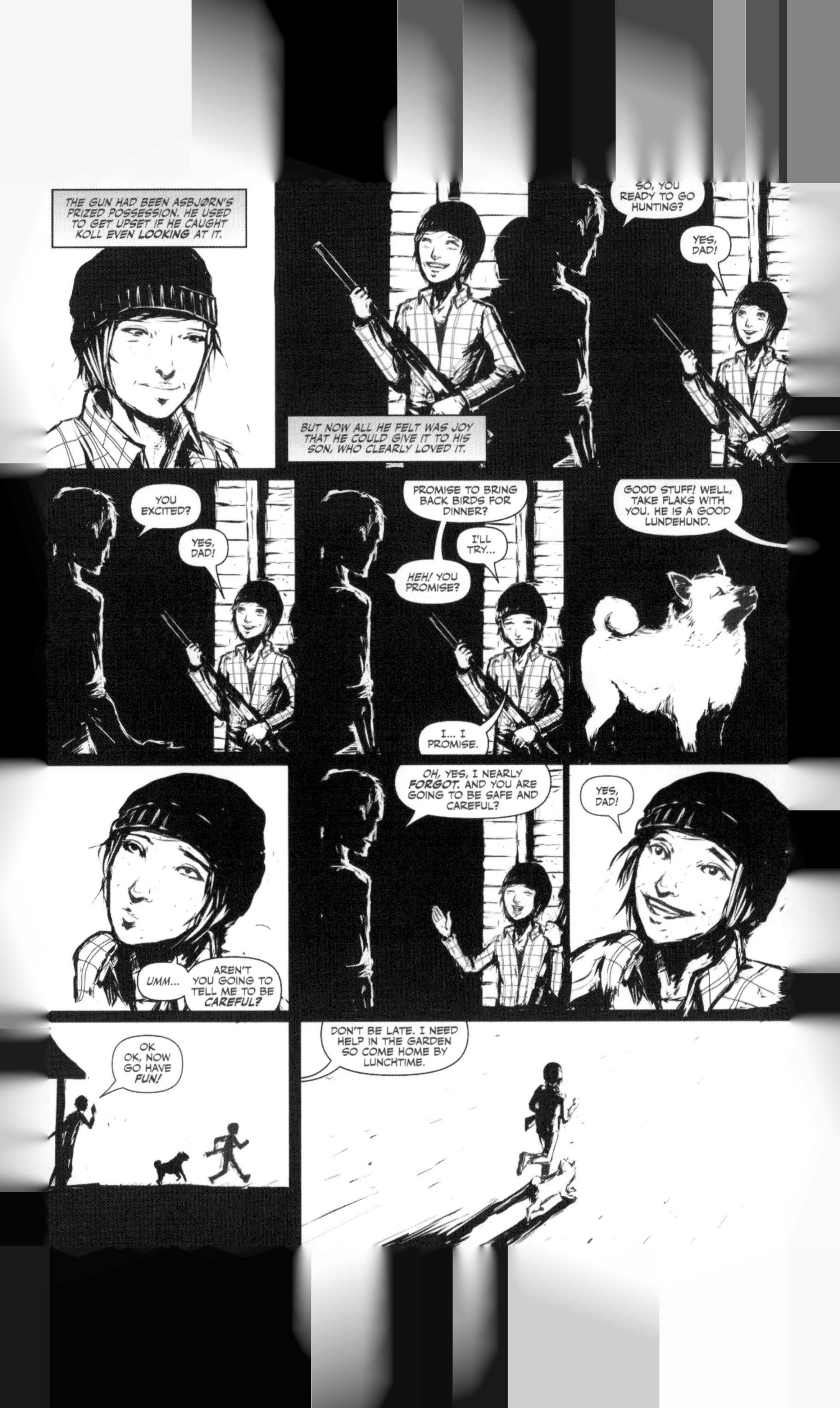

THE GUN HAD BEEN ASBJØRN'S PRIZED POSSESSION. HE USED TO GET UPSET IF HE CAUGHT KOLL EVEN LOOKING AT IT.
BUT NOW ALL HE FELT WAS JOY THAT HE COULD GIVE IT TO HIS SON, WHO CLEARLY LOVED IT.
SO, YOU READY TO GO HUNTING?
YES, DAD!
YOU EXCITED?
YES, DAD!
PROMISE TO BRING BACK BIRDS FOR DINNER?
I'LL TRY...
HEH! YOU PROMISE?
I... I PROMISE.
GOOD STUFF! WELL, TAKE FLAKS WITH YOU. HE IS A GOOD LUNDEHUND.
UMM...
AREN'T YOU GOING TO TELL ME TO BE CAREFUL?
OH, YES, I NEARLY FORGOT. AND YOU ARE GOING TO BE SAFE AND CAREFUL?
YES, DAD!
OK OK, NOW GO HAVE FUN!
DON'T BE LATE. I NEED HELP IN THE GARDEN SO COME HOME BY LUNCHTIME.

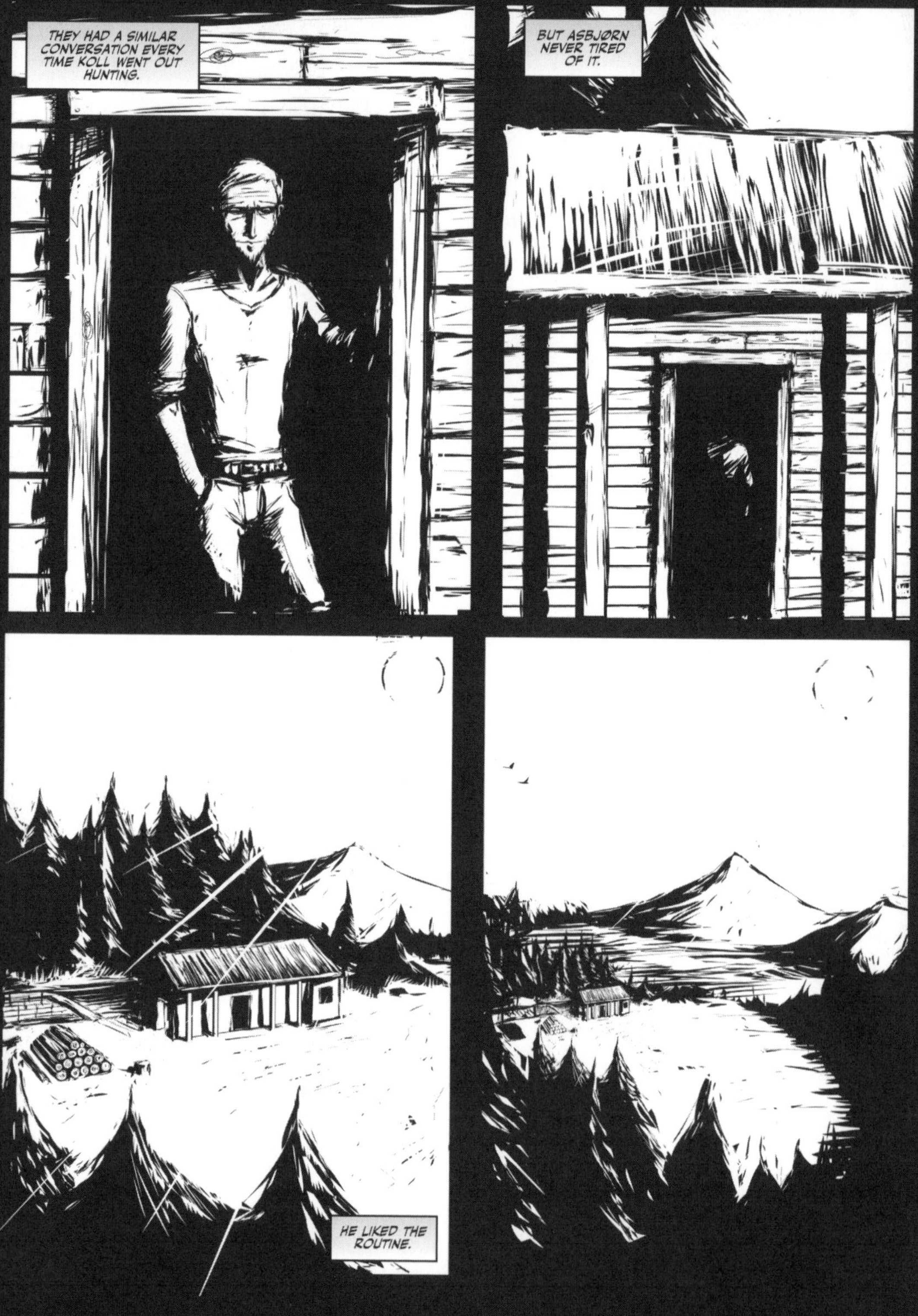
THEY HAD A SIMILAR CONVERSATION EVERY TIME KOLL WENT OUT HUNTING.
BUT ASBJØRN NEVER TIRED OF IT.
HE LIKED THE ROUTINE.

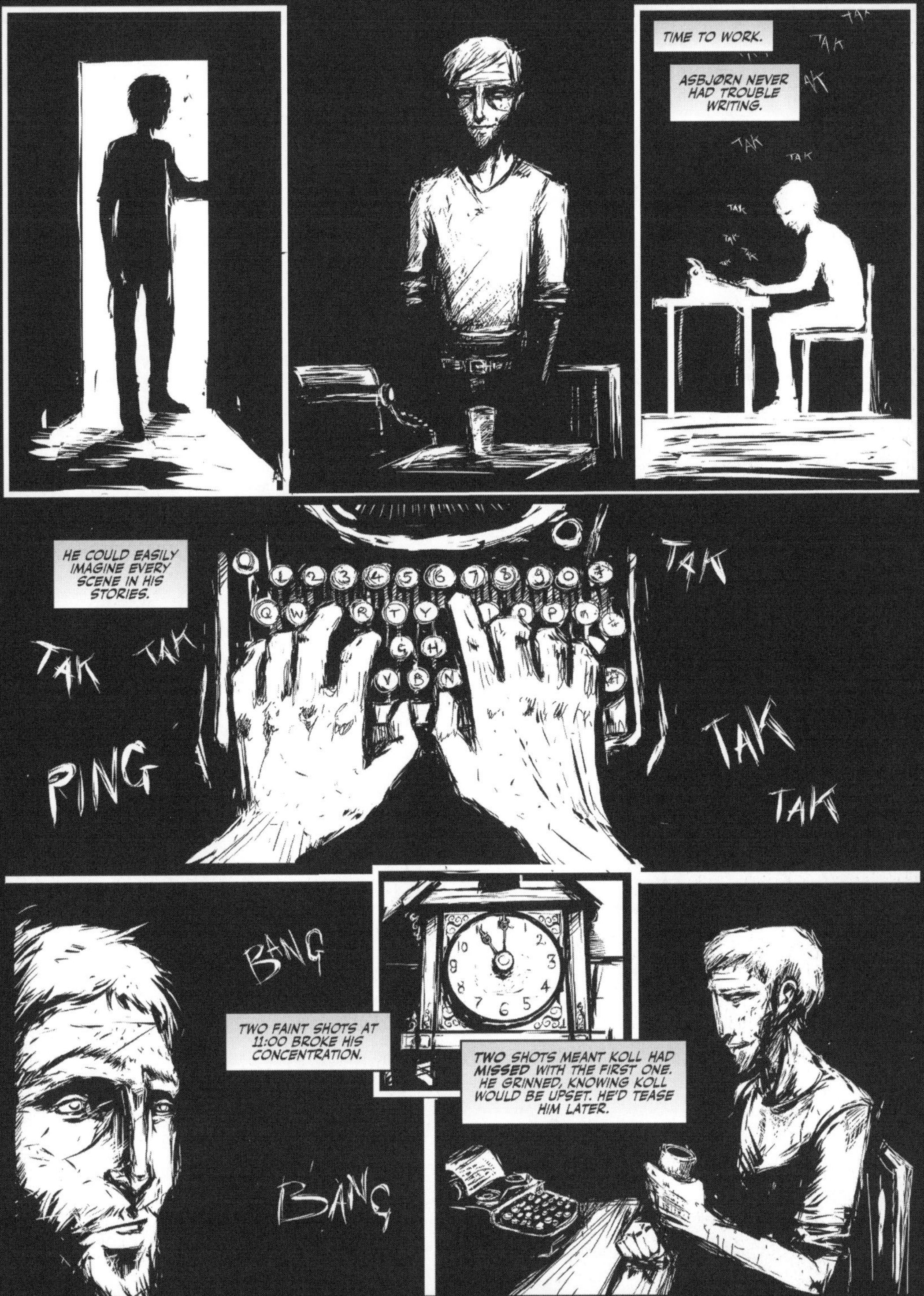
TIME TO WORK.
ASBJØRN NEVER HAD TROUBLE WRITING.
TAK
TAK
TAK
TAK
TAK
HE COULD EASILY IMAGINE EVERY SCENE IN HIS STORIES.
TAK
TAK
TAK
PING
TAK
TAK
BANG
TWO FAINT SHOTS AT 11:00 BROKE HIS CONCENTRATION.
BANG
TWO SHOTS MEANT KOLL HAD MISSED WITH THE FIRST ONE. HE GRINNED, KNOWING KOLL WOULD BE UPSET. HE'D TEASE HIM LATER.

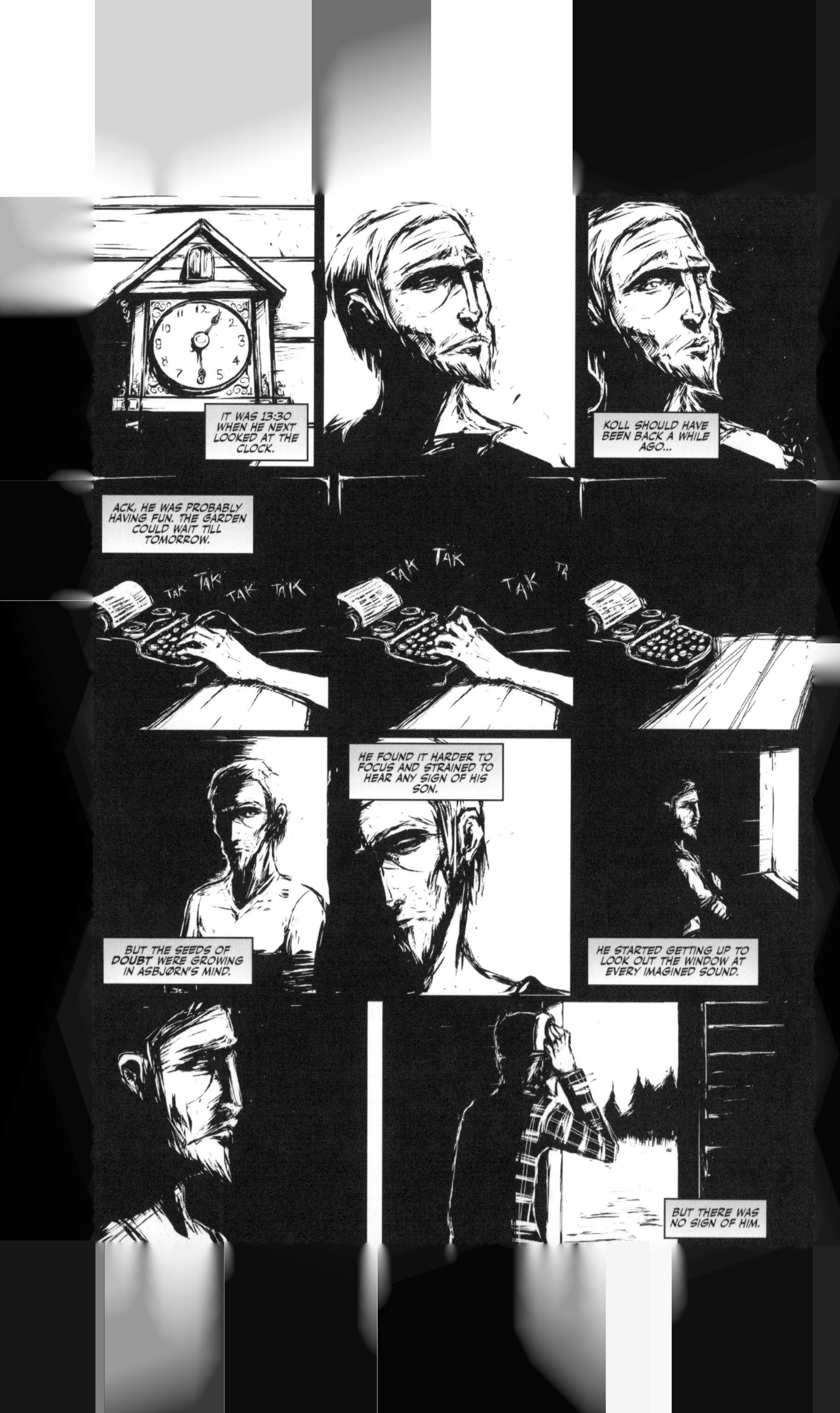
IT WAS 13:30 WHEN HE NEXT LOOKED AT THE CLOCK.
KOLL SHOULD HAVE BEEN BACK A WHILE AGO...
ACK, HE WAS PROBABLY HAVING FUN. THE GARDEN COULD WAIT TILL TOMORROW.
TAK TAK TAK TAK
TAK TAK TAK
BUT THE SEEDS OF DOUBT WERE GROWING IN ASBJØRN'S MIND.
HE FOUND IT HARDER TO FOCUS AND STRAINED TO HEAR ANY SIGN OF HIS SON.
HE STARTED GETTING UP TO LOOK OUT THE WINDOW AT EVERY IMAGINED SOUND.
BUT THERE WAS NO SIGN OF HIM.

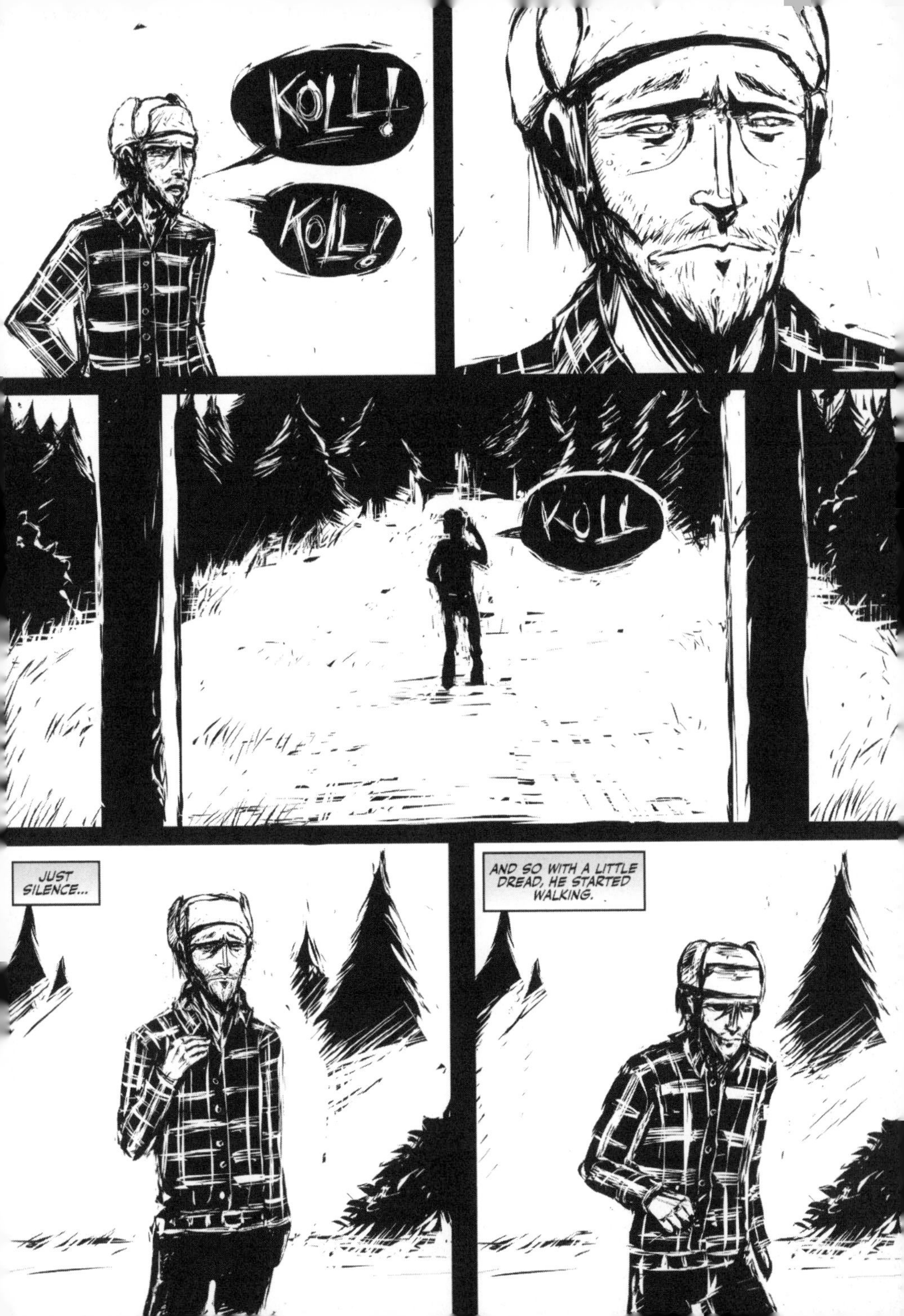
KOLL!
KOLL!
KOLL
JUST SILENCE...
AND SO WITH A LITTLE DREAD, HE STARTED WALKING.

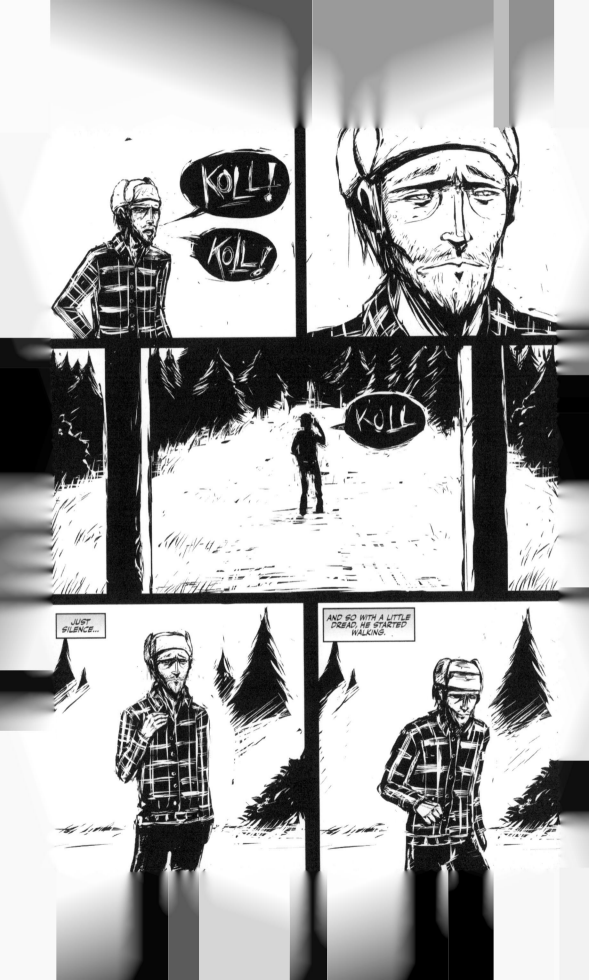

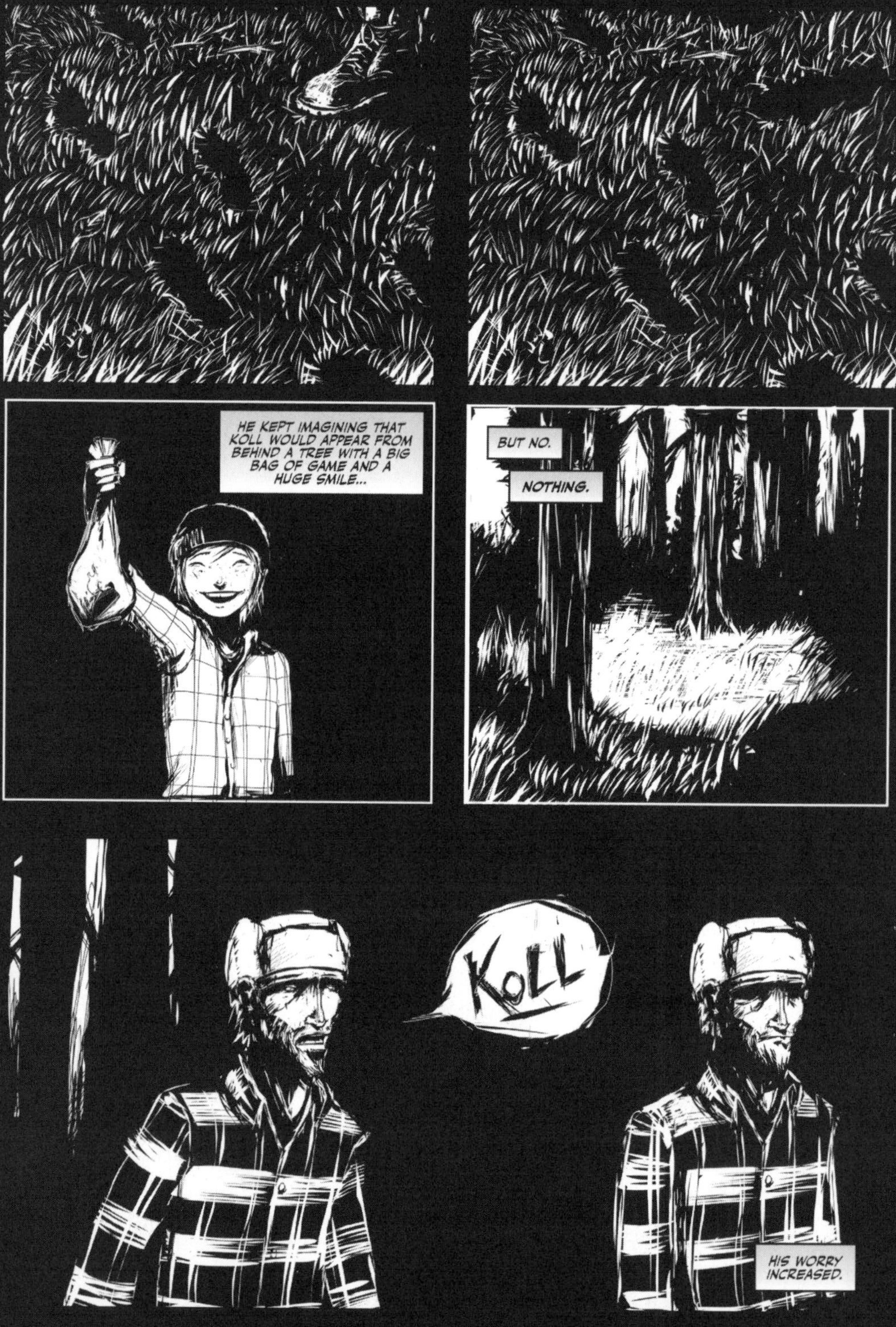

HE KEPT IMAGINING THAT KOLL WOULD APPEAR FROM BEHIND A TREE WITH A BIG BAG OF GAME AND A HUGE SMILE...
BUT NO.
NOTHING.
KOLL
HIS WORRY INCREASED.

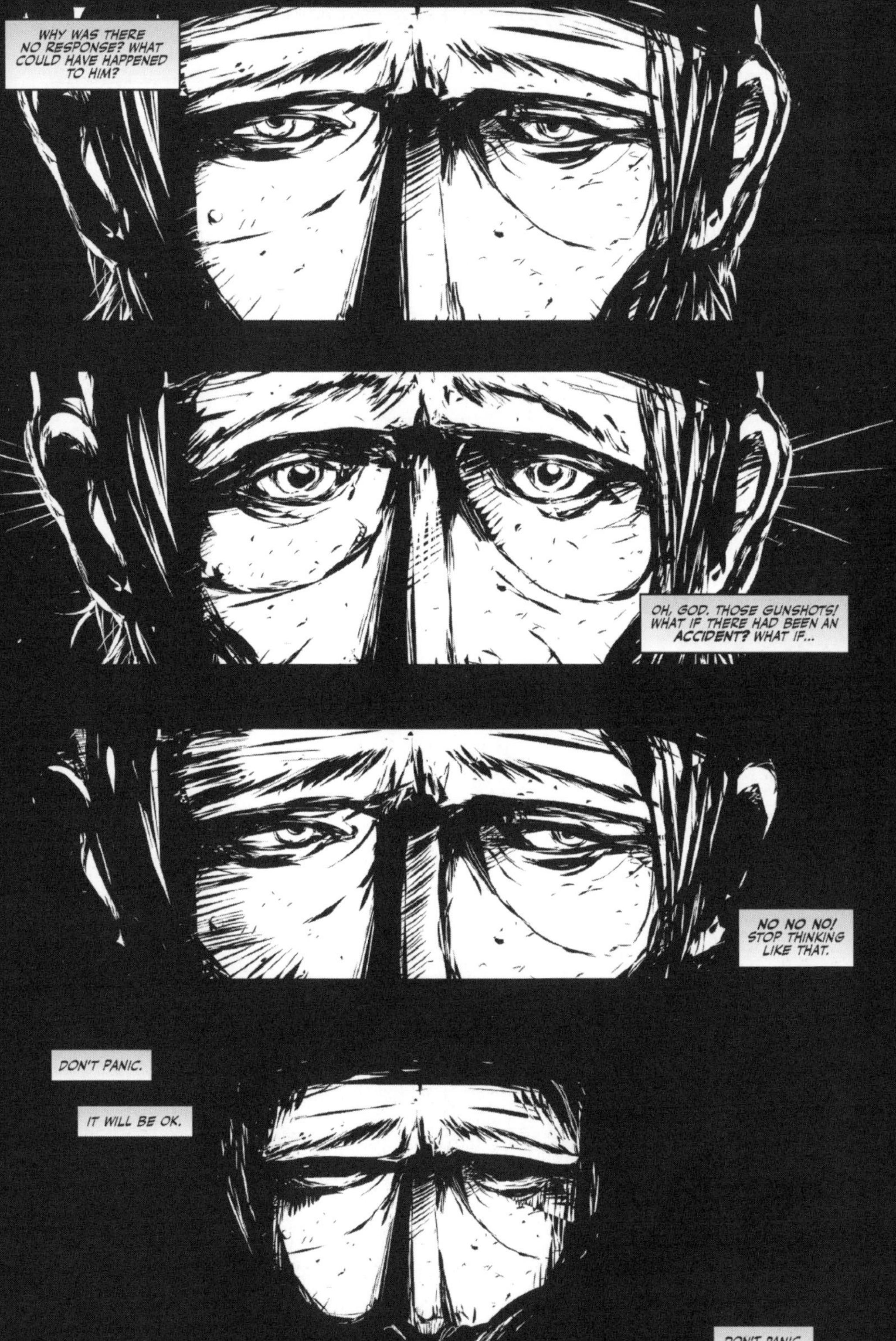
WHY WAS THERE NO RESPONSE? WHAT COULD HAVE HAPPENED TO HIM?
OH, GOD. THOSE GUNSHOTS! WHAT IF THERE HAD BEEN AN ACCIDENT? WHAT IF...
NO NO NO! STOP THINKING LIKE THAT.
DON'T PANIC.
IT WILL BE OK.
DON'T PANIC.

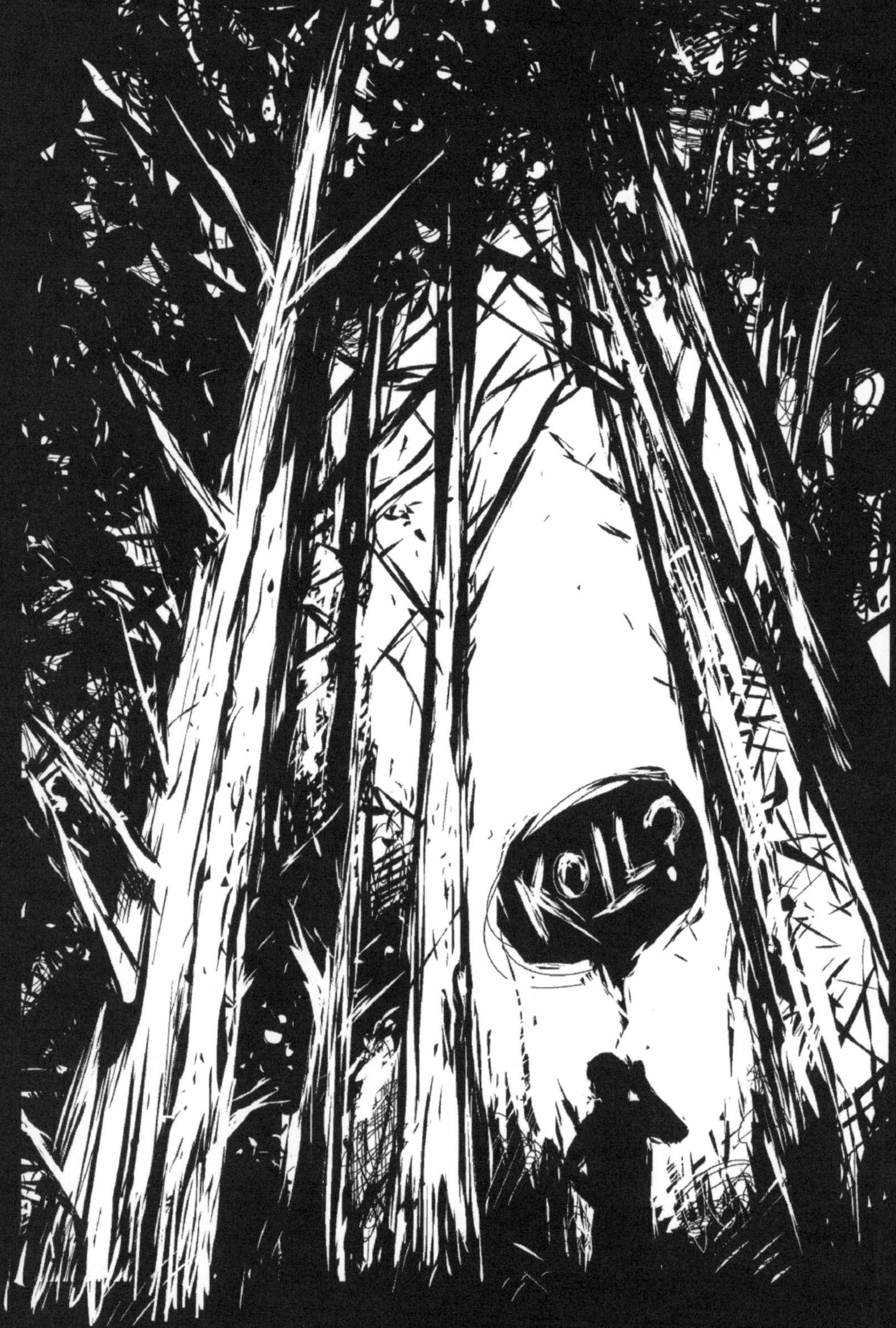
KOIL?

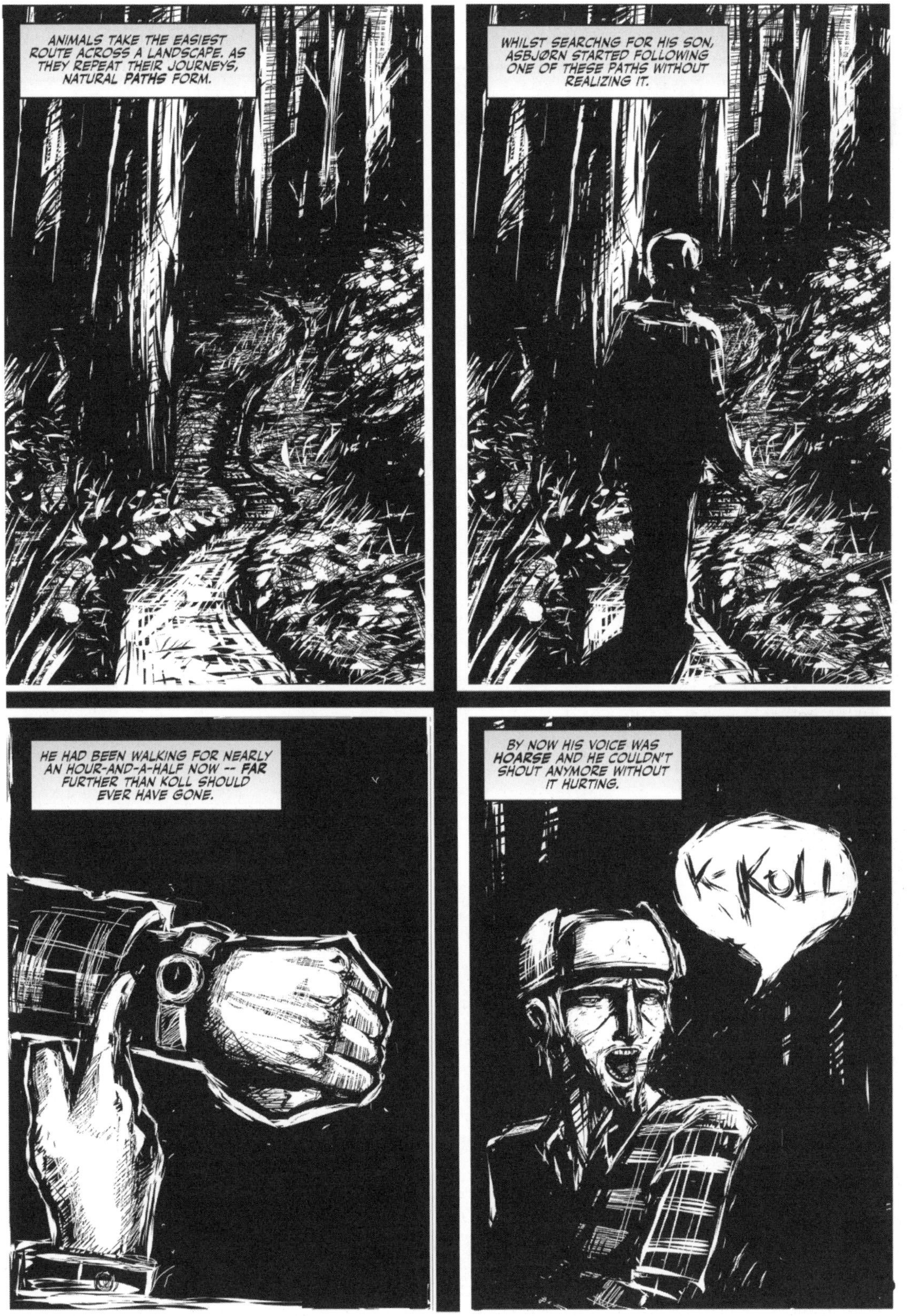

ANIMALS TAKE THE EASIEST ROUTE ACROSS A LANDSCAPE. AS THEY REPEAT THEIR JOURNEYS, NATURAL PATHS FORM.
WHILST SEARCHNG FOR HIS SON, ASBJØRN STARTED FOLLOWING ONE OF THESE PATHS WITHOUT REALIZING IT.
HE HAD BEEN WALKING FOR NEARLY AN HOUR-AND-A-HALF NOW -- FAR FURTHER THAN KOLL SHOULD EVER HAVE GONE.
BY NOW HIS VOICE WAS HOARSE AND HE COULDN'T SHOUT ANYMORE WITHOUT IT HURTING.
K-KOLL

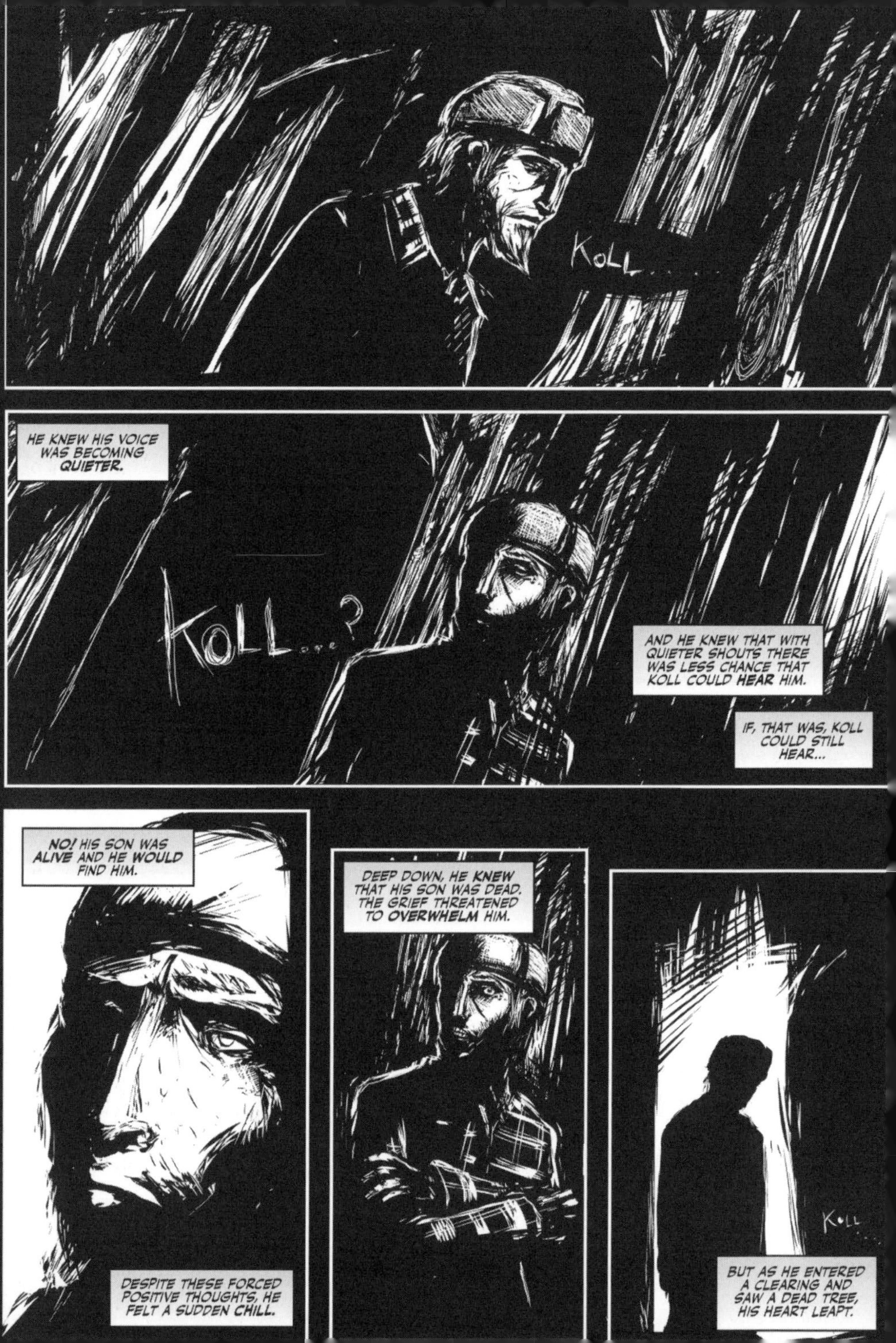
KOLL...
HE KNEW HIS VOICE WAS BECOMING QUIETER.
KOLL...?
AND HE KNEW THAT WITH QUIETER SHOUTS THERE WAS LESS CHANCE THAT KOLL COULD HEAR HIM.
IF, THAT WAS, KOLL COULD STILL HEAR...
NO! HIS SON WAS ALIVE AND HE WOULD FIND HIM.
DESPITE THESE FORCED POSITIVE THOUGHTS, HE FELT A SUDDEN CHILL.
DEEP DOWN, HE KNEW THAT HIS SON WAS DEAD. THE GRIEF THREATENED TO OVERWHELM HIM.
KOLL...
BUT AS HE ENTERED A CLEARING AND SAW A DEAD TREE, HIS HEART LEAPT.

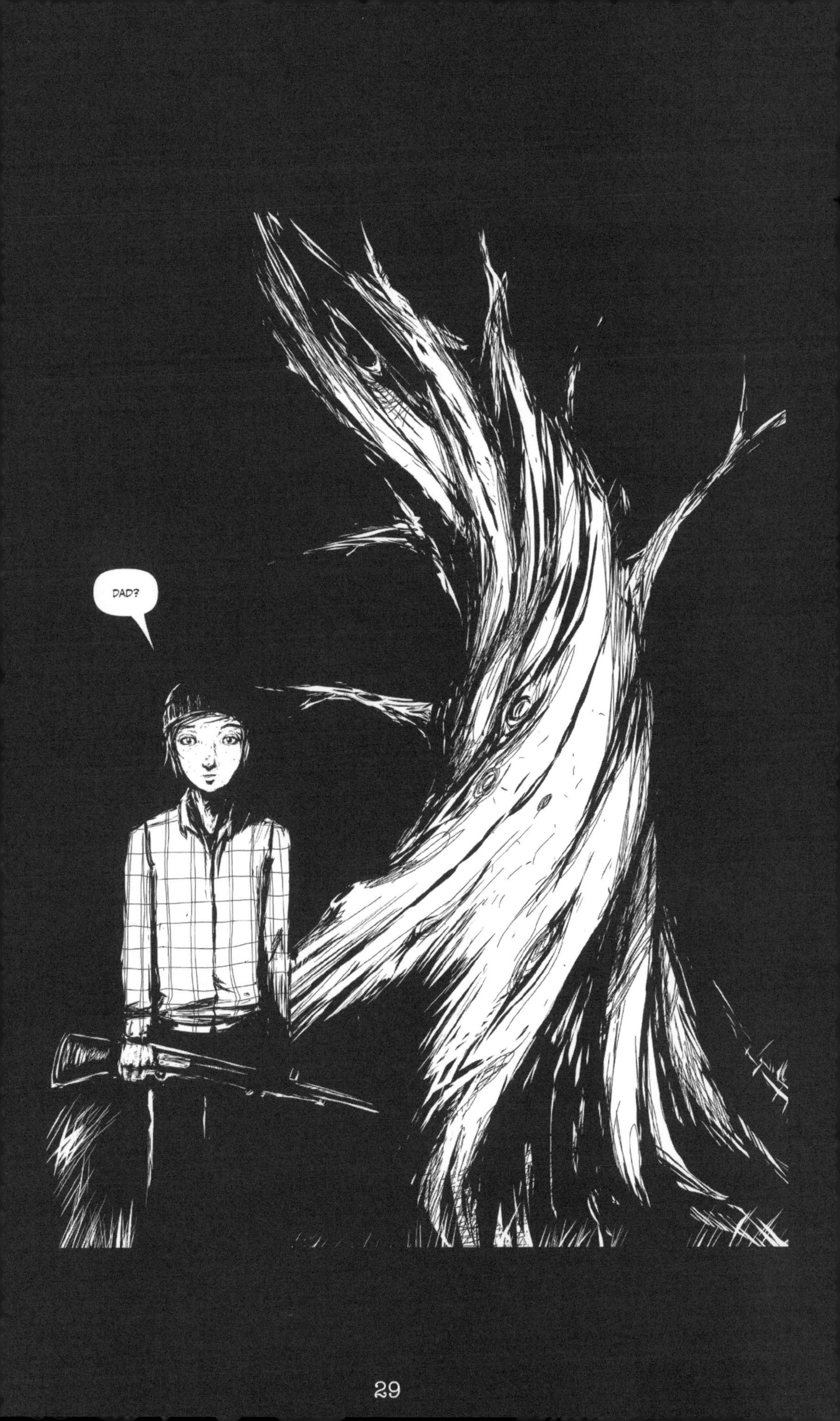
DAD?

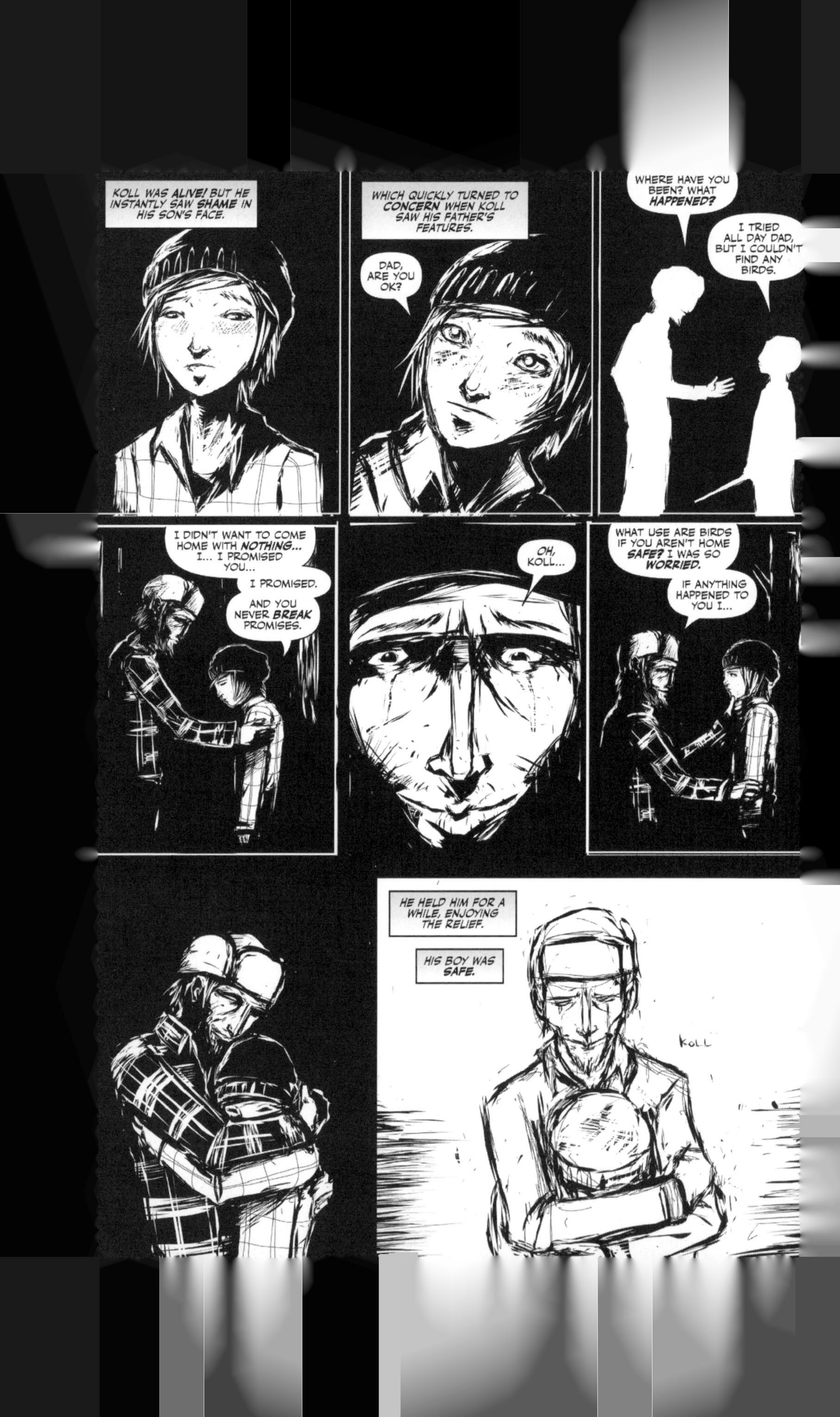
KOLL WAS ALIVE! BUT HE INSTANTLY SAW SHAME IN HIS SON'S FACE.
WHICH QUICKLY TURNED TO CONCERN WHEN KOLL SAW HIS FATHER'S FEATURES.
DAD, ARE YOU OK?
WHERE HAVE YOU BEEN? WHAT HAPPENED?
I TRIED ALL DAY DAD, BUT I COULDN'T FIND ANY BIRDS.
I DIDN'T WANT TO COME HOME WITH NOTHING... I... I PROMISED YOU...
I PROMISED.
AND YOU NEVER BREAK PROMISES.
OH, KOLL...
WHAT USE ARE BIRDS IF YOU AREN'T HOME SAFE? I WAS SO WORRIED.
IF ANYTHING HAPPENED TO YOU I...
HE HELD HIM FOR A WHILE, ENJOYING THE RELIEF.
HIS BOY WAS SAFE.
KOLL

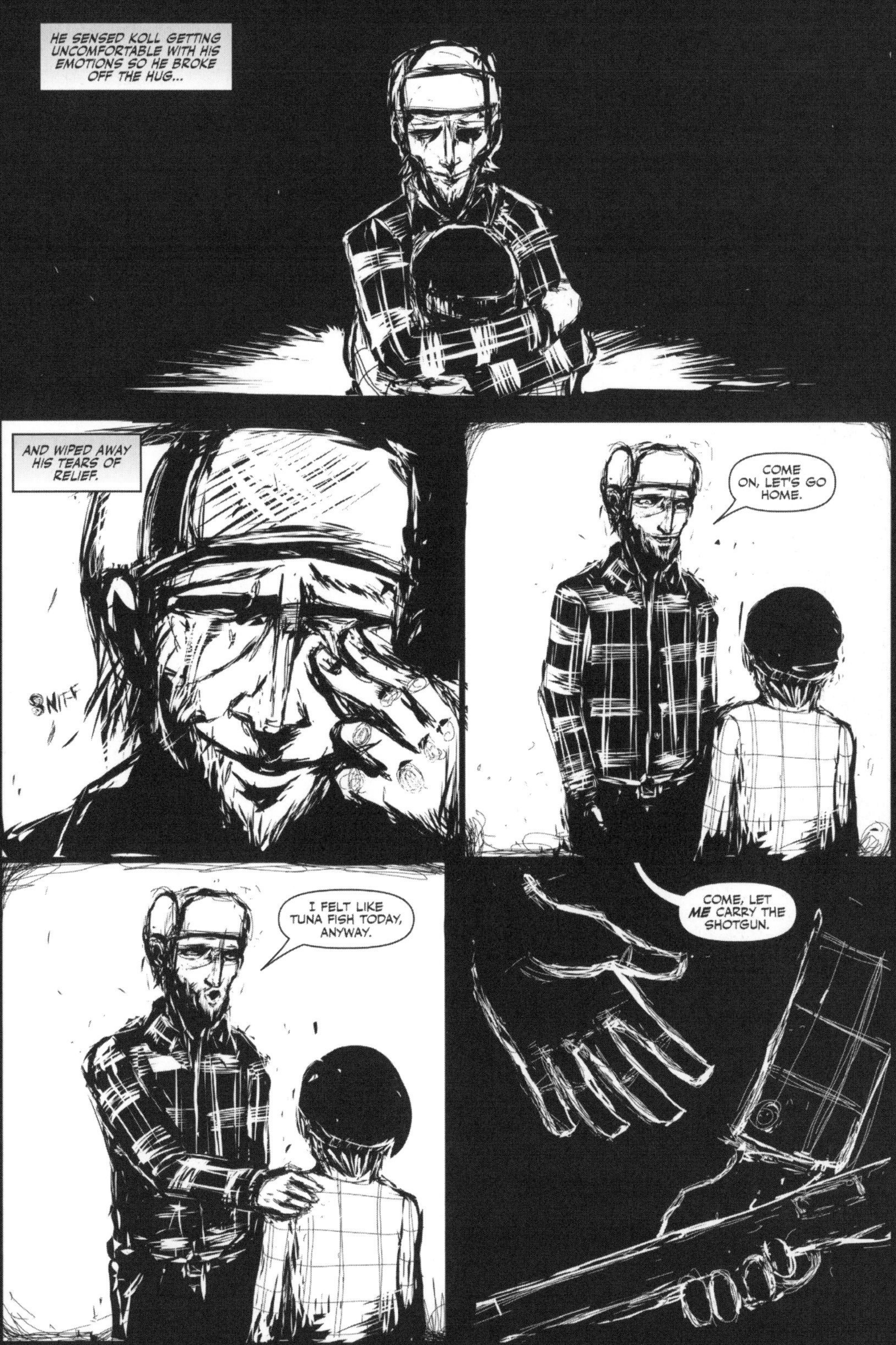
HE SENSED KOLL GETTING UNCOMFORTABLE WITH HIS EMOTIONS SO HE BROKE OFF THE HUG...
AND WIPED AWAY HIS TEARS OF RELIEF.
SNIFF
COME ON, LET'S GO HOME.
I FELT LIKE TUNA FISH TODAY, ANYWAY.
COME, LET *ME* CARRY THE SHOTGUN.

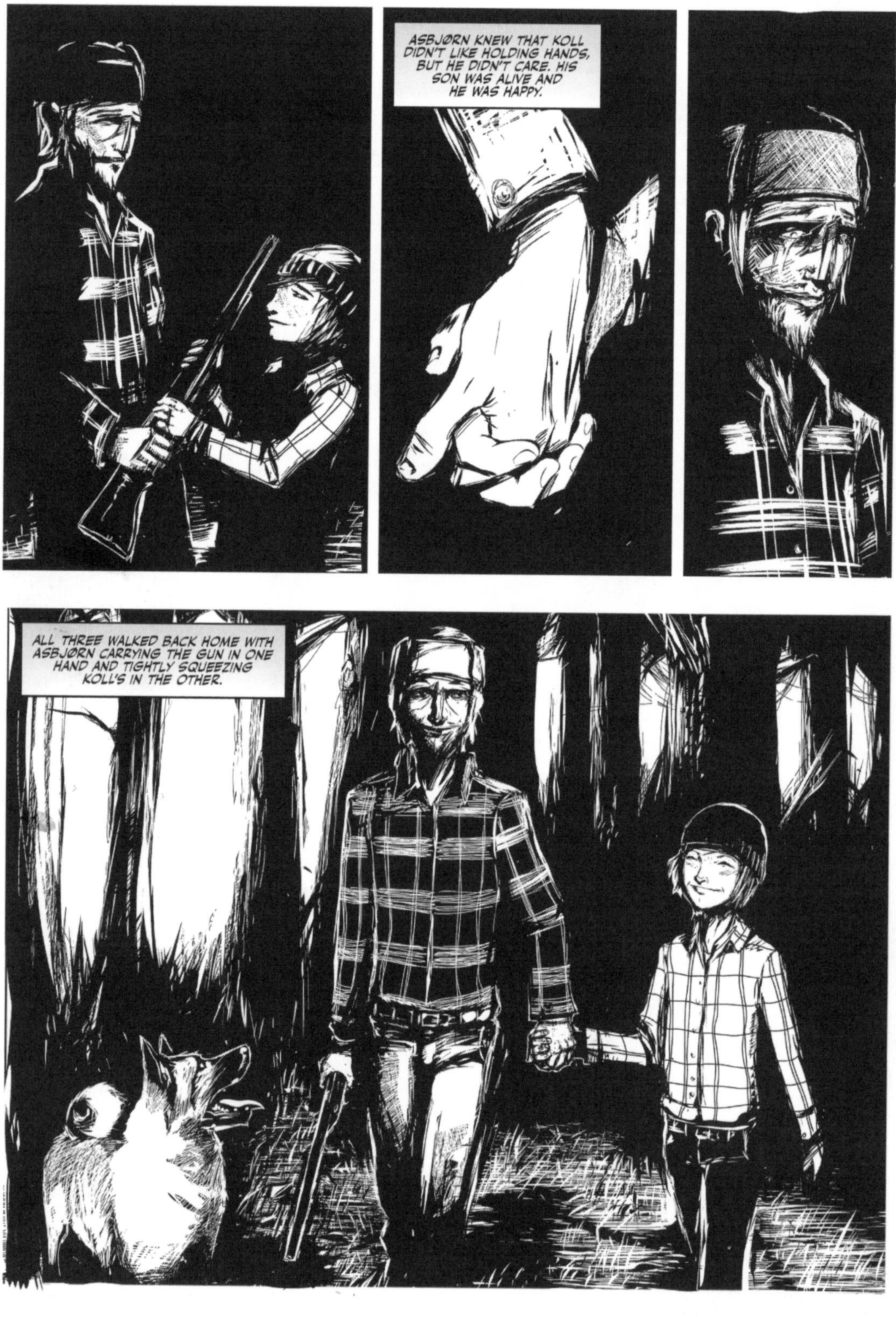
ASBJØRN KNEW THAT KOLL DIDN'T LIKE HOLDING HANDS, BUT HE DIDN'T CARE. HIS SON WAS ALIVE AND HE WAS HAPPY.
ALL THREE WALKED BACK HOME WITH ASBJØRN CARRYING THE GUN IN ONE HAND AND TIGHTLY SQUEEZING KOLL'S IN THE OTHER.

ONLY...

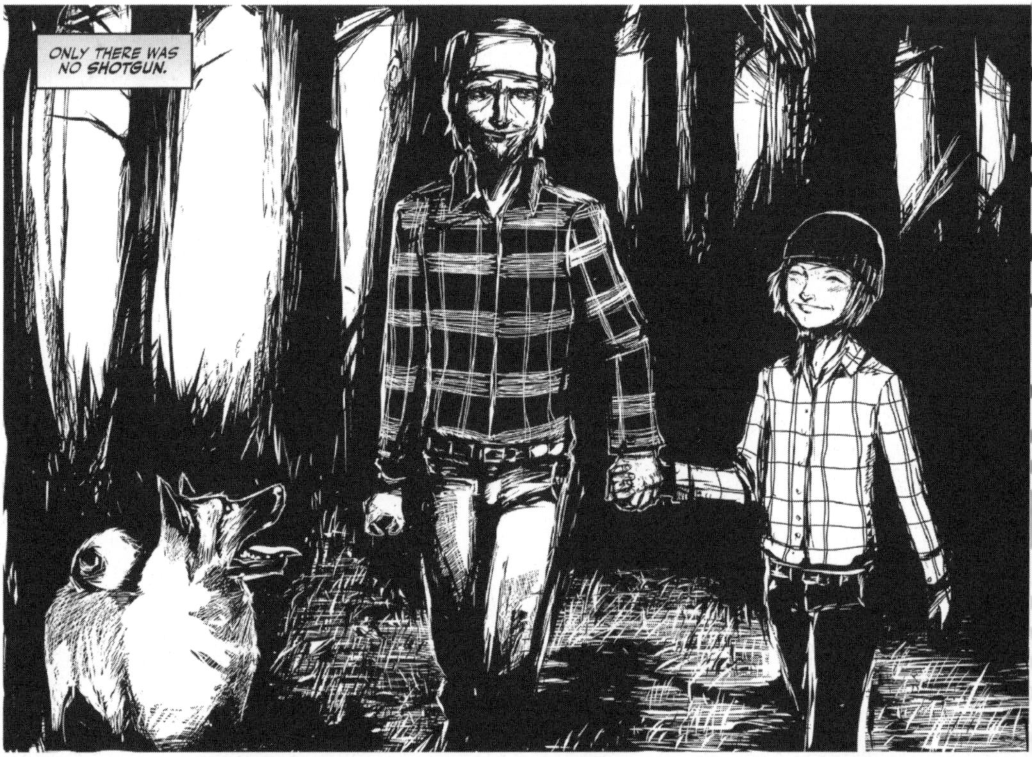
ONLY THERE WAS NO SHOTGUN.

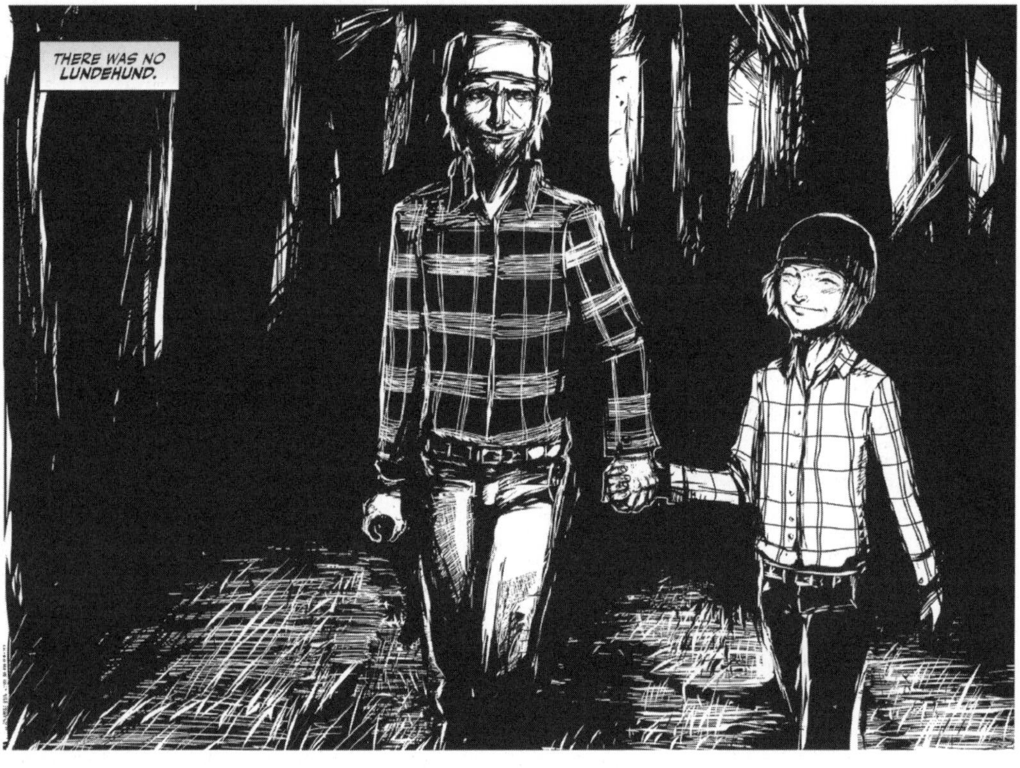
THERE WAS NO LUNDEHUND.

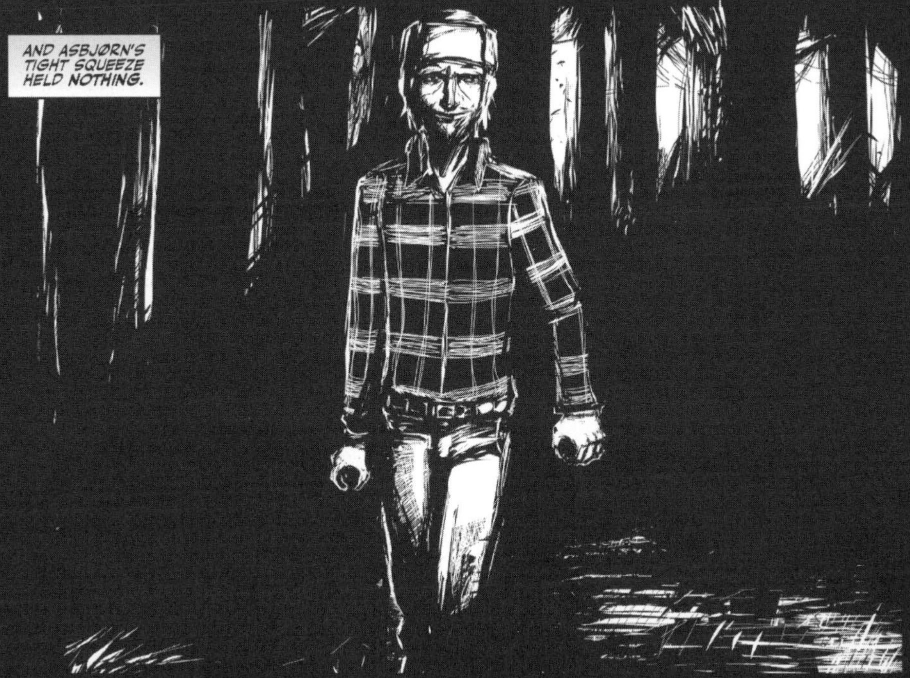
AND ASBJØRN'S TIGHT SQUEEZE HELD NOTHING.

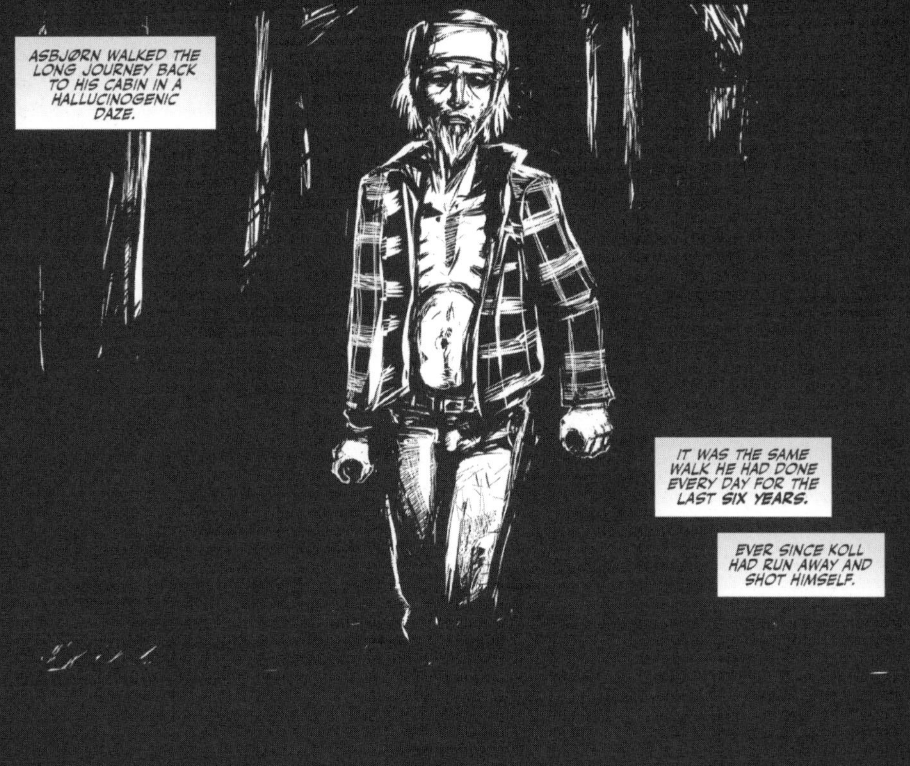
ASBJØRN WALKED THE LONG JOURNEY BACK TO HIS CABIN IN A HALLUCINOGENIC DAZE.
IT WAS THE SAME WALK HE HAD DONE EVERY DAY FOR THE LAST SIX YEARS.
EVER SINCE KOLL HAD RUN AWAY AND SHOT HIMSELF.

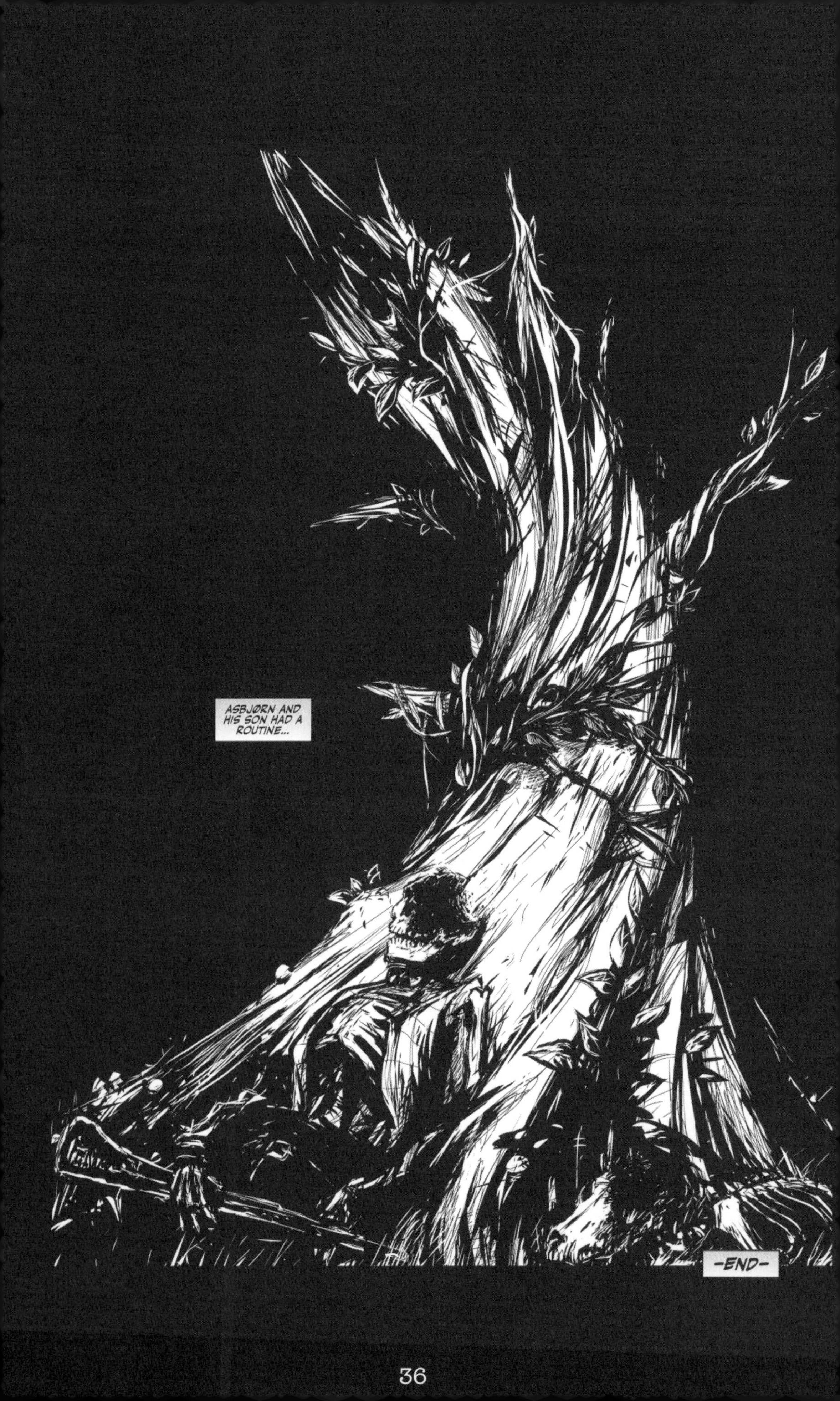
ASBJØRN AND HIS SON HAD A ROUTINE...
-END-

A Lighter Note...

In the 3rd century BC, Ashoka abolished the slave trade and encouraged people to treat slaves well in the Maurya Empire, which covered the majority of India. He stopped short of abolishing slavery itself.

In 1963, the UAE abolished slavery and was one of the last countries to do so.

As of 2011, there are more human slaves alive than at any other time in human history.

Writer/Creator
Neil Gibson

Illustrator
Heru Prasetyo Djalal

www.tpub.co.uk

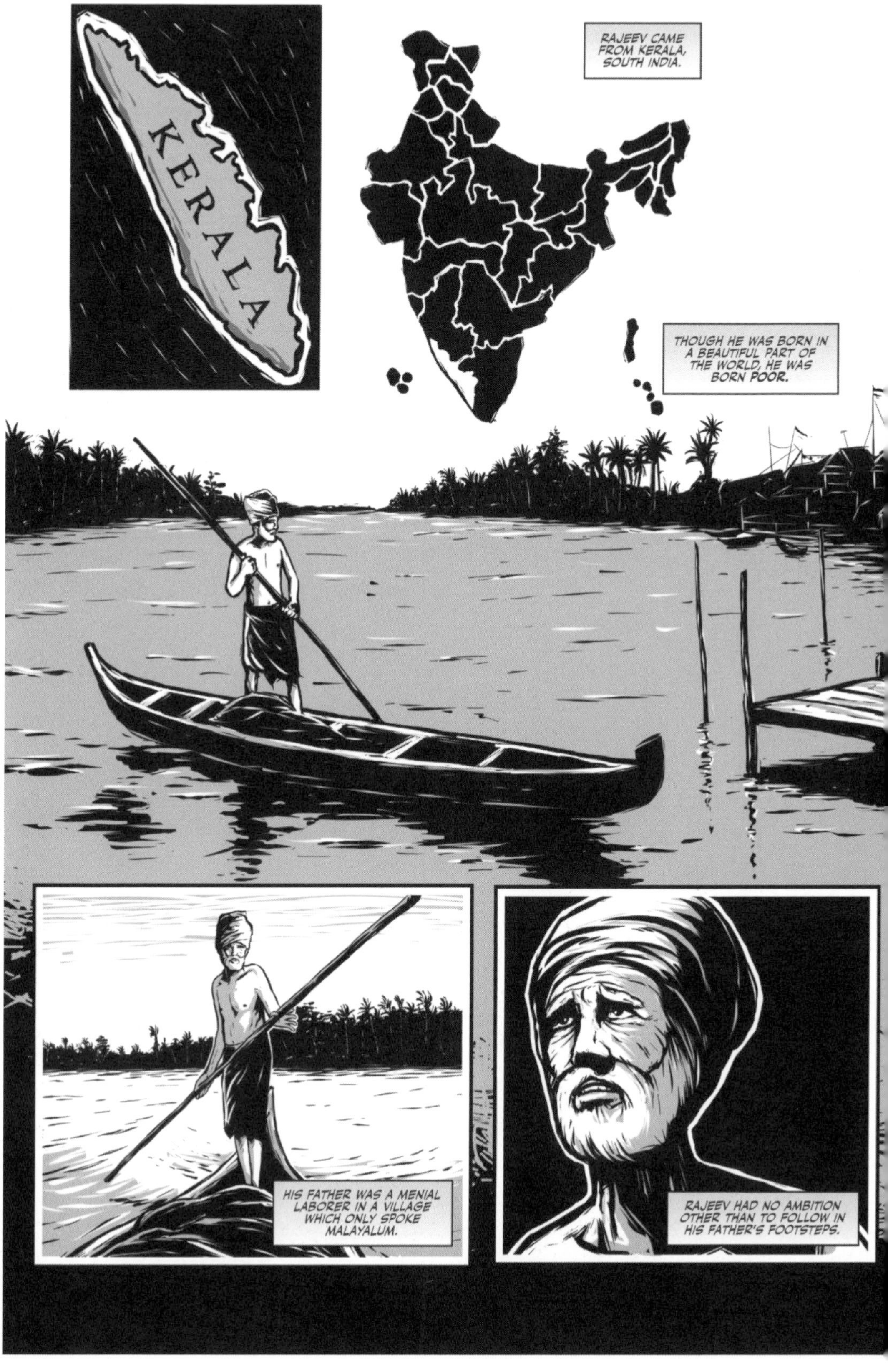
KERALA
RAJEEV CAME FROM KERALA, SOUTH INDIA.
THOUGH HE WAS BORN IN A BEAUTIFUL PART OF THE WORLD, HE WAS BORN POOR.
HIS FATHER WAS A MENIAL LABORER IN A VILLAGE WHICH ONLY SPOKE MALAYALUM.
RAJEEV HAD NO AMBITION OTHER THAN TO FOLLOW IN HIS FATHER'S FOOTSTEPS.

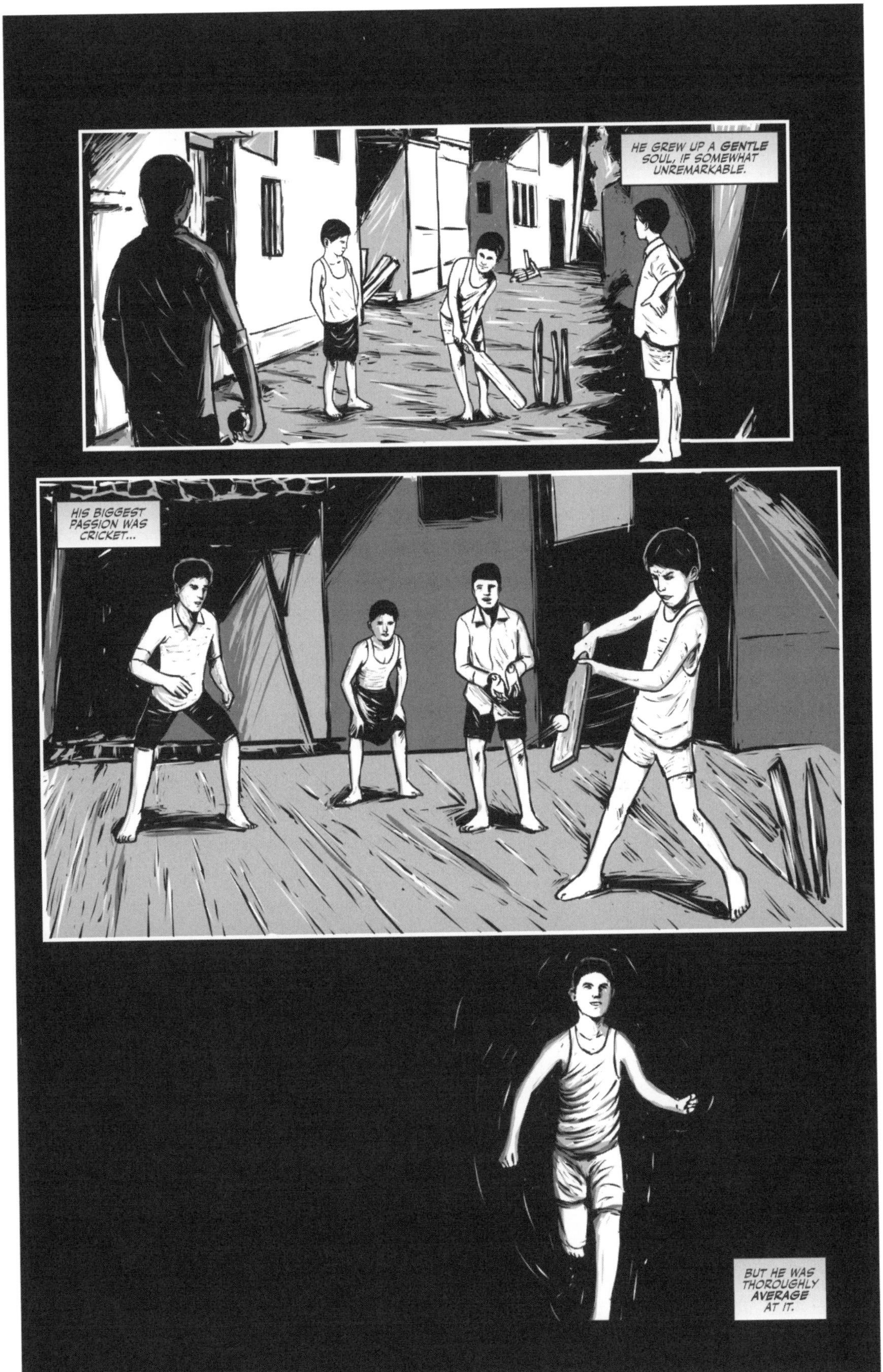
HE GREW UP A GENTLE SOUL, IF SOMEWHAT UNREMARKABLE.
HIS BIGGEST PASSION WAS CRICKET...
BUT HE WAS THOROUGHLY AVERAGE AT IT.

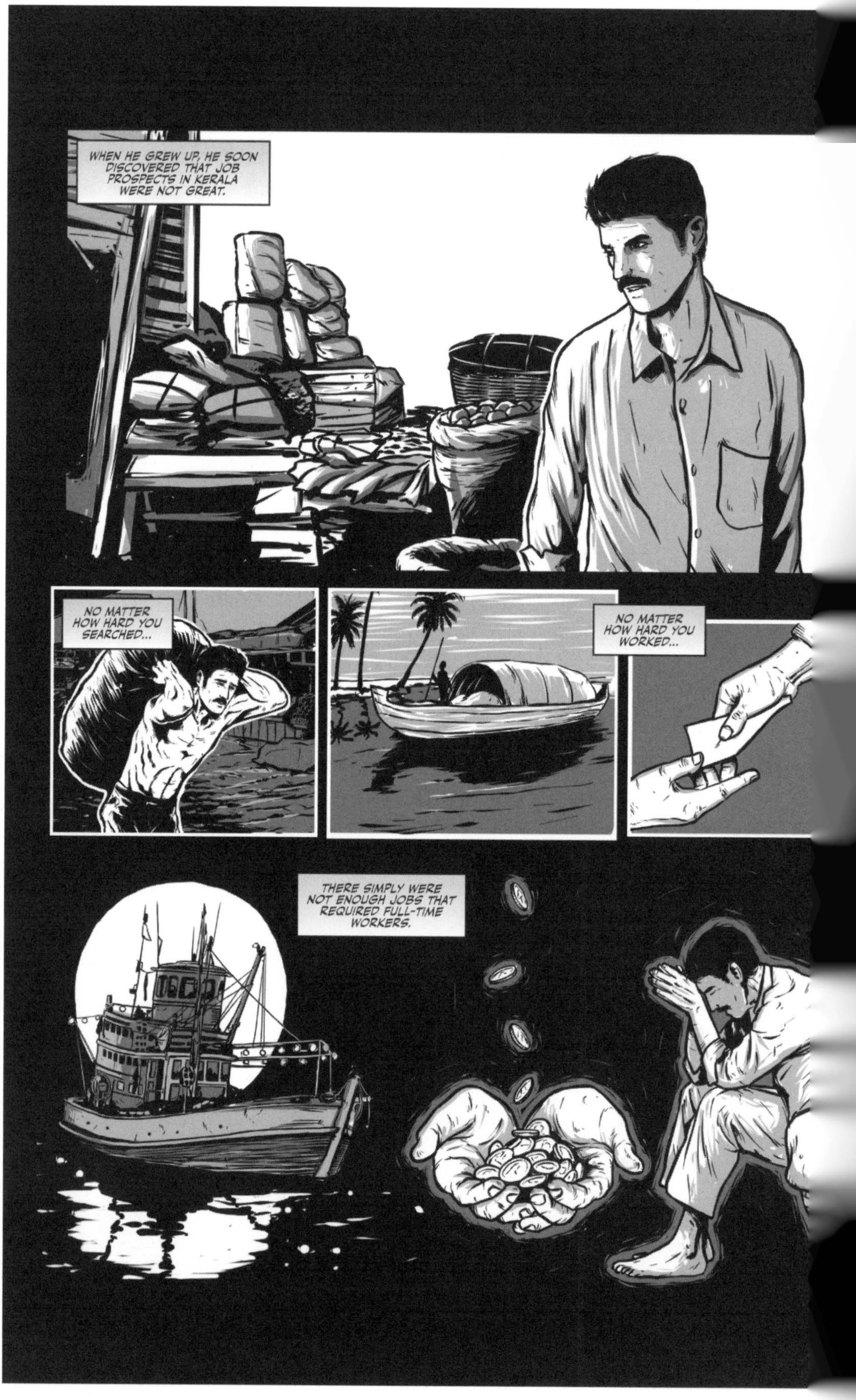
WHEN HE GREW UP, HE SOON DISCOVERED THAT JOB PROSPECTS IN KERALA WERE NOT GREAT.
NO MATTER HOW HARD YOU SEARCHED...
NO MATTER HOW HARD YOU WORKED...
THERE SIMPLY WERE NOT ENOUGH JOBS THAT REQUIRED FULL-TIME WORKERS.

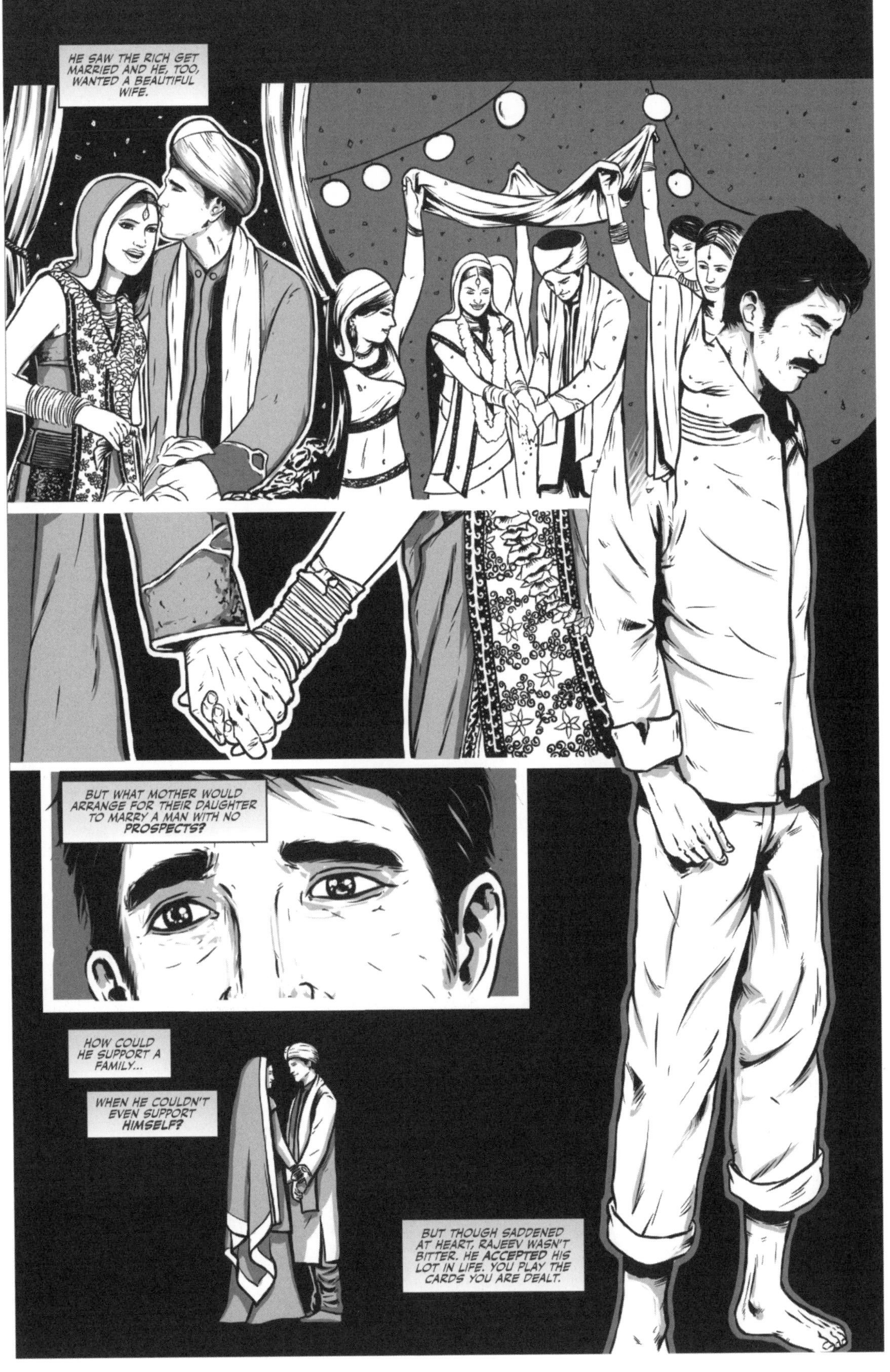
HE SAW THE RICH GET MARRIED AND HE, TOO, WANTED A BEAUTIFUL WIFE.
BUT WHAT MOTHER WOULD ARRANGE FOR THEIR DAUGHTER TO MARRY A MAN WITH NO PROSPECTS?
HOW COULD HE SUPPORT A FAMILY...
WHEN HE COULDN'T EVEN SUPPORT HIMSELF?
BUT THOUGH SADDENED AT HEART, RAJEEV WASN'T BITTER. HE ACCEPTED HIS LOT IN LIFE. YOU PLAY THE CARDS YOU ARE DEALT.

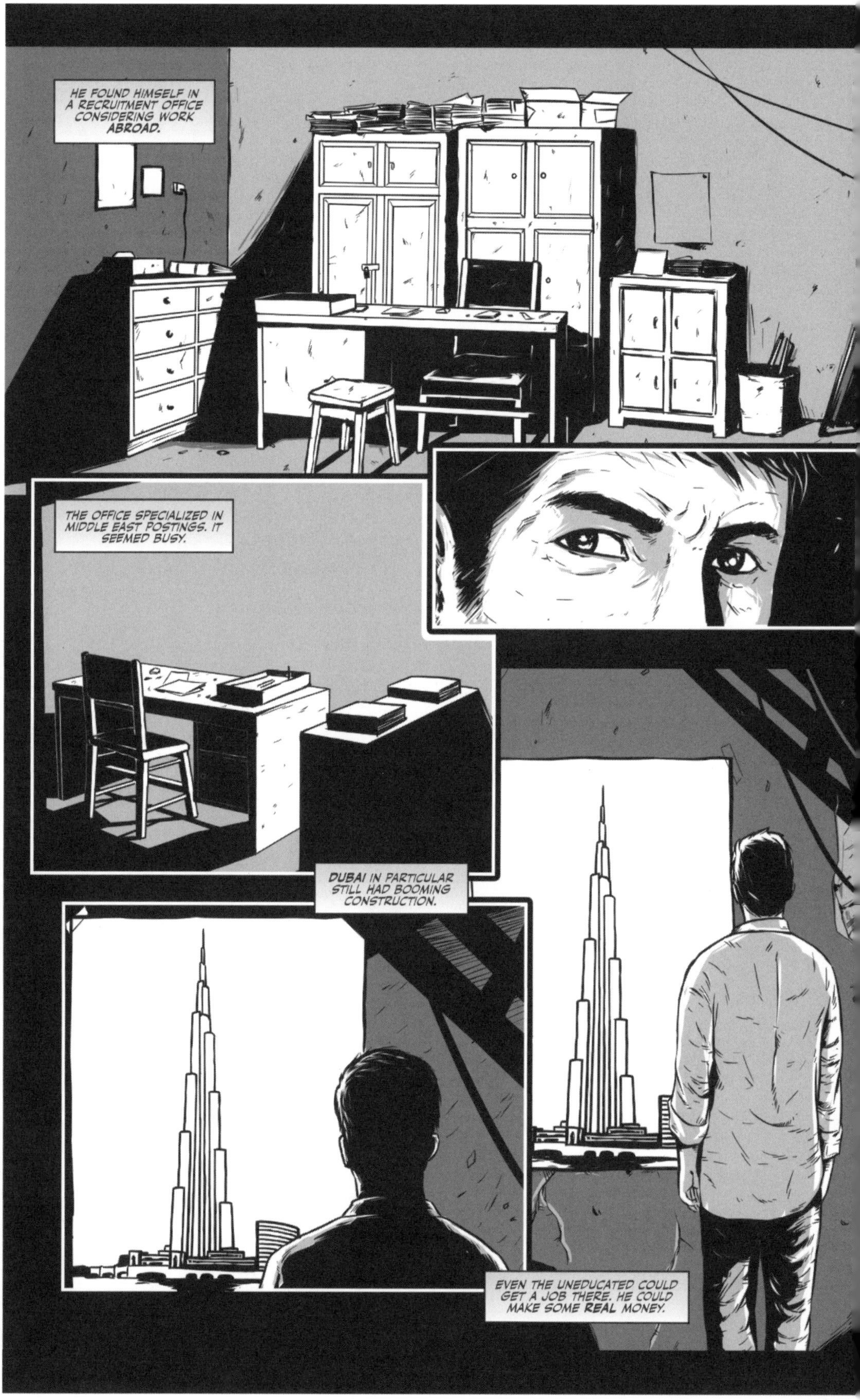
HE FOUND HIMSELF IN A RECRUITMENT OFFICE CONSIDERING WORK ABROAD.
THE OFFICE SPECIALIZED IN MIDDLE EAST POSTINGS. IT SEEMED BUSY.
DUBAI IN PARTICULAR STILL HAD BOOMING CONSTRUCTION.
EVEN THE UNEDUCATED COULD GET A JOB THERE. HE COULD MAKE SOME REAL MONEY.

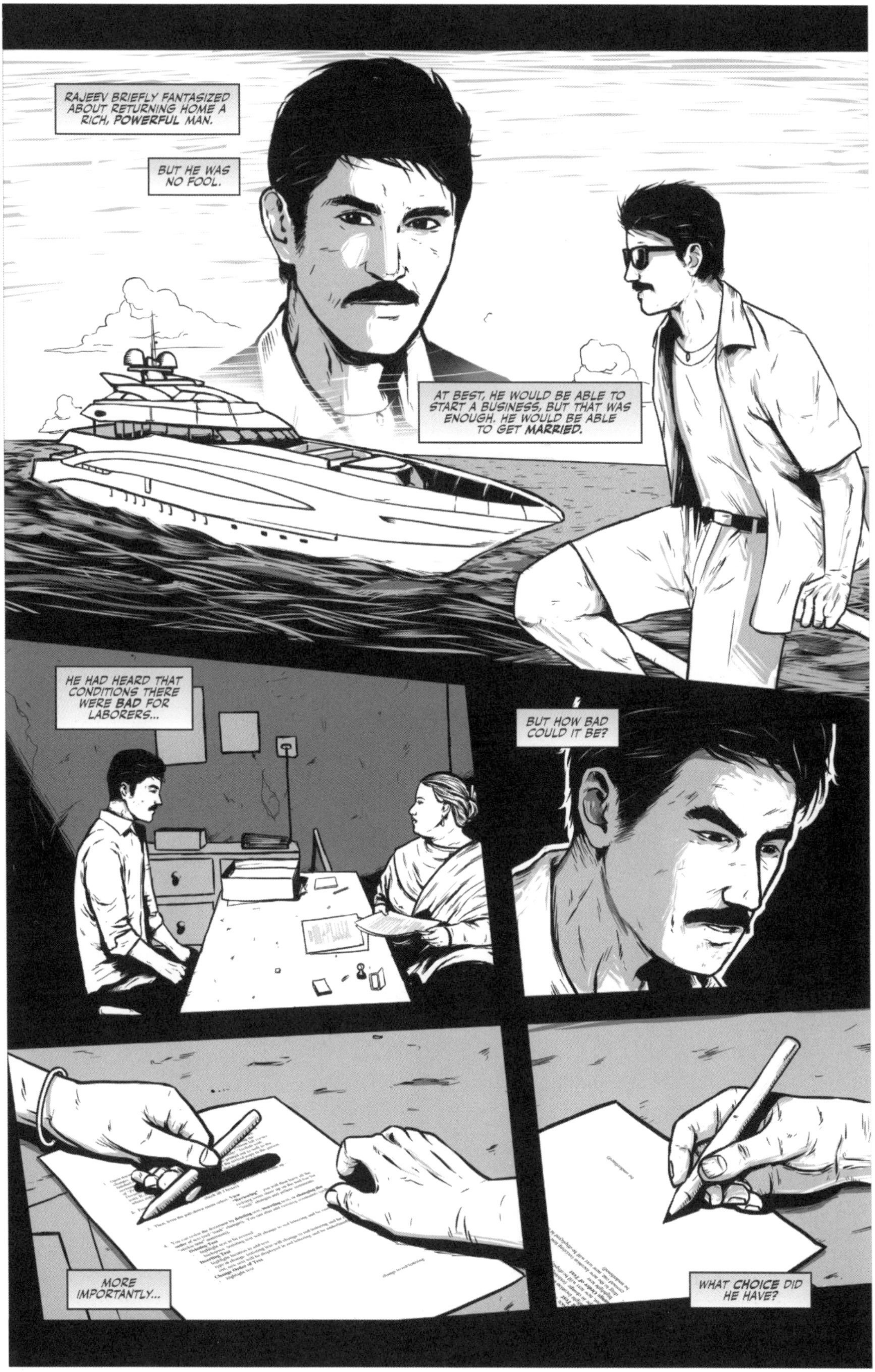
RAJEEV BRIEFLY FANTASIZED ABOUT RETURNING HOME A RICH, POWERFUL MAN.
BUT HE WAS NO FOOL.
AT BEST, HE WOULD BE ABLE TO START A BUSINESS, BUT THAT WAS ENOUGH. HE WOULD BE ABLE TO GET MARRIED.
HE HAD HEARD THAT CONDITIONS THERE WERE BAD FOR LABORERS...
BUT HOW BAD COULD IT BE?
MORE IMPORTANTLY...
WHAT CHOICE DID HE HAVE?

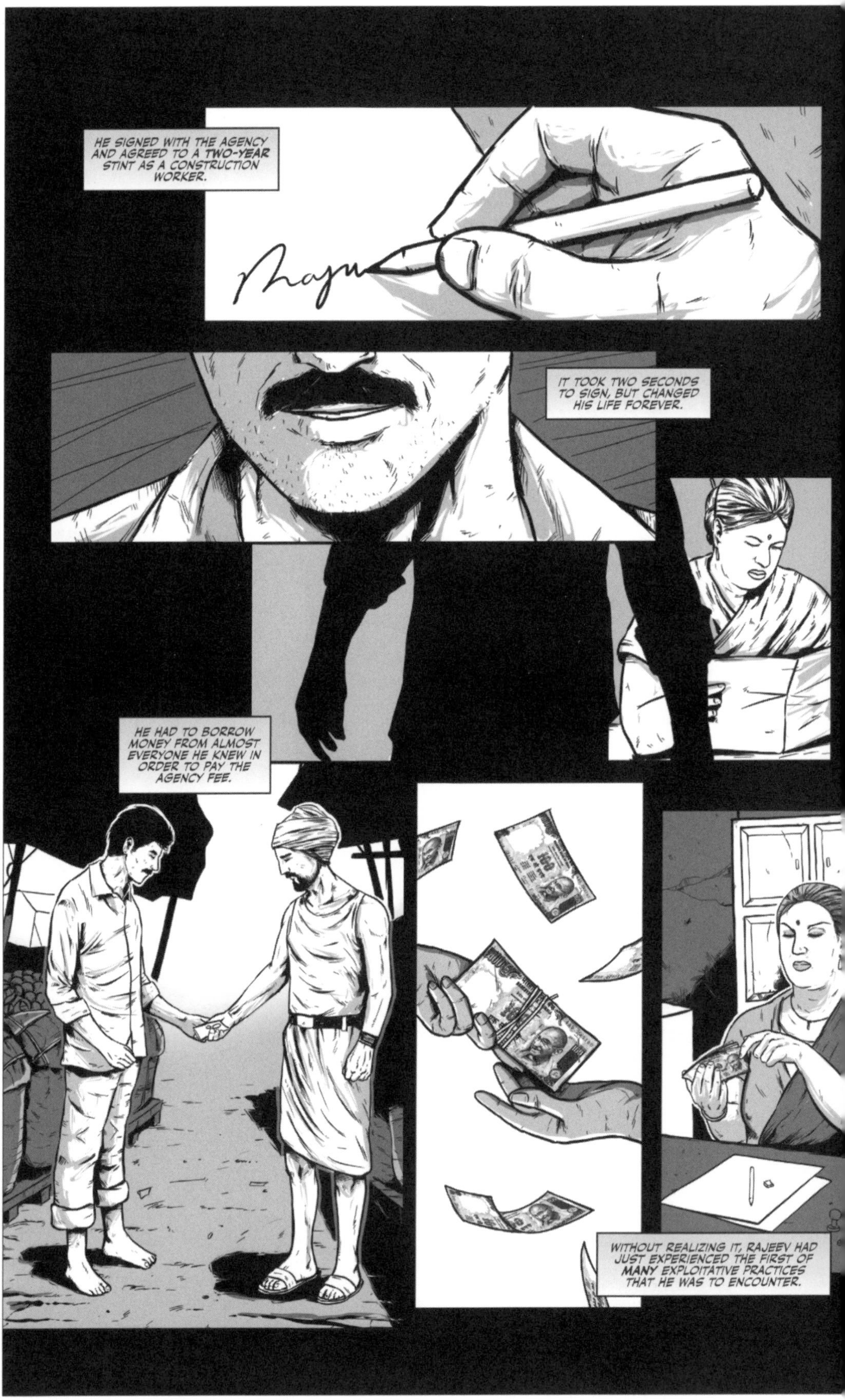
HE SIGNED WITH THE AGENCY AND AGREED TO A TWO-YEAR STINT AS A CONSTRUCTION WORKER.
IT TOOK TWO SECONDS TO SIGN, BUT CHANGED HIS LIFE FOREVER.
HE HAD TO BORROW MONEY FROM ALMOST EVERYONE HE KNEW IN ORDER TO PAY THE AGENCY FEE.
WITHOUT REALIZING IT, RAJEEV HAD JUST EXPERIENCED THE FIRST OF MANY EXPLOITATIVE PRACTICES THAT HE WAS TO ENCOUNTER.

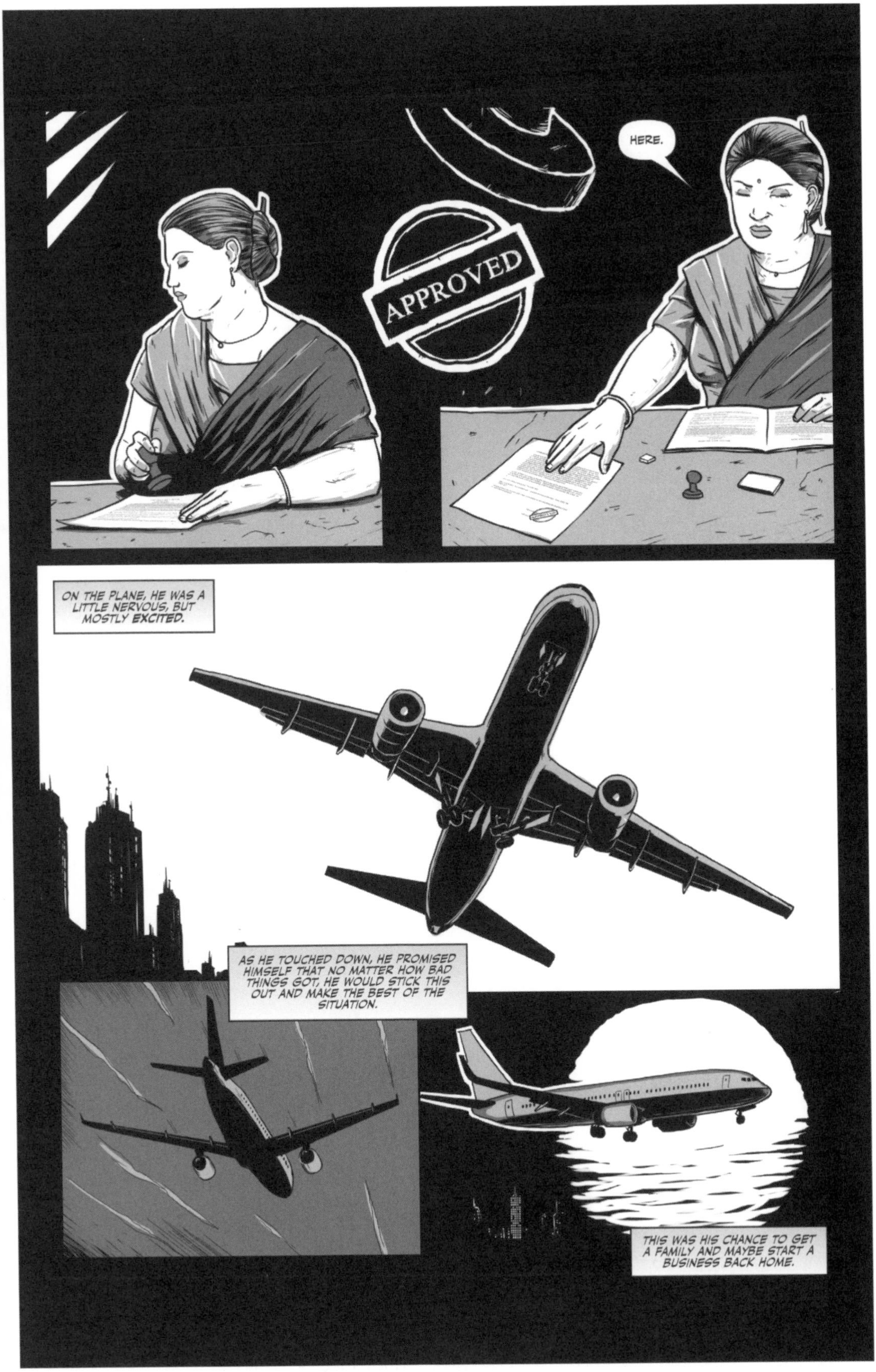
APPROVED
HERE.
ON THE PLANE, HE WAS A LITTLE NERVOUS, BUT MOSTLY EXCITED.
AS HE TOUCHED DOWN, HE PROMISED HIMSELF THAT NO MATTER HOW BAD THINGS GOT, HE WOULD STICK THIS OUT AND MAKE THE BEST OF THE SITUATION.
THIS WAS HIS CHANCE TO GET A FAMILY AND MAYBE START A BUSINESS BACK HOME.

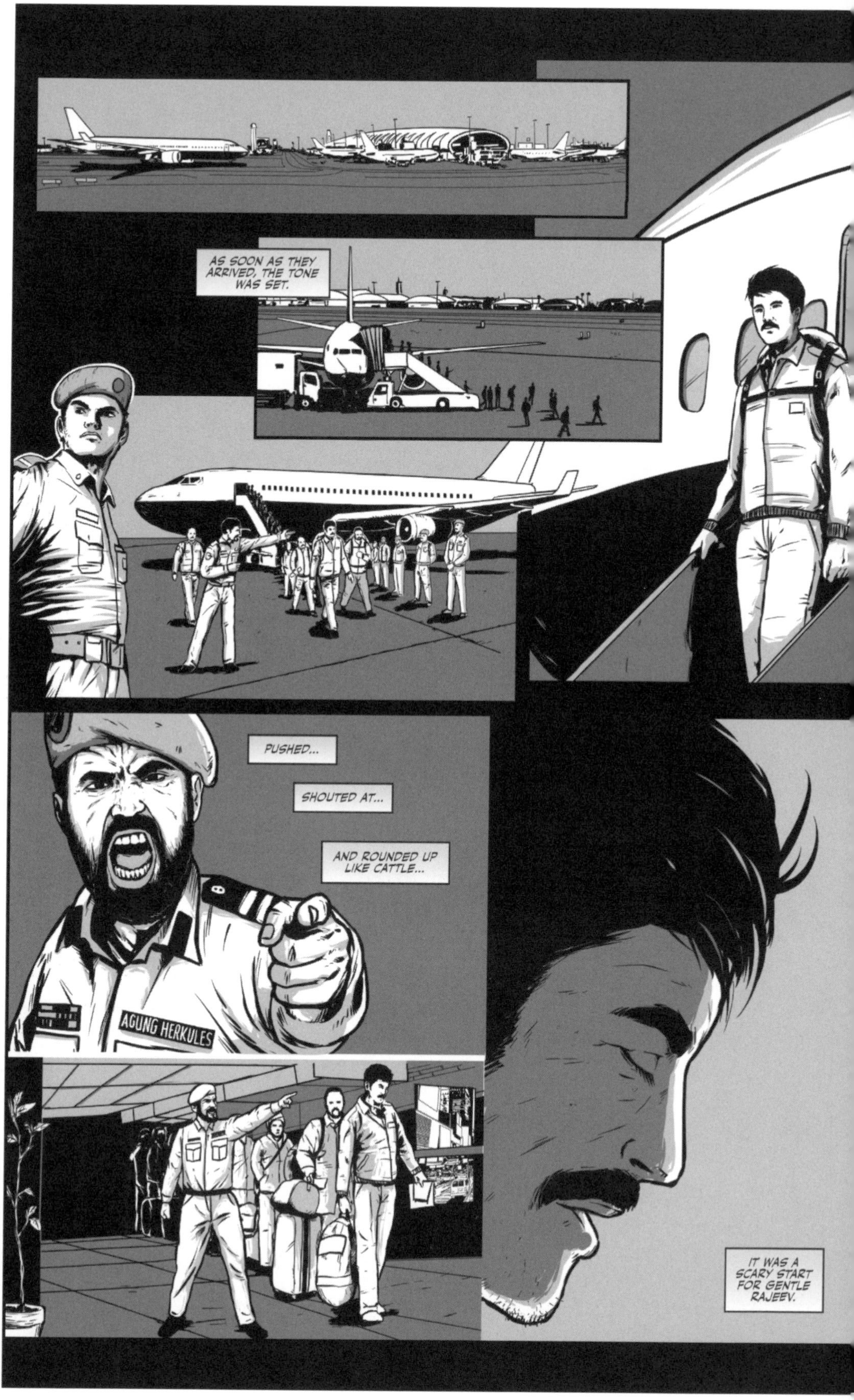
AS SOON AS THEY ARRIVED, THE TONE WAS SET.
PUSHED...
SHOUTED AT...
AND ROUNDED UP LIKE CATTLE...
AGUNG HERKULES
IT WAS A SCARY START FOR GENTLE RAJEEV.

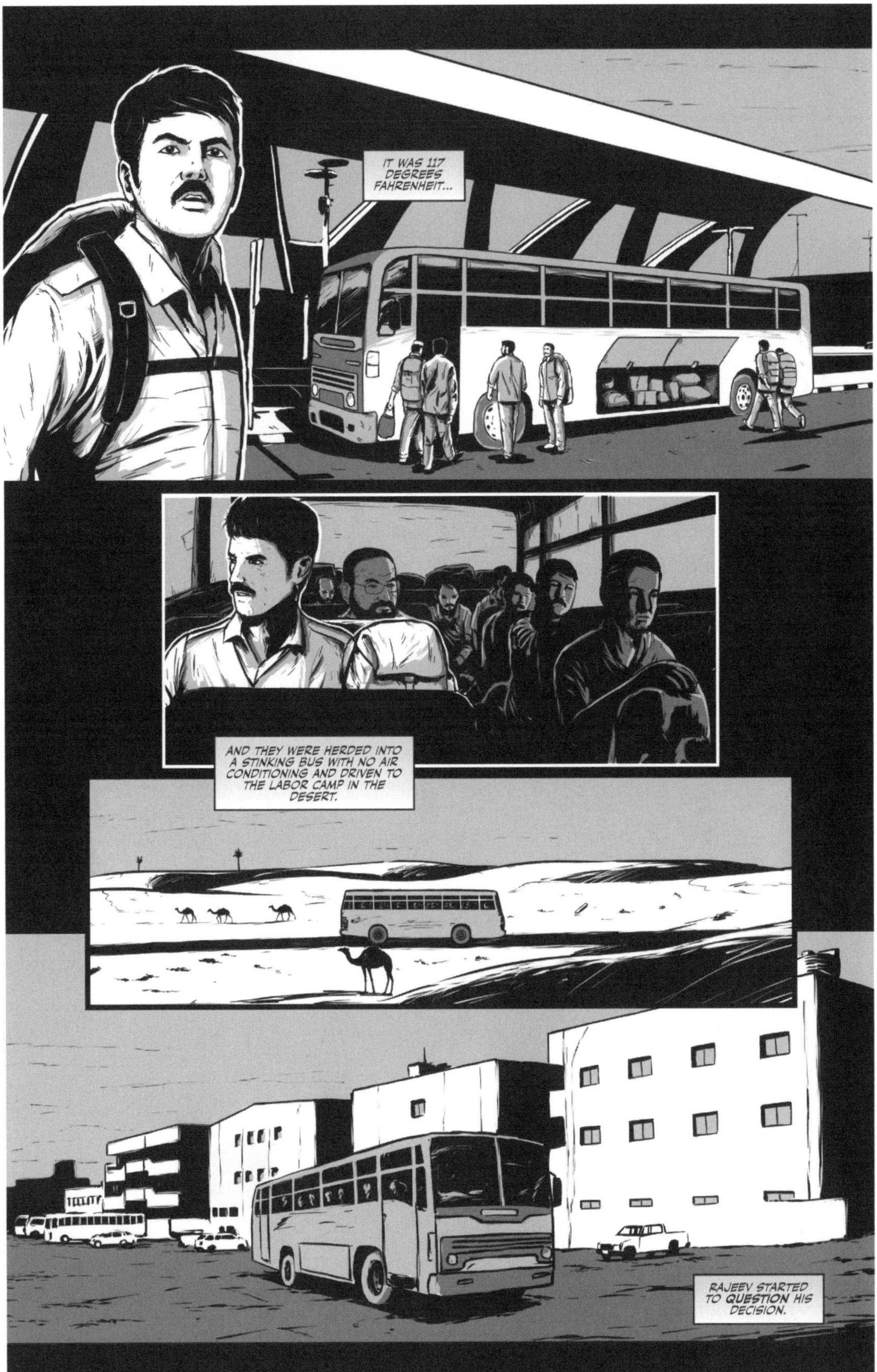
IT WAS 117 DEGREES FAHRENHEIT...
AND THEY WERE HERDED INTO A STINKING BUS WITH NO AIR CONDITIONING AND DRIVEN TO THE LABOR CAMP IN THE DESERT.
RAJEEV STARTED TO **QUESTION** HIS DECISION.

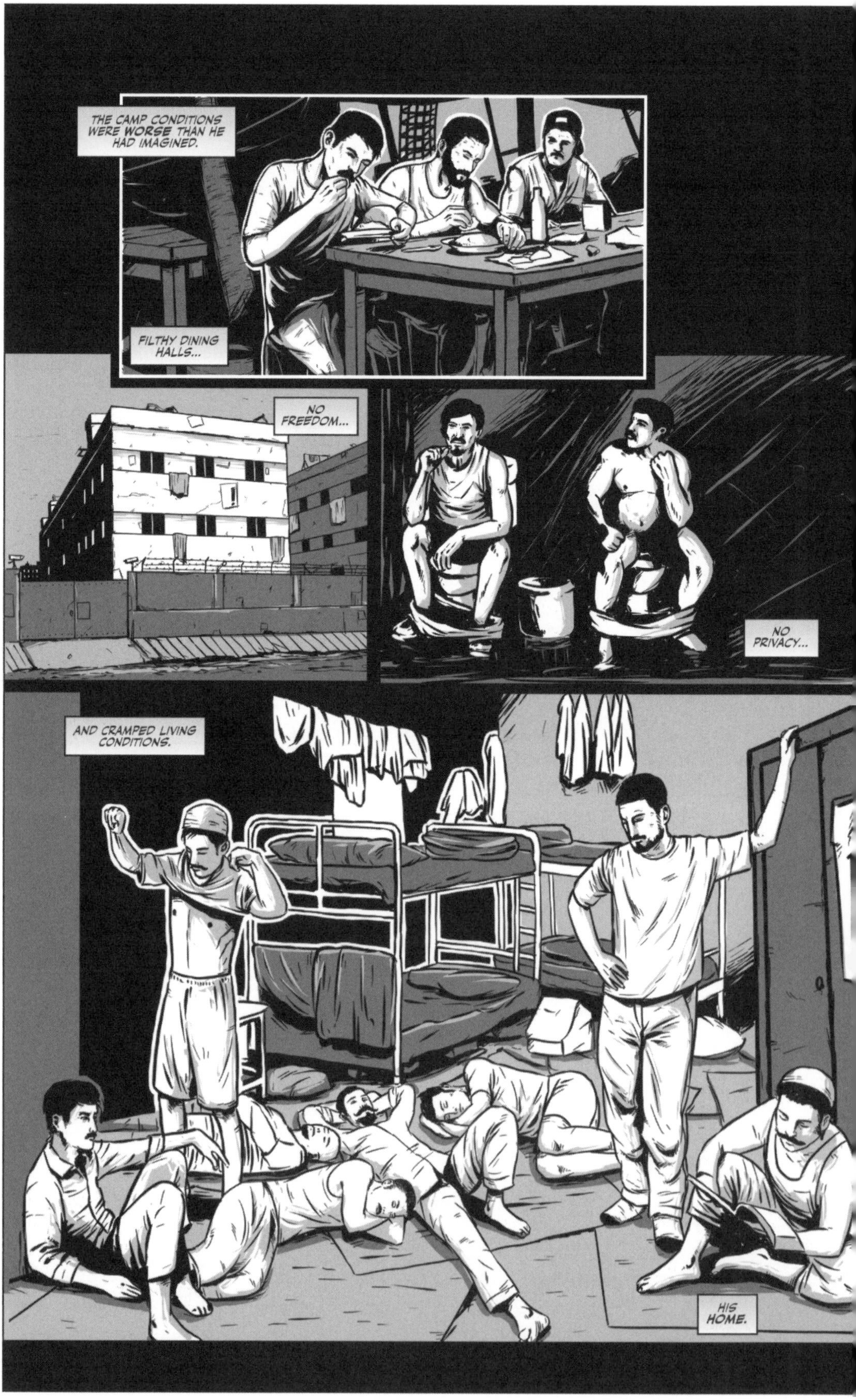
THE CAMP CONDITIONS WERE WORSE THAN HE HAD IMAGINED.
FILTHY DINING HALLS...
NO FREEDOM...
NO PRIVACY...
AND CRAMPED LIVING CONDITIONS.
HIS HOME.

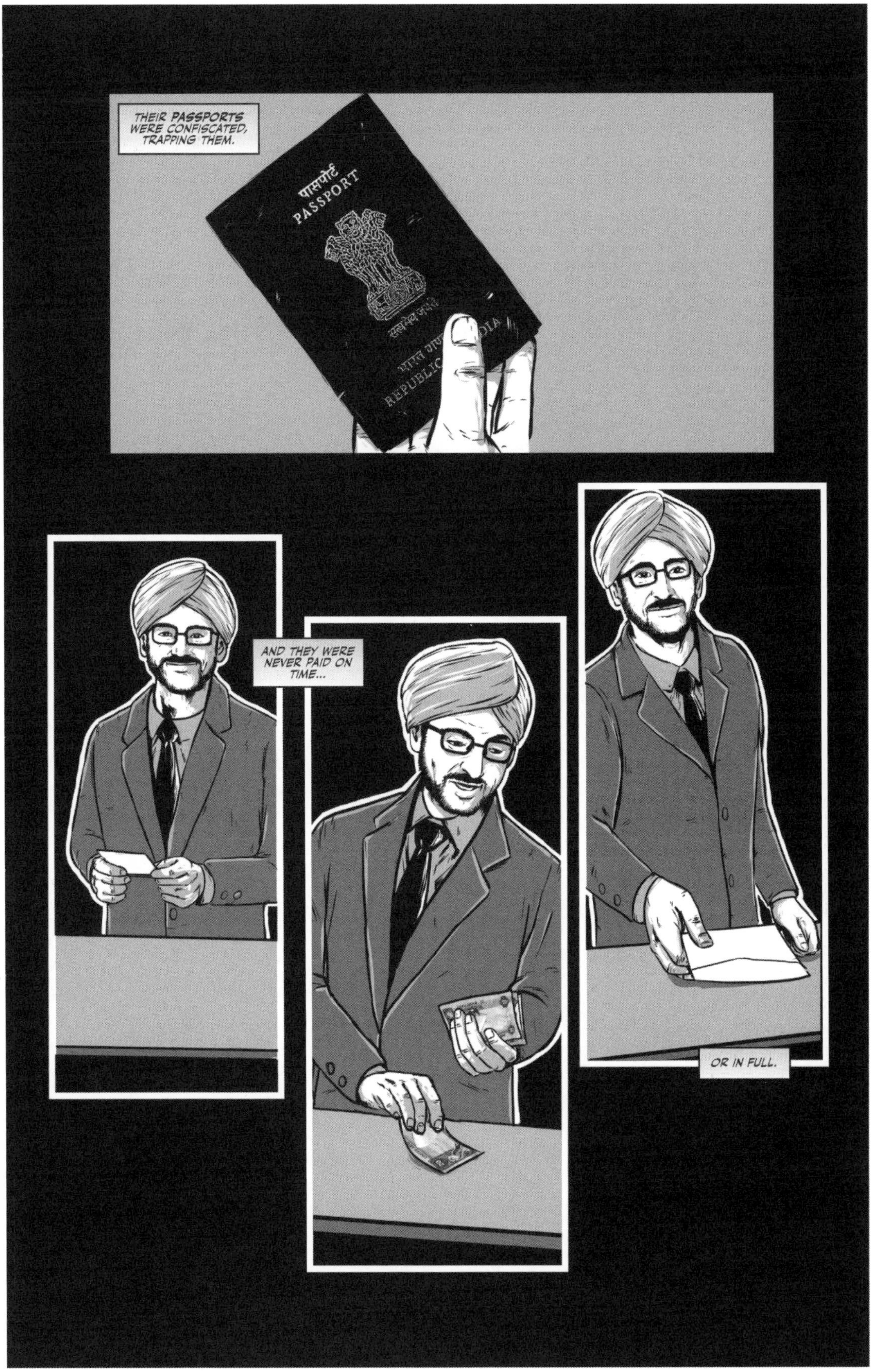
THEIR PASSPORTS WERE CONFISCATED, TRAPPING THEM.
पासपोर्ट
PASSPORT
REPUBLIC OF INDIA
AND THEY WERE NEVER PAID ON TIME...
OR IN FULL.

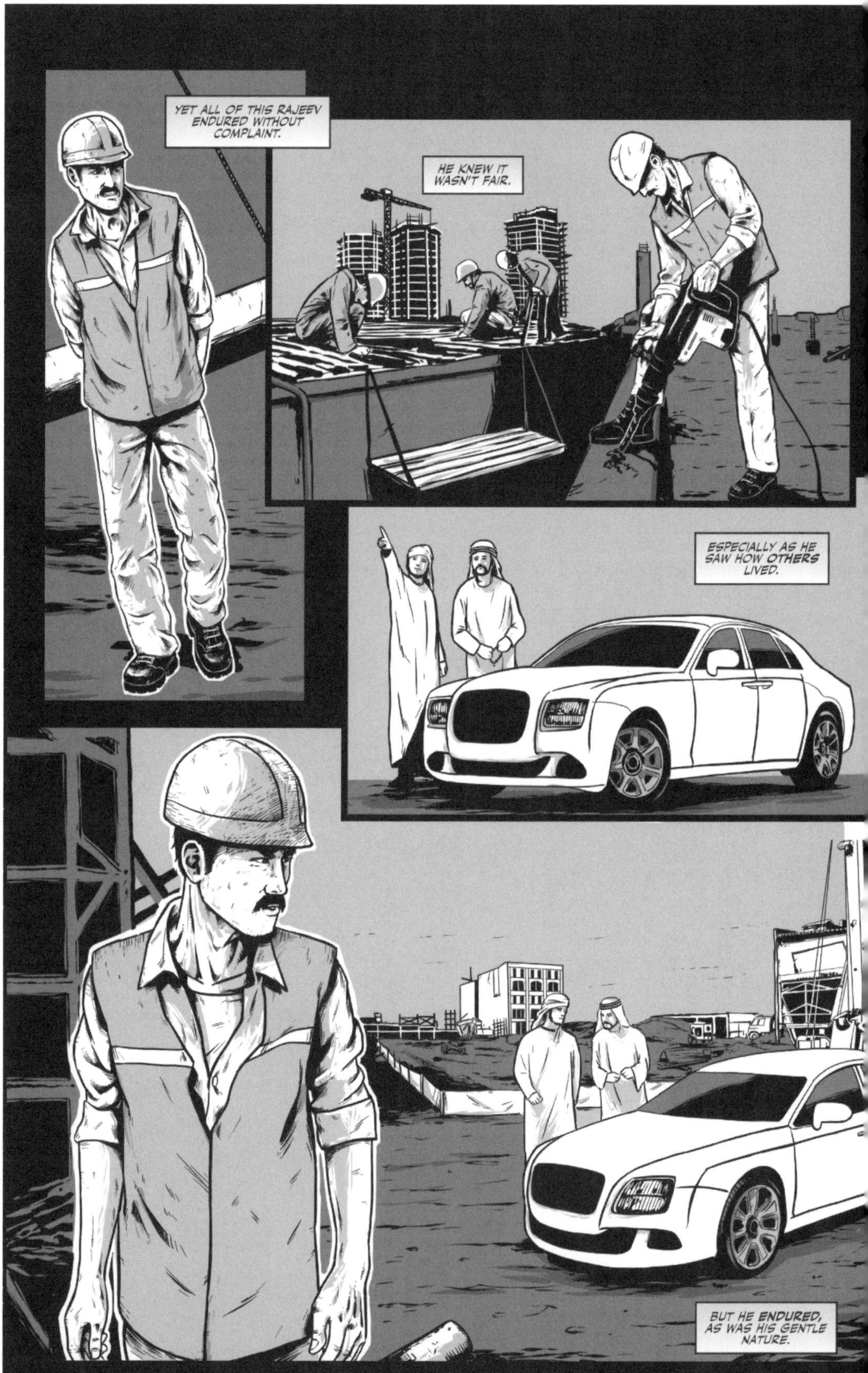
YET ALL OF THIS RAJEEV ENDURED WITHOUT COMPLAINT.
HE KNEW IT WASN'T FAIR.
ESPECIALLY AS HE SAW HOW OTHERS LIVED.
BUT HE ENDURED, AS WAS HIS GENTLE NATURE.

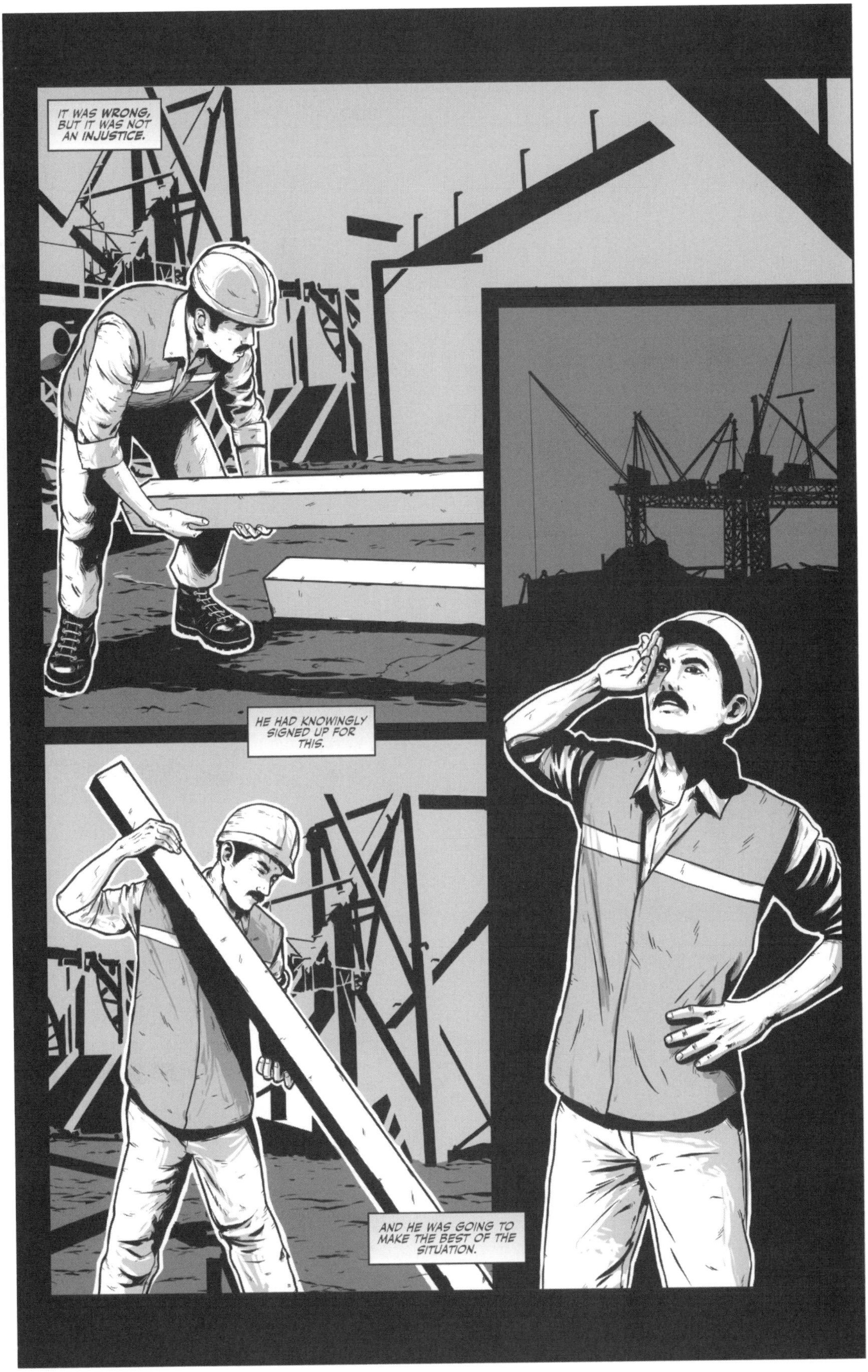
IT WAS WRONG, BUT IT WAS NOT AN INJUSTICE.
HE HAD KNOWINGLY SIGNED UP FOR THIS.
AND HE WAS GOING TO MAKE THE BEST OF THE SITUATION.

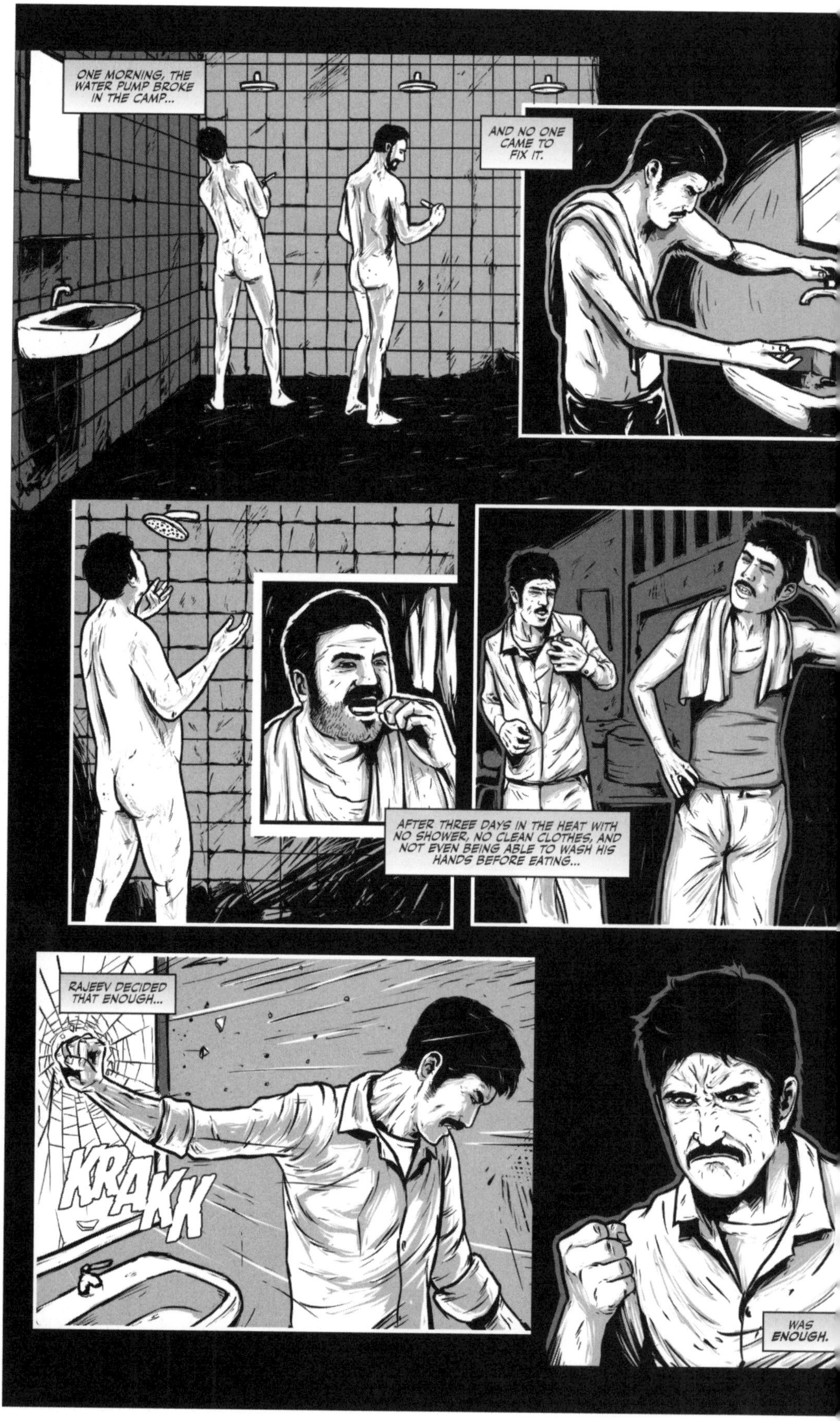
ONE MORNING, THE WATER PUMP BROKE IN THE CAMP...
AND NO ONE CAME TO FIX IT.
AFTER THREE DAYS IN THE HEAT WITH NO SHOWER, NO CLEAN CLOTHES, AND NOT EVEN BEING ABLE TO WASH HIS HANDS BEFORE EATING...
RAJEEV DECIDED THAT ENOUGH...
KRAKK
WAS ENOUGH.

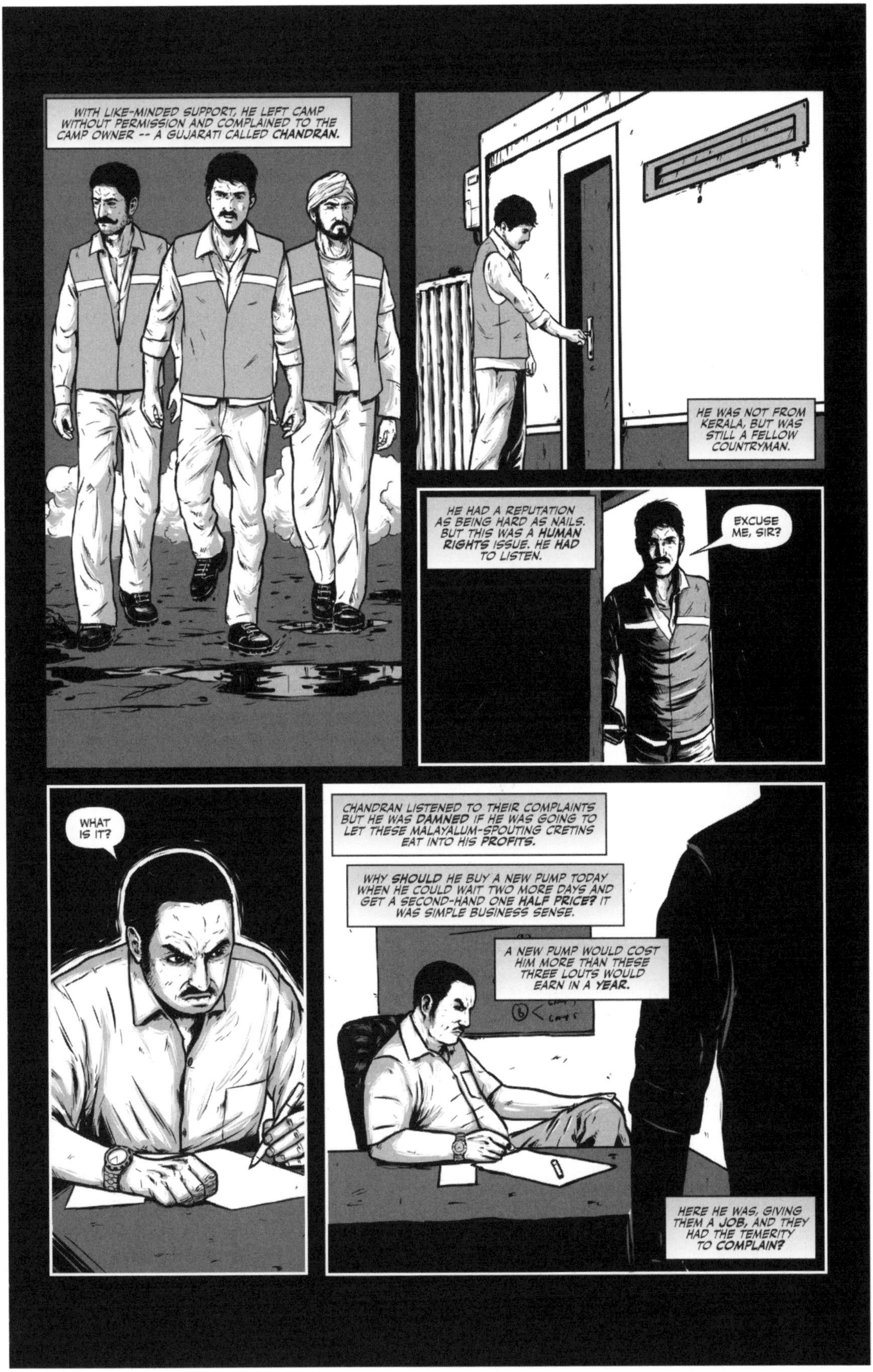

WITH LIKE-MINDED SUPPORT, HE LEFT CAMP WITHOUT PERMISSION AND COMPLAINED TO THE CAMP OWNER -- A GUJARATI CALLED CHANDRAN.
HE WAS NOT FROM KERALA, BUT WAS STILL A FELLOW COUNTRYMAN.
HE HAD A REPUTATION AS BEING HARD AS NAILS. BUT THIS WAS A HUMAN RIGHTS ISSUE. HE HAD TO LISTEN.
EXCUSE ME, SIR?
WHAT IS IT?
CHANDRAN LISTENED TO THEIR COMPLAINTS BUT HE WAS DAMNED IF HE WAS GOING TO LET THESE MALAYALUM-SPOUTING CRETINS EAT INTO HIS PROFITS.
WHY SHOULD HE BUY A NEW PUMP TODAY WHEN HE COULD WAIT TWO MORE DAYS AND GET A SECOND-HAND ONE HALF PRICE? IT WAS SIMPLE BUSINESS SENSE.
A NEW PUMP WOULD COST HIM MORE THAN THESE THREE LOUTS WOULD EARN IN A YEAR.
HERE HE WAS, GIVING THEM A JOB, AND THEY HAD THE TEMERITY TO COMPLAIN?

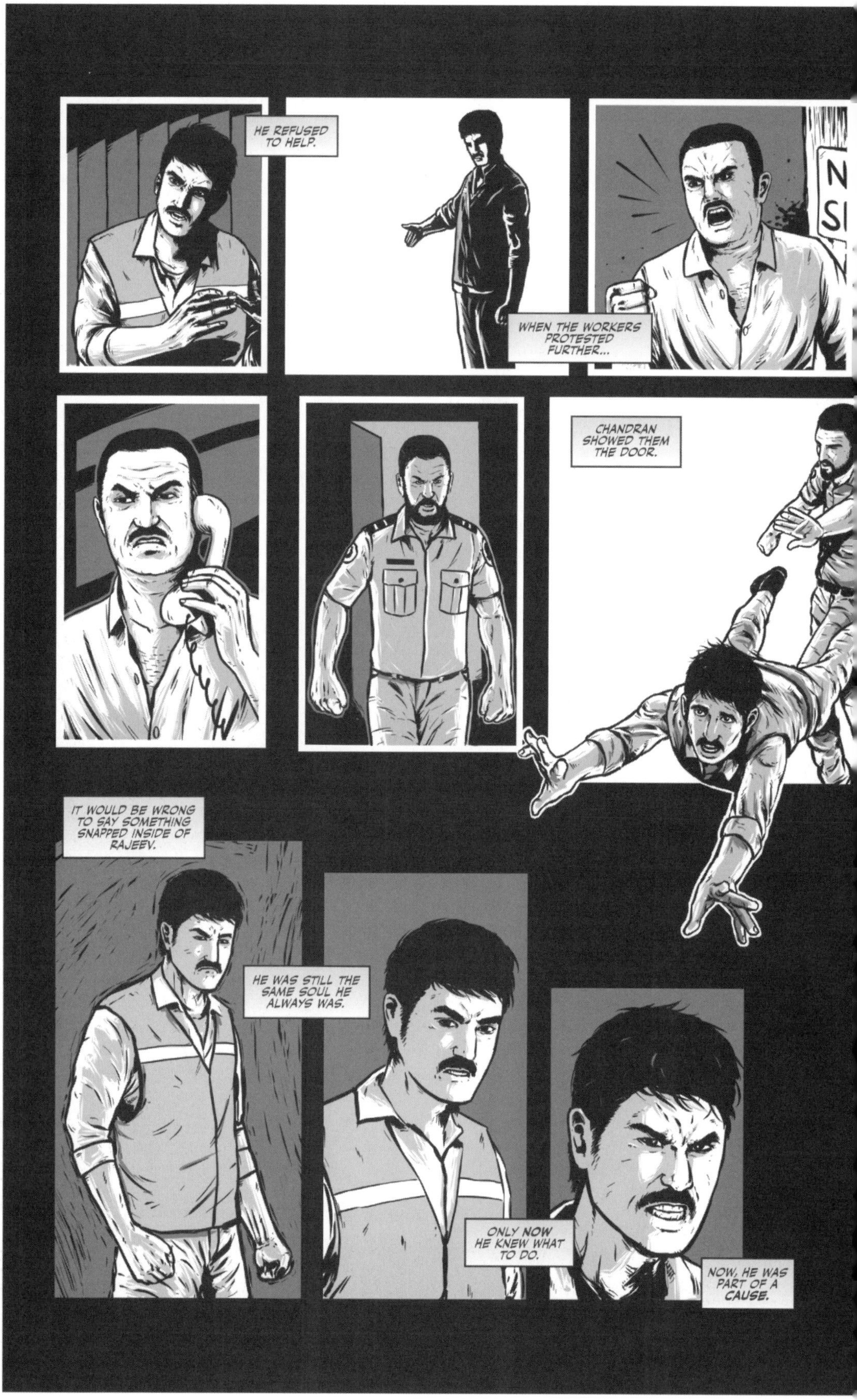
HE REFUSED TO HELP.
WHEN THE WORKERS PROTESTED FURTHER...
CHANDRAN SHOWED THEM THE DOOR.
IT WOULD BE WRONG TO SAY SOMETHING SNAPPED INSIDE OF RAJEEV.
HE WAS STILL THE SAME SOUL HE ALWAYS WAS.
ONLY NOW HE KNEW WHAT TO DO.
NOW, HE WAS PART OF A CAUSE.

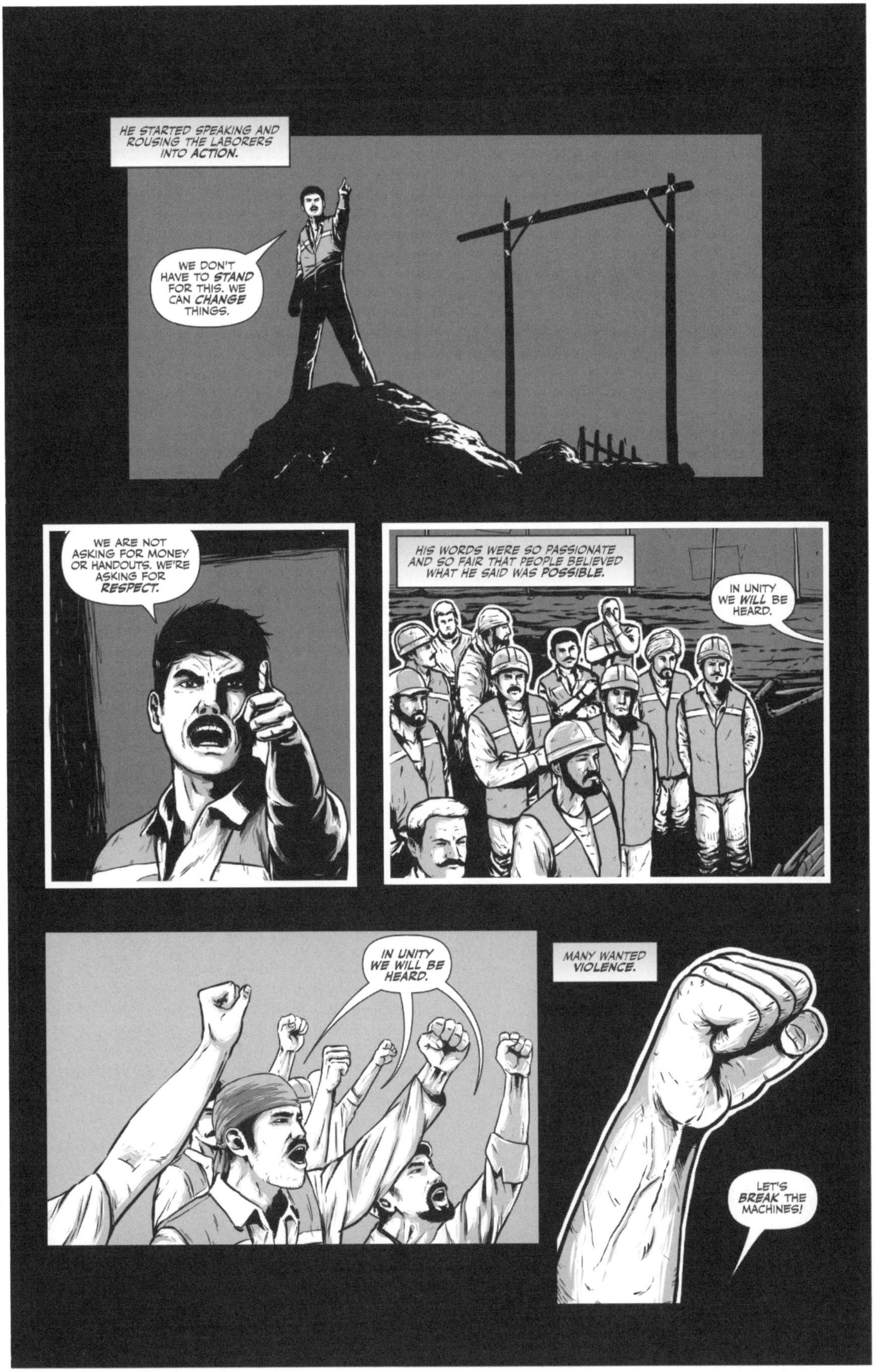

HE STARTED SPEAKING AND ROUSING THE LABORERS INTO ACTION.
WE DON'T HAVE TO STAND FOR THIS. WE CAN CHANGE THINGS.
WE ARE NOT ASKING FOR MONEY OR HANDOUTS. WE'RE ASKING FOR RESPECT.
HIS WORDS WERE SO PASSIONATE AND SO FAIR THAT PEOPLE BELIEVED WHAT HE SAID WAS POSSIBLE.
IN UNITY WE WILL BE HEARD.
IN UNITY WE WILL BE HEARD.
MANY WANTED VIOLENCE.
LET'S BREAK THE MACHINES!

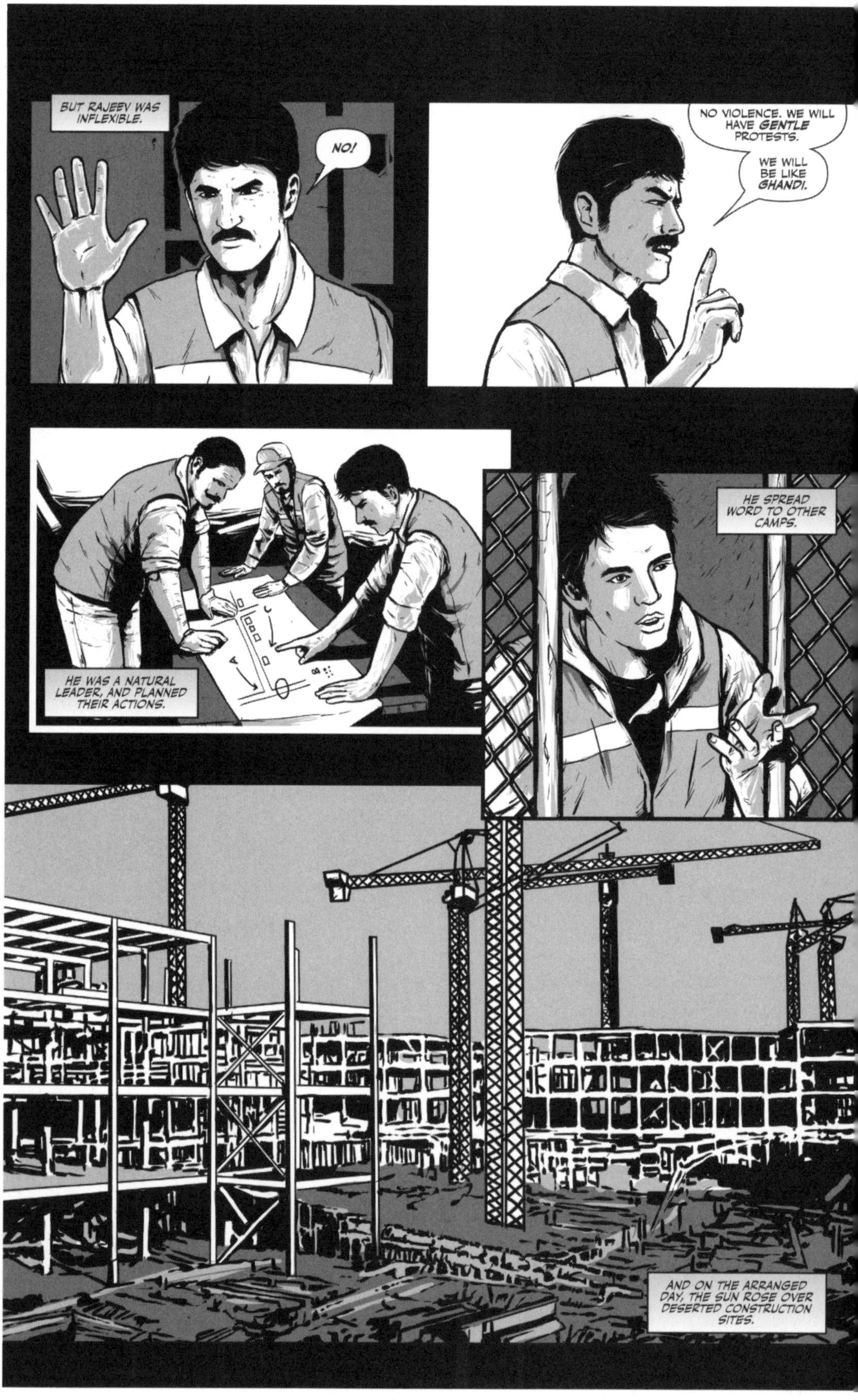
BUT RAJEEV WAS INFLEXIBLE.
NO!
NO VIOLENCE. WE WILL HAVE GENTLE PROTESTS.
WE WILL BE LIKE GHANDI.
HE WAS A NATURAL LEADER, AND PLANNED THEIR ACTIONS.
HE SPREAD WORD TO OTHER CAMPS.
AND ON THE ARRANGED DAY, THE SUN ROSE OVER DESERTED CONSTRUCTION SITES.

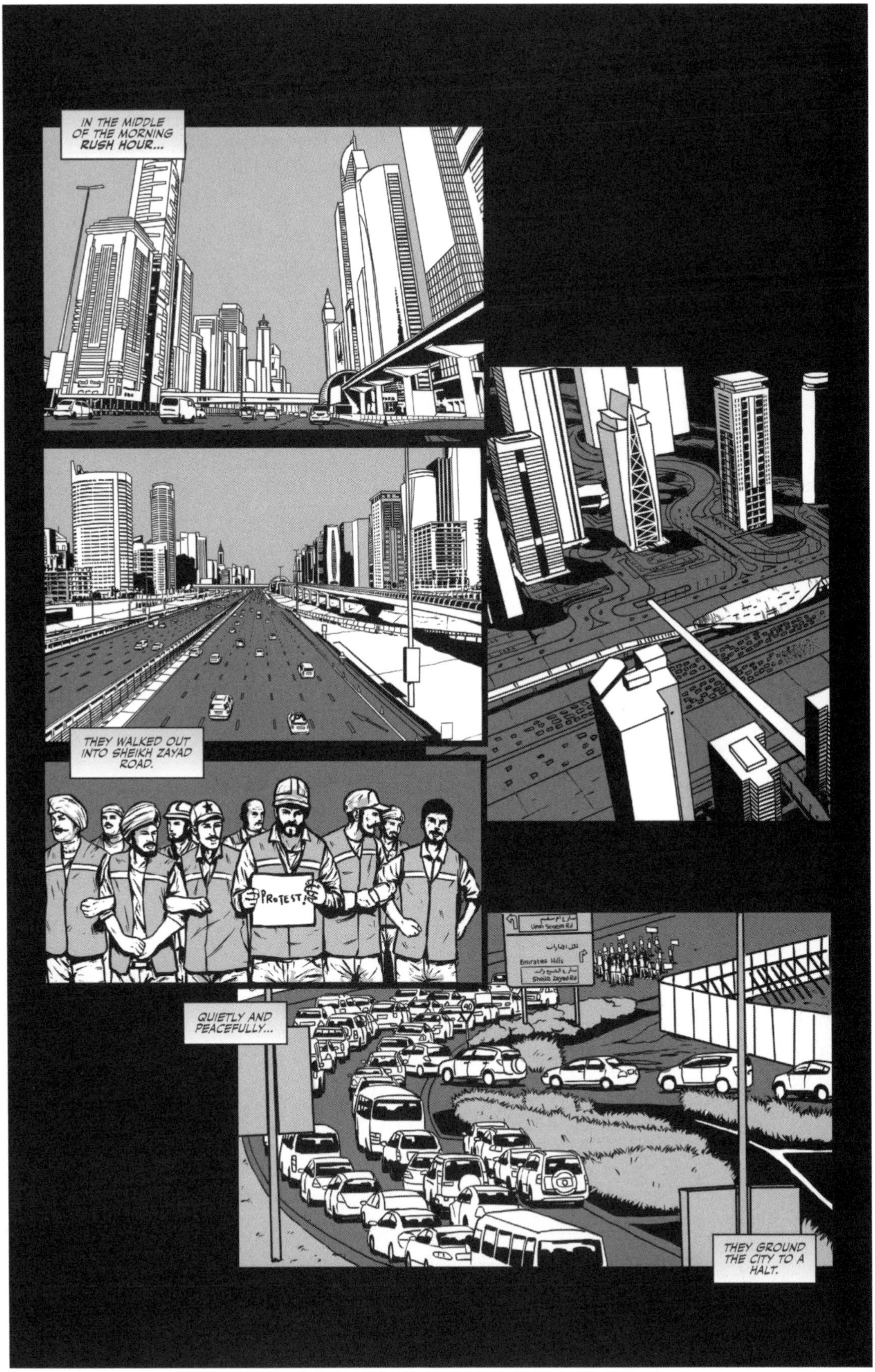
IN THE MIDDLE OF THE MORNING RUSH HOUR...
THEY WALKED OUT INTO SHEIKH ZAYAD ROAD.
PROTEST!
QUIETLY AND PEACEFULLY...
Emirates Hills
Sheikh Zayed Rd
THEY GROUND THE CITY TO A HALT.

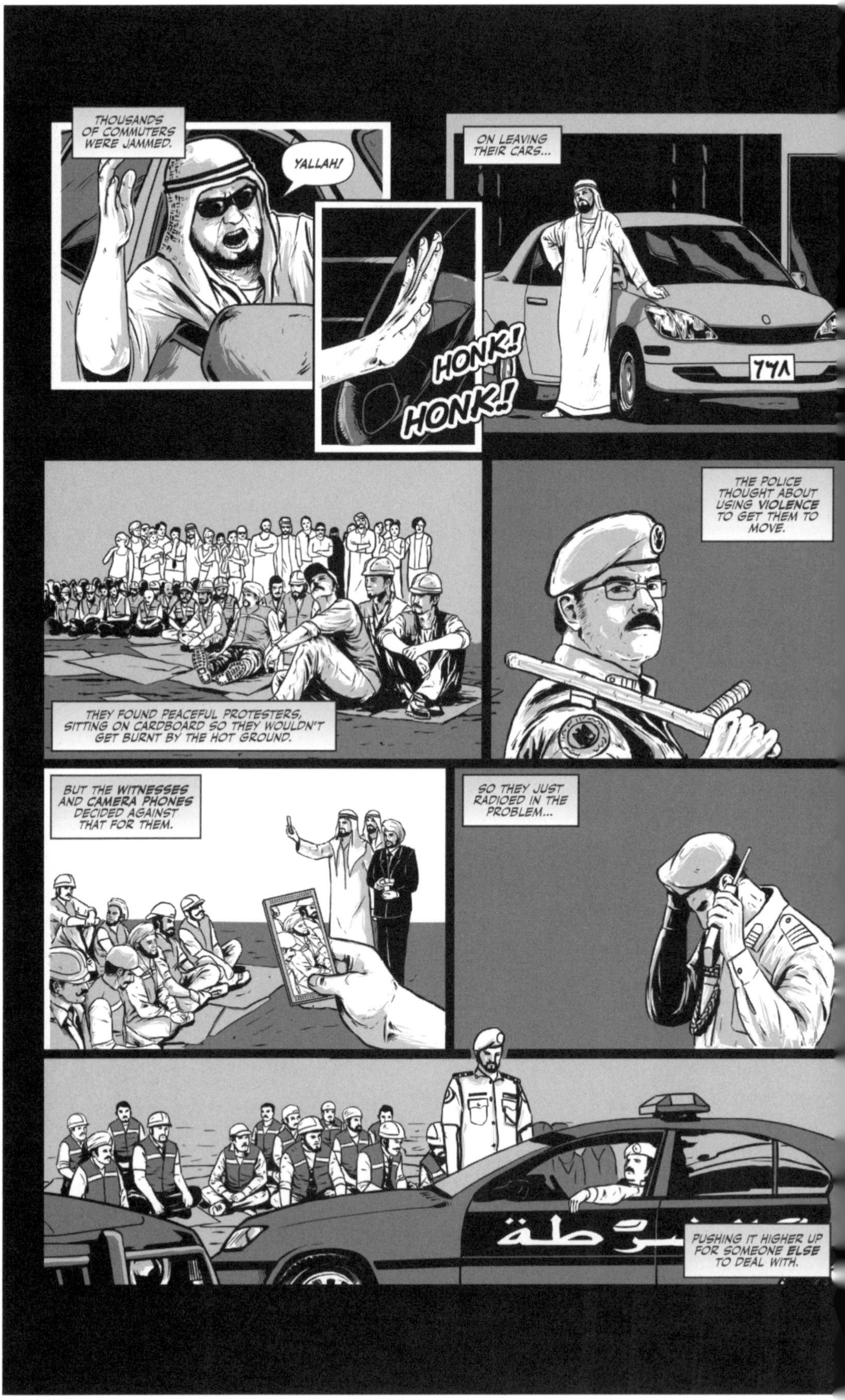
THOUSANDS OF COMMUTERS WERE JAMMED.
YALLAH!
HONK! HONK!
ON LEAVING THEIR CARS...
٦٦٨
THEY FOUND PEACEFUL PROTESTERS, SITTING ON CARDBOARD SO THEY WOULDN'T GET BURNT BY THE HOT GROUND.
THE POLICE THOUGHT ABOUT USING VIOLENCE TO GET THEM TO MOVE.
BUT THE WITNESSES AND CAMERA PHONES DECIDED AGAINST THAT FOR THEM.
SO THEY JUST RADIOED IN THE PROBLEM...
PUSHING IT HIGHER UP FOR SOMEONE ELSE TO DEAL WITH.

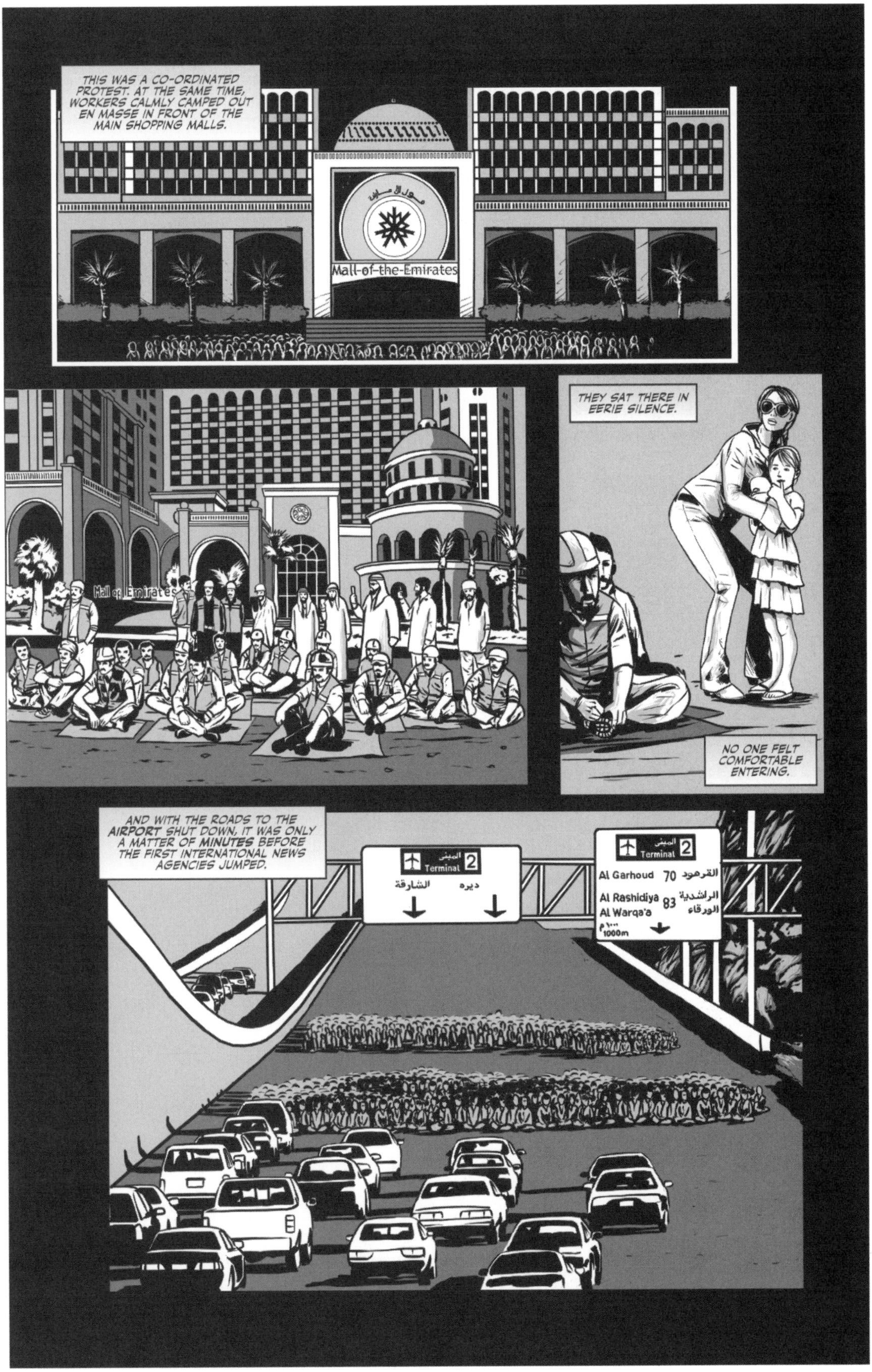
THIS WAS A CO-ORDINATED PROTEST. AT THE SAME TIME, WORKERS CALMLY CAMPED OUT EN MASSE IN FRONT OF THE MAIN SHOPPING MALLS.
Mall-of-the-Emirates
Mall of Emirates
THEY SAT THERE IN EERIE SILENCE.
NO ONE FELT COMFORTABLE ENTERING.
AND WITH THE ROADS TO THE AIRPORT SHUT DOWN, IT WAS ONLY A MATTER OF MINUTES BEFORE THE FIRST INTERNATIONAL NEWS AGENCIES JUMPED.
Terminal 2
الشارقة
ديره
Terminal 2
Al Garhoud 70 القرهود
Al Rashidiya 83 الراشدية
Al Warqa'a الورقاء
1000m

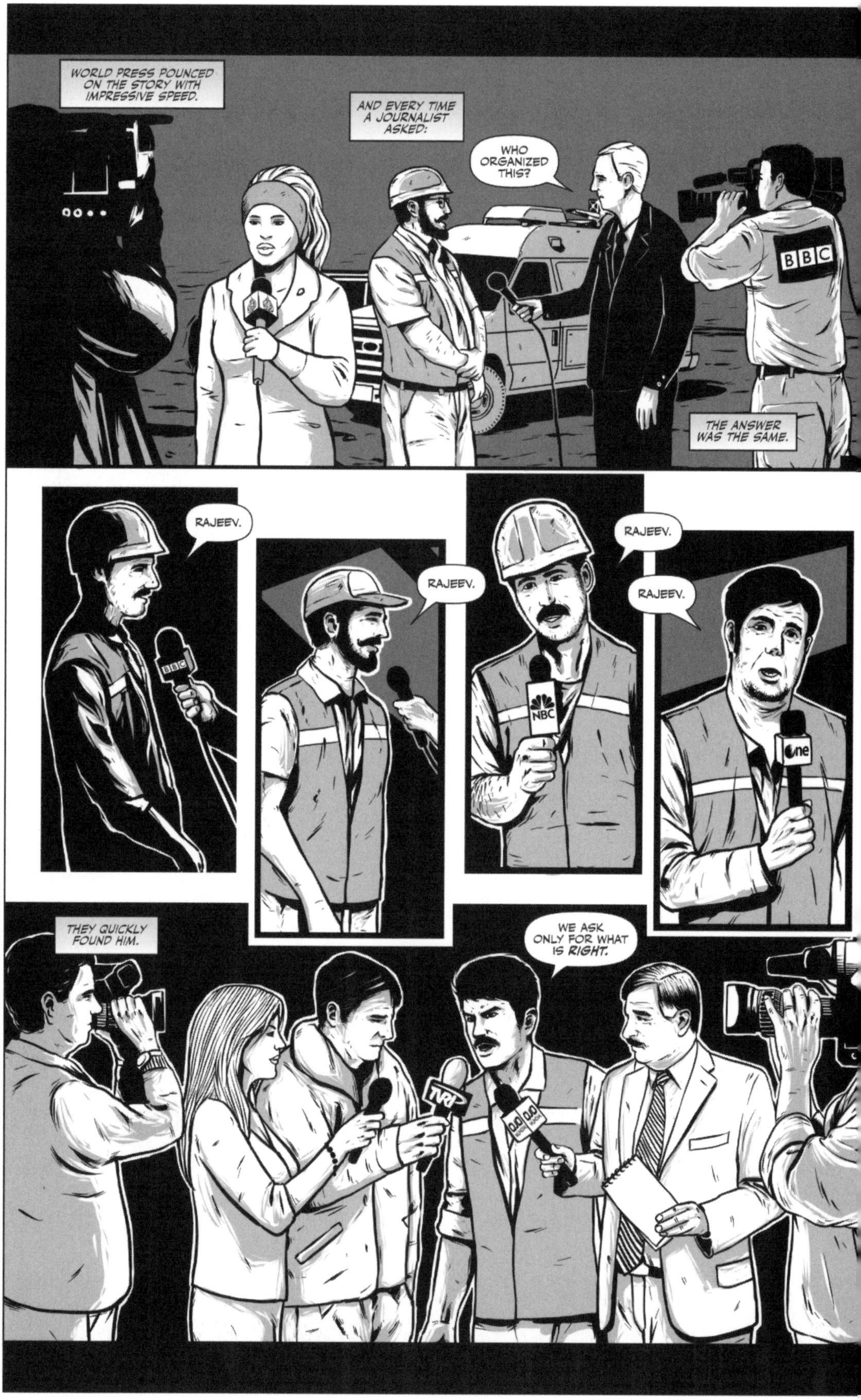
WORLD PRESS POUNCED ON THE STORY WITH IMPRESSIVE SPEED.
AND EVERY TIME A JOURNALIST ASKED:
WHO ORGANIZED THIS?
BBC
THE ANSWER WAS THE SAME.
RAJEEV.
BBC
RAJEEV.
RAJEEV.
NBC
RAJEEV.
One
THEY QUICKLY FOUND HIM.
WE ASK ONLY FOR WHAT IS *RIGHT*.

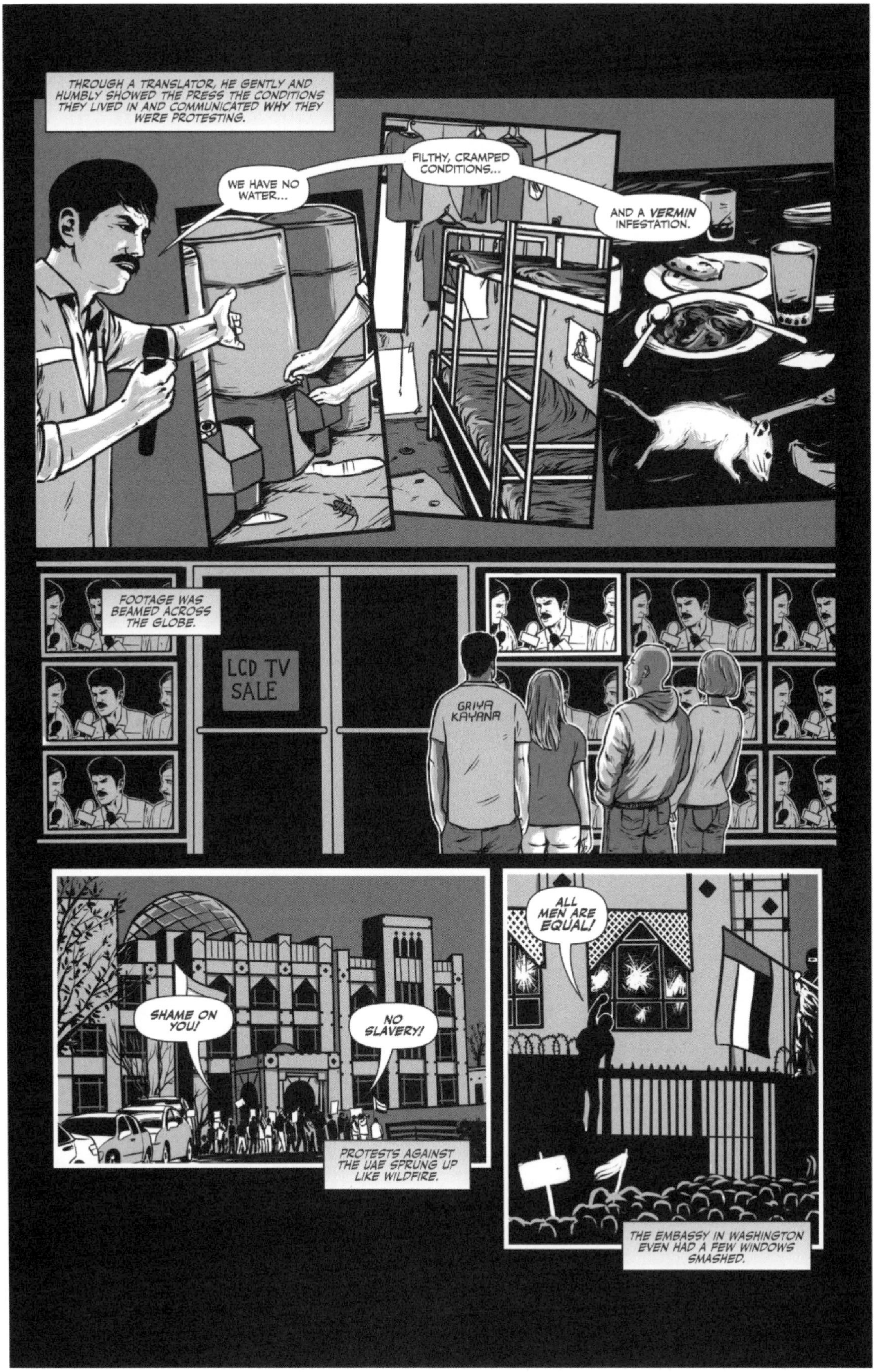
THROUGH A TRANSLATOR, HE GENTLY AND HUMBLY SHOWED THE PRESS THE CONDITIONS THEY LIVED IN AND COMMUNICATED WHY THEY WERE PROTESTING.
WE HAVE NO WATER...
FILTHY, CRAMPED CONDITIONS...
AND A VERMIN INFESTATION.
FOOTAGE WAS BEAMED ACROSS THE GLOBE.
LCD TV SALE
GRIYA KAYANA
SHAME ON YOU!
NO SLAVERY!
PROTESTS AGAINST THE UAE SPRUNG UP LIKE WILDFIRE.
ALL MEN ARE EQUAL!
THE EMBASSY IN WASHINGTON EVEN HAD A FEW WINDOWS SMASHED.

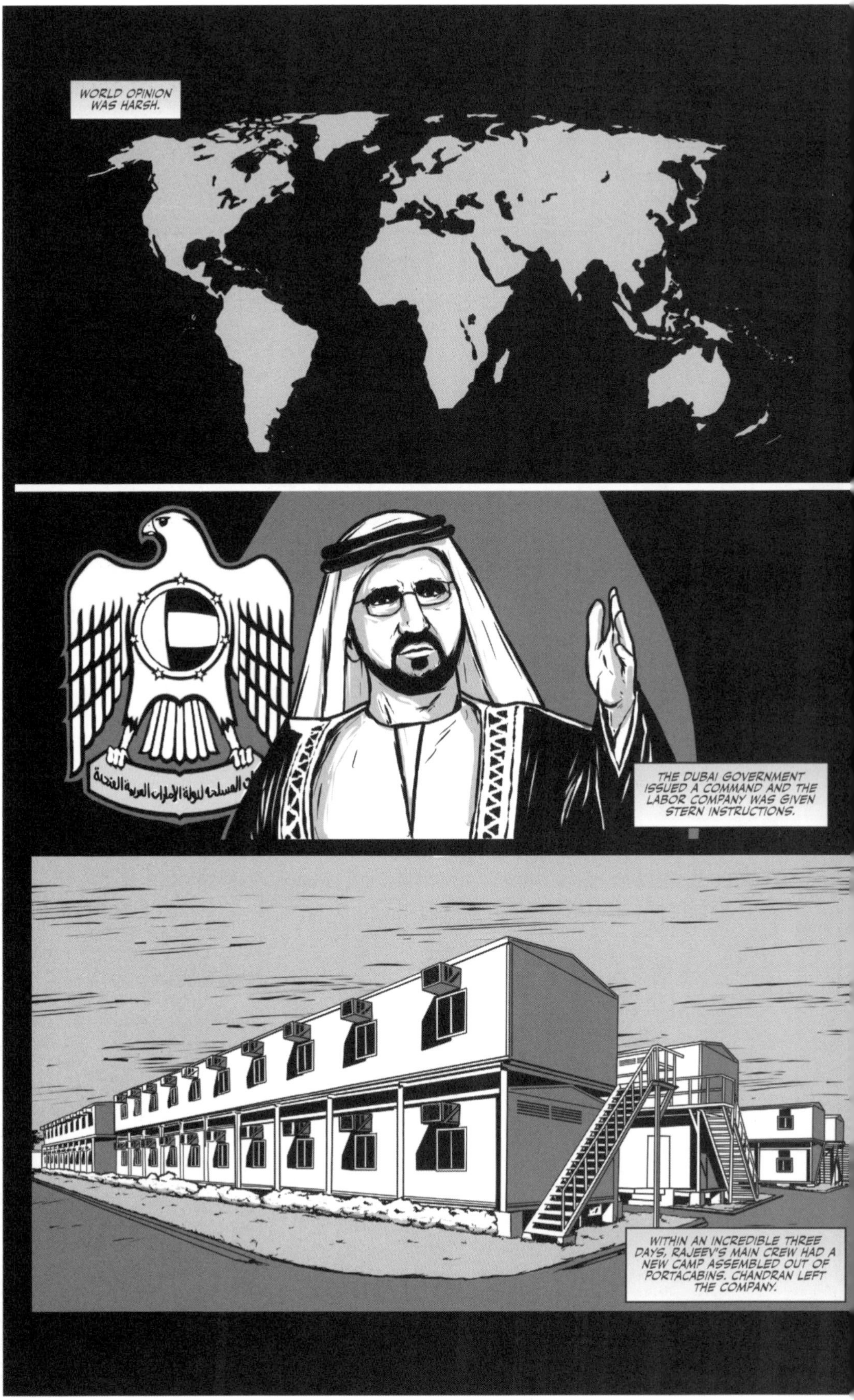
WORLD OPINION WAS HARSH.
THE DUBAI GOVERNMENT ISSUED A COMMAND AND THE LABOR COMPANY WAS GIVEN STERN INSTRUCTIONS.
WITHIN AN INCREDIBLE THREE DAYS, RAJEEV'S MAIN CREW HAD A NEW CAMP ASSEMBLED OUT OF PORTACABINS. CHANDRAN LEFT THE COMPANY.

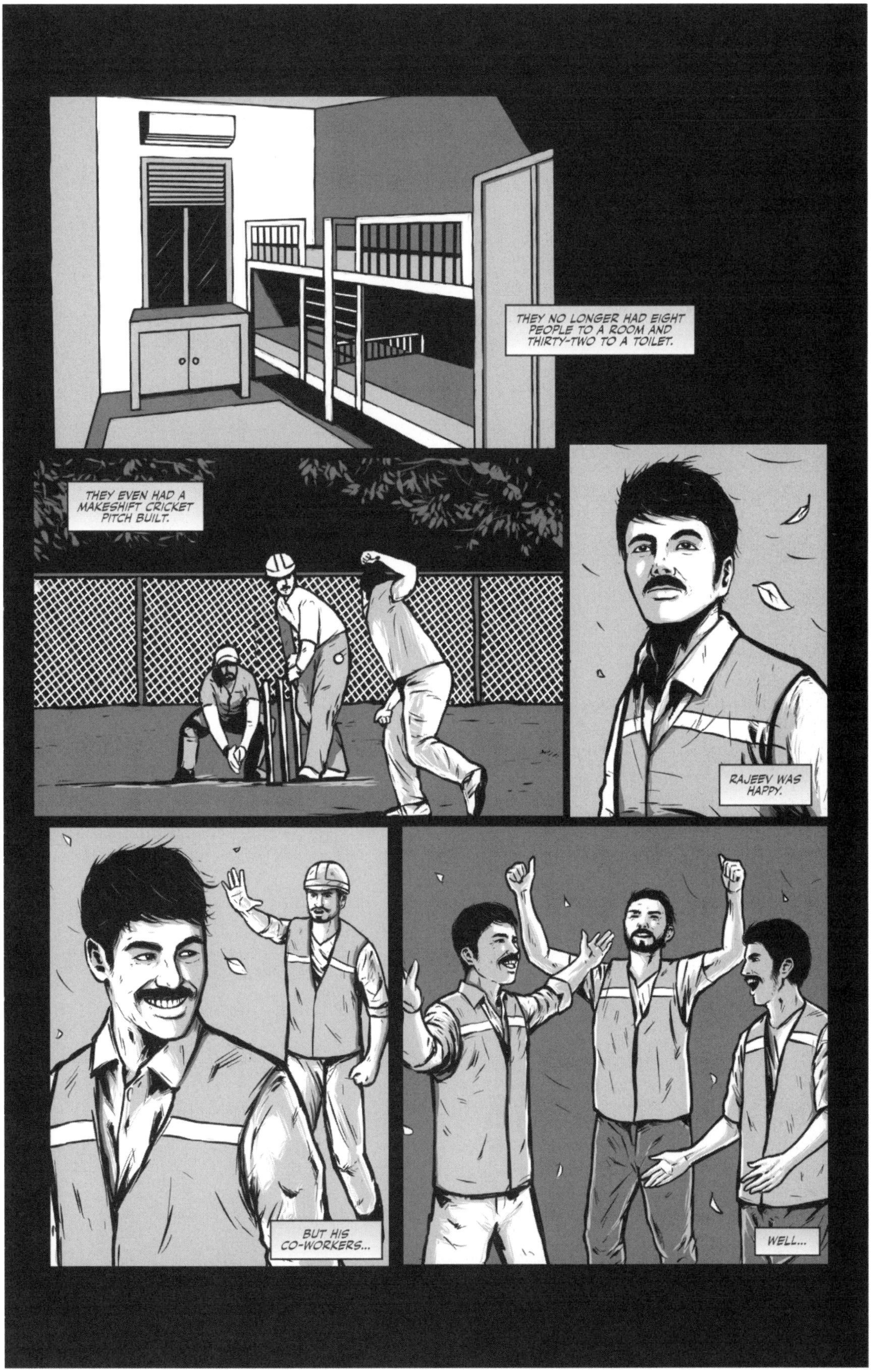
THEY NO LONGER HAD EIGHT PEOPLE TO A ROOM AND THIRTY-TWO TO A TOILET.
THEY EVEN HAD A MAKESHIFT CRICKET PITCH BUILT.
RAJEEV WAS HAPPY.
BUT HIS CO-WORKERS...
WELL...

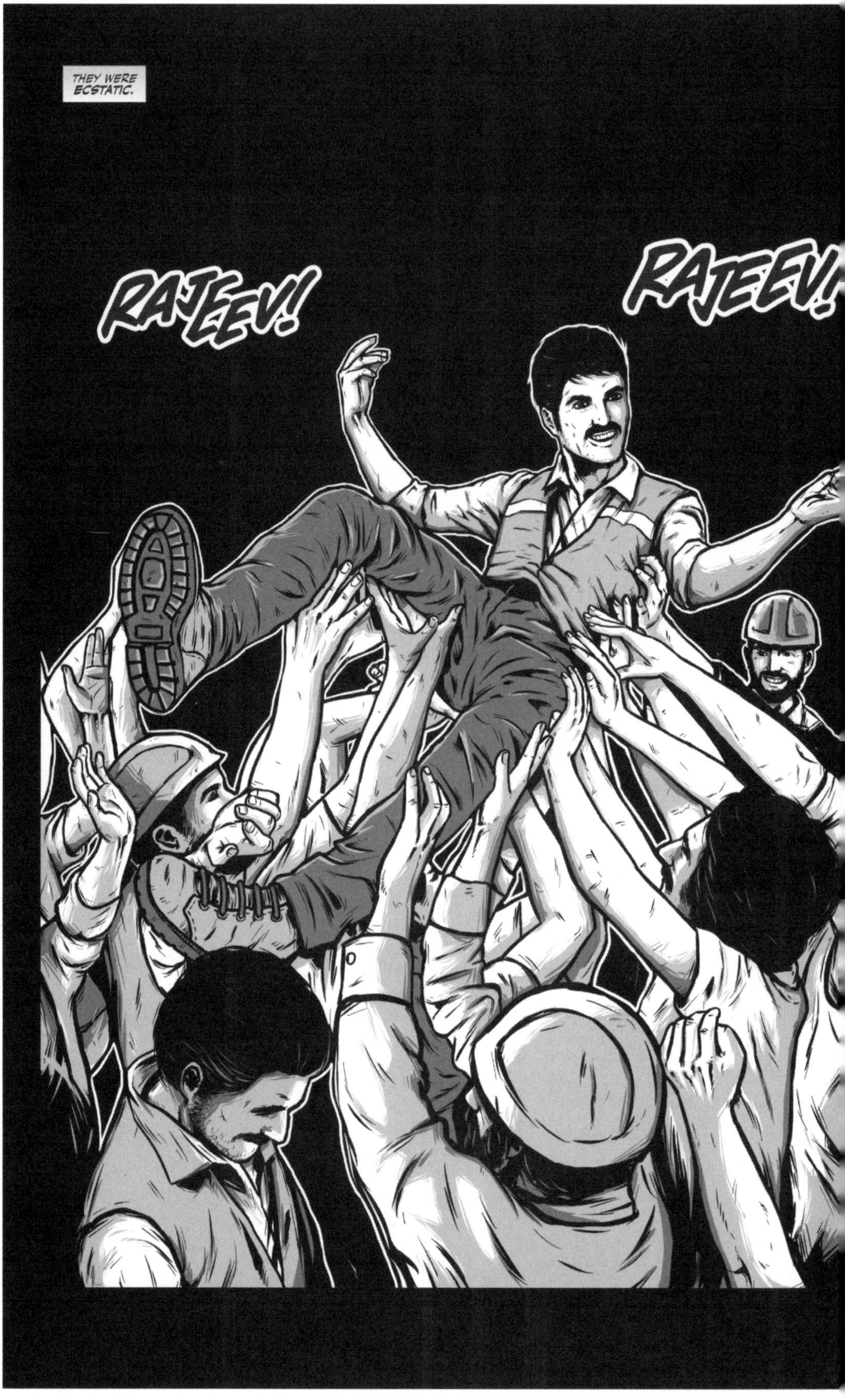
THEY WERE ECSTATIC.
RAJEEV!
RAJEEV!

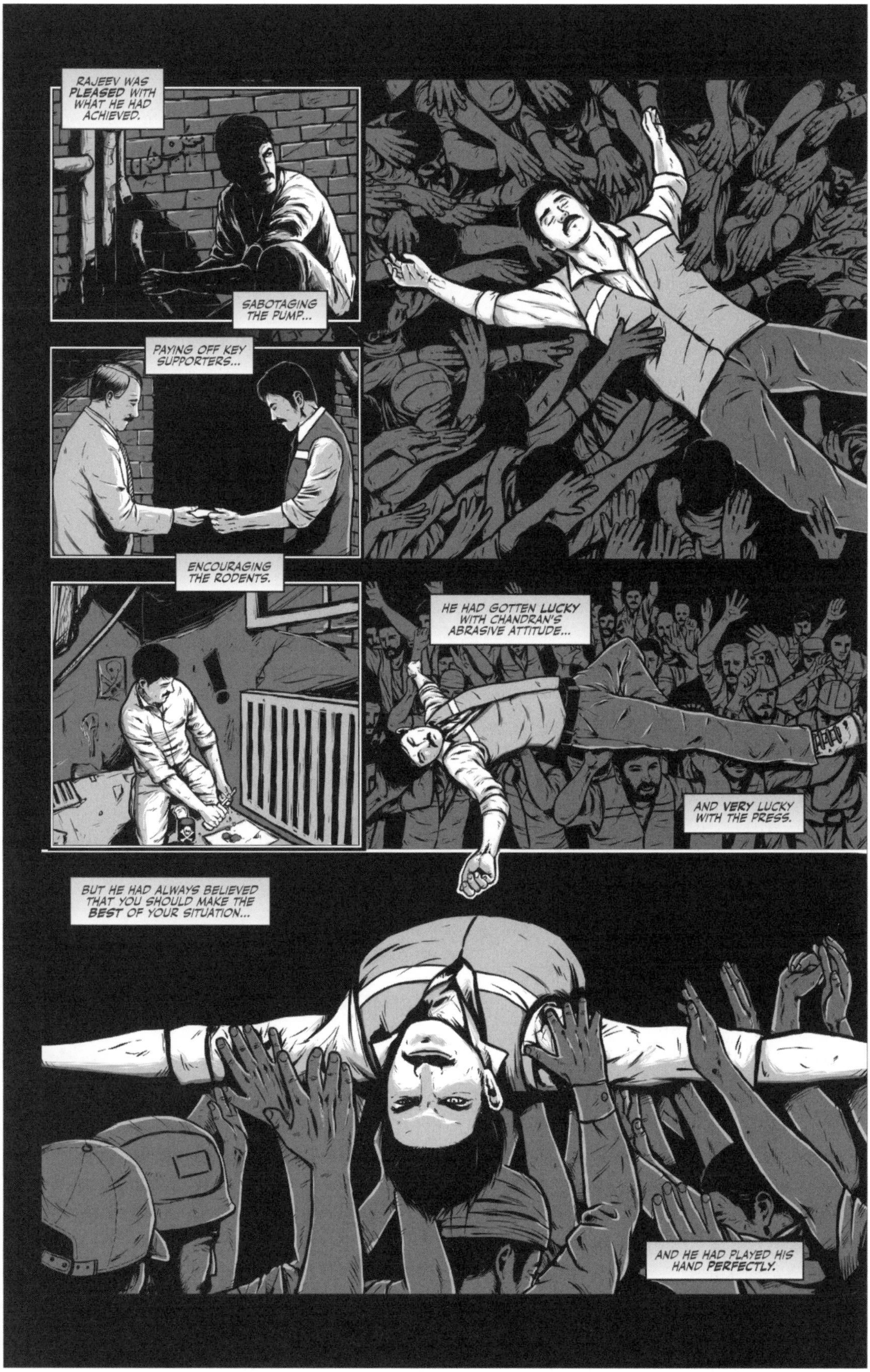
RAJEEV WAS PLEASED WITH WHAT HE HAD ACHIEVED.
SABOTAGING THE PUMP...
PAYING OFF KEY SUPPORTERS...
ENCOURAGING THE RODENTS.
HE HAD GOTTEN LUCKY WITH CHANDRAN'S ABRASIVE ATTITUDE...
AND VERY LUCKY WITH THE PRESS.
BUT HE HAD ALWAYS BELIEVED THAT YOU SHOULD MAKE THE BEST OF YOUR SITUATION...
AND HE HAD PLAYED HIS HAND PERFECTLY.

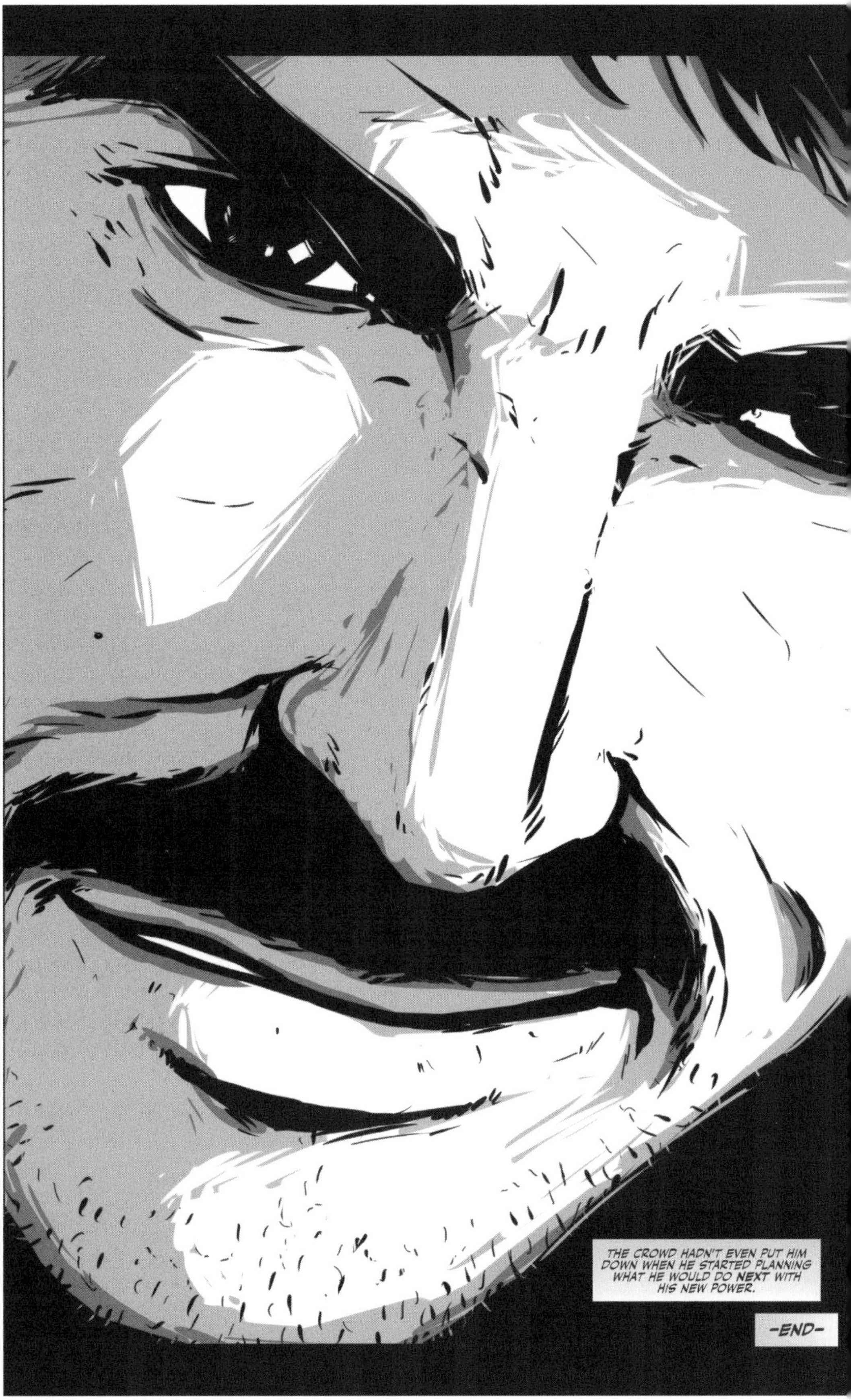
THE CROWD HADN'T EVEN PUT HIM DOWN WHEN HE STARTED PLANNING WHAT HE WOULD DO **NEXT** WITH HIS NEW POWER.
-END-

Windowpayne...

"Rodrigo is one of the most eligible bachelors on the planet. Wealthy, generous, great to look at even with his scar, and utterly mysterious."

-Plug-in Magazine

Writer/Creator
Neil Gibson

Illustrator
Jan Wijngaard

www.tpub.co.uk

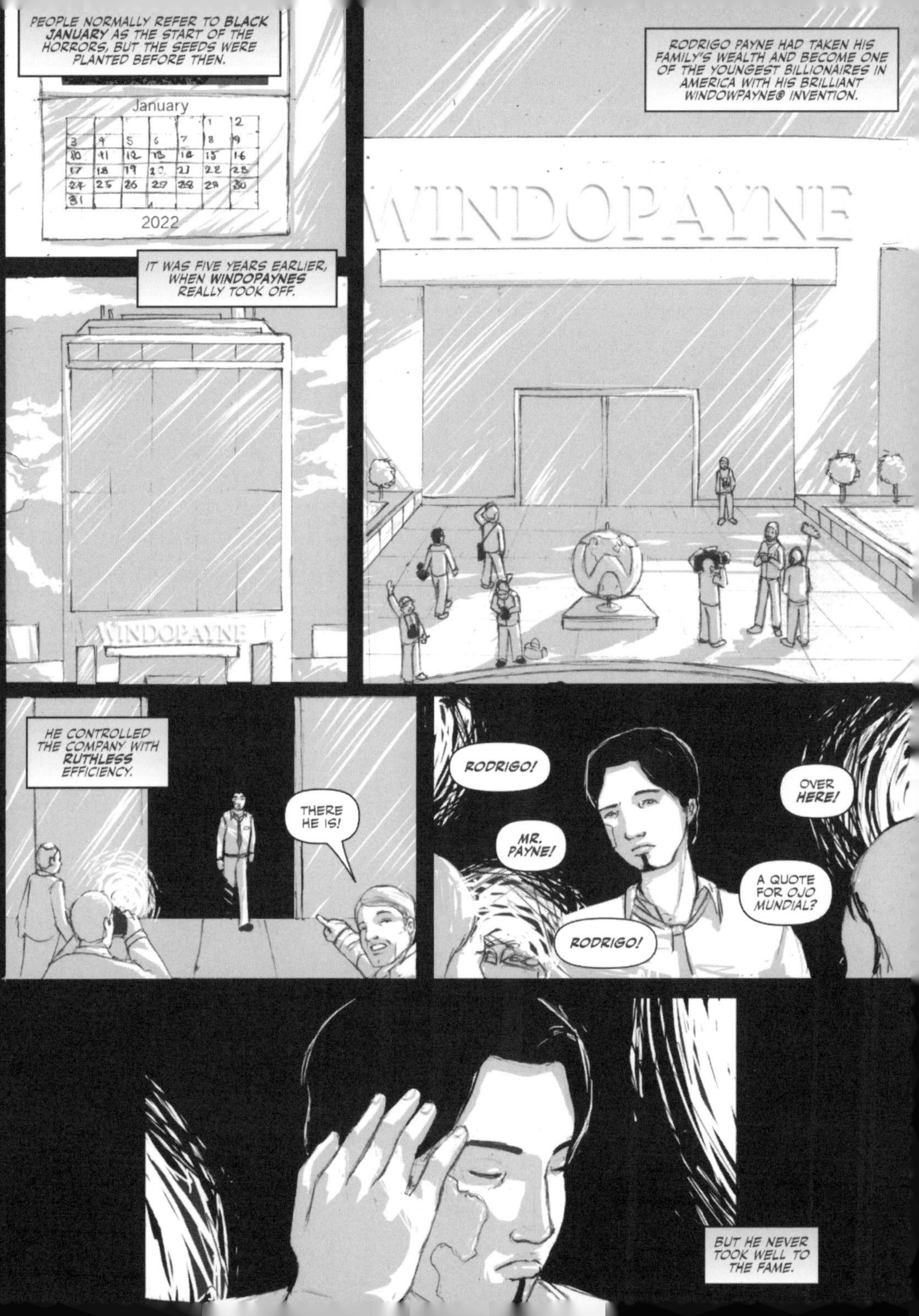

PEOPLE NORMALLY REFER TO BLACK JANUARY AS THE START OF THE HORRORS, BUT THE SEEDS WERE PLANTED BEFORE THEN.
January
2022
RODRIGO PAYNE HAD TAKEN HIS FAMILY'S WEALTH AND BECOME ONE OF THE YOUNGEST BILLIONAIRES IN AMERICA WITH HIS BRILLIANT WINDOWPAYNE® INVENTION.
WINDOPAYNE
IT WAS FIVE YEARS EARLIER, WHEN WINDOPAYNES REALLY TOOK OFF.
WINDOPAYNE
HE CONTROLLED THE COMPANY WITH RUTHLESS EFFICIENCY.
THERE HE IS!
RODRIGO!
MR. PAYNE!
OVER HERE!
A QUOTE FOR OJO MUNDIAL?
RODRIGO!
BUT HE NEVER TOOK WELL TO THE FAME.

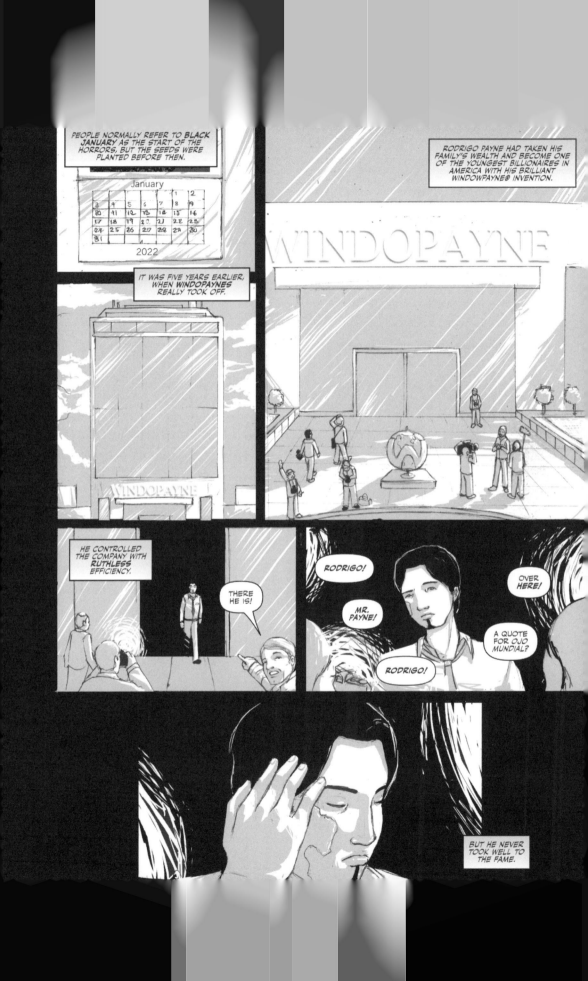

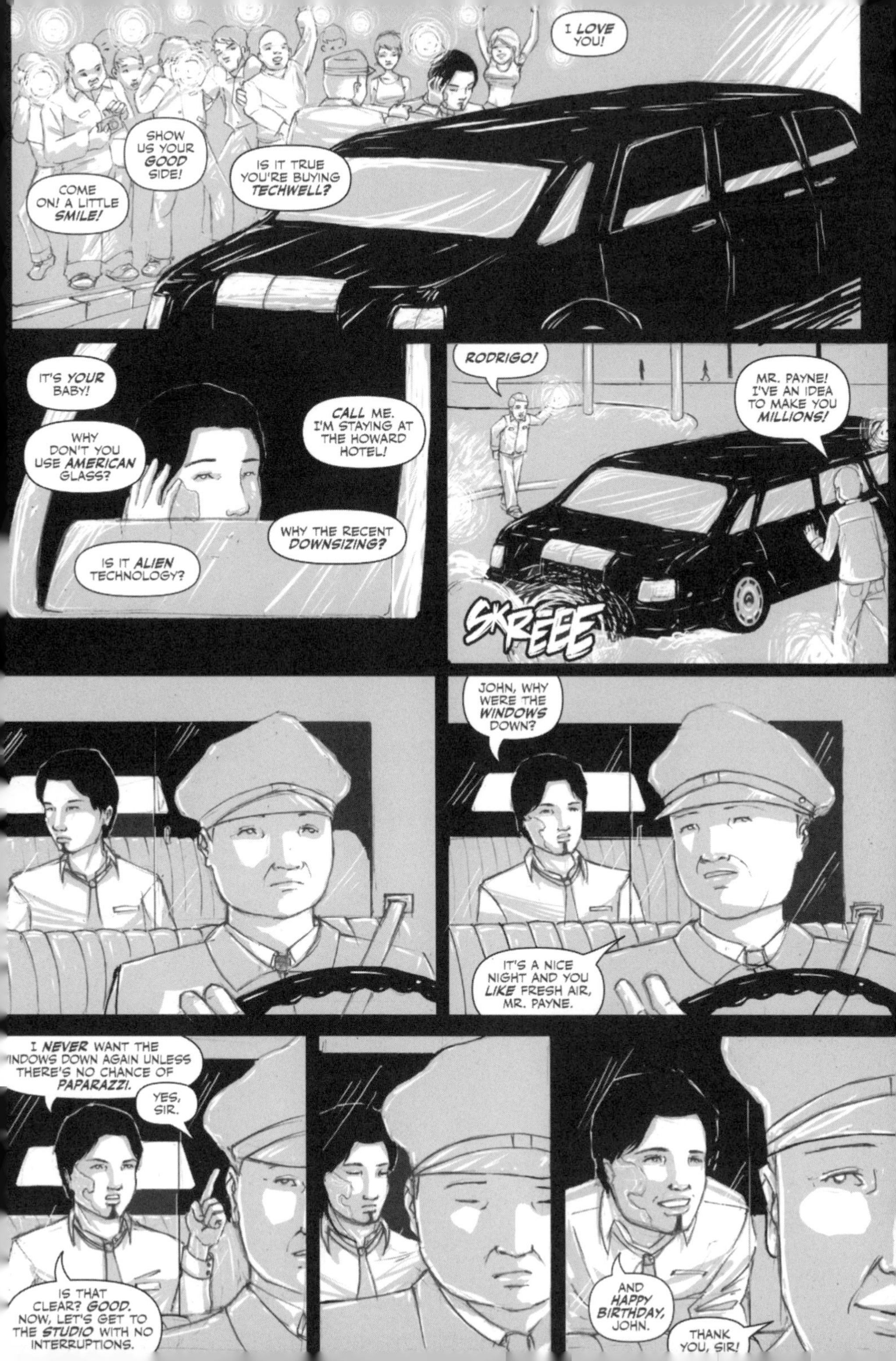
I LOVE YOU!
SHOW US YOUR GOOD SIDE!
COME ON! A LITTLE SMILE!
IS IT TRUE YOU'RE BUYING TECHWELL?
IT'S YOUR BABY!
WHY DON'T YOU USE AMERICAN GLASS?
CALL ME. I'M STAYING AT THE HOWARD HOTEL!
WHY THE RECENT DOWNSIZING?
IS IT ALIEN TECHNOLOGY?
RODRIGO!
MR. PAYNE! I'VE AN IDEA TO MAKE YOU MILLIONS!
SKREEEE
JOHN, WHY WERE THE WINDOWS DOWN?
IT'S A NICE NIGHT AND YOU LIKE FRESH AIR, MR. PAYNE.
I NEVER WANT THE WINDOWS DOWN AGAIN UNLESS THERE'S NO CHANCE OF PAPARAZZI.
YES, SIR.
IS THAT CLEAR? GOOD. NOW, LET'S GET TO THE STUDIO WITH NO INTERRUPTIONS.
AND HAPPY BIRTHDAY, JOHN.
THANK YOU, SIR!

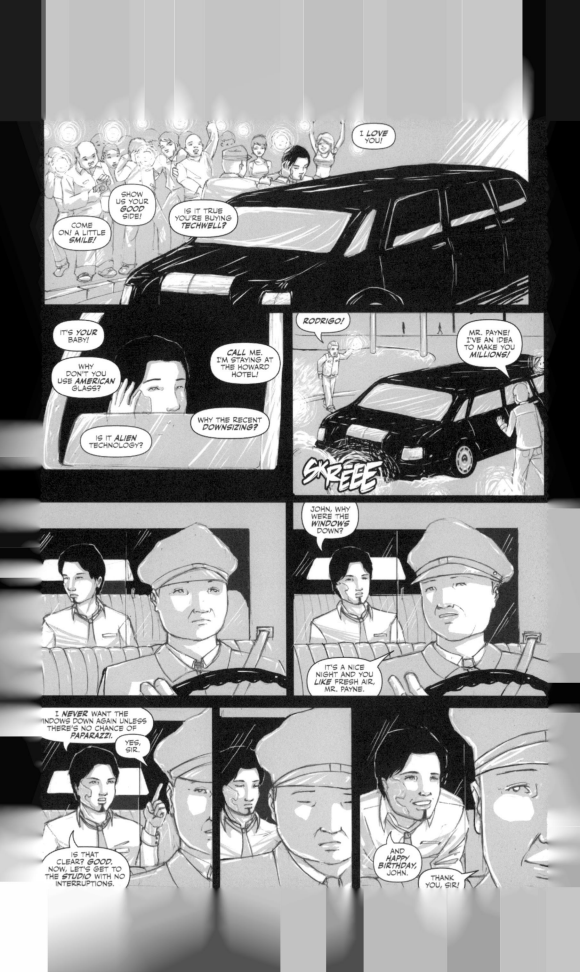

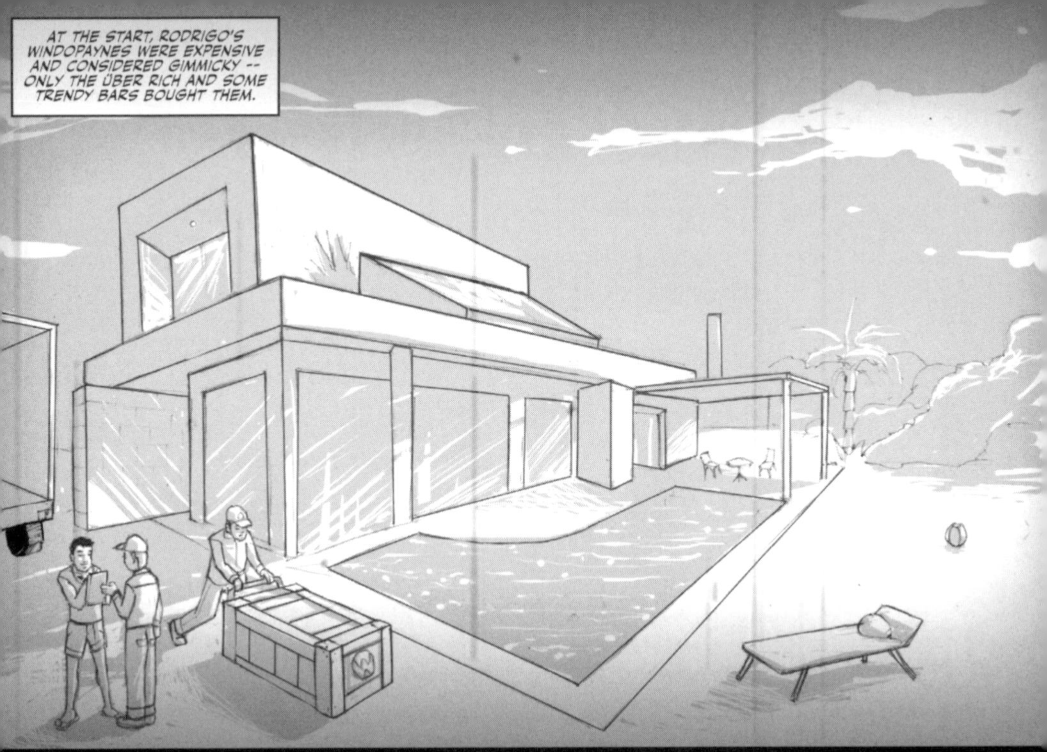
AT THE START, RODRIGO'S WINDOPAYNES WERE EXPENSIVE AND CONSIDERED GIMMICKY -- ONLY THE ÜBER RICH AND SOME TRENDY BARS BOUGHT THEM.

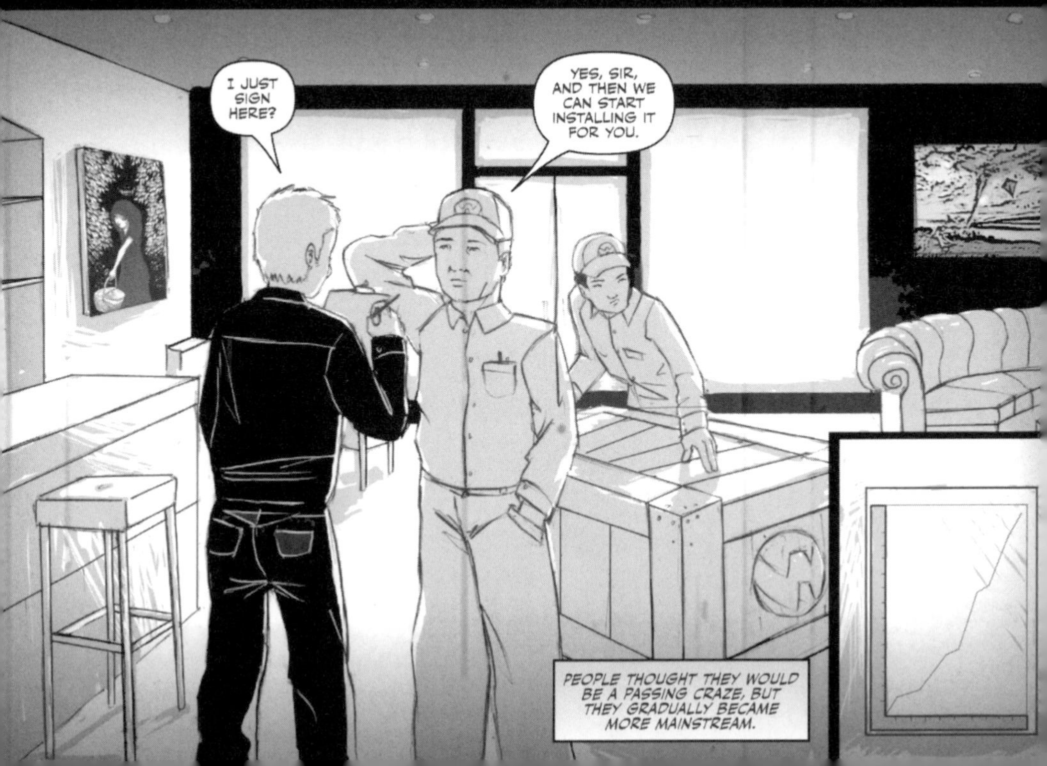
I JUST SIGN HERE?
YES, SIR, AND THEN WE CAN START INSTALLING IT FOR YOU.
PEOPLE THOUGHT THEY WOULD BE A PASSING CRAZE, BUT THEY GRADUALLY BECAME MORE MAINSTREAM.

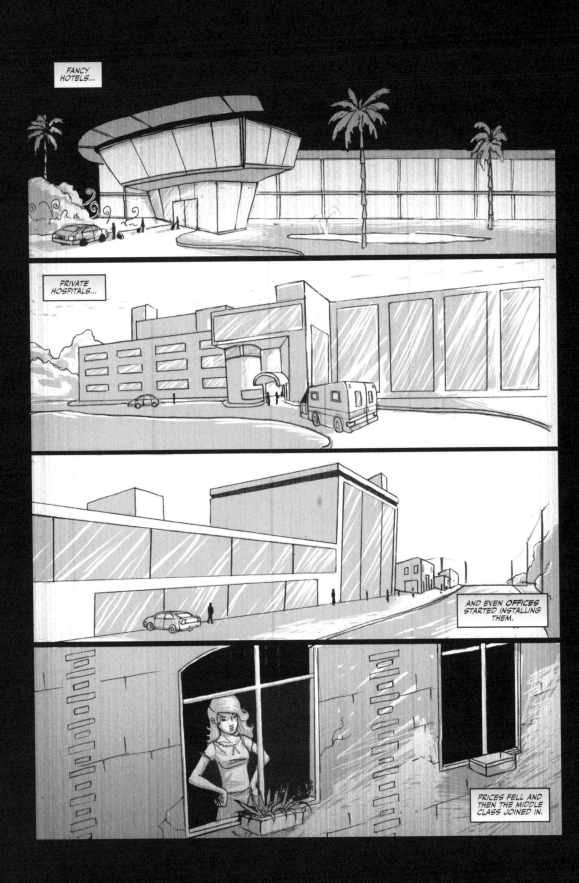

FANCY HOTELS...

PRIVATE HOSPITALS...

AND EVEN OFFICES STARTED INSTALLING THEM.

PRICES FELL AND THEN THE MIDDLE CLASS JOINED IN.

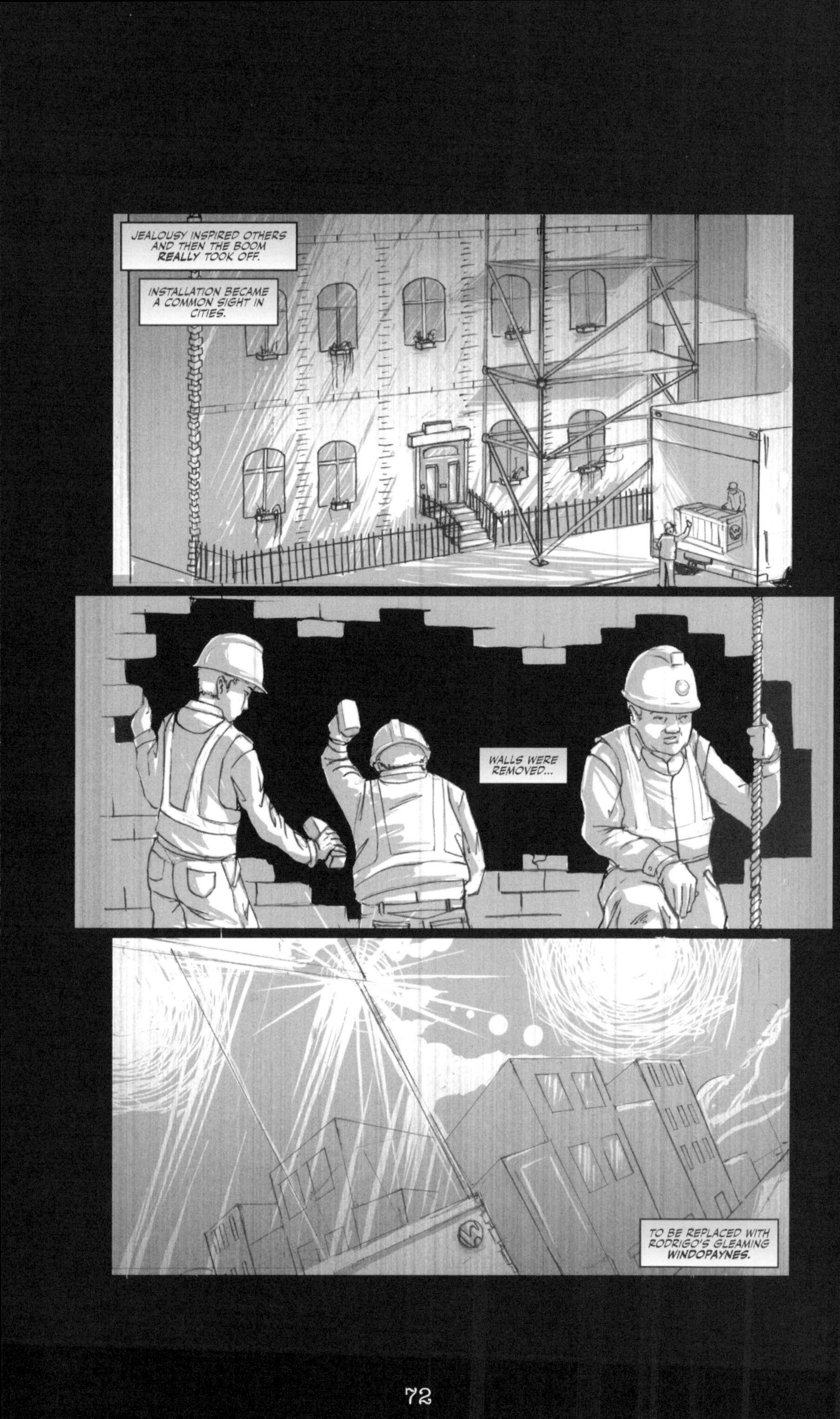
JEALOUSY INSPIRED OTHERS AND THEN THE BOOM REALLY TOOK OFF.
INSTALLATION BECAME A COMMON SIGHT IN CITIES.
WALLS WERE REMOVED...
TO BE REPLACED WITH RODRIGO'S GLEAMING WINDOPAYNES.

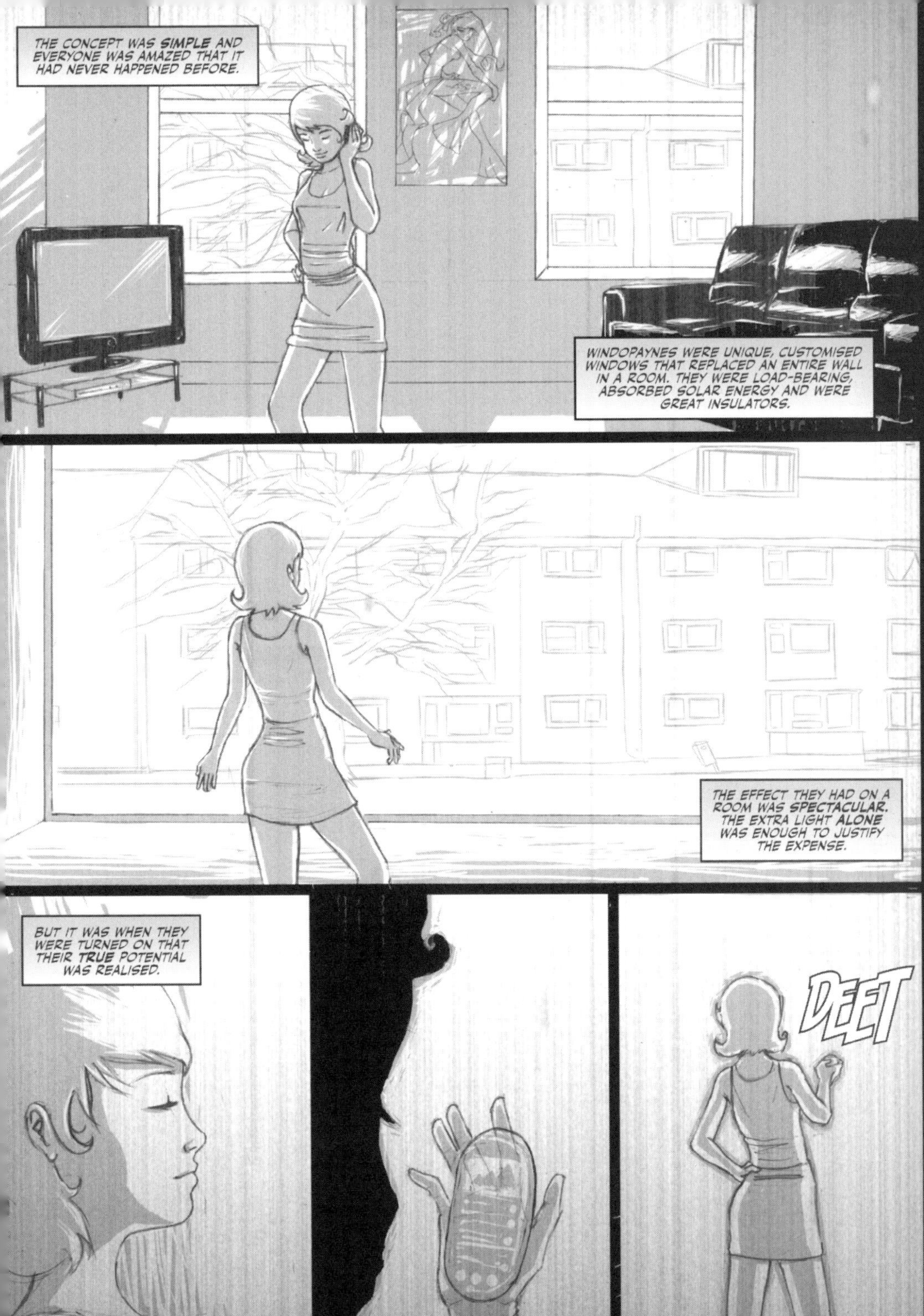
THE CONCEPT WAS SIMPLE AND EVERYONE WAS AMAZED THAT IT HAD NEVER HAPPENED BEFORE.
WINDOPAYNES WERE UNIQUE, CUSTOMISED WINDOWS THAT REPLACED AN ENTIRE WALL IN A ROOM. THEY WERE LOAD-BEARING, ABSORBED SOLAR ENERGY AND WERE GREAT INSULATORS.
THE EFFECT THEY HAD ON A ROOM WAS SPECTACULAR. THE EXTRA LIGHT ALONE WAS ENOUGH TO JUSTIFY THE EXPENSE.
BUT IT WAS WHEN THEY WERE TURNED ON THAT THEIR TRUE POTENTIAL WAS REALISED.
DEET

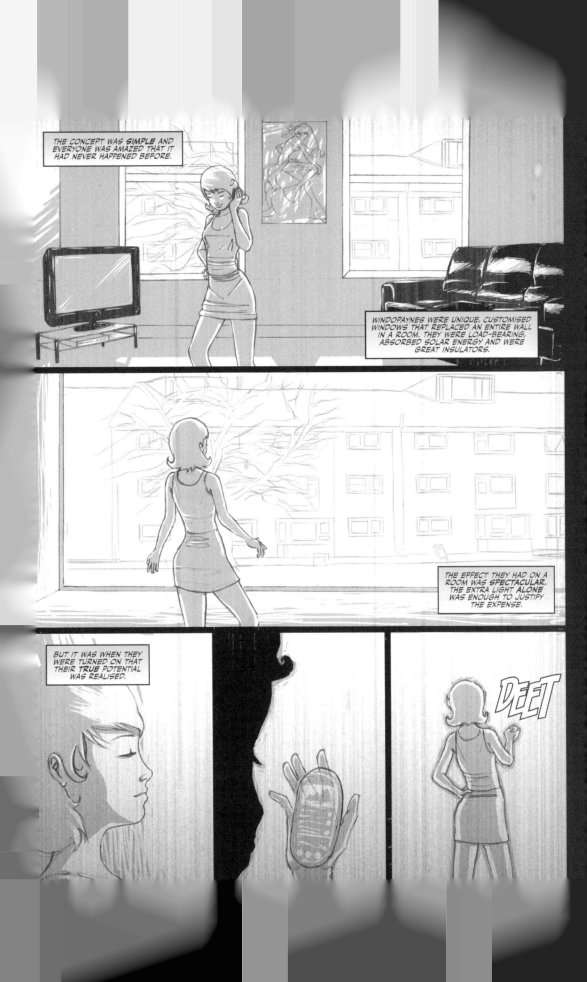

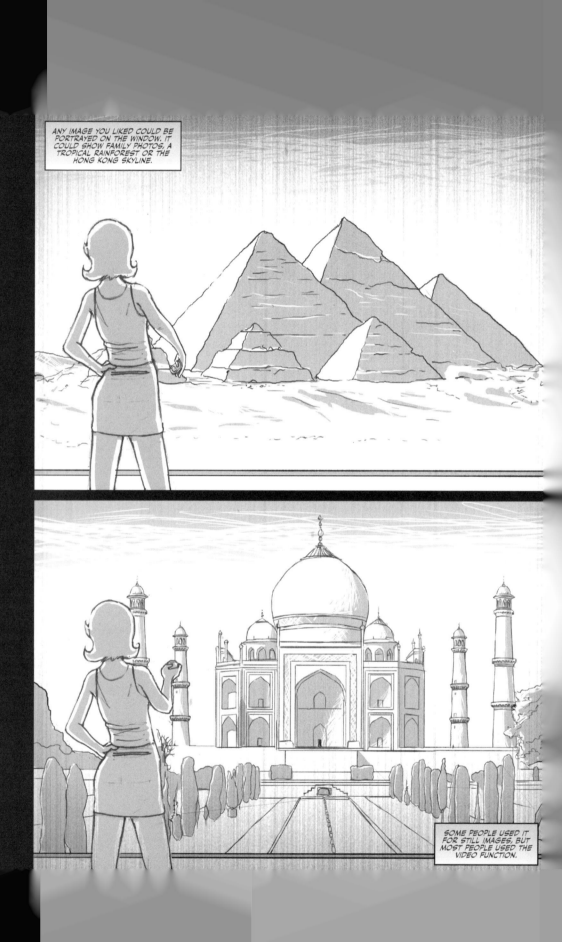

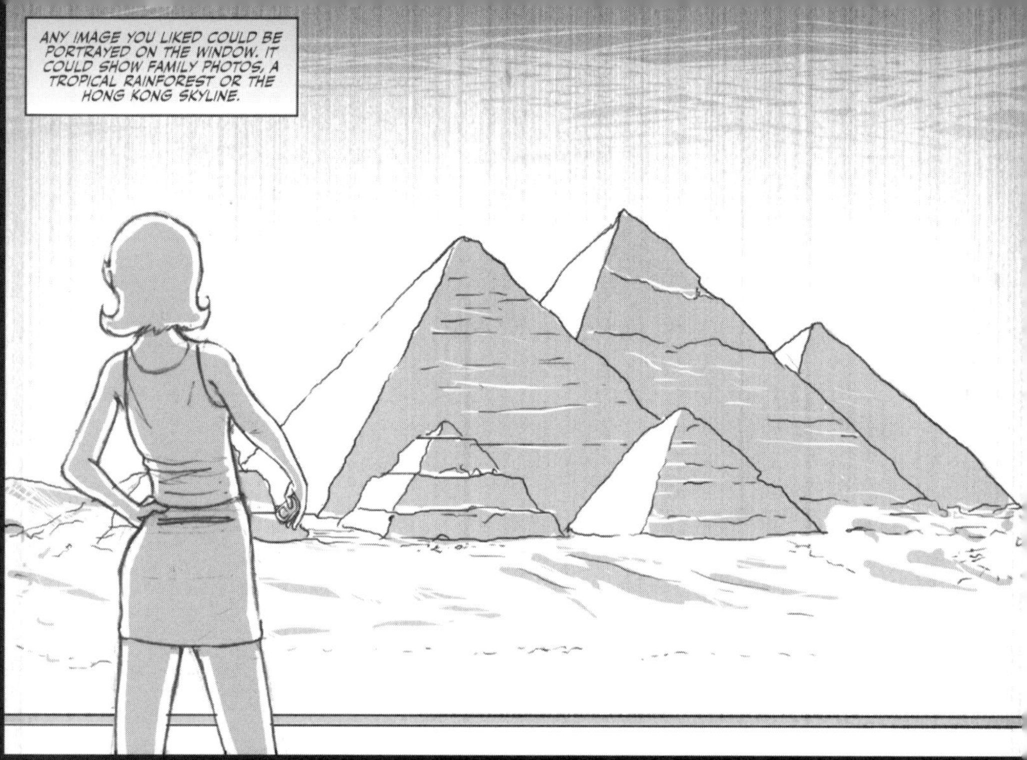
ANY IMAGE YOU LIKED COULD BE PORTRAYED ON THE WINDOW. IT COULD SHOW FAMILY PHOTOS, A TROPICAL RAINFOREST OR THE HONG KONG SKYLINE.

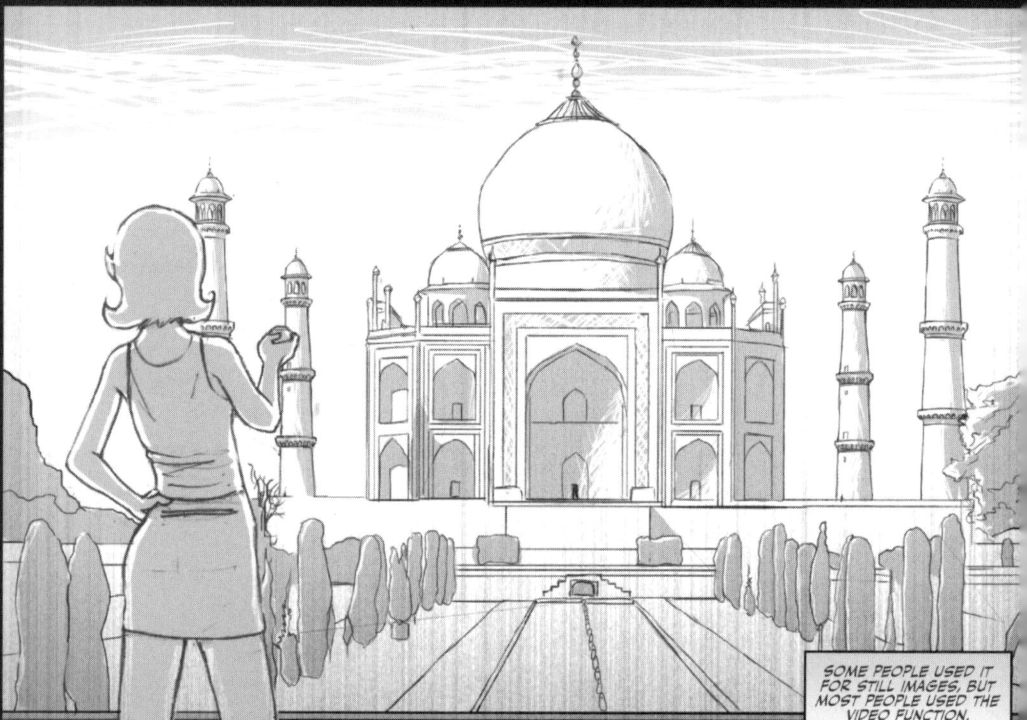
SOME PEOPLE USED IT FOR STILL IMAGES, BUT MOST PEOPLE USED THE VIDEO FUNCTION.

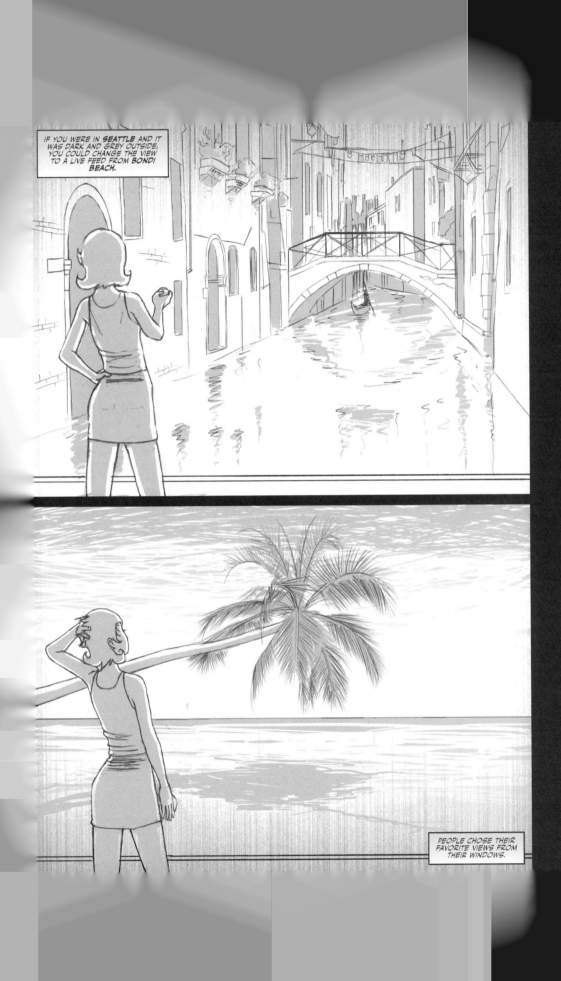

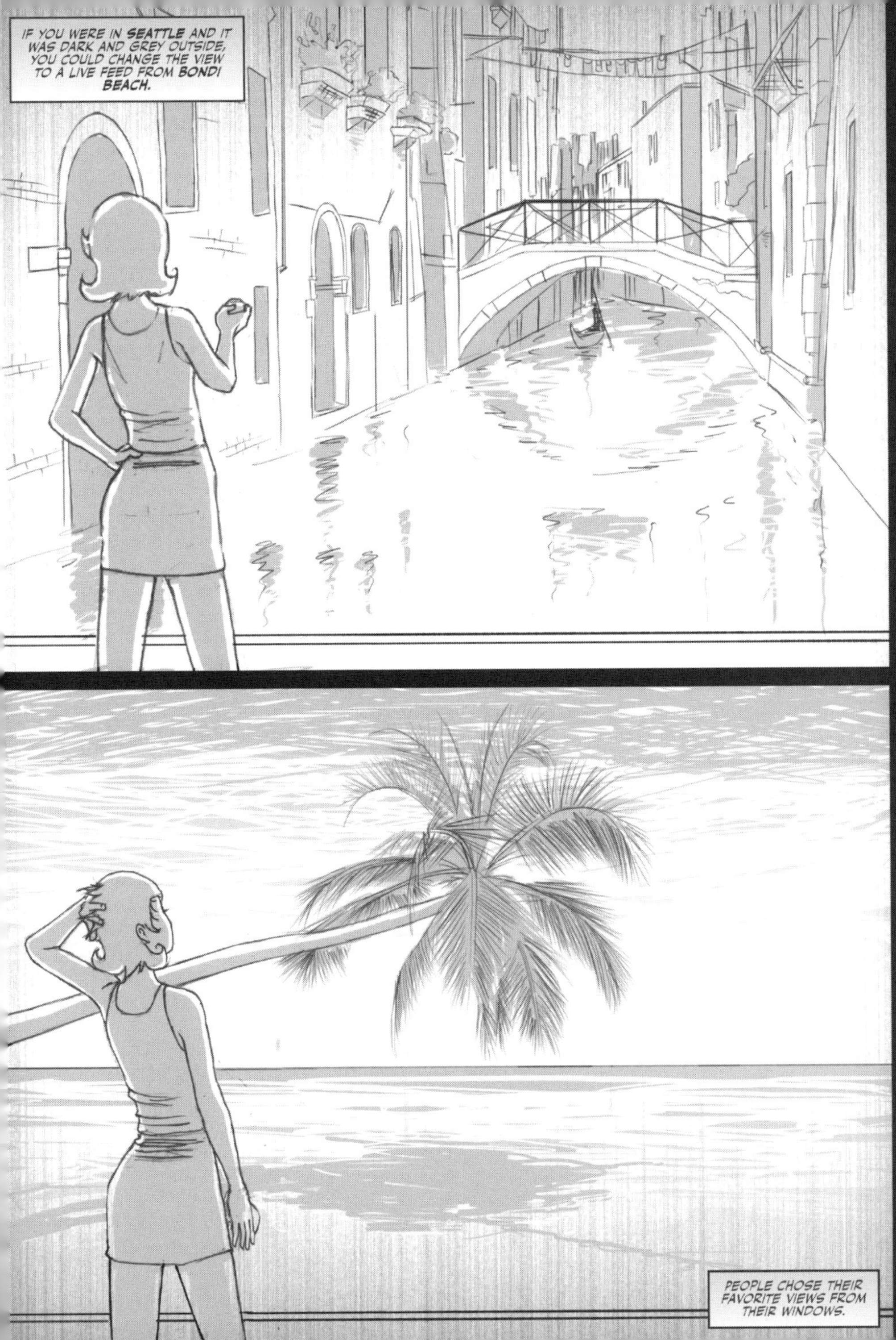
IF YOU WERE IN SEATTLE AND IT WAS DARK AND GREY OUTSIDE, YOU COULD CHANGE THE VIEW TO A LIVE FEED FROM BONDI BEACH.
PEOPLE CHOSE THEIR FAVORITE VIEWS FROM THEIR WINDOWS.

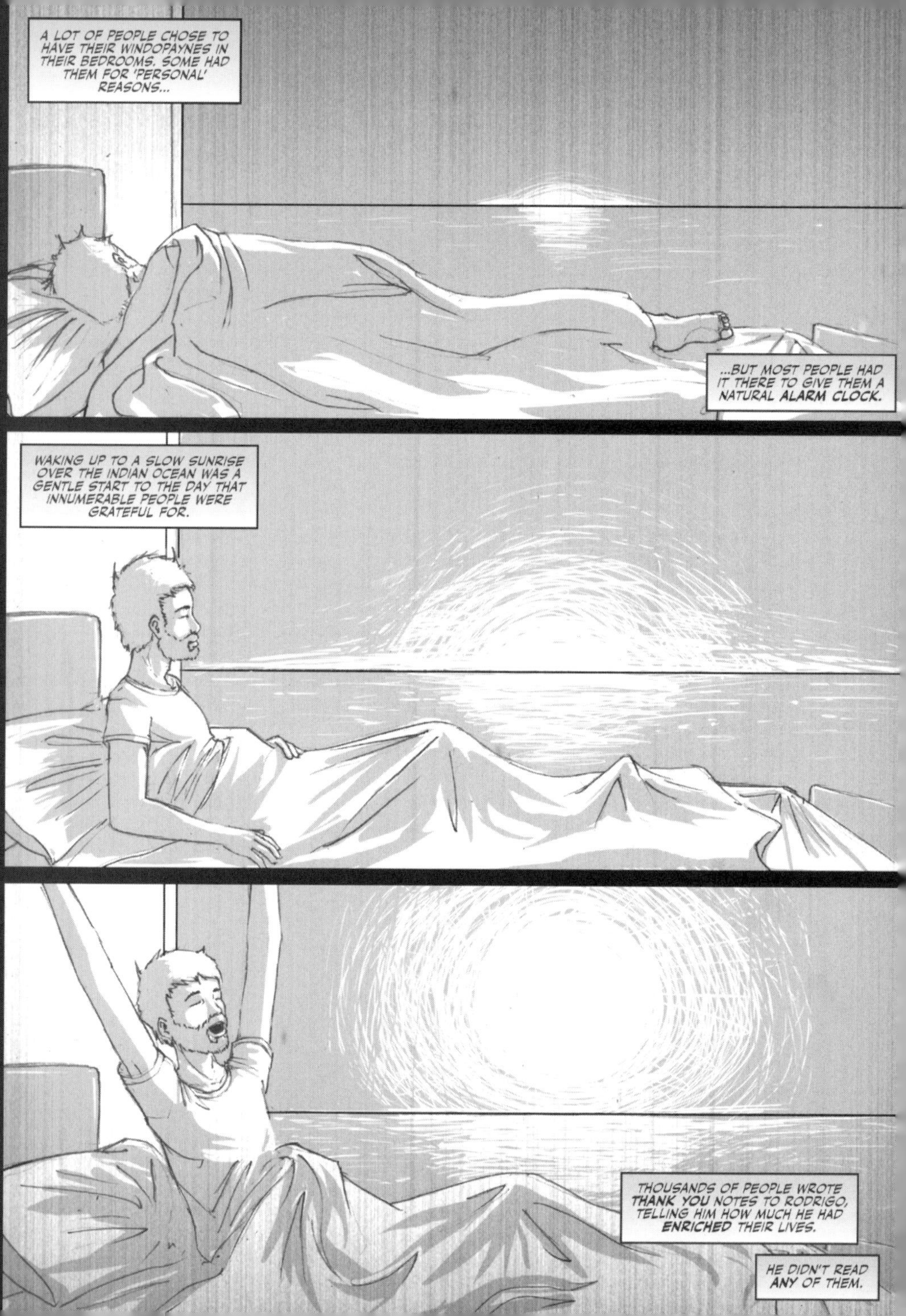
A LOT OF PEOPLE CHOSE TO HAVE THEIR WINDOPAYNES IN THEIR BEDROOMS. SOME HAD THEM FOR 'PERSONAL' REASONS...
...BUT MOST PEOPLE HAD IT THERE TO GIVE THEM A NATURAL ALARM CLOCK.
WAKING UP TO A SLOW SUNRISE OVER THE INDIAN OCEAN WAS A GENTLE START TO THE DAY THAT INNUMERABLE PEOPLE WERE GRATEFUL FOR.
THOUSANDS OF PEOPLE WROTE THANK YOU NOTES TO RODRIGO, TELLING HIM HOW MUCH HE HAD ENRICHED THEIR LIVES.
HE DIDN'T READ ANY OF THEM.

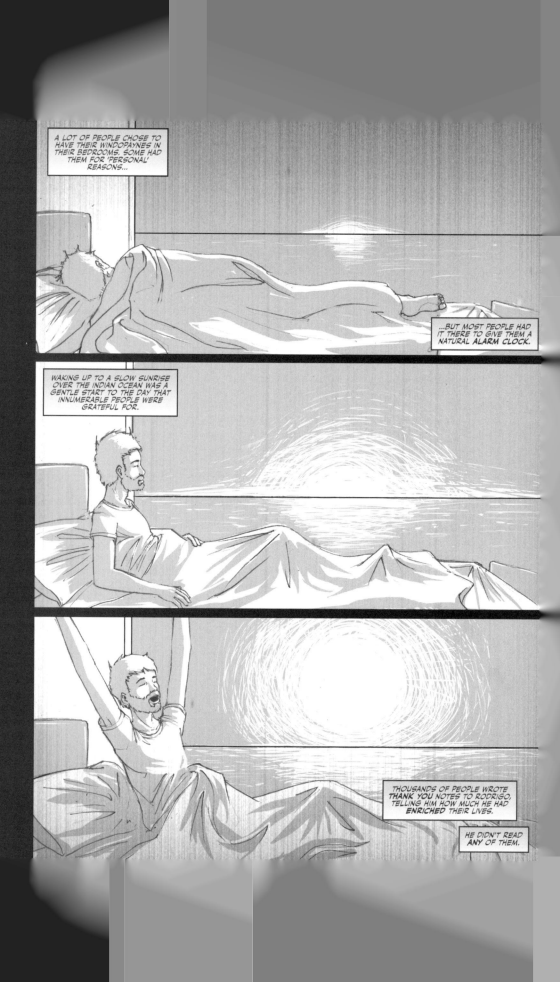

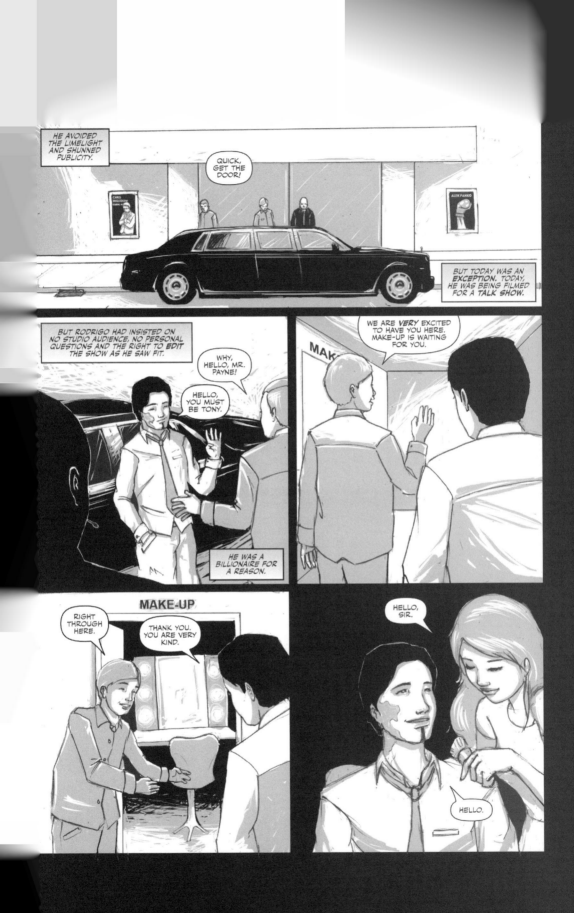

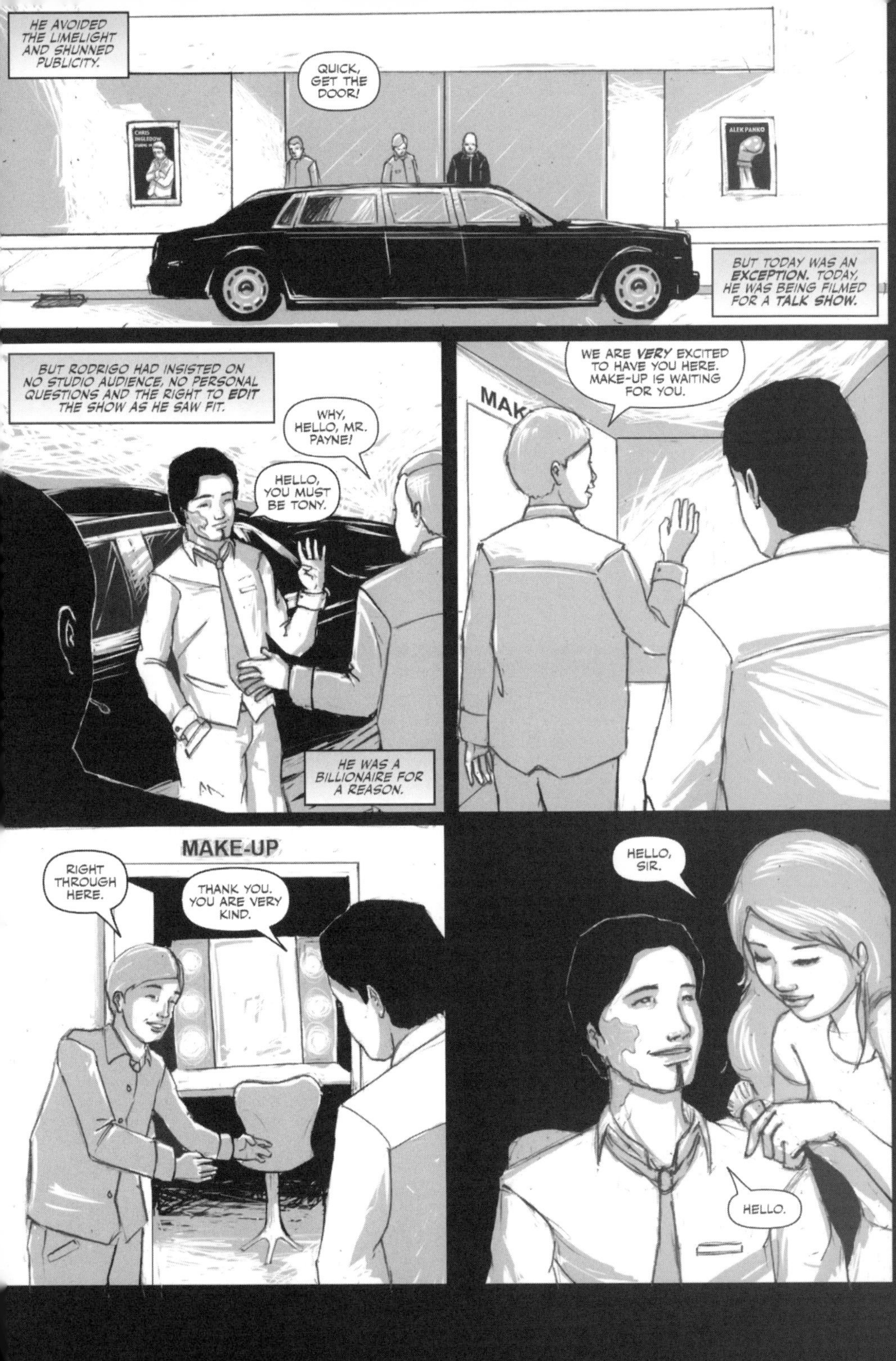
HE AVOIDED THE LIMELIGHT AND SHUNNED PUBLICITY.
QUICK, GET THE DOOR!
ALEK PANKO
BUT TODAY WAS AN EXCEPTION. TODAY, HE WAS BEING FILMED FOR A TALK SHOW.
BUT RODRIGO HAD INSISTED ON NO STUDIO AUDIENCE, NO PERSONAL QUESTIONS AND THE RIGHT TO EDIT THE SHOW AS HE SAW FIT.
WHY, HELLO, MR. PAYNE!
HELLO, YOU MUST BE TONY.
HE WAS A BILLIONAIRE FOR A REASON.
WE ARE VERY EXCITED TO HAVE YOU HERE. MAKE-UP IS WAITING FOR YOU.
MAKE-UP
RIGHT THROUGH HERE.
THANK YOU. YOU ARE VERY KIND.
HELLO, SIR.
HELLO.

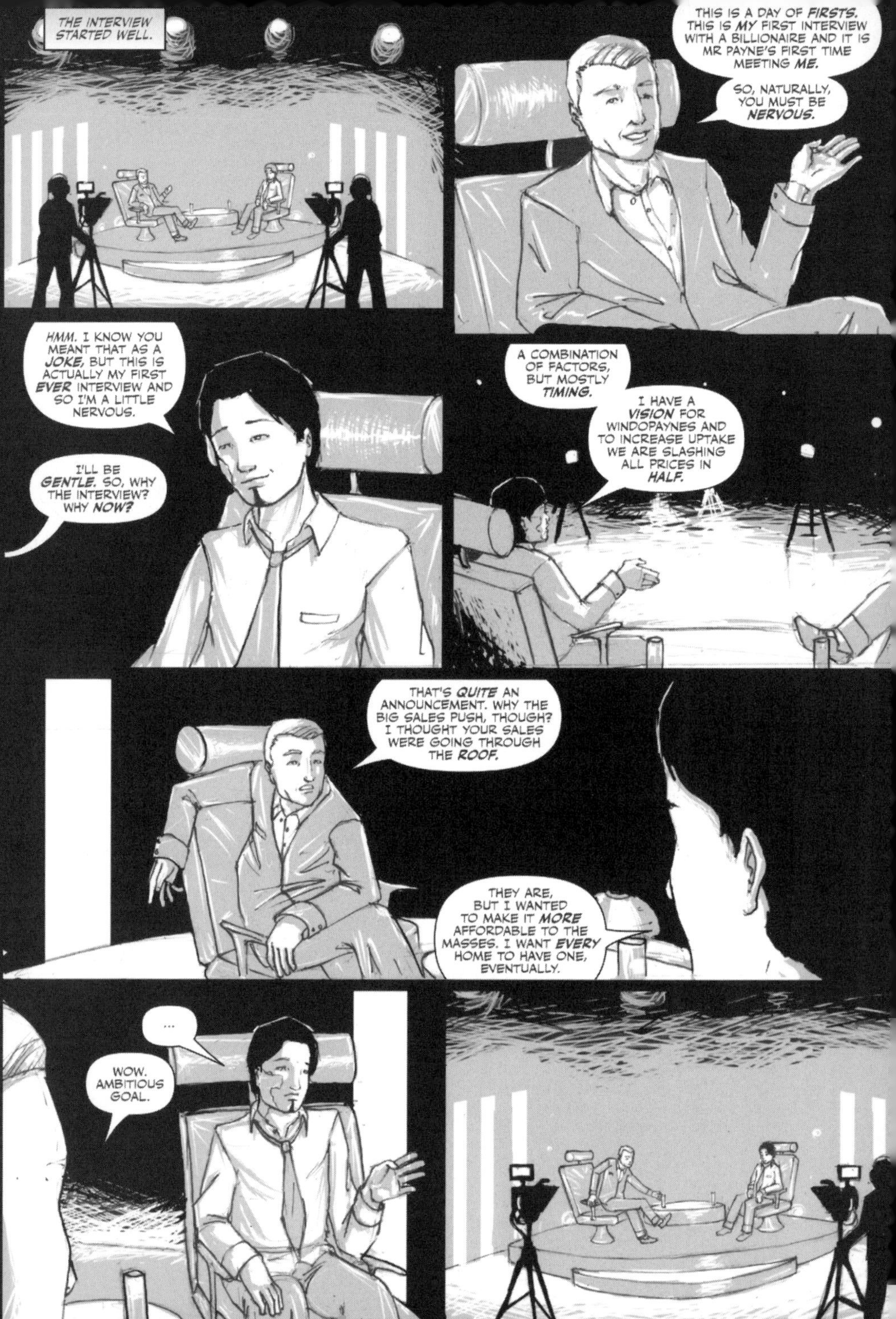
THE INTERVIEW STARTED WELL.
THIS IS A DAY OF FIRSTS. THIS IS MY FIRST INTERVIEW WITH A BILLIONAIRE AND IT IS MR PAYNE'S FIRST TIME MEETING ME.
SO, NATURALLY, YOU MUST BE NERVOUS.
HMM. I KNOW YOU MEANT THAT AS A JOKE, BUT THIS IS ACTUALLY MY FIRST EVER INTERVIEW AND SO I'M A LITTLE NERVOUS.
I'LL BE GENTLE. SO, WHY THE INTERVIEW? WHY NOW?
A COMBINATION OF FACTORS, BUT MOSTLY TIMING.
I HAVE A VISION FOR WINDOPAYNES AND TO INCREASE UPTAKE WE ARE SLASHING ALL PRICES IN HALF.
THAT'S QUITE AN ANNOUNCEMENT. WHY THE BIG SALES PUSH, THOUGH? I THOUGHT YOUR SALES WERE GOING THROUGH THE ROOF.
THEY ARE, BUT I WANTED TO MAKE IT MORE AFFORDABLE TO THE MASSES. I WANT EVERY HOME TO HAVE ONE, EVENTUALLY.
...
WOW. AMBITIOUS GOAL.

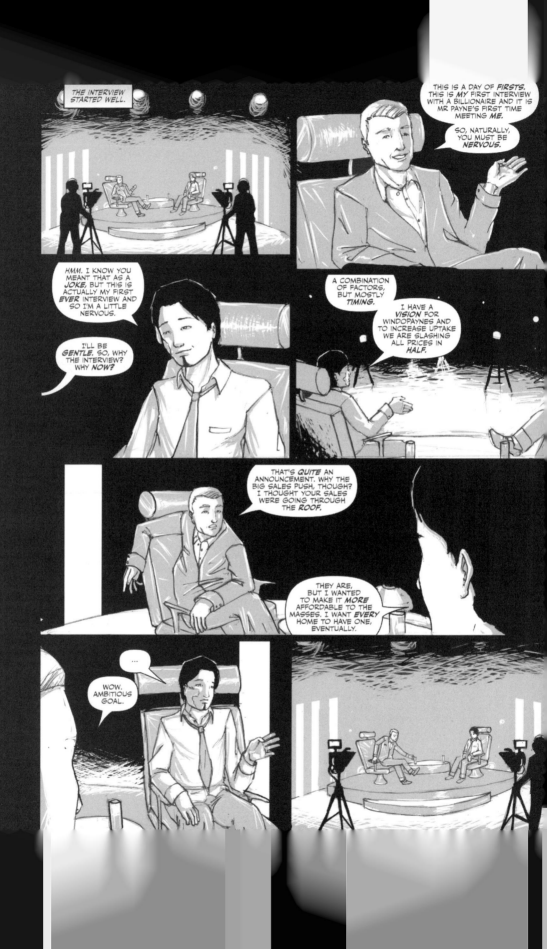

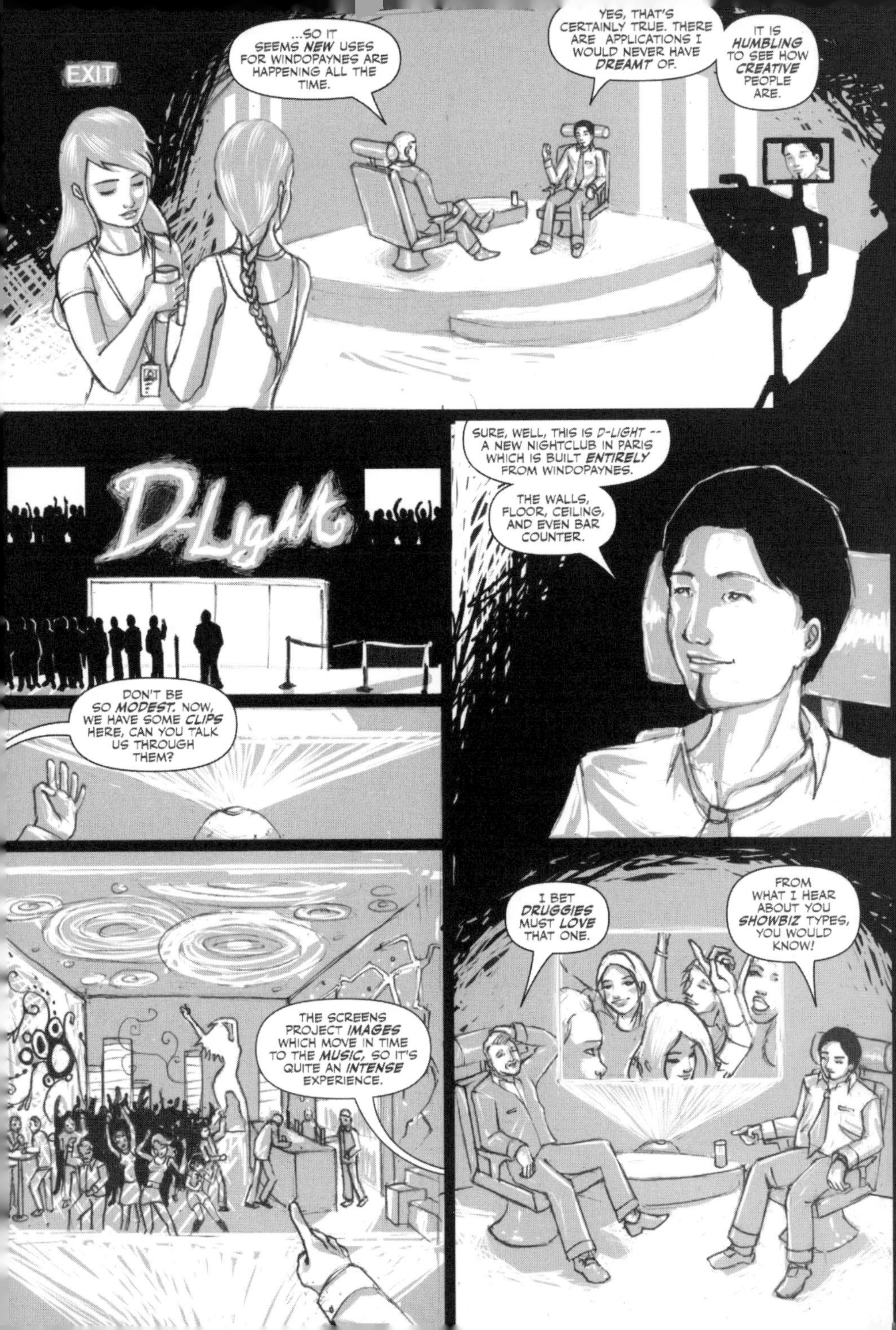

EXIT
...SO IT SEEMS NEW USES FOR WINDOPAYNES ARE HAPPENING ALL THE TIME.
YES, THAT'S CERTAINLY TRUE. THERE ARE APPLICATIONS I WOULD NEVER HAVE DREAMT OF.
IT IS HUMBLING TO SEE HOW CREATIVE PEOPLE ARE.
D-Light
DON'T BE SO MODEST. NOW, WE HAVE SOME CLIPS HERE, CAN YOU TALK US THROUGH THEM?
SURE, WELL, THIS IS D-LIGHT -- A NEW NIGHTCLUB IN PARIS WHICH IS BUILT ENTIRELY FROM WINDOPAYNES.
THE WALLS, FLOOR, CEILING, AND EVEN BAR COUNTER.
THE SCREENS PROJECT IMAGES WHICH MOVE IN TIME TO THE MUSIC, SO IT'S QUITE AN INTENSE EXPERIENCE.
I BET DRUGGIES MUST LOVE THAT ONE.
FROM WHAT I HEAR ABOUT YOU SHOWBIZ TYPES, YOU WOULD KNOW!

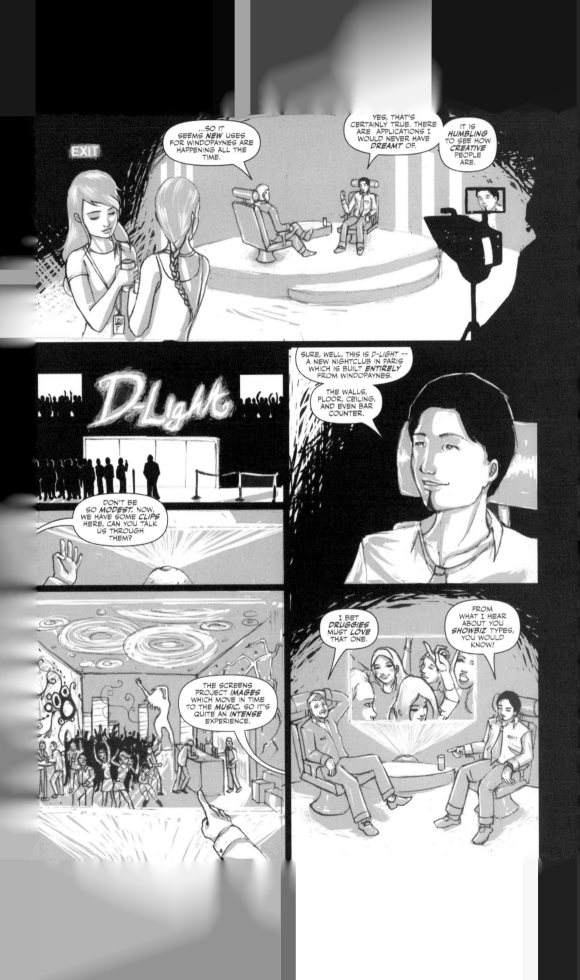

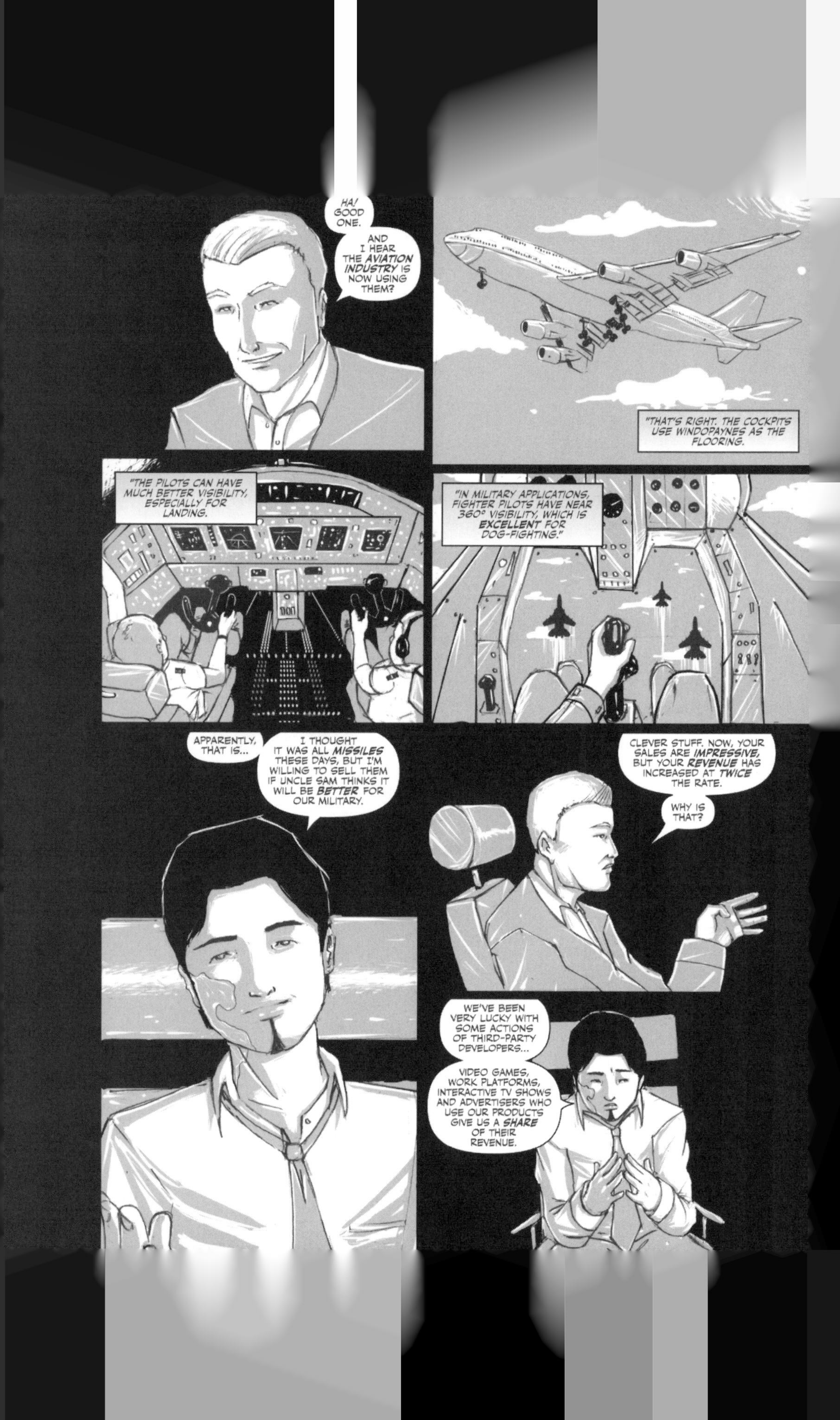

HA! GOOD ONE.
AND I HEAR THE AVIATION INDUSTRY IS NOW USING THEM?
"THAT'S RIGHT. THE COCKPITS USE WINDOPAYNES AS THE FLOORING.
"THE PILOTS CAN HAVE MUCH BETTER VISIBILITY, ESPECIALLY FOR LANDING.
"IN MILITARY APPLICATIONS, FIGHTER PILOTS HAVE NEAR 360° VISIBILITY, WHICH IS EXCELLENT FOR DOG-FIGHTING."
APPARENTLY, THAT IS...
I THOUGHT IT WAS ALL MISSILES THESE DAYS, BUT I'M WILLING TO SELL THEM IF UNCLE SAM THINKS IT WILL BE BETTER FOR OUR MILITARY.
CLEVER STUFF. NOW, YOUR SALES ARE IMPRESSIVE, BUT YOUR REVENUE HAS INCREASED AT TWICE THE RATE.
WHY IS THAT?
WE'VE BEEN VERY LUCKY WITH SOME ACTIONS OF THIRD-PARTY DEVELOPERS...
VIDEO GAMES, WORK PLATFORMS, INTERACTIVE TV SHOWS AND ADVERTISERS WHO USE OUR PRODUCTS GIVE US A SHARE OF THEIR REVENUE.

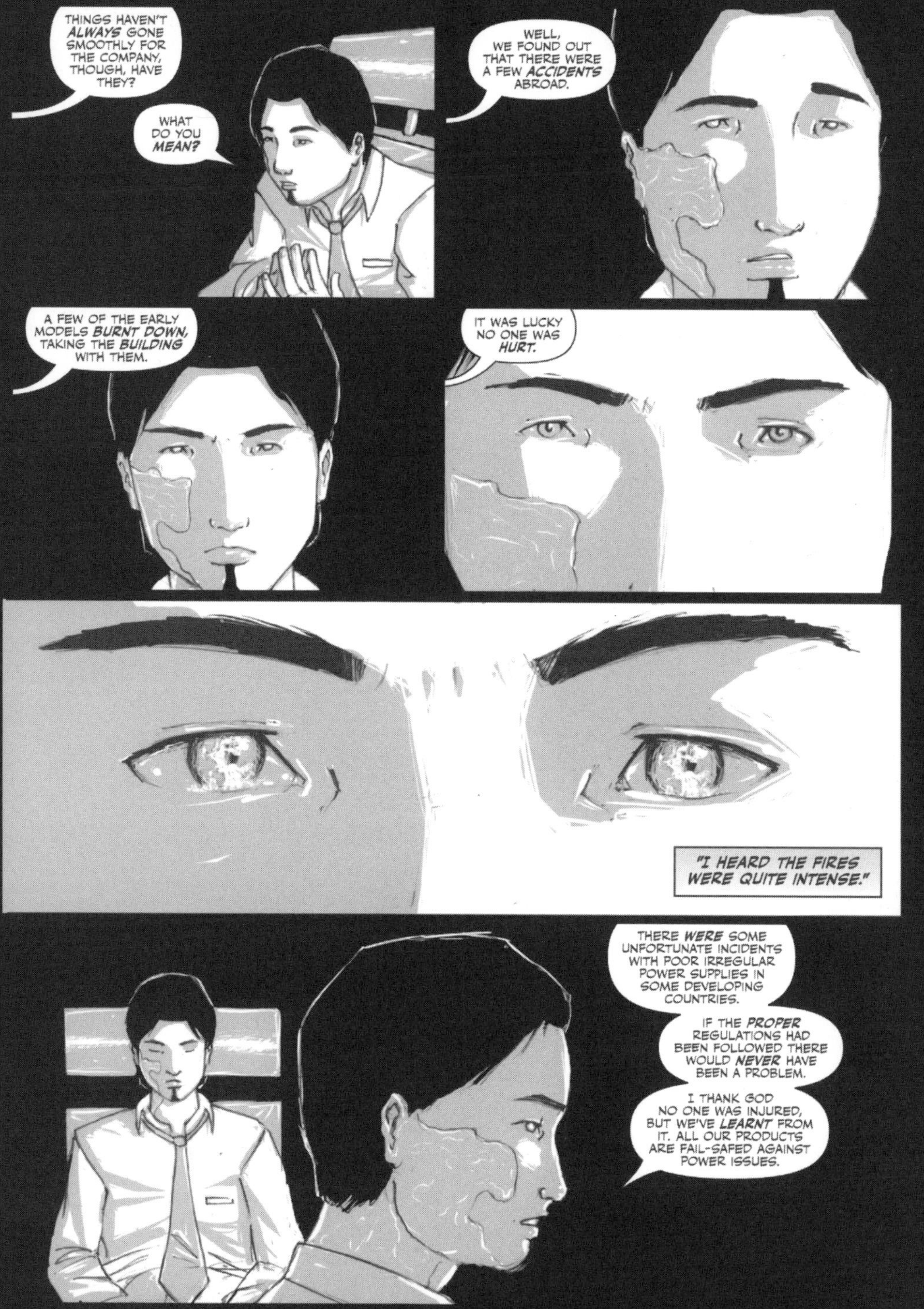
THINGS HAVEN'T ALWAYS GONE SMOOTHLY FOR THE COMPANY, THOUGH, HAVE THEY?
WHAT DO YOU MEAN?
WELL, WE FOUND OUT THAT THERE WERE A FEW ACCIDENTS ABROAD.
A FEW OF THE EARLY MODELS BURNT DOWN, TAKING THE BUILDING WITH THEM.
IT WAS LUCKY NO ONE WAS HURT.
"I HEARD THE FIRES WERE QUITE INTENSE."
THERE WERE SOME UNFORTUNATE INCIDENTS WITH POOR IRREGULAR POWER SUPPLIES IN SOME DEVELOPING COUNTRIES.
IF THE PROPER REGULATIONS HAD BEEN FOLLOWED THERE WOULD NEVER HAVE BEEN A PROBLEM.
I THANK GOD NO ONE WAS INJURED, BUT WE'VE LEARNT FROM IT. ALL OUR PRODUCTS ARE FAIL-SAFED AGAINST POWER ISSUES.

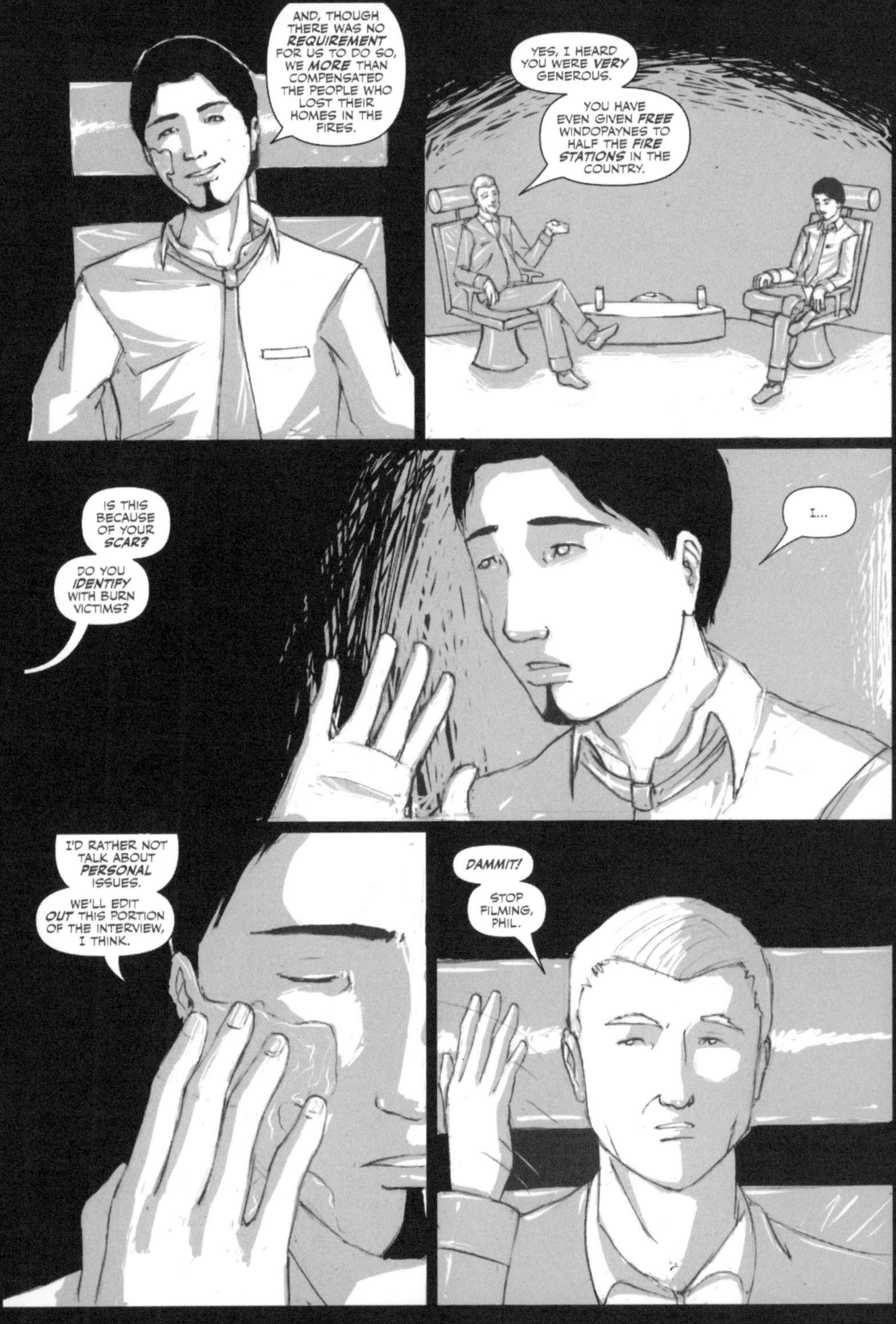
AND, THOUGH THERE WAS NO REQUIREMENT FOR US TO DO SO, WE MORE THAN COMPENSATED THE PEOPLE WHO LOST THEIR HOMES IN THE FIRES.
YES, I HEARD YOU WERE VERY GENEROUS.
YOU HAVE EVEN GIVEN FREE WINDOPAYNES TO HALF THE FIRE STATIONS IN THE COUNTRY.
IS THIS BECAUSE OF YOUR SCAR?
DO YOU IDENTIFY WITH BURN VICTIMS?
I...
I'D RATHER NOT TALK ABOUT PERSONAL ISSUES.
WE'LL EDIT OUT THIS PORTION OF THE INTERVIEW, I THINK.
DAMMIT!
STOP FILMING, PHIL.

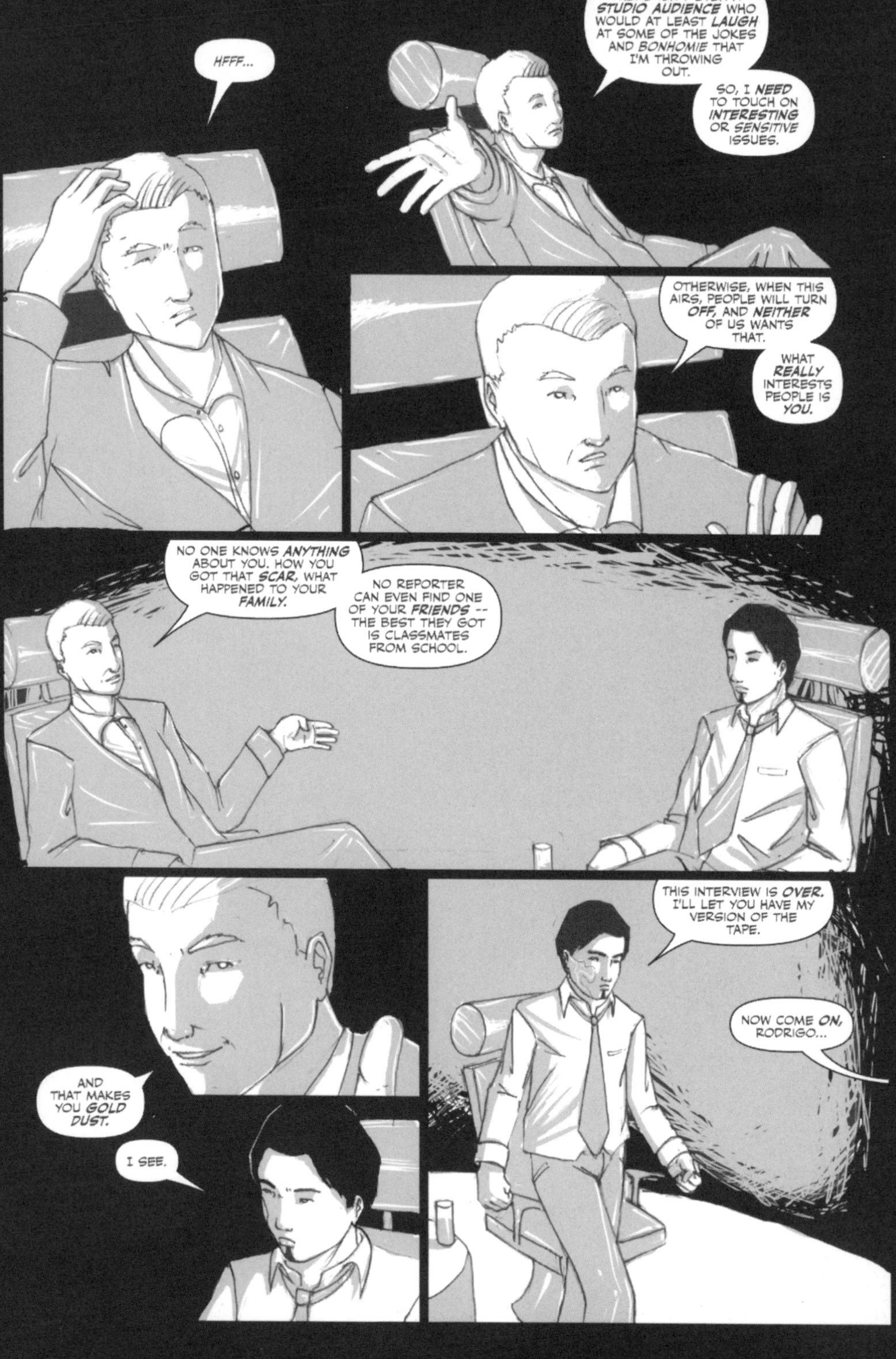
HFFF...
THERE ISN'T EVEN A STUDIO AUDIENCE WHO WOULD AT LEAST LAUGH AT SOME OF THE JOKES AND BONHOMIE THAT I'M THROWING OUT.
SO, I NEED TO TOUCH ON INTERESTING OR SENSITIVE ISSUES.
OTHERWISE, WHEN THIS AIRS, PEOPLE WILL TURN OFF, AND NEITHER OF US WANTS THAT.
WHAT REALLY INTERESTS PEOPLE IS YOU.
NO ONE KNOWS ANYTHING ABOUT YOU. HOW YOU GOT THAT SCAR, WHAT HAPPENED TO YOUR FAMILY.
NO REPORTER CAN EVEN FIND ONE OF YOUR FRIENDS -- THE BEST THEY GOT IS CLASSMATES FROM SCHOOL.
AND THAT MAKES YOU GOLD DUST.
I SEE.
THIS INTERVIEW IS OVER. I'LL LET YOU HAVE MY VERSION OF THE TAPE.
NOW COME ON, RODRIGO...

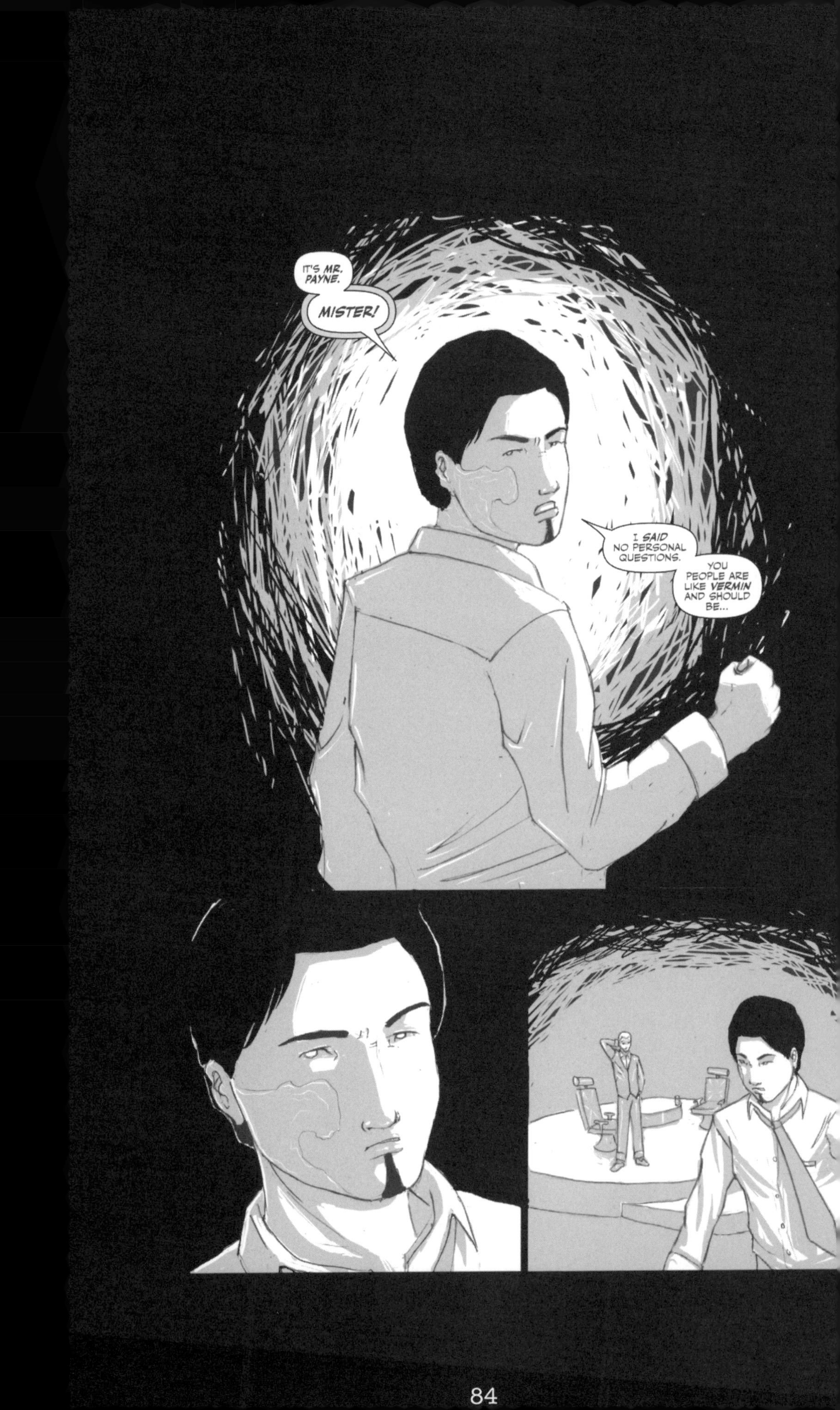
IT'S MR. PAYNE.
MISTER!
I SAID NO PERSONAL QUESTIONS.
YOU PEOPLE ARE LIKE VERMIN AND SHOULD BE...

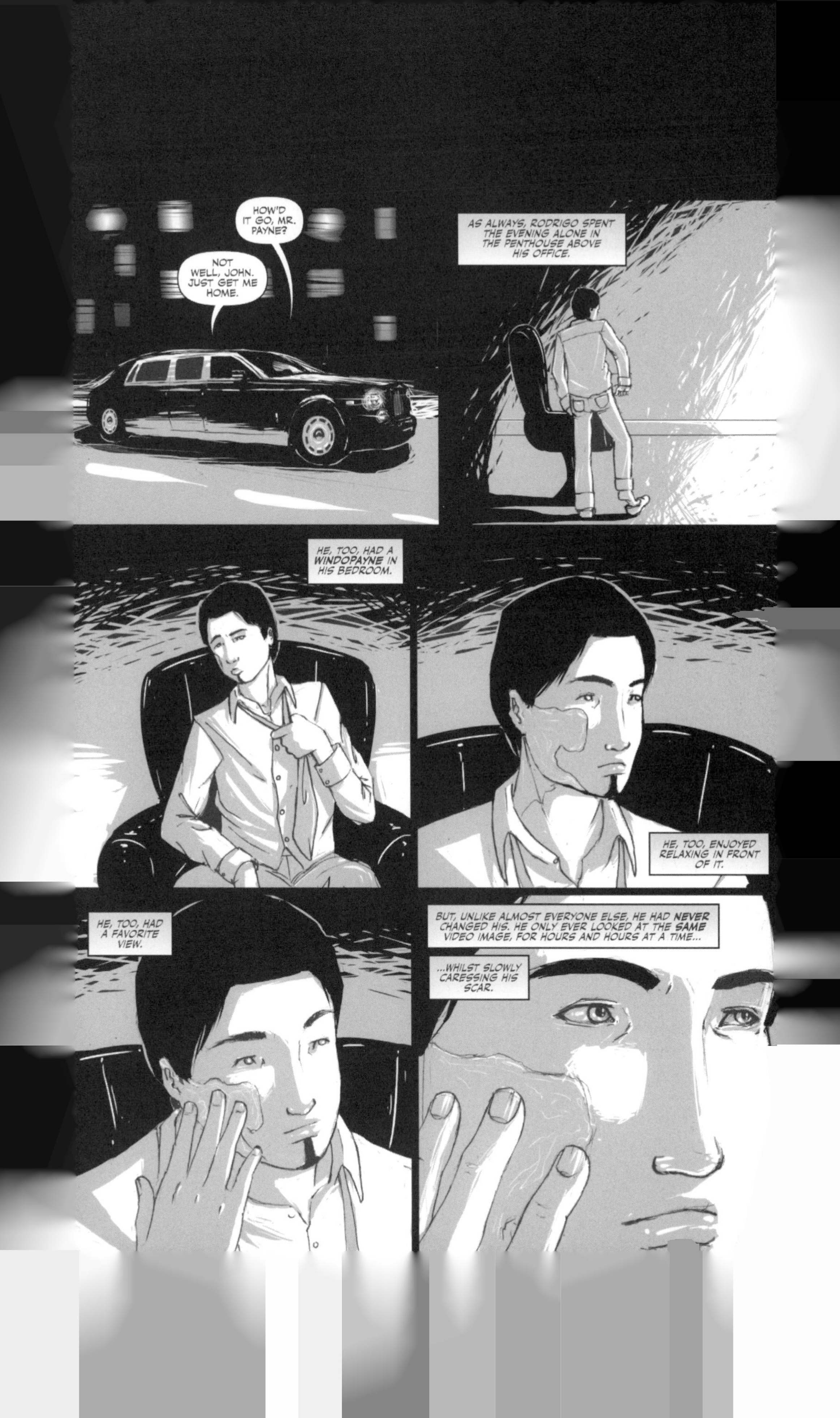
HOW'D IT GO, MR. PAYNE?
NOT WELL, JOHN. JUST GET ME HOME.
AS ALWAYS, RODRIGO SPENT THE EVENING ALONE IN THE PENTHOUSE ABOVE HIS OFFICE.
HE, TOO, HAD A WINDOPAYNE IN HIS BEDROOM.
HE, TOO, ENJOYED RELAXING IN FRONT OF IT.
HE, TOO, HAD A FAVORITE VIEW.
BUT, UNLIKE ALMOST EVERYONE ELSE, HE HAD NEVER CHANGED HIS. HE ONLY EVER LOOKED AT THE SAME VIDEO IMAGE, FOR HOURS AND HOURS AT A TIME...
...WHILST SLOWLY CARESSING HIS SCAR.

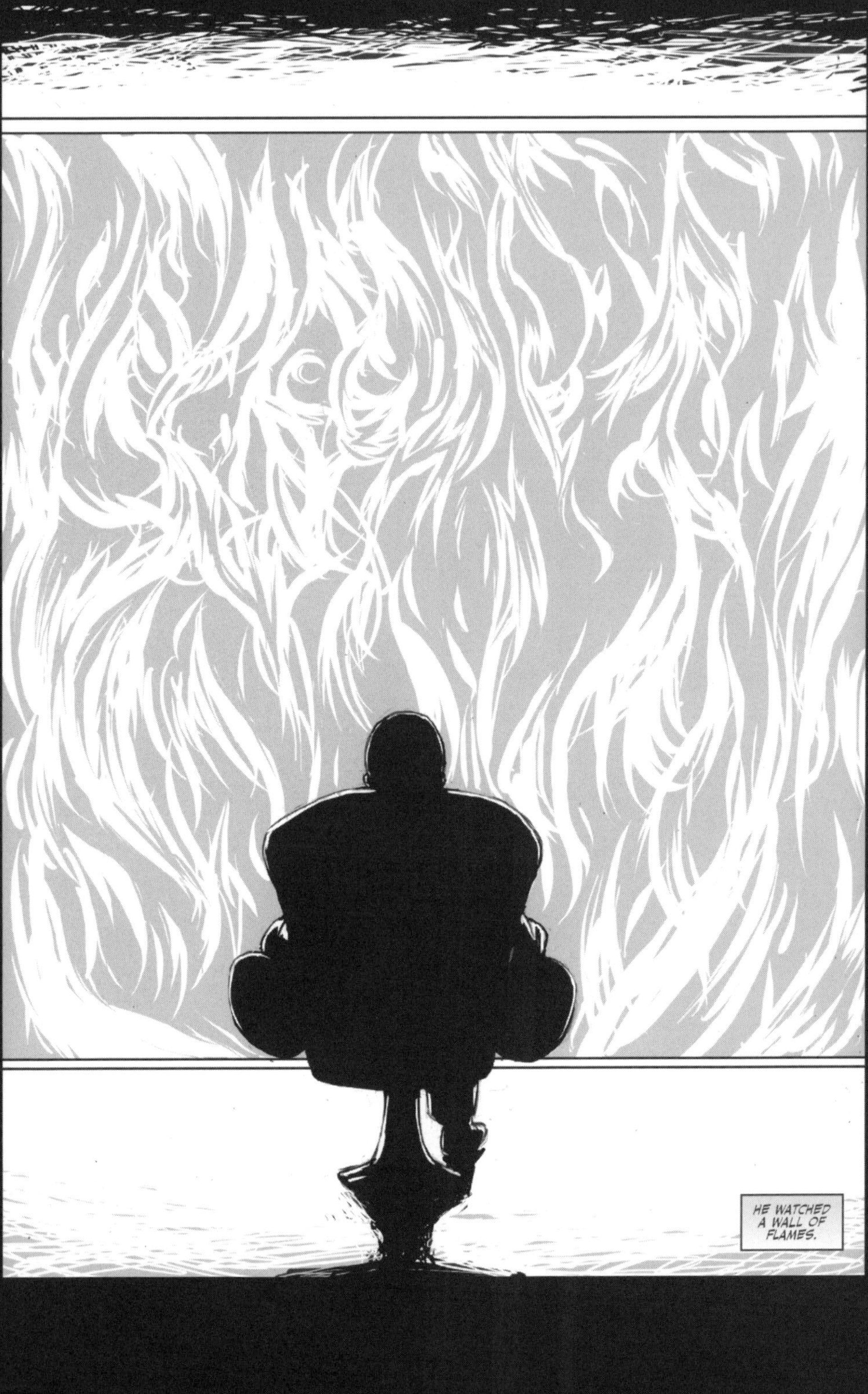
HE WATCHED A WALL OF FLAMES.

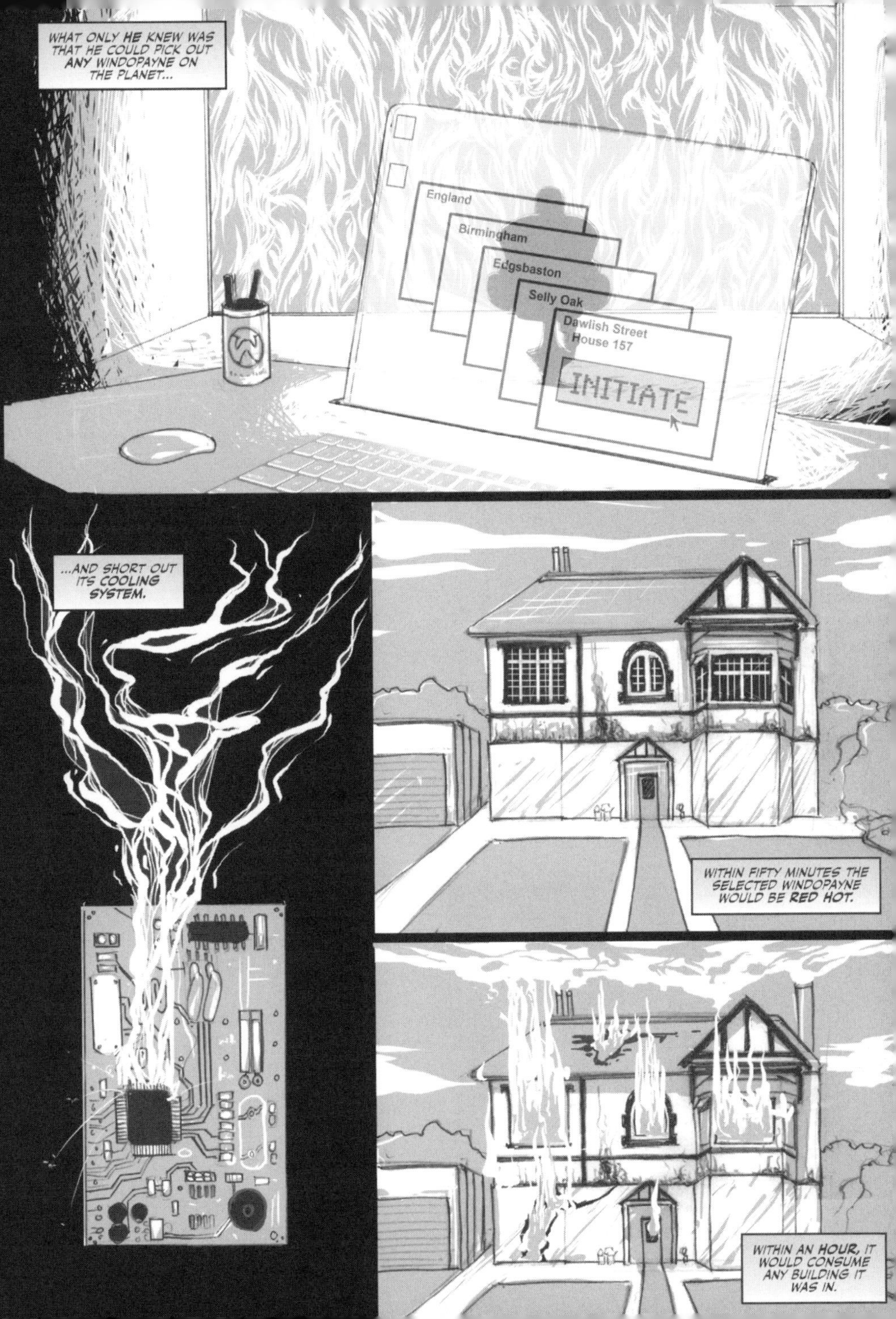

WHAT ONLY HE KNEW WAS THAT HE COULD PICK OUT ANY WINDOPAYNE ON THE PLANET...
England
Birmingham
Edgsbaston
Selly Oak
Dawlish Street
House 157
INITIATE
...AND SHORT OUT ITS COOLING SYSTEM.
WITHIN FIFTY MINUTES THE SELECTED WINDOPAYNE WOULD BE RED HOT.
WITHIN AN HOUR, IT WOULD CONSUME ANY BUILDING IT WAS IN.

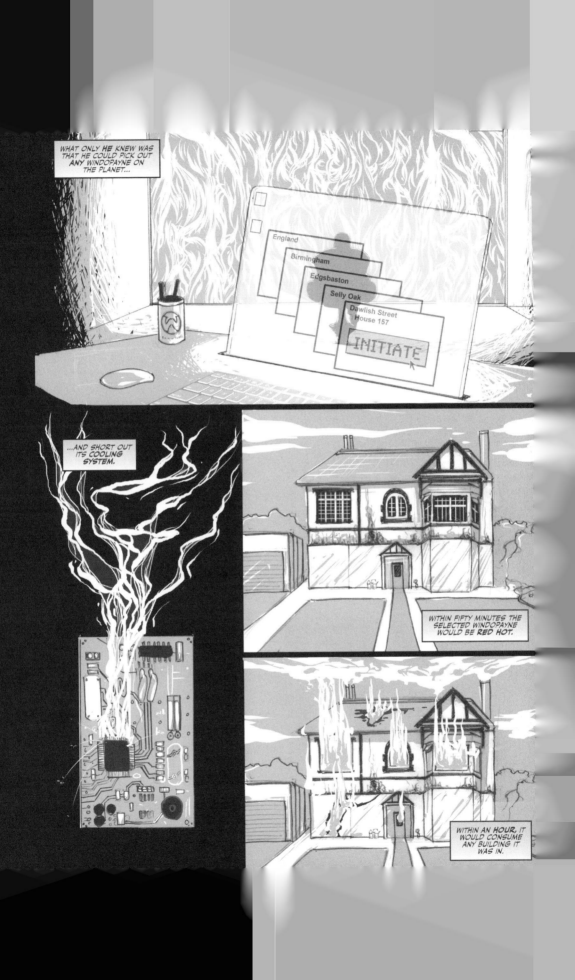

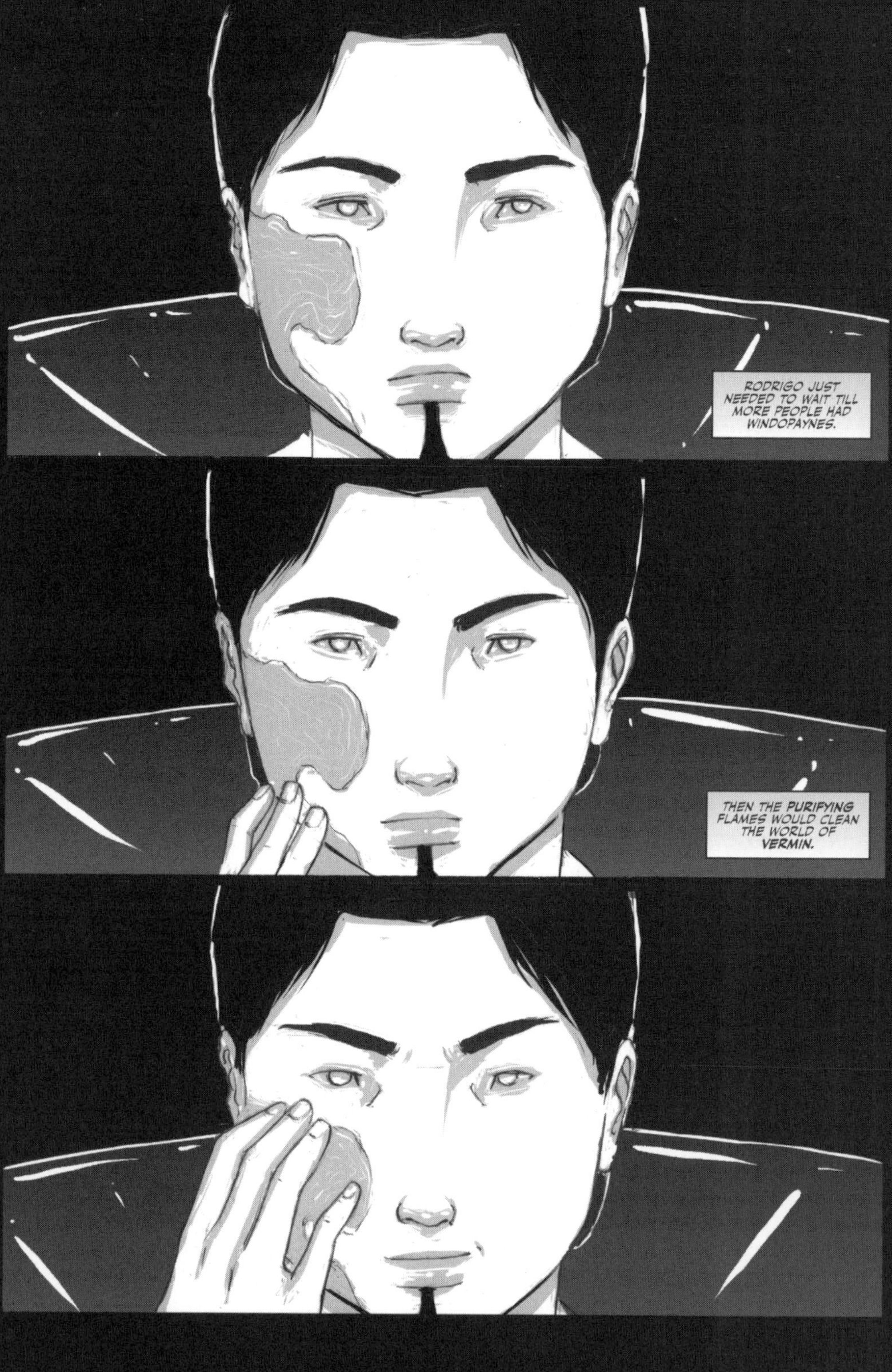
RODRIGO JUST NEEDED TO WAIT TILL MORE PEOPLE HAD WINDOPAYNES.
THEN THE PURIFYING FLAMES WOULD CLEAN THE WORLD OF VERMIN.

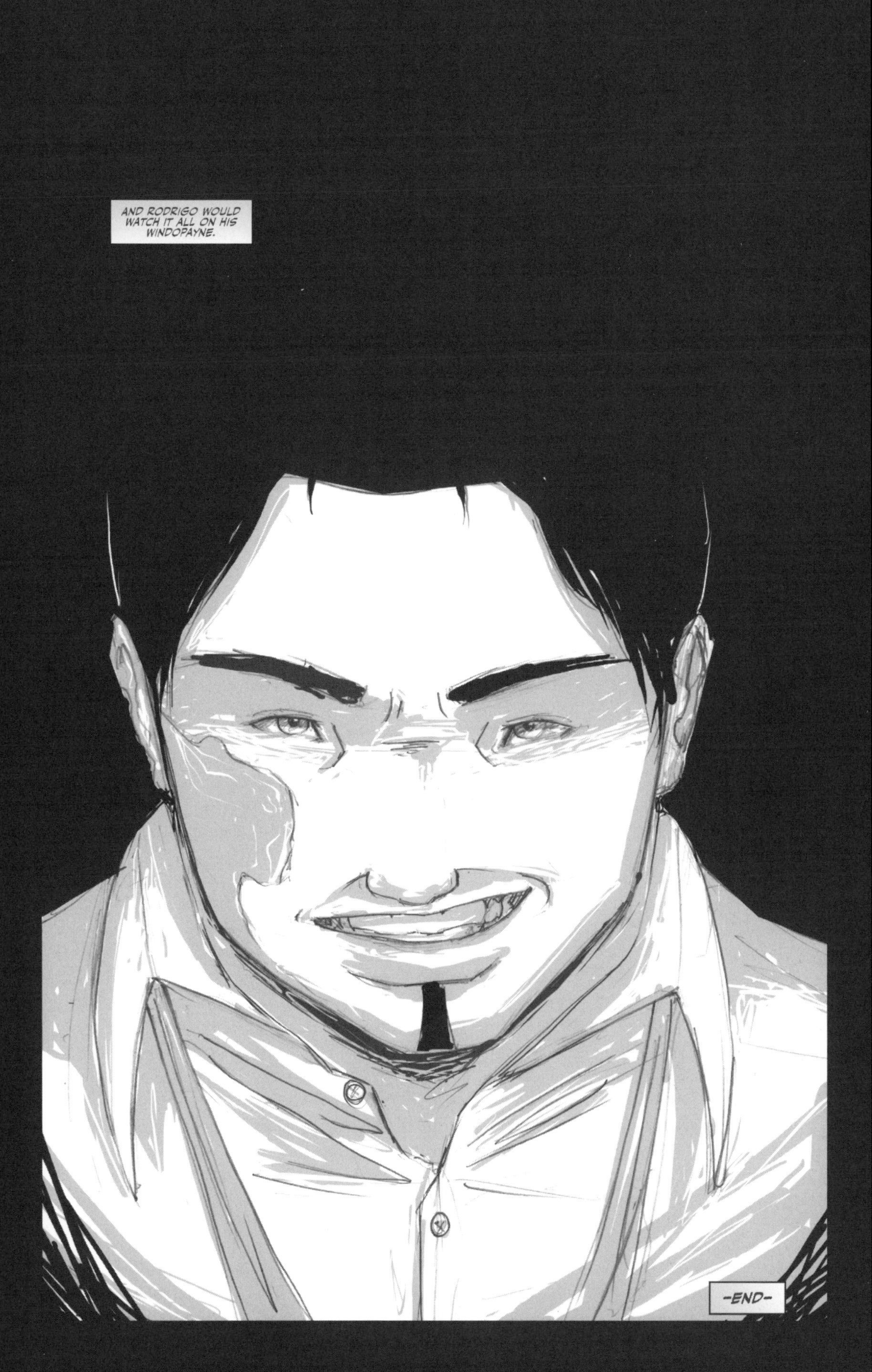
AND RODRIGO WOULD WATCH IT ALL ON HIS WINDOPAYNE.
-END-

The Game...

"Keep trying, hold on, and always, always, always believe in yourself, because if you don't, then who will, sweetie?"

-Marilyn Monroe

Writer/Creator
Neil Gibson

Illustrator
Ant Mercer

www.tpub.co.uk

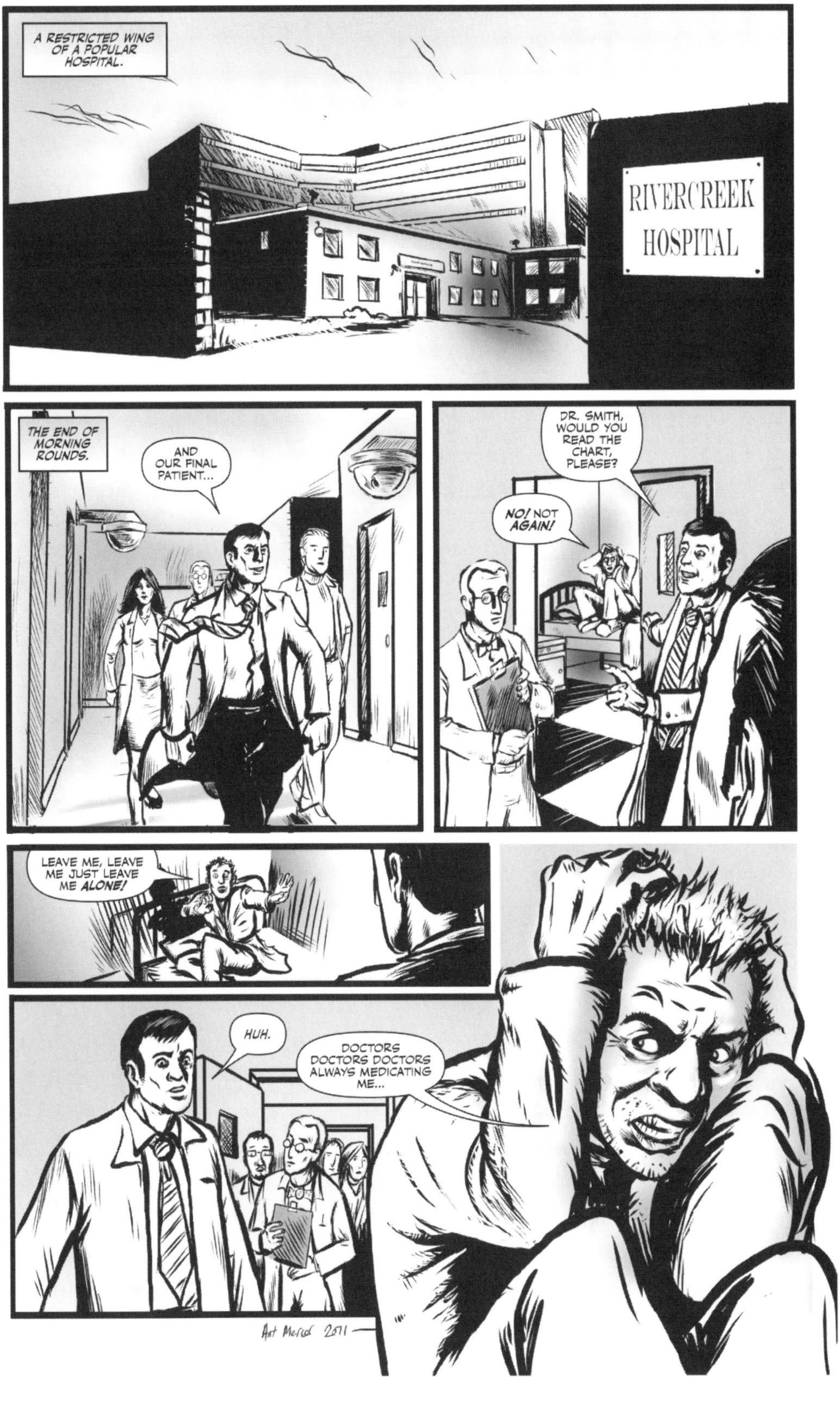
A RESTRICTED WING OF A POPULAR HOSPITAL.
RIVERCREEK HOSPITAL
THE END OF MORNING ROUNDS.
AND OUR FINAL PATIENT...
DR. SMITH, WOULD YOU READ THE CHART, PLEASE?
NO! NOT AGAIN!
LEAVE ME, LEAVE ME JUST LEAVE ME ALONE!
HUH.
DOCTORS DOCTORS DOCTORS ALWAYS MEDICATING ME...
Art Mercer 2011

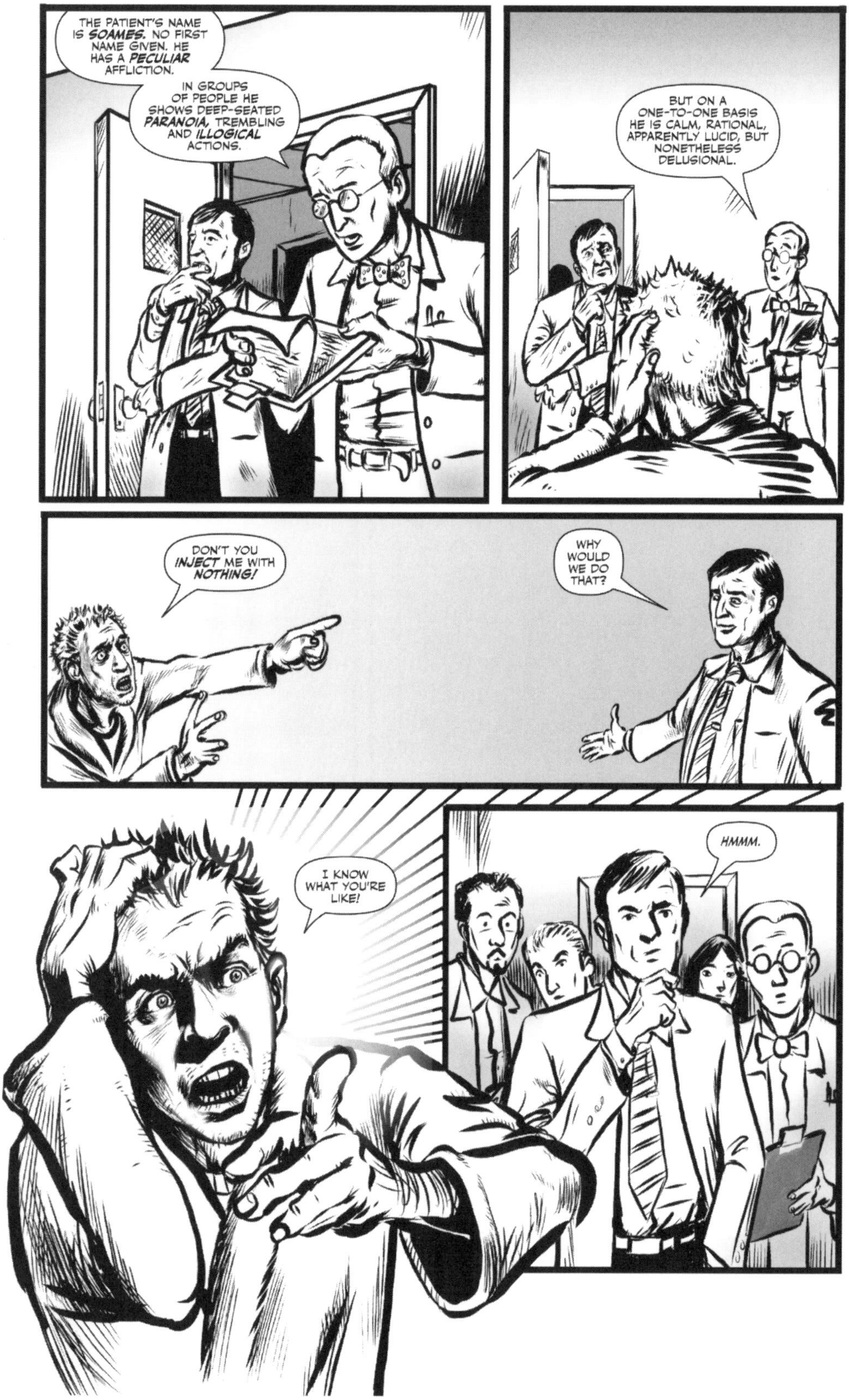
THE PATIENT'S NAME IS SOAMES. NO FIRST NAME GIVEN. HE HAS A PECULIAR AFFLICTION.
IN GROUPS OF PEOPLE HE SHOWS DEEP-SEATED PARANOIA, TREMBLING AND ILLOGICAL ACTIONS.
BUT ON A ONE-TO-ONE BASIS HE IS CALM, RATIONAL, APPARENTLY LUCID, BUT NONETHELESS DELUSIONAL.
DON'T YOU INJECT ME WITH NOTHING!
WHY WOULD WE DO THAT?
I KNOW WHAT YOU'RE LIKE!
HMMM.

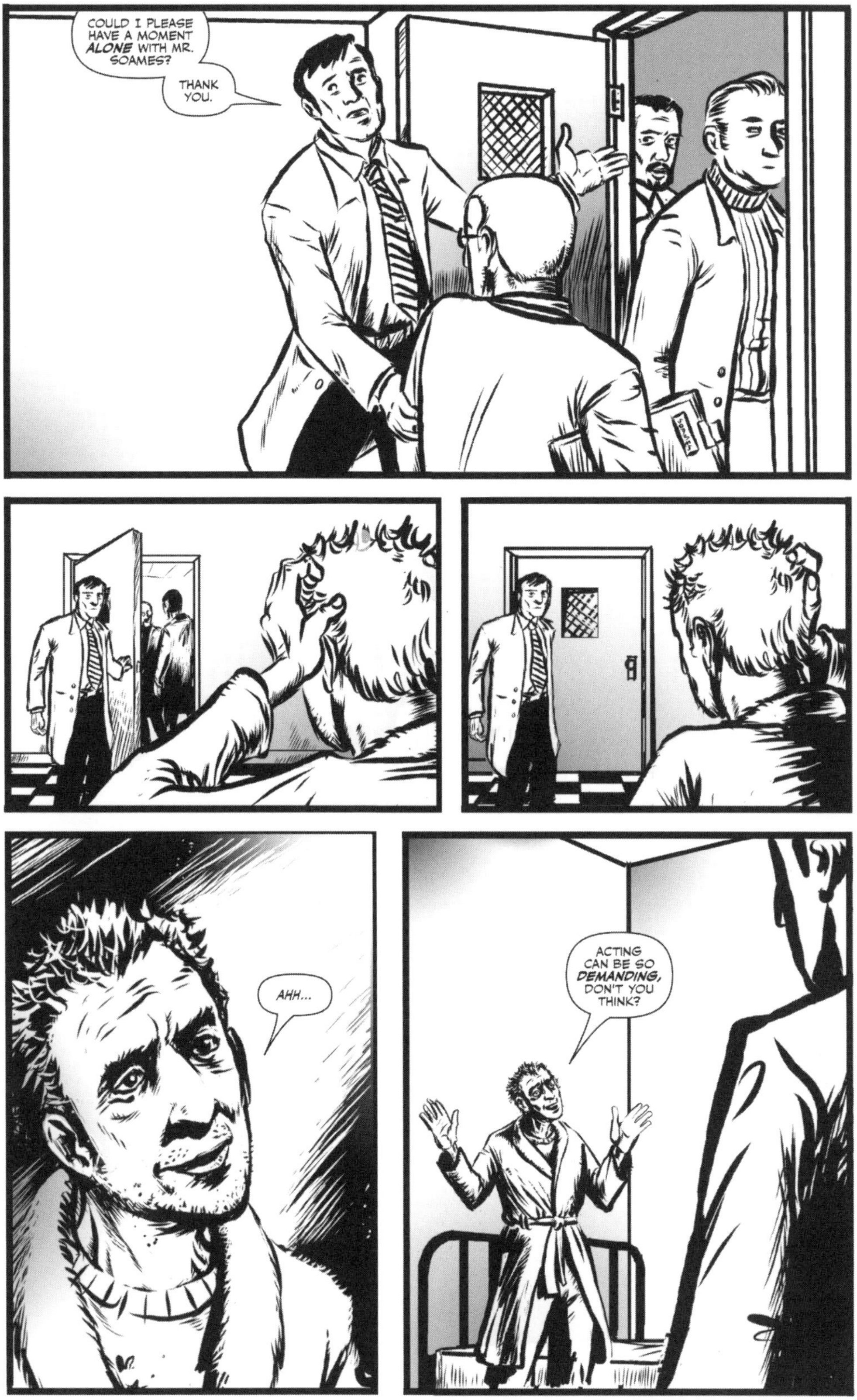
COULD I PLEASE HAVE A MOMENT ALONE WITH MR. SOAMES?
THANK YOU.
AHH...
ACTING CAN BE SO DEMANDING, DON'T YOU THINK?

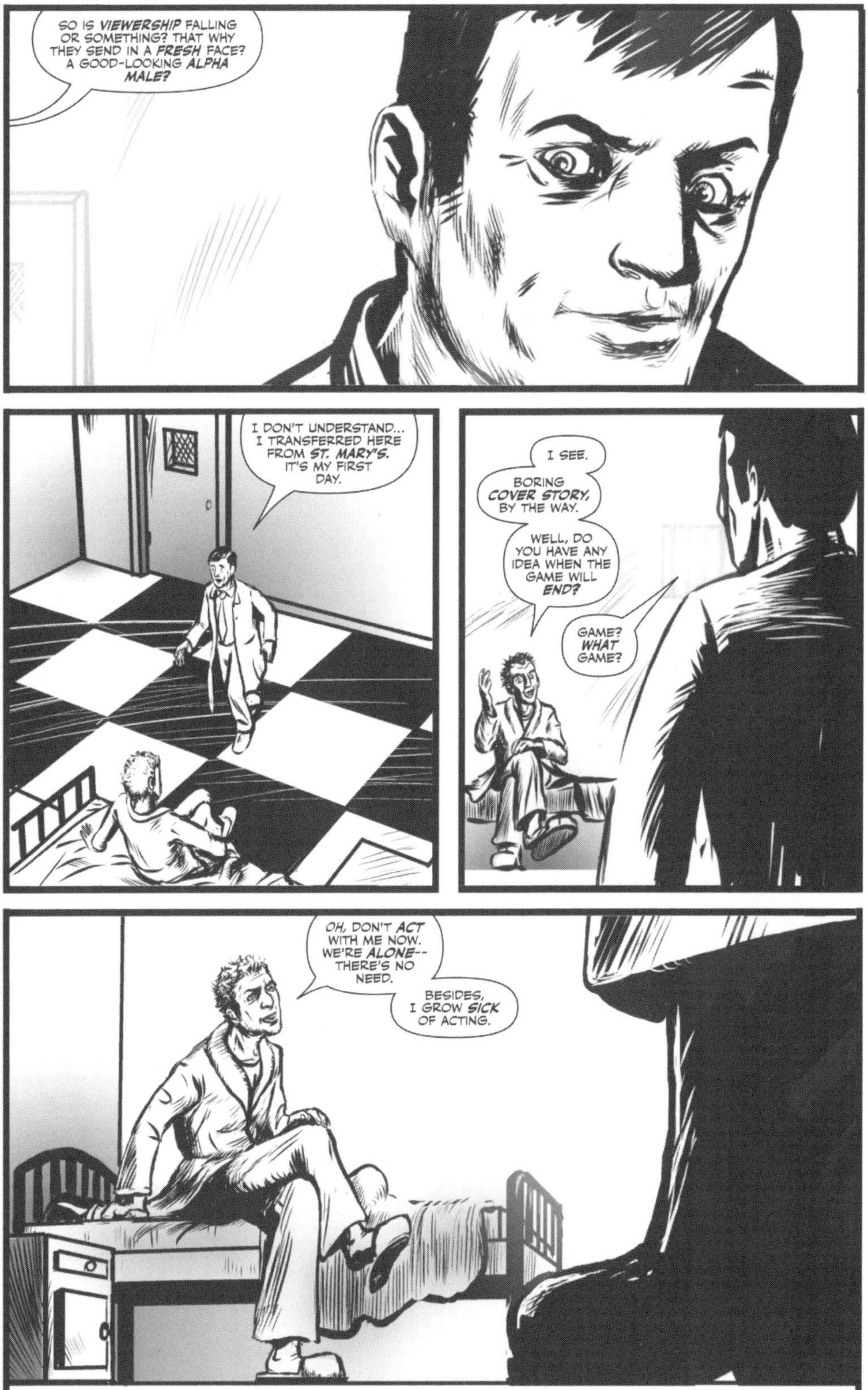
SO IS VIEWERSHIP FALLING OR SOMETHING? THAT WHY THEY SEND IN A FRESH FACE? A GOOD-LOOKING ALPHA MALE?
I DON'T UNDERSTAND... I TRANSFERRED HERE FROM ST. MARY'S. IT'S MY FIRST DAY.
I SEE.
BORING COVER STORY, BY THE WAY.
WELL, DO YOU HAVE ANY IDEA WHEN THE GAME WILL END?
GAME? WHAT GAME?
OH, DON'T ACT WITH ME NOW. WE'RE ALONE-- THERE'S NO NEED.
BESIDES, I GROW SICK OF ACTING.

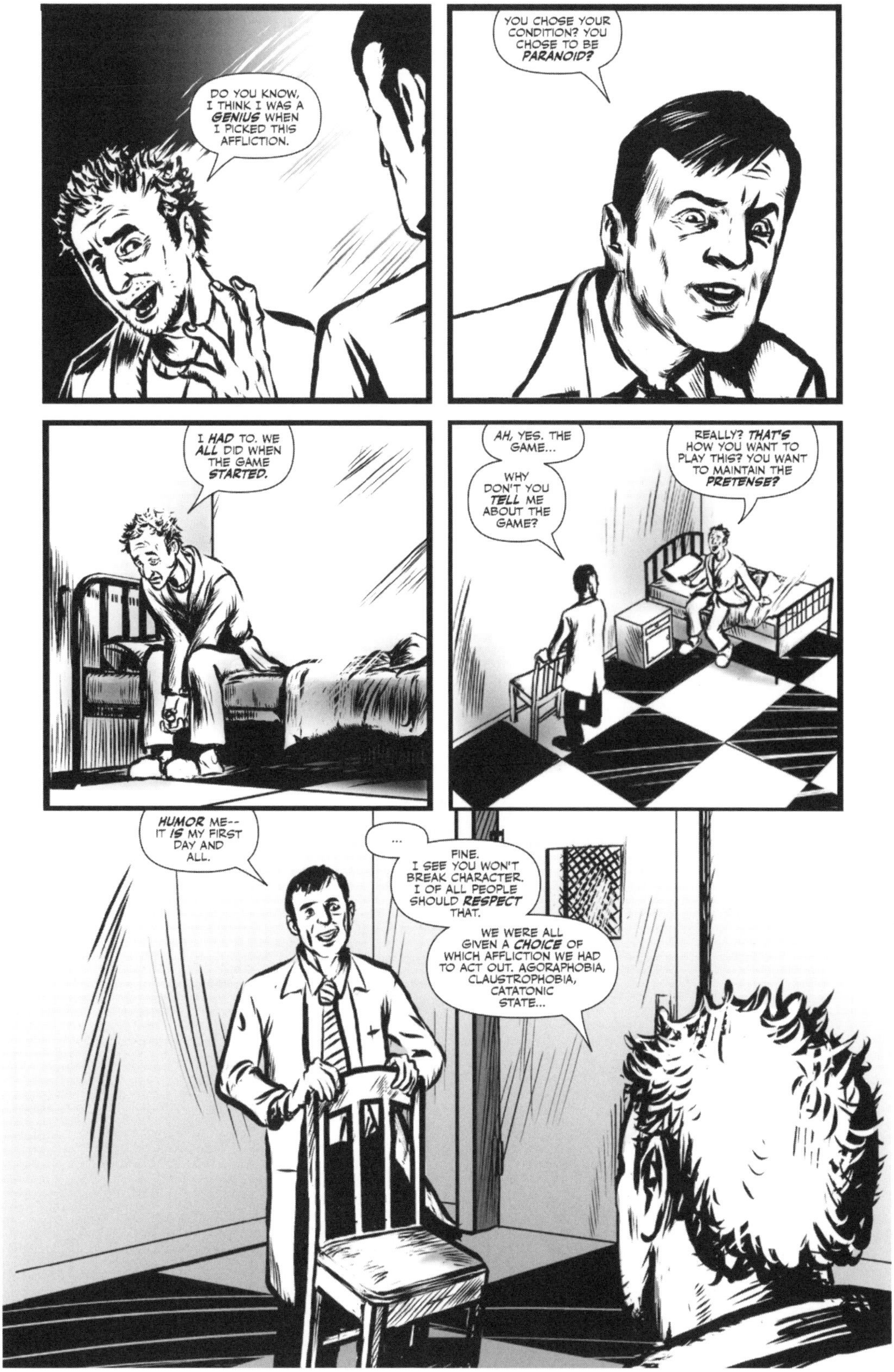
DO YOU KNOW, I THINK I WAS A GENIUS WHEN I PICKED THIS AFFLICTION.
YOU CHOSE YOUR CONDITION? YOU CHOSE TO BE PARANOID?
I HAD TO. WE ALL DID WHEN THE GAME STARTED.
AH, YES. THE GAME...
WHY DON'T YOU TELL ME ABOUT THE GAME?
REALLY? THAT'S HOW YOU WANT TO PLAY THIS? YOU WANT TO MAINTAIN THE PRETENSE?
HUMOR ME-- IT IS MY FIRST DAY AND ALL.
...
FINE. I SEE YOU WON'T BREAK CHARACTER. I OF ALL PEOPLE SHOULD RESPECT THAT.
WE WERE ALL GIVEN A CHOICE OF WHICH AFFLICTION WE HAD TO ACT OUT. AGORAPHOBIA, CLAUSTROPHOBIA, CATATONIC STATE...

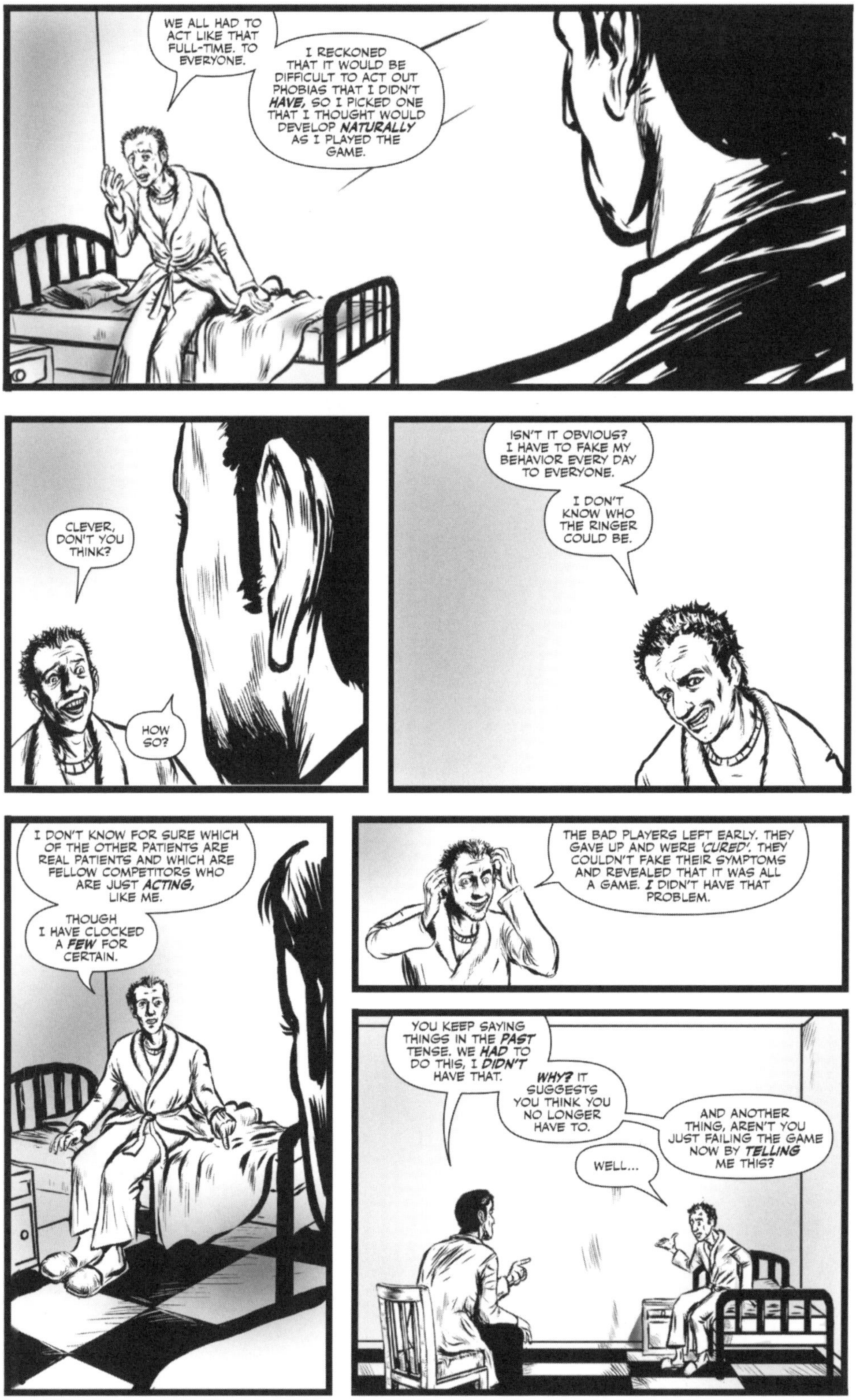
WE ALL HAD TO ACT LIKE THAT FULL-TIME. TO EVERYONE.
I RECKONED THAT IT WOULD BE DIFFICULT TO ACT OUT PHOBIAS THAT I DIDN'T *HAVE,* SO I PICKED ONE THAT I THOUGHT WOULD DEVELOP *NATURALLY* AS I PLAYED THE GAME.
CLEVER, DON'T YOU THINK?
HOW SO?
ISN'T IT OBVIOUS? I HAVE TO FAKE MY BEHAVIOR EVERY DAY TO EVERYONE.
I DON'T KNOW WHO THE RINGER COULD BE.
I DON'T KNOW FOR SURE WHICH OF THE OTHER PATIENTS ARE REAL PATIENTS AND WHICH ARE FELLOW COMPETITORS WHO ARE JUST *ACTING,* LIKE ME.
THOUGH I HAVE CLOCKED A *FEW* FOR CERTAIN.
THE BAD PLAYERS LEFT EARLY. THEY GAVE UP AND WERE *'CURED'.* THEY COULDN'T FAKE THEIR SYMPTOMS AND REVEALED THAT IT WAS ALL A GAME. *I* DIDN'T HAVE THAT PROBLEM.
YOU KEEP SAYING THINGS IN THE *PAST* TENSE. WE *HAD* TO DO THIS, I *DIDN'T* HAVE THAT.
WHY? IT SUGGESTS YOU THINK YOU NO LONGER HAVE TO.
AND ANOTHER THING, AREN'T YOU JUST FAILING THE GAME NOW BY *TELLING* ME THIS?
WELL...

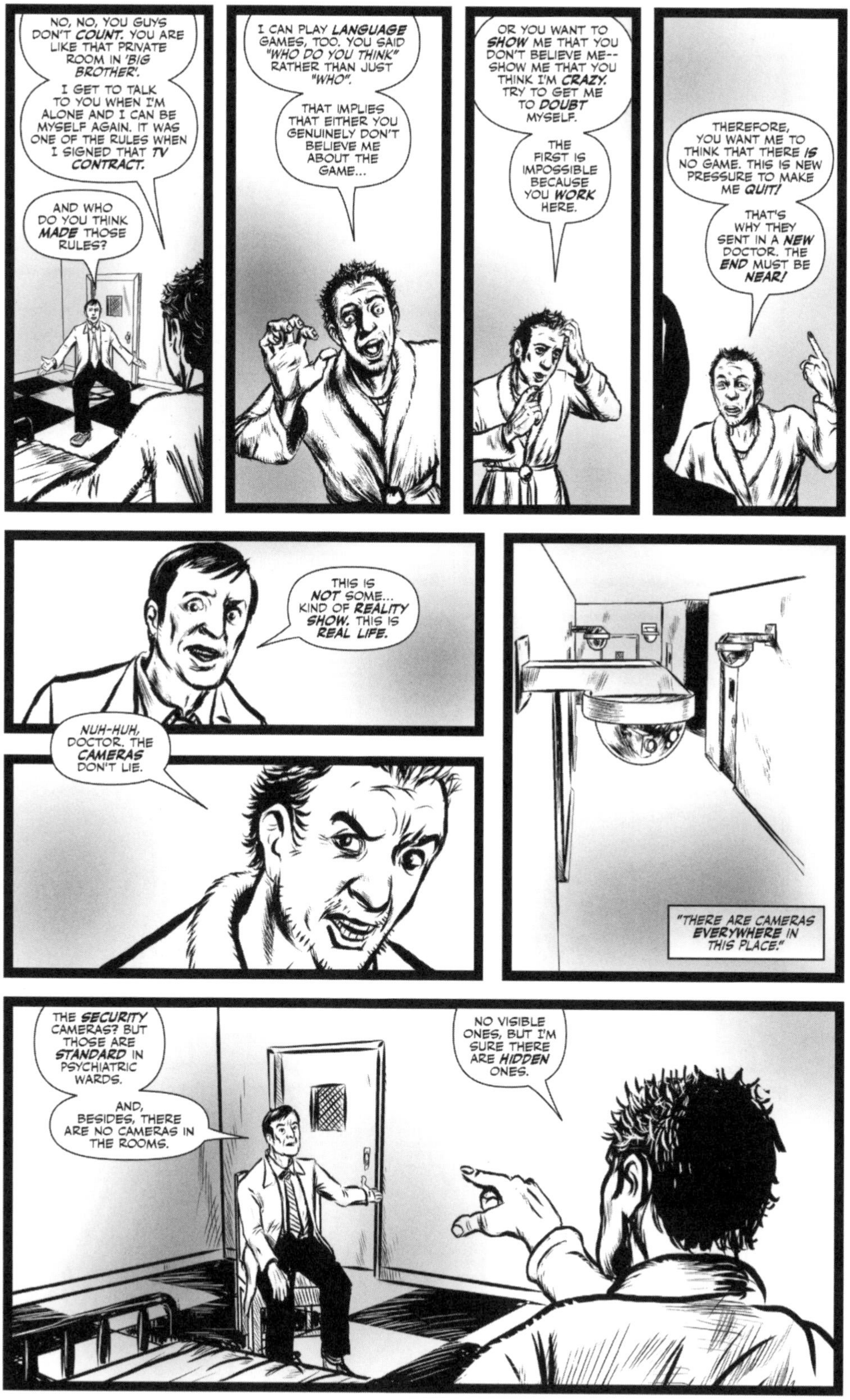
NO, NO, YOU GUYS DON'T COUNT. YOU ARE LIKE THAT PRIVATE ROOM IN 'BIG BROTHER'.
I GET TO TALK TO YOU WHEN I'M ALONE AND I CAN BE MYSELF AGAIN. IT WAS ONE OF THE RULES WHEN I SIGNED THAT TV CONTRACT.
AND WHO DO YOU THINK MADE THOSE RULES?
I CAN PLAY LANGUAGE GAMES, TOO. YOU SAID "WHO DO YOU THINK" RATHER THAN JUST "WHO".
THAT IMPLIES THAT EITHER YOU GENUINELY DON'T BELIEVE ME ABOUT THE GAME...
OR YOU WANT TO SHOW ME THAT YOU DON'T BELIEVE ME-- SHOW ME THAT YOU THINK I'M CRAZY. TRY TO GET ME TO DOUBT MYSELF.
THE FIRST IS IMPOSSIBLE BECAUSE YOU WORK HERE.
THEREFORE, YOU WANT ME TO THINK THAT THERE IS NO GAME. THIS IS NEW PRESSURE TO MAKE ME QUIT!
THAT'S WHY THEY SENT IN A NEW DOCTOR. THE END MUST BE NEAR!
THIS IS NOT SOME... KIND OF REALITY SHOW. THIS IS REAL LIFE.
NUH-HUH, DOCTOR. THE CAMERAS DON'T LIE.
"THERE ARE CAMERAS EVERYWHERE IN THIS PLACE."
THE SECURITY CAMERAS? BUT THOSE ARE STANDARD IN PSYCHIATRIC WARDS.
AND, BESIDES, THERE ARE NO CAMERAS IN THE ROOMS.
NO VISIBLE ONES, BUT I'M SURE THERE ARE HIDDEN ONES.

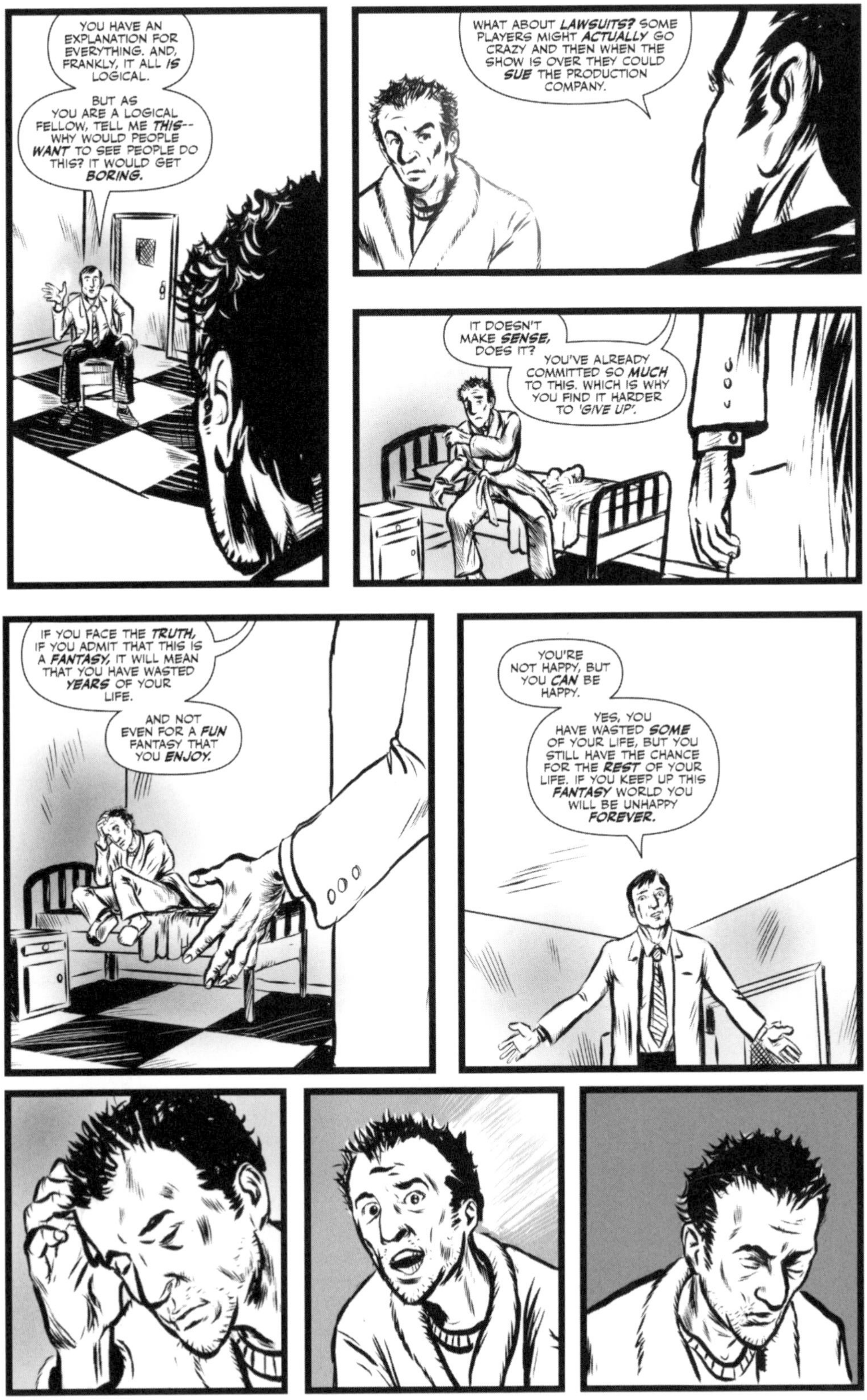
YOU HAVE AN EXPLANATION FOR EVERYTHING. AND, FRANKLY, IT ALL IS LOGICAL.
BUT AS YOU ARE A LOGICAL FELLOW, TELL ME THIS-- WHY WOULD PEOPLE WANT TO SEE PEOPLE DO THIS? IT WOULD GET BORING.
WHAT ABOUT LAWSUITS? SOME PLAYERS MIGHT ACTUALLY GO CRAZY AND THEN WHEN THE SHOW IS OVER THEY COULD SUE THE PRODUCTION COMPANY.
IT DOESN'T MAKE SENSE, DOES IT?
YOU'VE ALREADY COMMITTED SO MUCH TO THIS. WHICH IS WHY YOU FIND IT HARDER TO 'GIVE UP'.
IF YOU FACE THE TRUTH, IF YOU ADMIT THAT THIS IS A FANTASY, IT WILL MEAN THAT YOU HAVE WASTED YEARS OF YOUR LIFE.
AND NOT EVEN FOR A FUN FANTASY THAT YOU ENJOY.
YOU'RE NOT HAPPY, BUT YOU CAN BE HAPPY.
YES, YOU HAVE WASTED SOME OF YOUR LIFE, BUT YOU STILL HAVE THE CHANCE FOR THE REST OF YOUR LIFE. IF YOU KEEP UP THIS FANTASY WORLD YOU WILL BE UNHAPPY FOREVER.

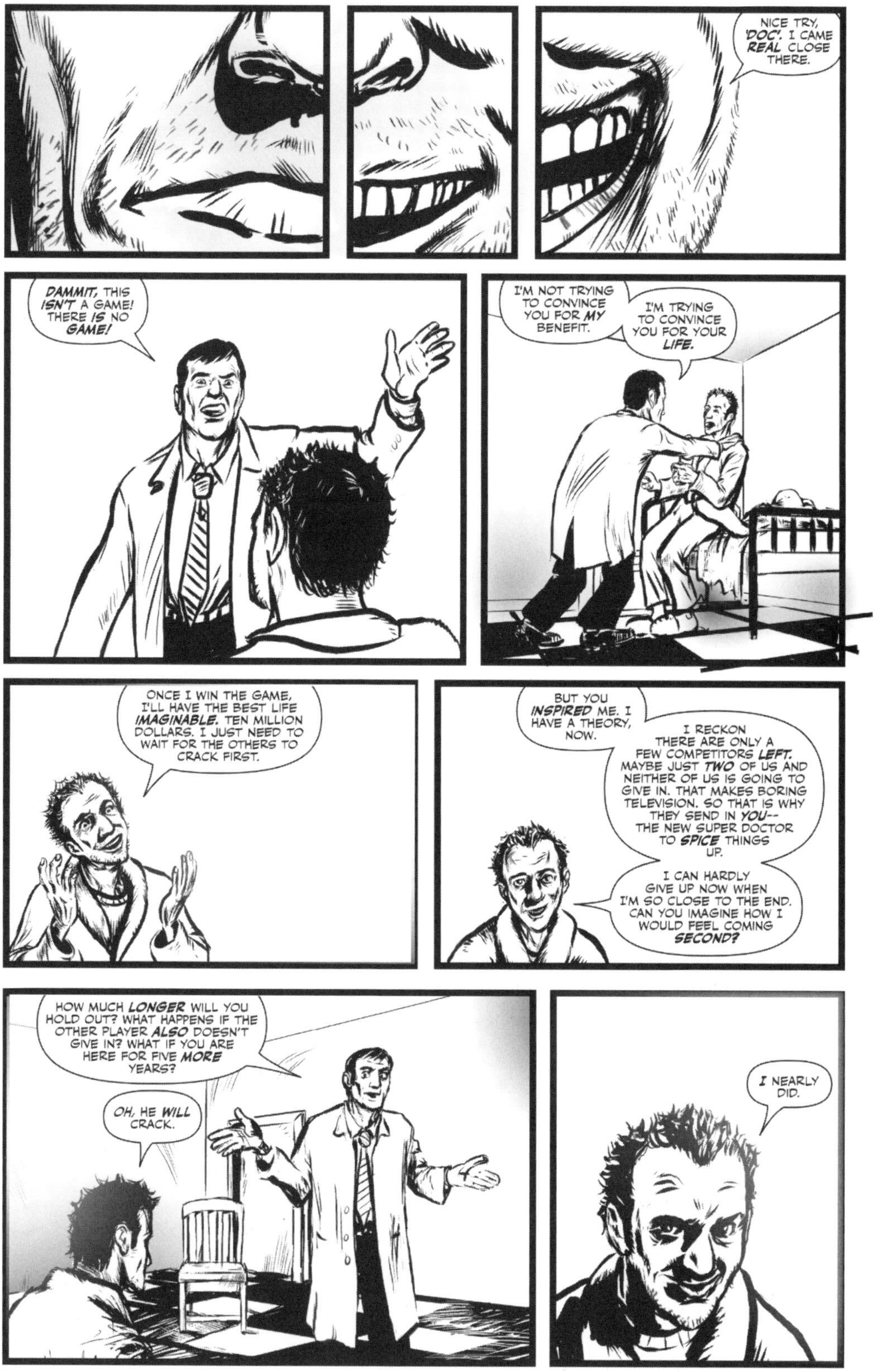
NICE TRY, 'DOC'. I CAME REAL CLOSE THERE.
DAMMIT, THIS ISN'T A GAME! THERE IS NO GAME!
I'M NOT TRYING TO CONVINCE YOU FOR MY BENEFIT.
I'M TRYING TO CONVINCE YOU FOR YOUR LIFE.
ONCE I WIN THE GAME, I'LL HAVE THE BEST LIFE IMAGINABLE. TEN MILLION DOLLARS. I JUST NEED TO WAIT FOR THE OTHERS TO CRACK FIRST.
BUT YOU INSPIRED ME. I HAVE A THEORY, NOW.
I RECKON THERE ARE ONLY A FEW COMPETITORS LEFT. MAYBE JUST TWO OF US AND NEITHER OF US IS GOING TO GIVE IN. THAT MAKES BORING TELEVISION. SO THAT IS WHY THEY SEND IN YOU-- THE NEW SUPER DOCTOR TO SPICE THINGS UP.
I CAN HARDLY GIVE UP NOW WHEN I'M SO CLOSE TO THE END. CAN YOU IMAGINE HOW I WOULD FEEL COMING SECOND?
HOW MUCH LONGER WILL YOU HOLD OUT? WHAT HAPPENS IF THE OTHER PLAYER ALSO DOESN'T GIVE IN? WHAT IF YOU ARE HERE FOR FIVE MORE YEARS?
OH, HE WILL CRACK.
I NEARLY DID.

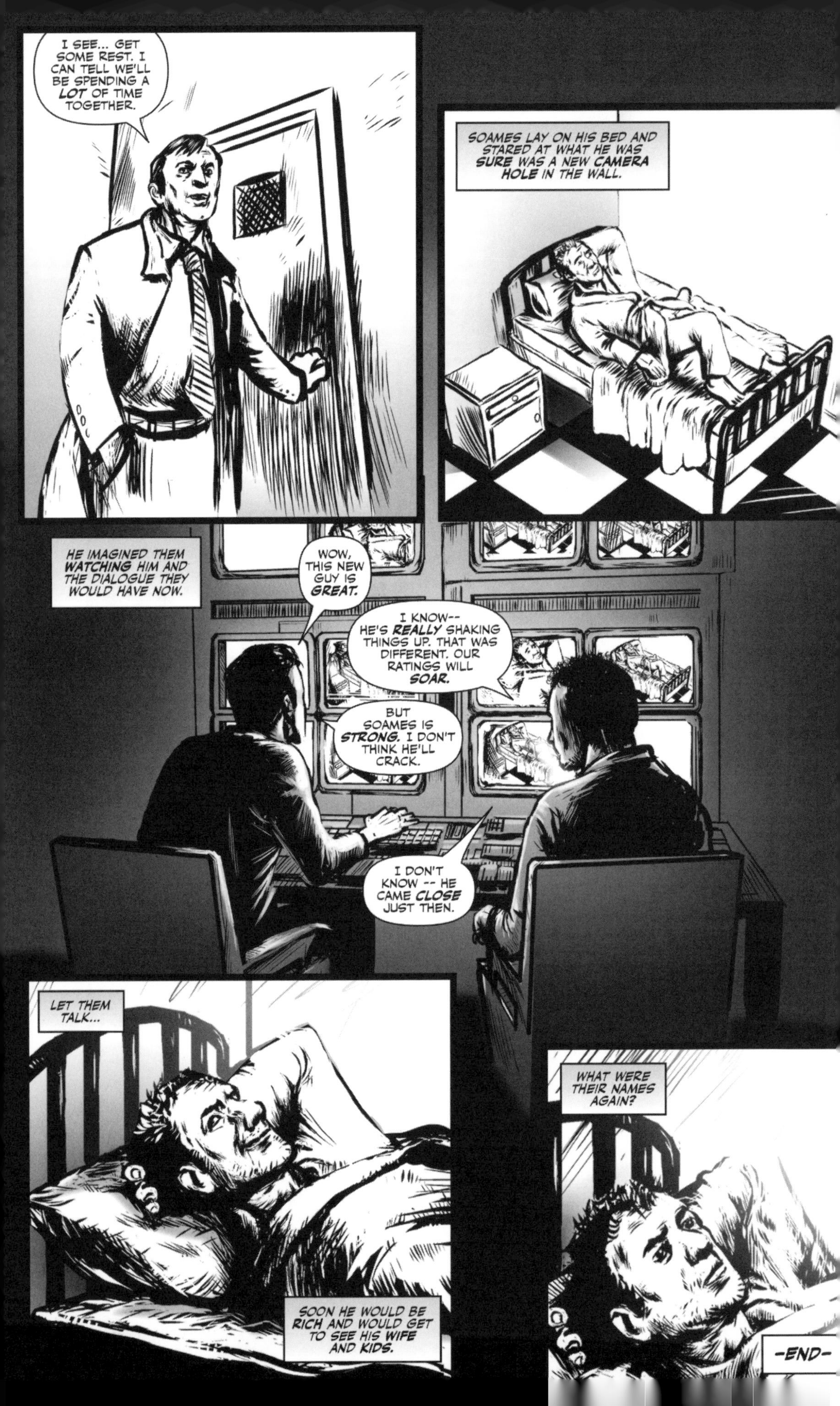
I SEE... GET SOME REST. I CAN TELL WE'LL BE SPENDING A LOT OF TIME TOGETHER.
SOAMES LAY ON HIS BED AND STARED AT WHAT HE WAS SURE WAS A NEW CAMERA HOLE IN THE WALL.
HE IMAGINED THEM WATCHING HIM AND THE DIALOGUE THEY WOULD HAVE NOW.
WOW, THIS NEW GUY IS GREAT.
I KNOW-- HE'S REALLY SHAKING THINGS UP. THAT WAS DIFFERENT. OUR RATINGS WILL SOAR.
BUT SOAMES IS STRONG. I DON'T THINK HE'LL CRACK.
I DON'T KNOW -- HE CAME CLOSE JUST THEN.
LET THEM TALK...
SOON HE WOULD BE RICH AND WOULD GET TO SEE HIS WIFE AND KIDS.
WHAT WERE THEIR NAMES AGAIN?
-END-

Blame...

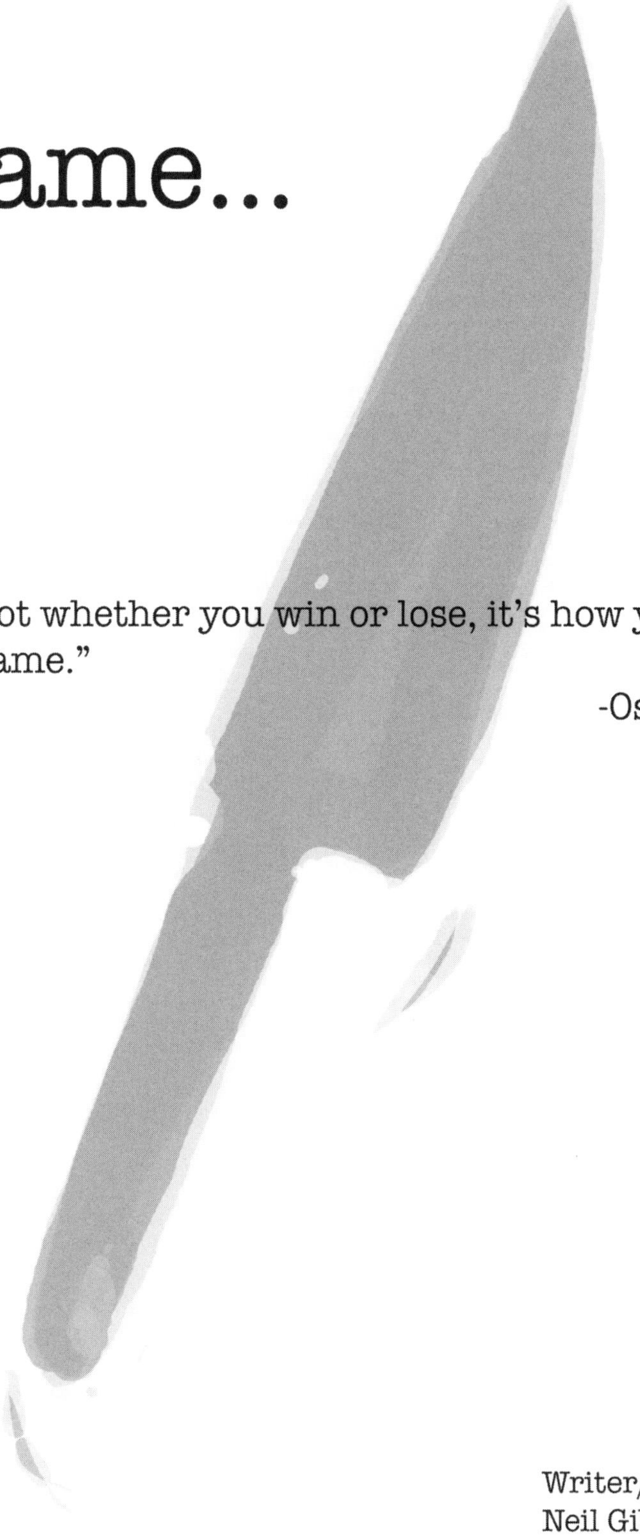

"It's not whether you win or lose, it's how you place the blame."

-Oscar Wilde

Writer/Creator
Neil Gibson

Illustrator
Atula Siriwardane

www.tpub.co.uk

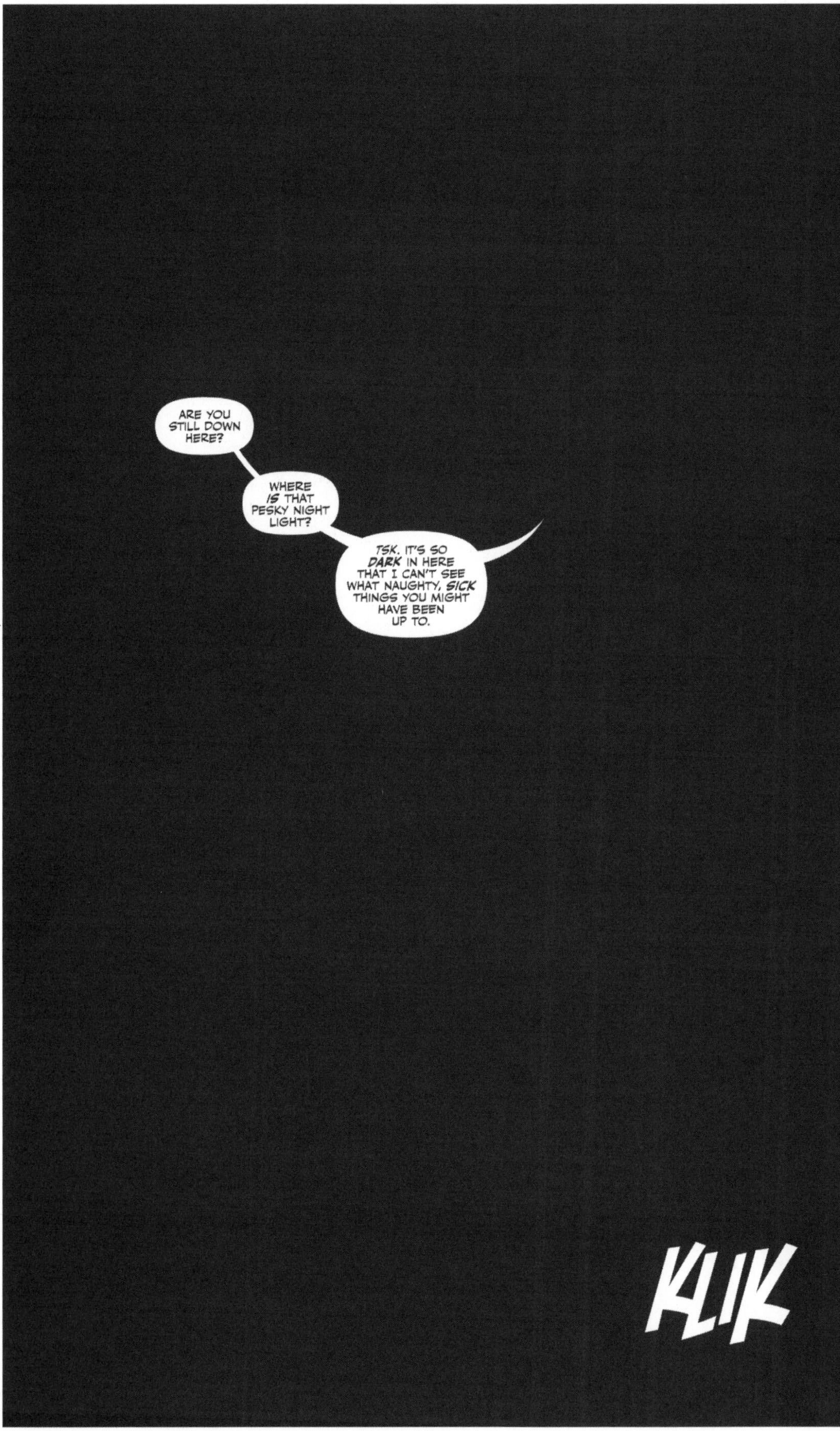

ARE YOU STILL DOWN HERE?
WHERE *IS* THAT PESKY NIGHT LIGHT?
TSK. IT'S SO *DARK* IN HERE THAT I CAN'T SEE WHAT NAUGHTY, *SICK* THINGS YOU MIGHT HAVE BEEN UP TO.
KLIK

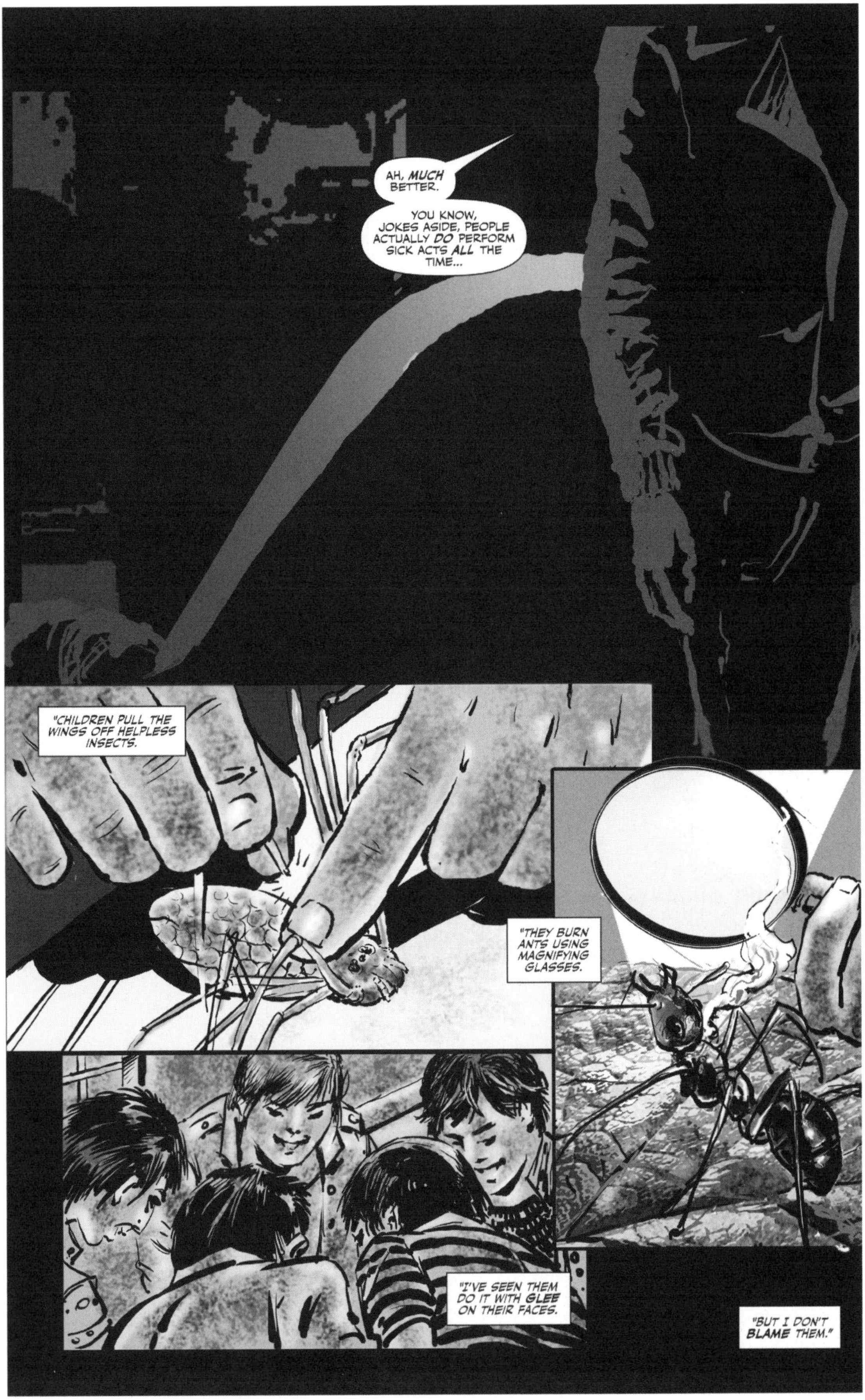

AH, MUCH BETTER.
YOU KNOW, JOKES ASIDE, PEOPLE ACTUALLY DO PERFORM SICK ACTS ALL THE TIME...
"CHILDREN PULL THE WINGS OFF HELPLESS INSECTS.
"THEY BURN ANTS USING MAGNIFYING GLASSES.
"I'VE SEEN THEM DO IT WITH GLEE ON THEIR FACES.
"BUT I DON'T BLAME THEM."

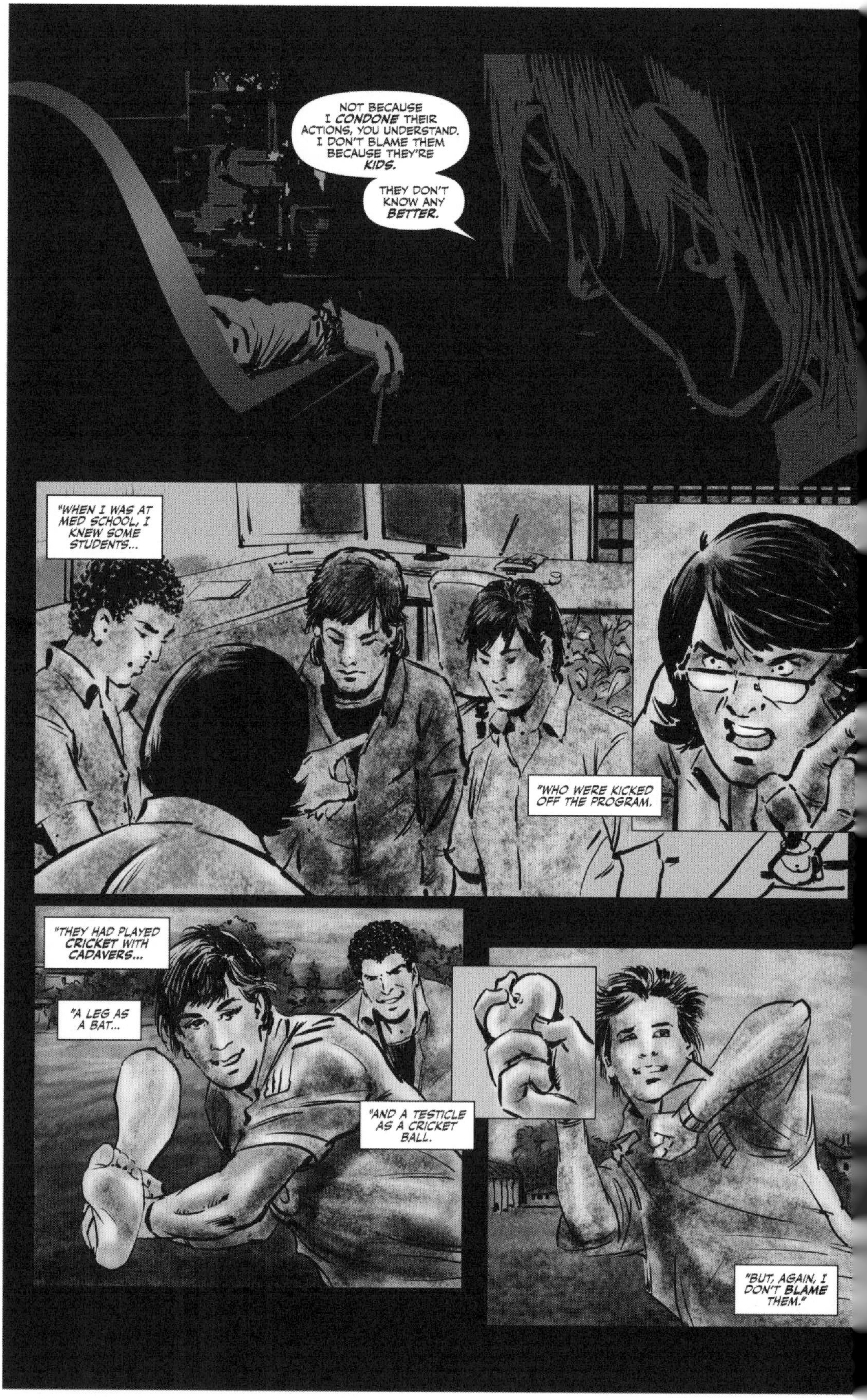
NOT BECAUSE I CONDONE THEIR ACTIONS, YOU UNDERSTAND. I DON'T BLAME THEM BECAUSE THEY'RE KIDS.
THEY DON'T KNOW ANY BETTER.
"WHEN I WAS AT MED SCHOOL, I KNEW SOME STUDENTS...
"WHO WERE KICKED OFF THE PROGRAM.
"THEY HAD PLAYED CRICKET WITH CADAVERS...
"A LEG AS A BAT...
"AND A TESTICLE AS A CRICKET BALL.
"BUT, AGAIN, I DON'T BLAME THEM."

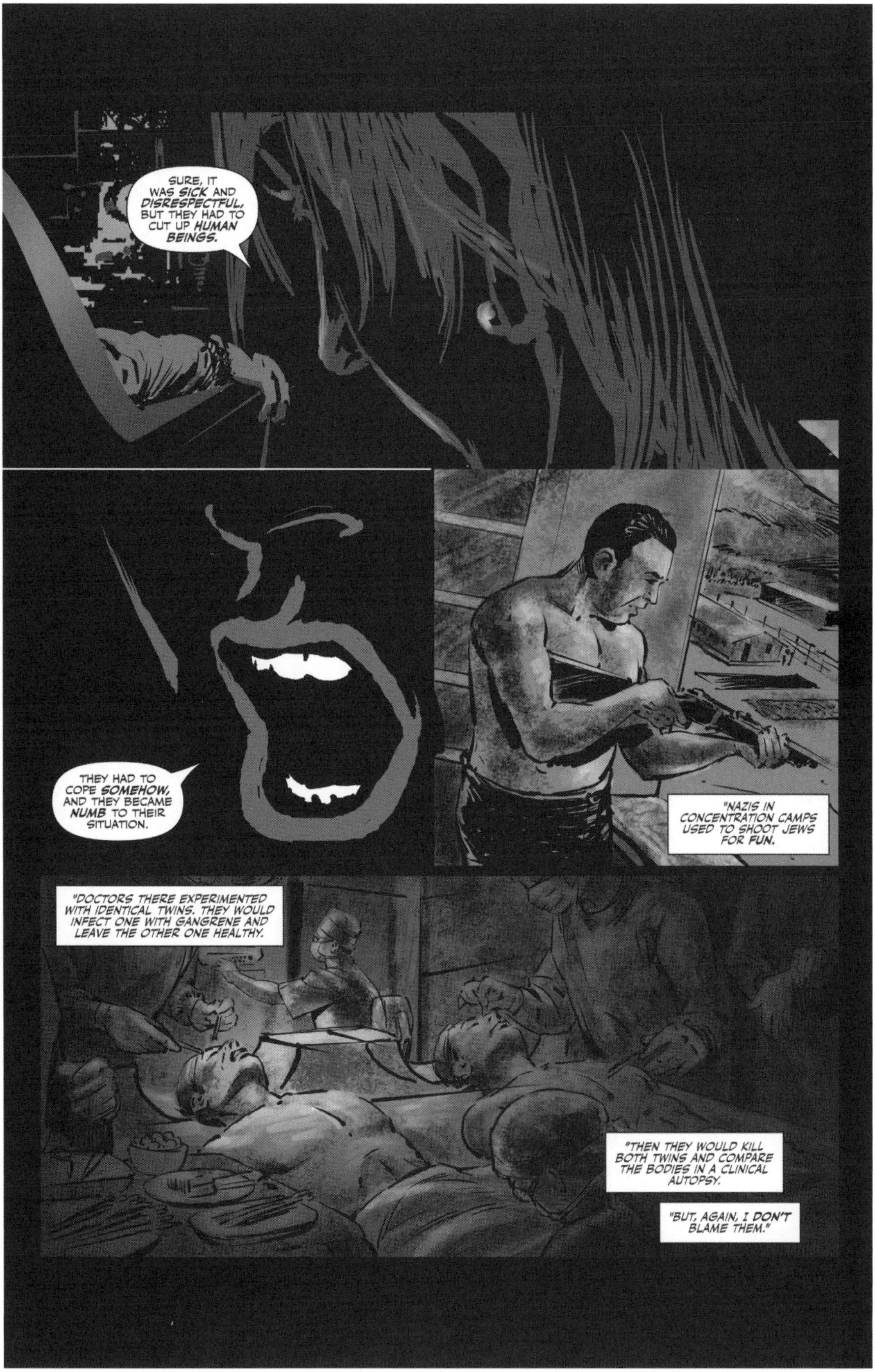
SURE, IT WAS SICK AND DISRESPECTFUL, BUT THEY HAD TO CUT UP HUMAN BEINGS.
THEY HAD TO COPE SOMEHOW, AND THEY BECAME NUMB TO THEIR SITUATION.
"NAZIS IN CONCENTRATION CAMPS USED TO SHOOT JEWS FOR FUN.
"DOCTORS THERE EXPERIMENTED WITH IDENTICAL TWINS. THEY WOULD INFECT ONE WITH GANGRENE AND LEAVE THE OTHER ONE HEALTHY.
"THEN THEY WOULD KILL BOTH TWINS AND COMPARE THE BODIES IN A CLINICAL AUTOPSY.
"BUT, AGAIN, I DON'T BLAME THEM."

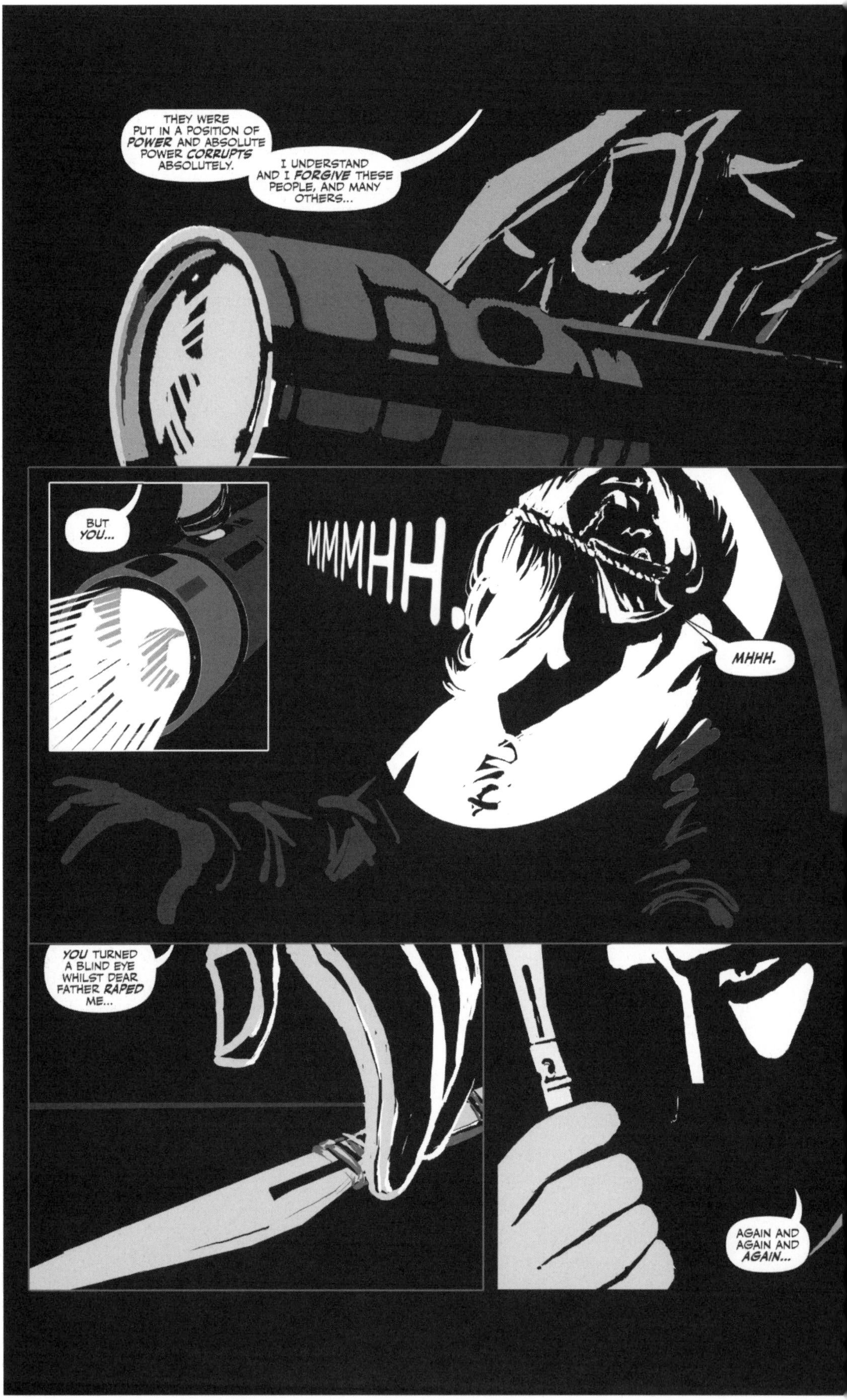
THEY WERE PUT IN A POSITION OF POWER AND ABSOLUTE POWER CORRUPTS ABSOLUTELY.
I UNDERSTAND AND I FORGIVE THESE PEOPLE, AND MANY OTHERS...
BUT YOU...
MMMHH.
MHHH.
YOU TURNED A BLIND EYE WHILST DEAR FATHER RAPED ME...
AGAIN AND AGAIN AND AGAIN...

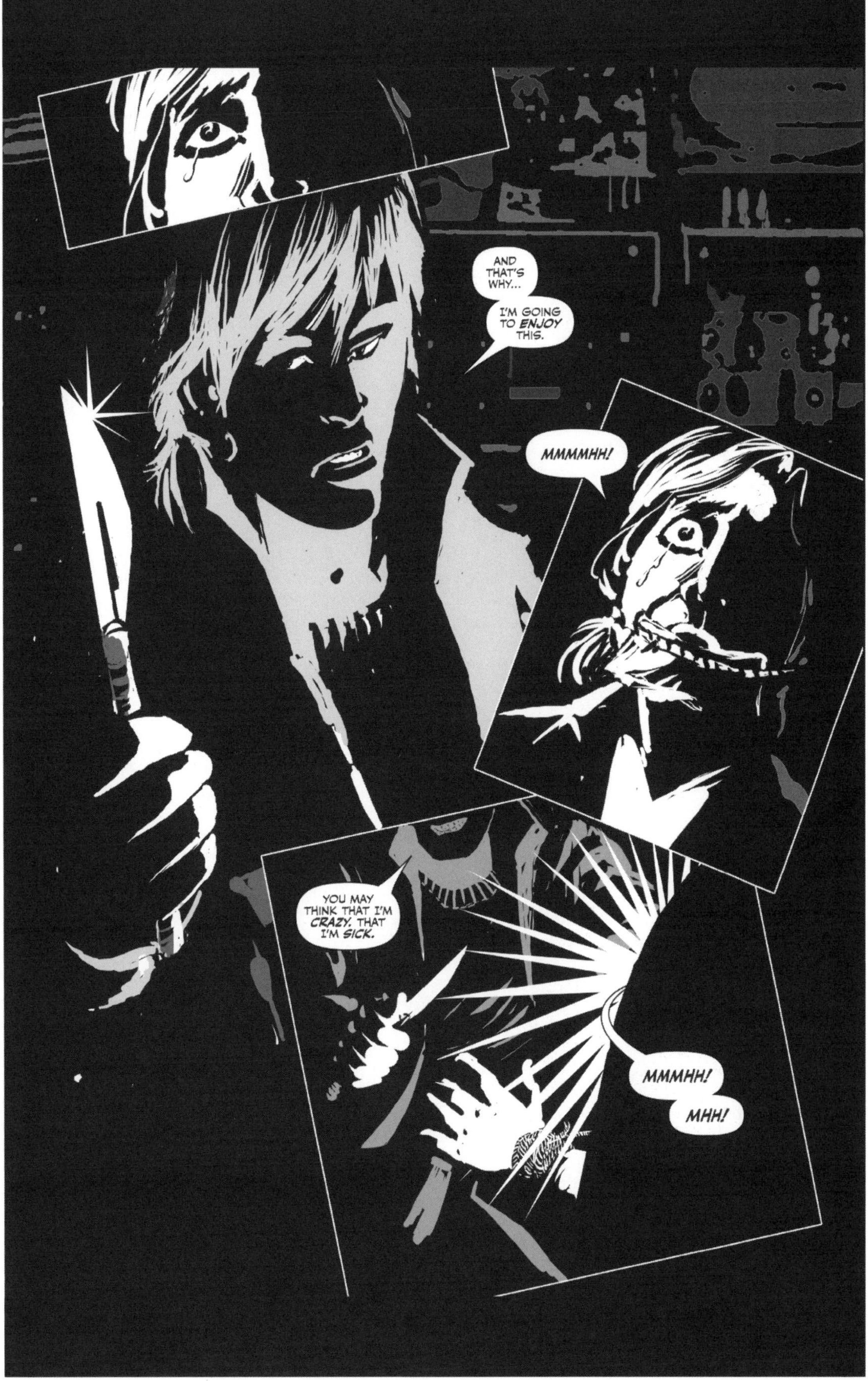
AND THAT'S WHY...
I'M GOING TO ENJOY THIS.
MMMMHH!
YOU MAY THINK THAT I'M CRAZY. THAT I'M SICK.
MMMHH!
MHH!

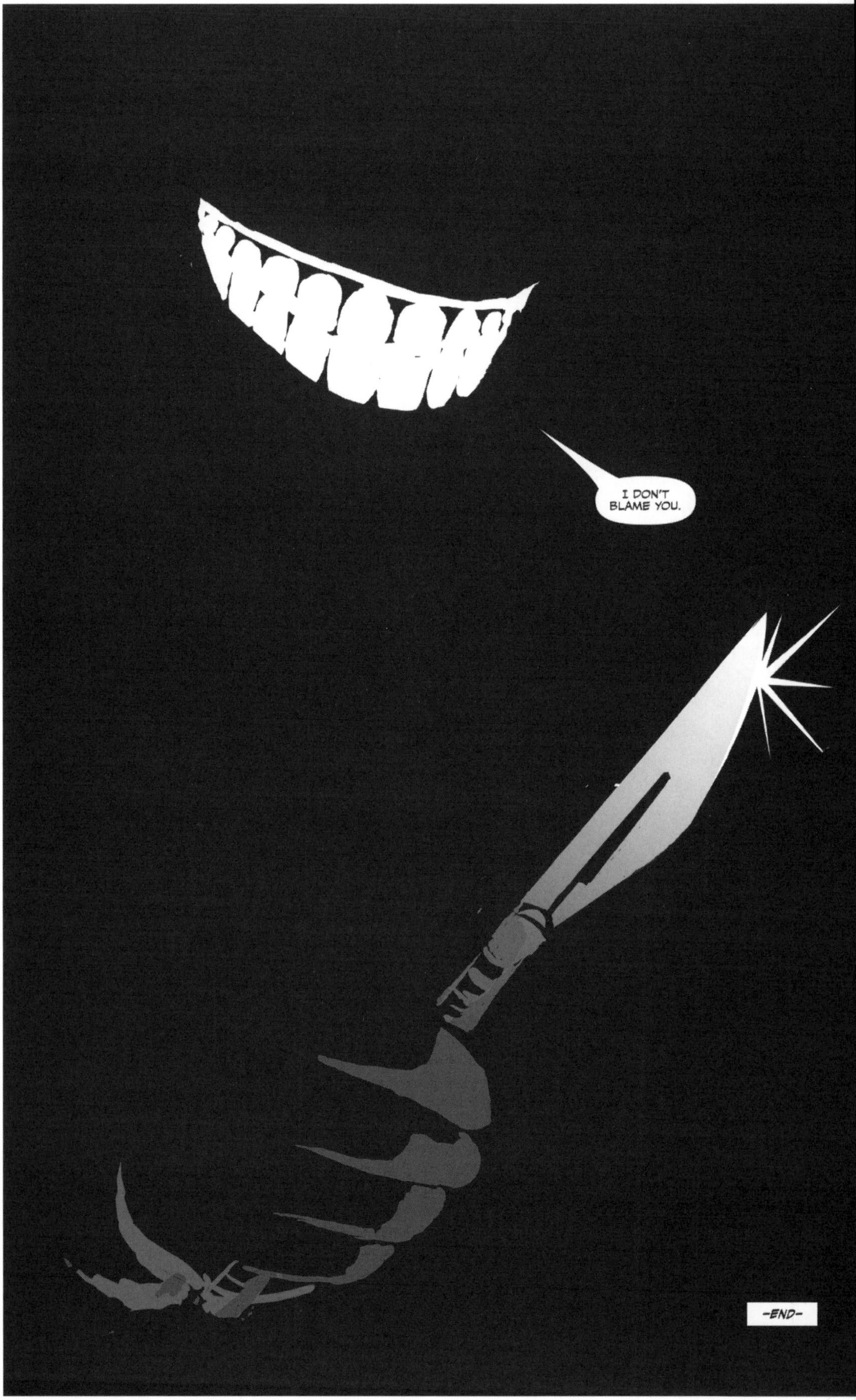
I DON'T BLAME YOU.
-END-

A Heavenly Note...

"The World's Muslim population is expected to increase by about 35% in the next 20 years, rising from 1.6bn in 2010 to 2.2bn by 2030."

-Pew Research Center Forum on Religion & Public Life

Writer/Creator
Neil Gibson

Illustrator
Heru Prasetyo Djalal

www.tpub.co.uk

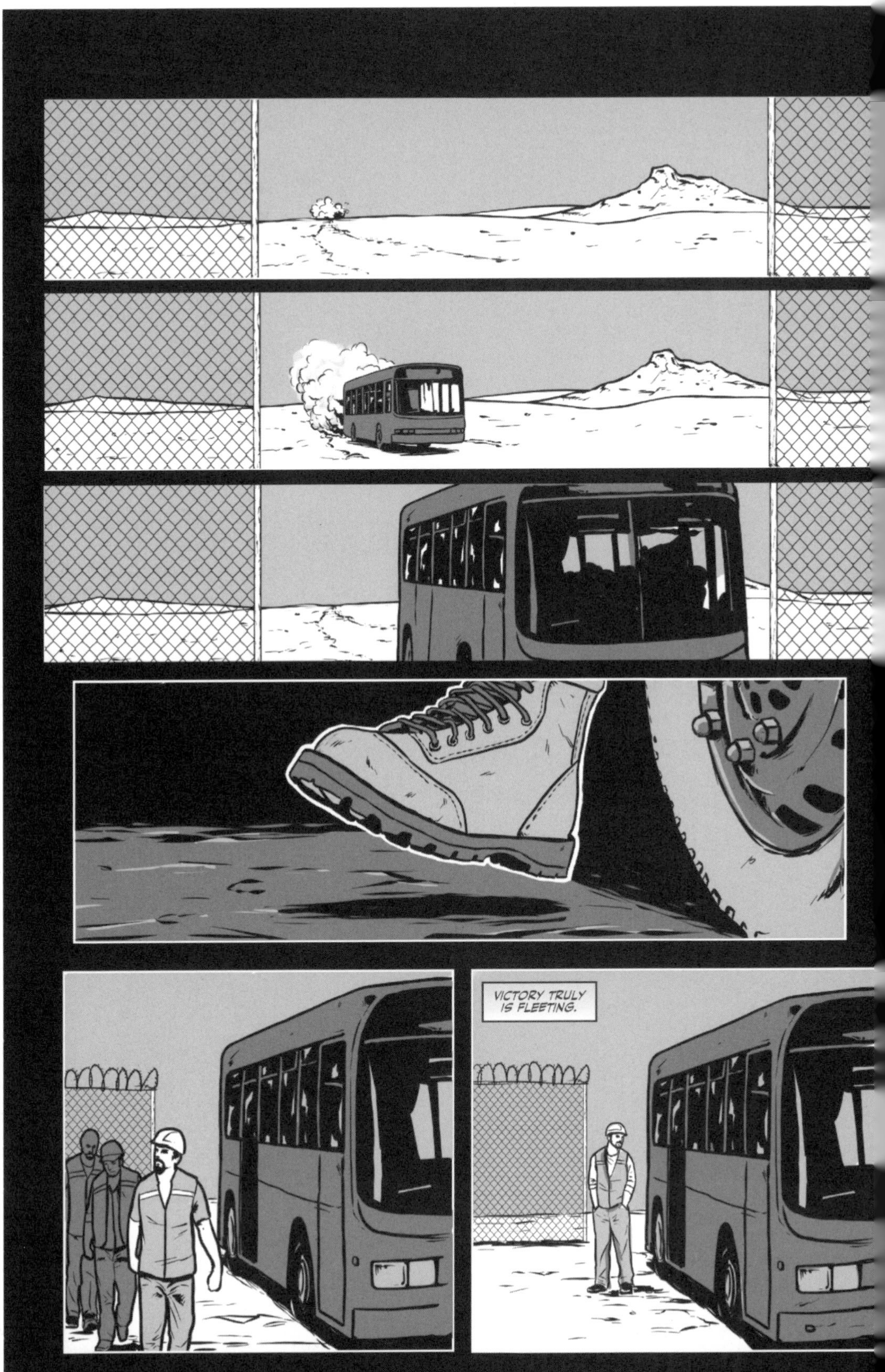
VICTORY TRULY
IS FLEETING.

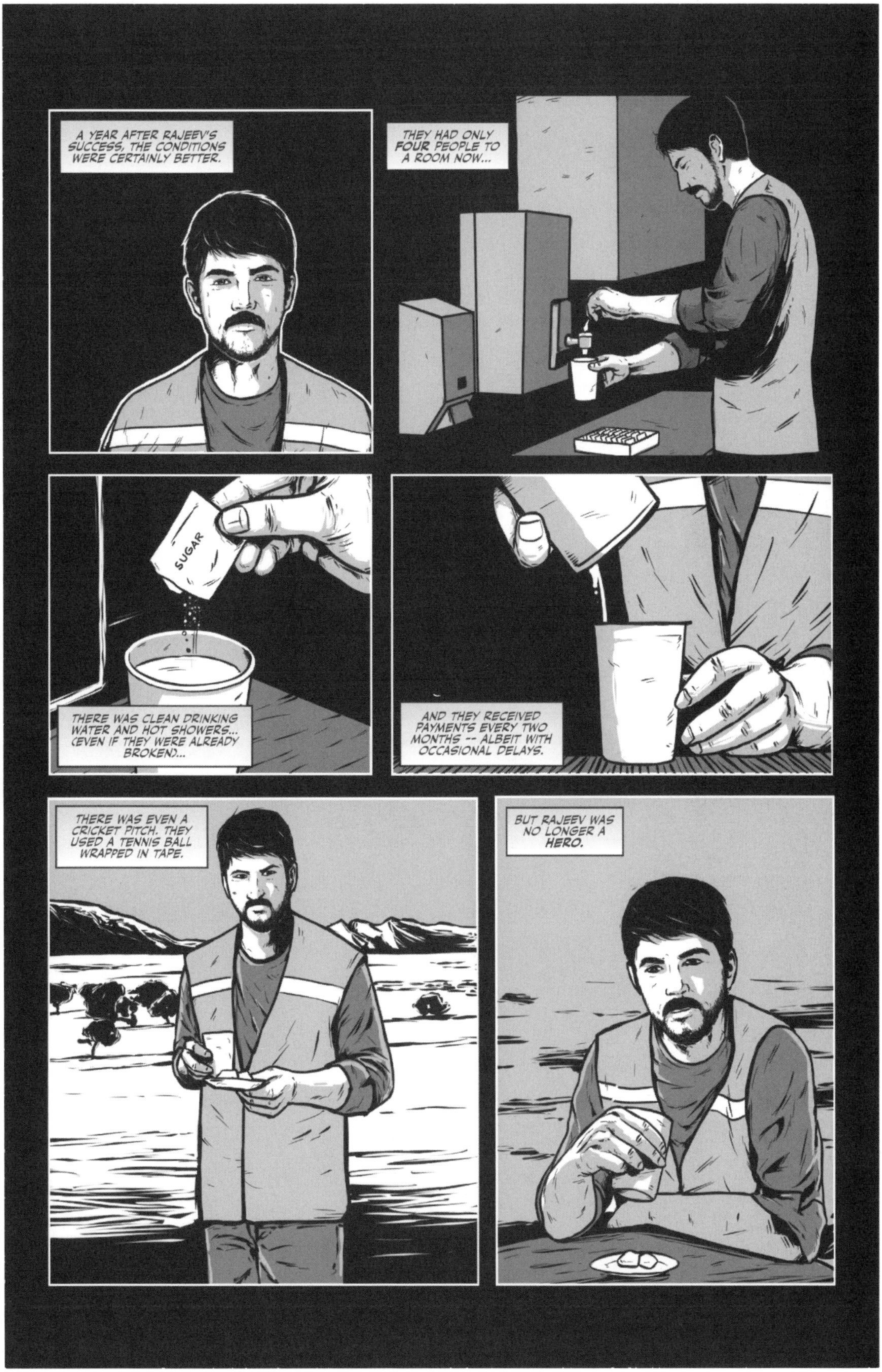
A YEAR AFTER RAJEEV'S SUCCESS, THE CONDITIONS WERE CERTAINLY BETTER.
THEY HAD ONLY FOUR PEOPLE TO A ROOM NOW...
SUGAR
THERE WAS CLEAN DRINKING WATER AND HOT SHOWERS... (EVEN IF THEY WERE ALREADY BROKEN)...
AND THEY RECEIVED PAYMENTS EVERY TWO MONTHS -- ALBEIT WITH OCCASIONAL DELAYS.
THERE WAS EVEN A CRICKET PITCH. THEY USED A TENNIS BALL WRAPPED IN TAPE.
BUT RAJEEV WAS NO LONGER A HERO.

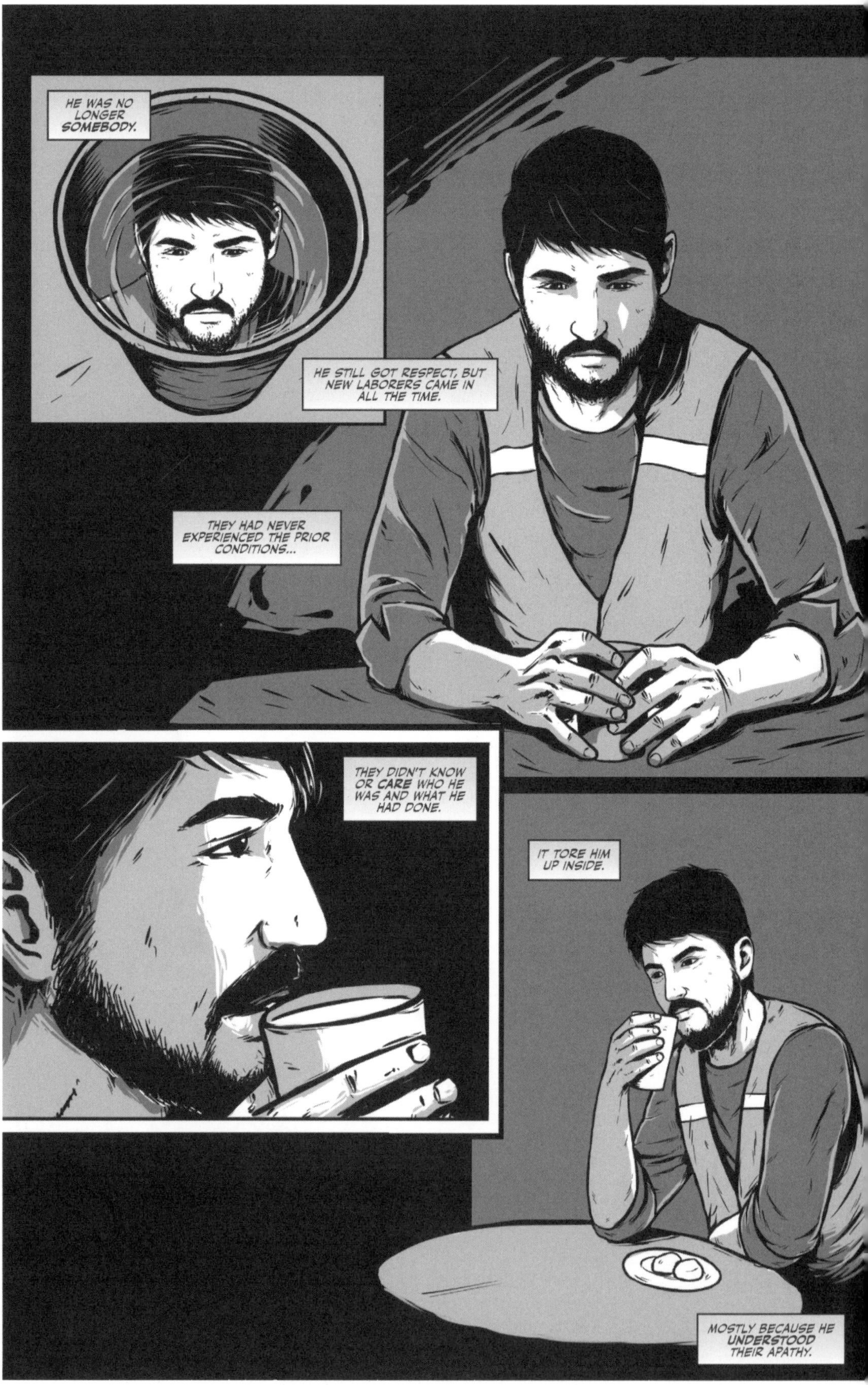
HE WAS NO LONGER SOMEBODY.
HE STILL GOT RESPECT, BUT NEW LABORERS CAME IN ALL THE TIME.
THEY HAD NEVER EXPERIENCED THE PRIOR CONDITIONS...
THEY DIDN'T KNOW OR CARE WHO HE WAS AND WHAT HE HAD DONE.
IT TORE HIM UP INSIDE.
MOSTLY BECAUSE HE UNDERSTOOD THEIR APATHY.

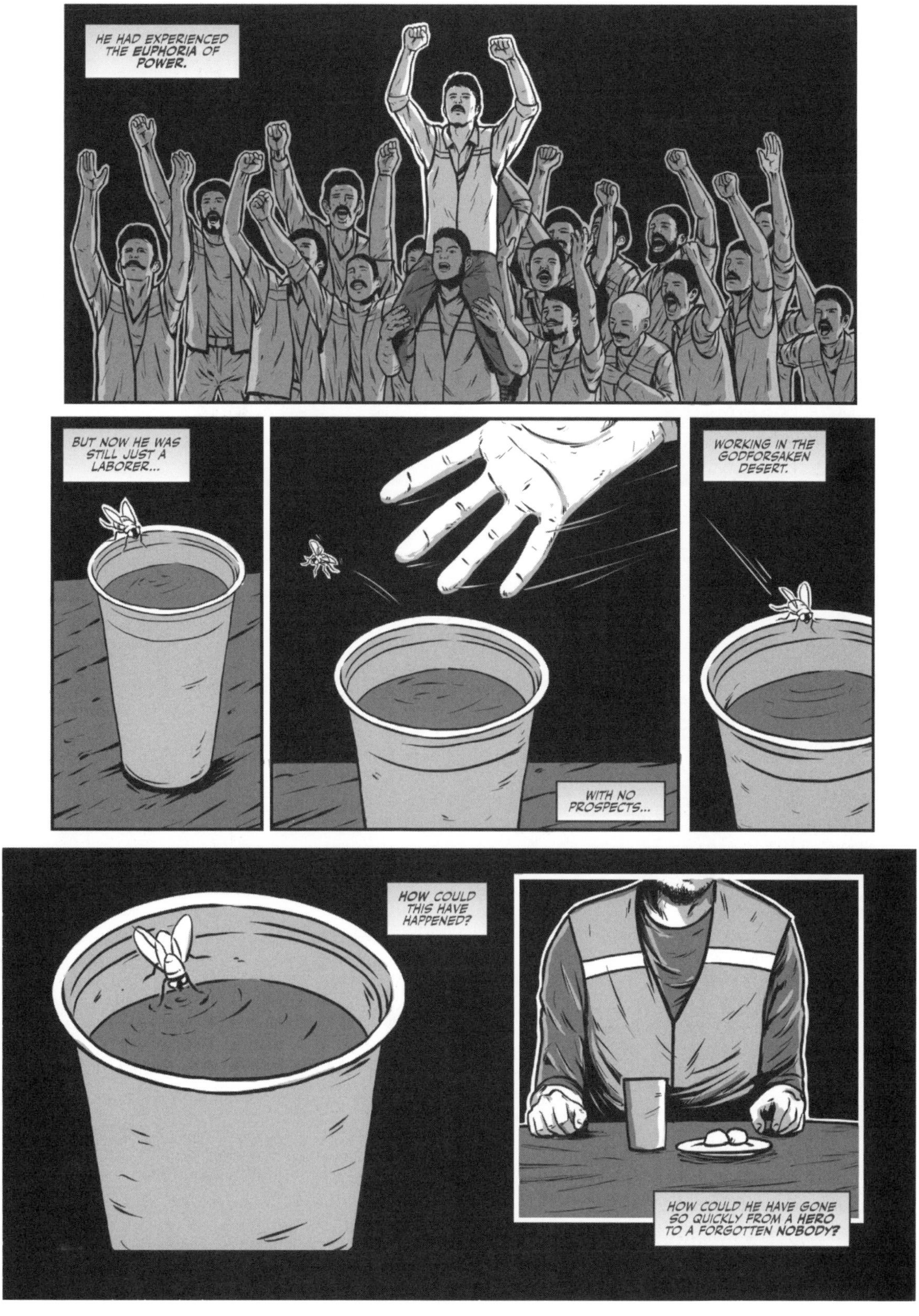
HE HAD EXPERIENCED THE EUPHORIA OF POWER.
BUT NOW HE WAS STILL JUST A LABORER...
WITH NO PROSPECTS...
WORKING IN THE GODFORSAKEN DESERT.
HOW COULD THIS HAVE HAPPENED?
HOW COULD HE HAVE GONE SO QUICKLY FROM A HERO TO A FORGOTTEN NOBODY?

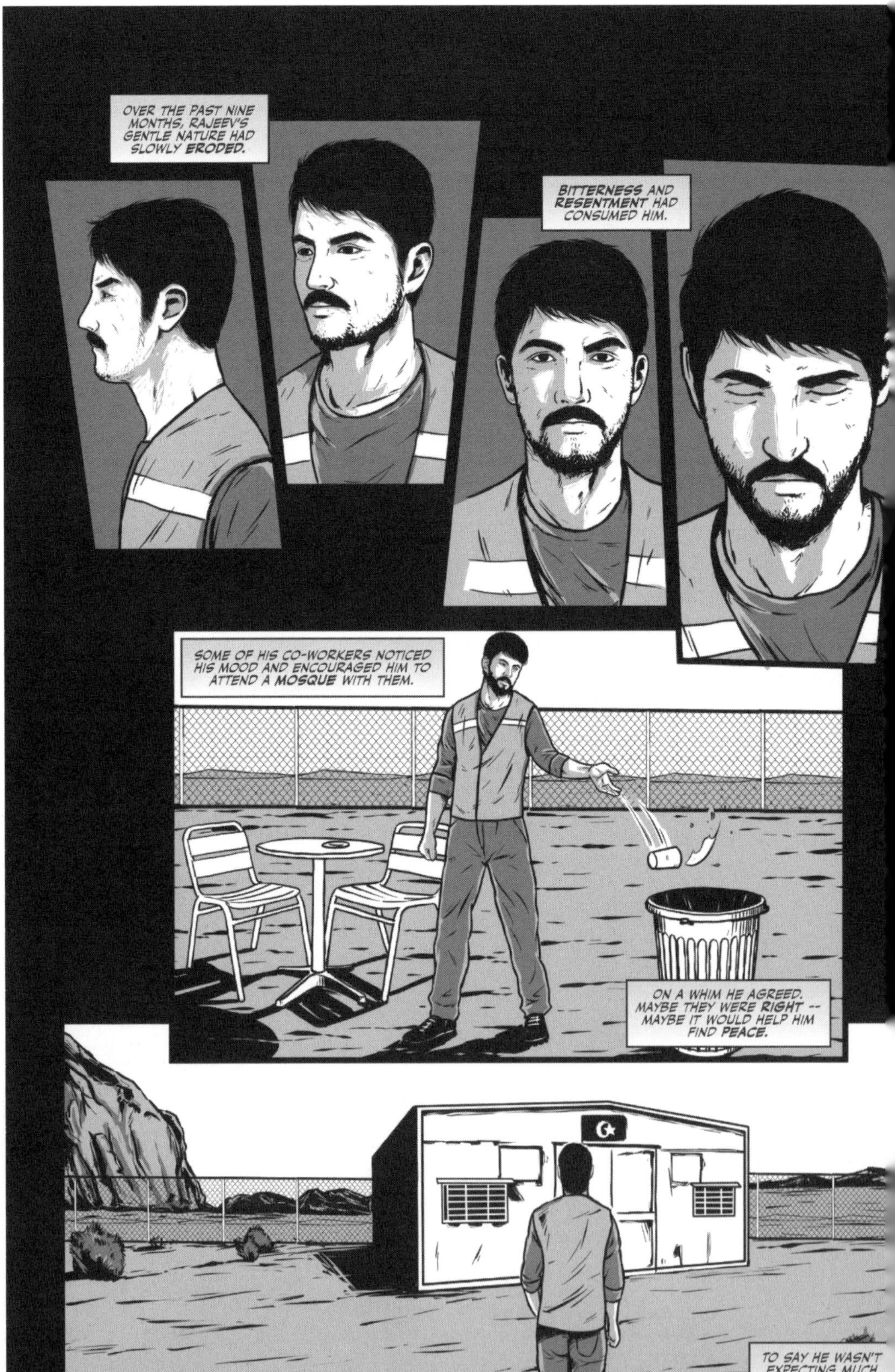

OVER THE PAST NINE MONTHS, RAJEEV'S GENTLE NATURE HAD SLOWLY ERODED.
BITTERNESS AND RESENTMENT HAD CONSUMED HIM.
SOME OF HIS CO-WORKERS NOTICED HIS MOOD AND ENCOURAGED HIM TO ATTEND A MOSQUE WITH THEM.
ON A WHIM HE AGREED. MAYBE THEY WERE RIGHT -- MAYBE IT WOULD HELP HIM FIND PEACE.
TO SAY HE WASN'T EXPECTING MUCH WOULD BE PUTTING IT VERY POLITELY.

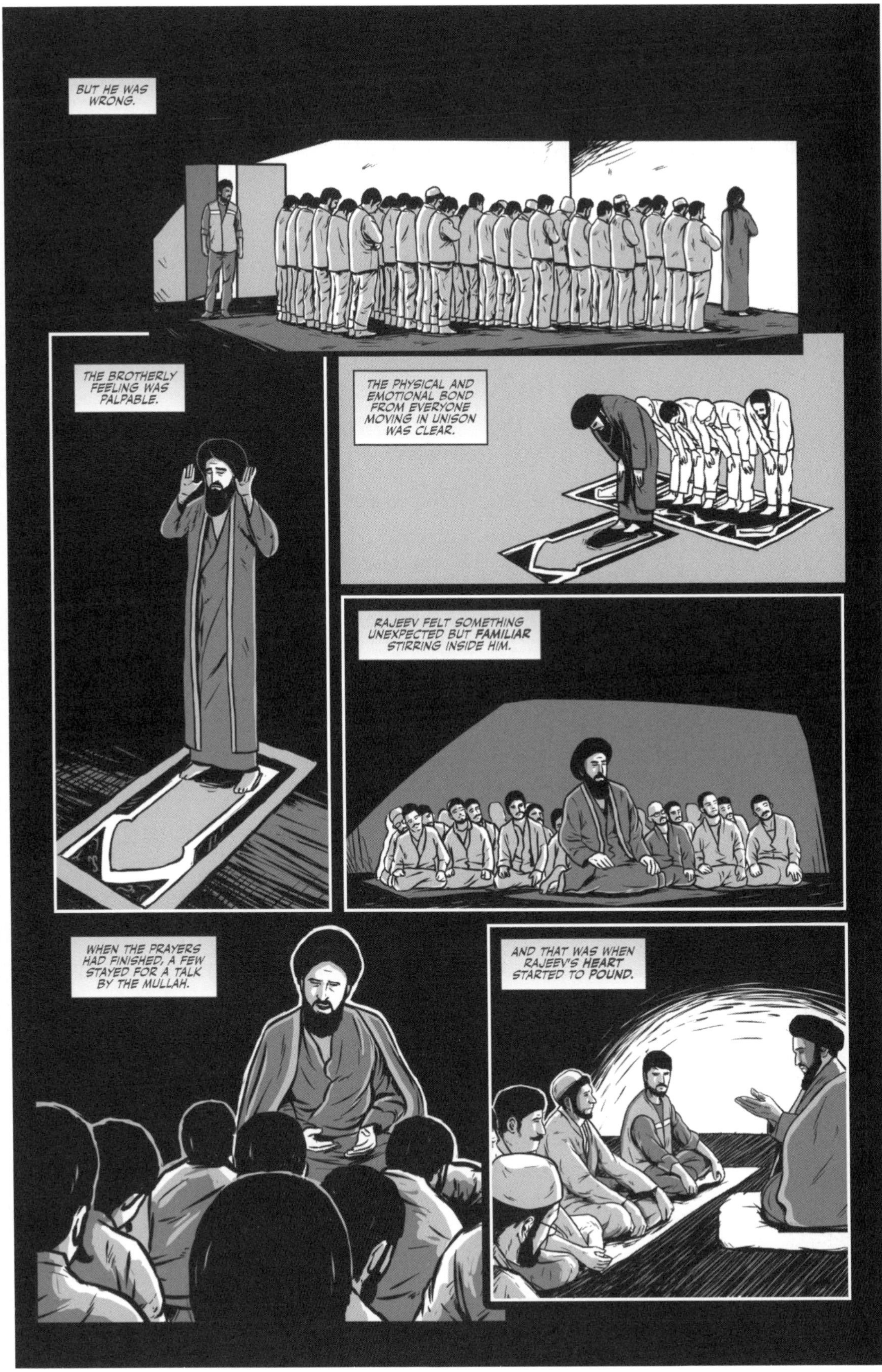
BUT HE WAS WRONG.
THE BROTHERLY FEELING WAS PALPABLE.
THE PHYSICAL AND EMOTIONAL BOND FROM EVERYONE MOVING IN UNISON WAS CLEAR.
RAJEEV FELT SOMETHING UNEXPECTED BUT FAMILIAR STIRRING INSIDE HIM.
WHEN THE PRAYERS HAD FINISHED, A FEW STAYED FOR A TALK BY THE MULLAH.
AND THAT WAS WHEN RAJEEV'S HEART STARTED TO POUND.

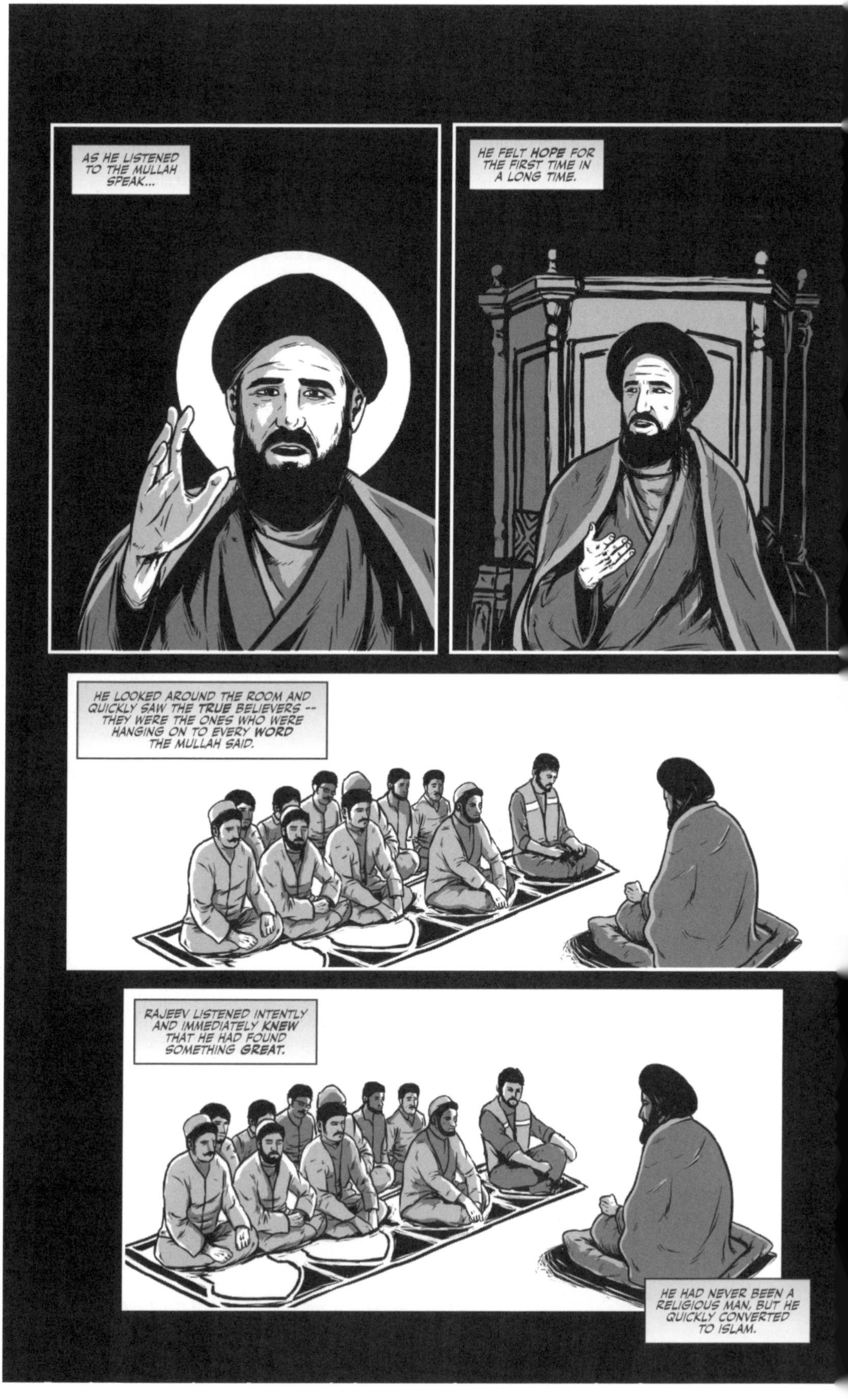
AS HE LISTENED TO THE MULLAH SPEAK...
HE FELT HOPE FOR THE FIRST TIME IN A LONG TIME.
HE LOOKED AROUND THE ROOM AND QUICKLY SAW THE TRUE BELIEVERS -- THEY WERE THE ONES WHO WERE HANGING ON TO EVERY WORD THE MULLAH SAID.
RAJEEV LISTENED INTENTLY AND IMMEDIATELY KNEW THAT HE HAD FOUND SOMETHING GREAT.
HE HAD NEVER BEEN A RELIGIOUS MAN, BUT HE QUICKLY CONVERTED TO ISLAM.

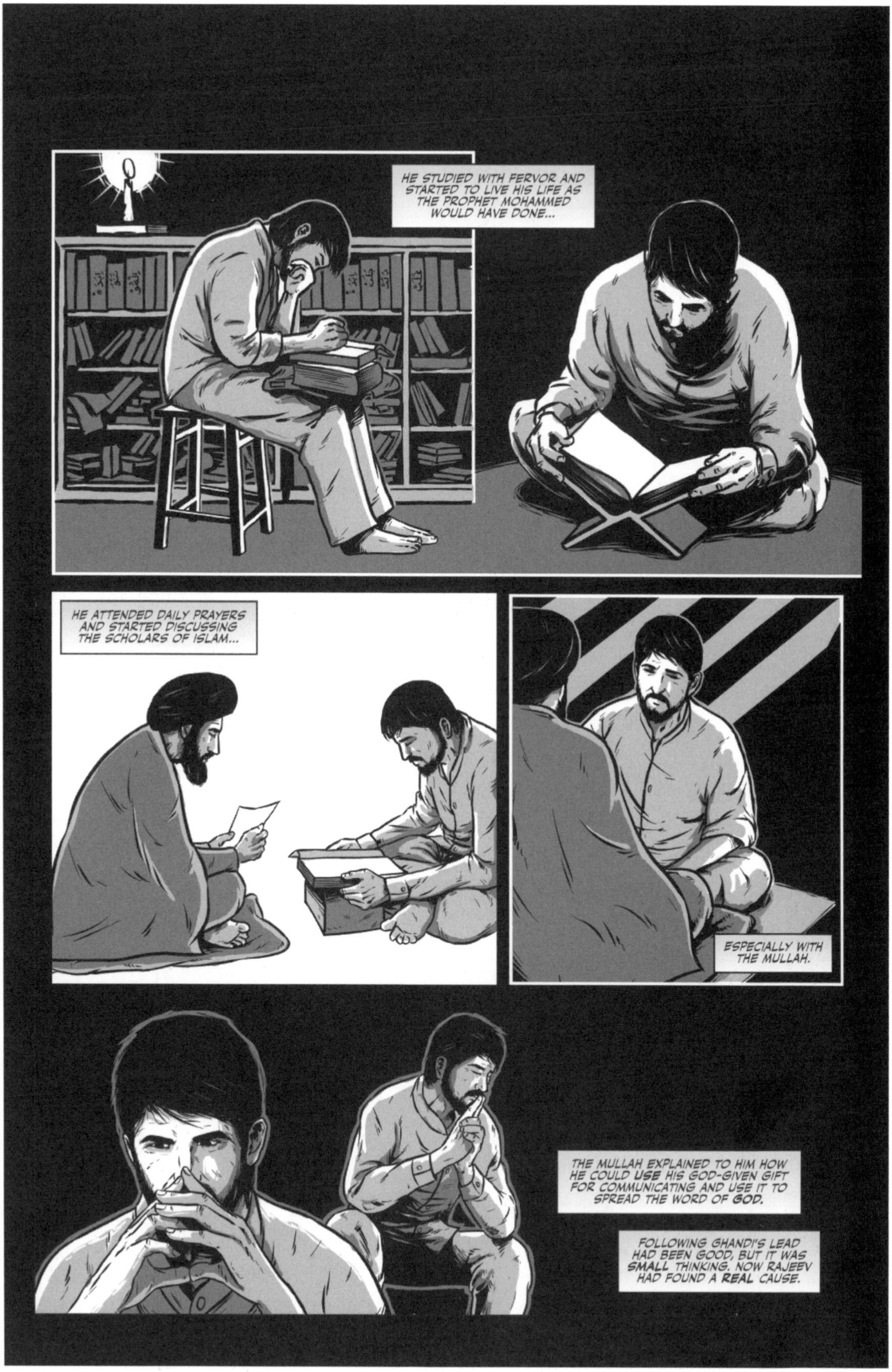
HE STUDIED WITH FERVOR AND STARTED TO LIVE HIS LIFE AS THE PROPHET MOHAMMED WOULD HAVE DONE...
HE ATTENDED DAILY PRAYERS AND STARTED DISCUSSING THE SCHOLARS OF ISLAM...
ESPECIALLY WITH THE MULLAH.
THE MULLAH EXPLAINED TO HIM HOW HE COULD USE HIS GOD-GIVEN GIFT FOR COMMUNICATING AND USE IT TO SPREAD THE WORD OF GOD.
FOLLOWING GHANDI'S LEAD HAD BEEN GOOD, BUT IT WAS SMALL THINKING. NOW RAJEEV HAD FOUND A REAL CAUSE.

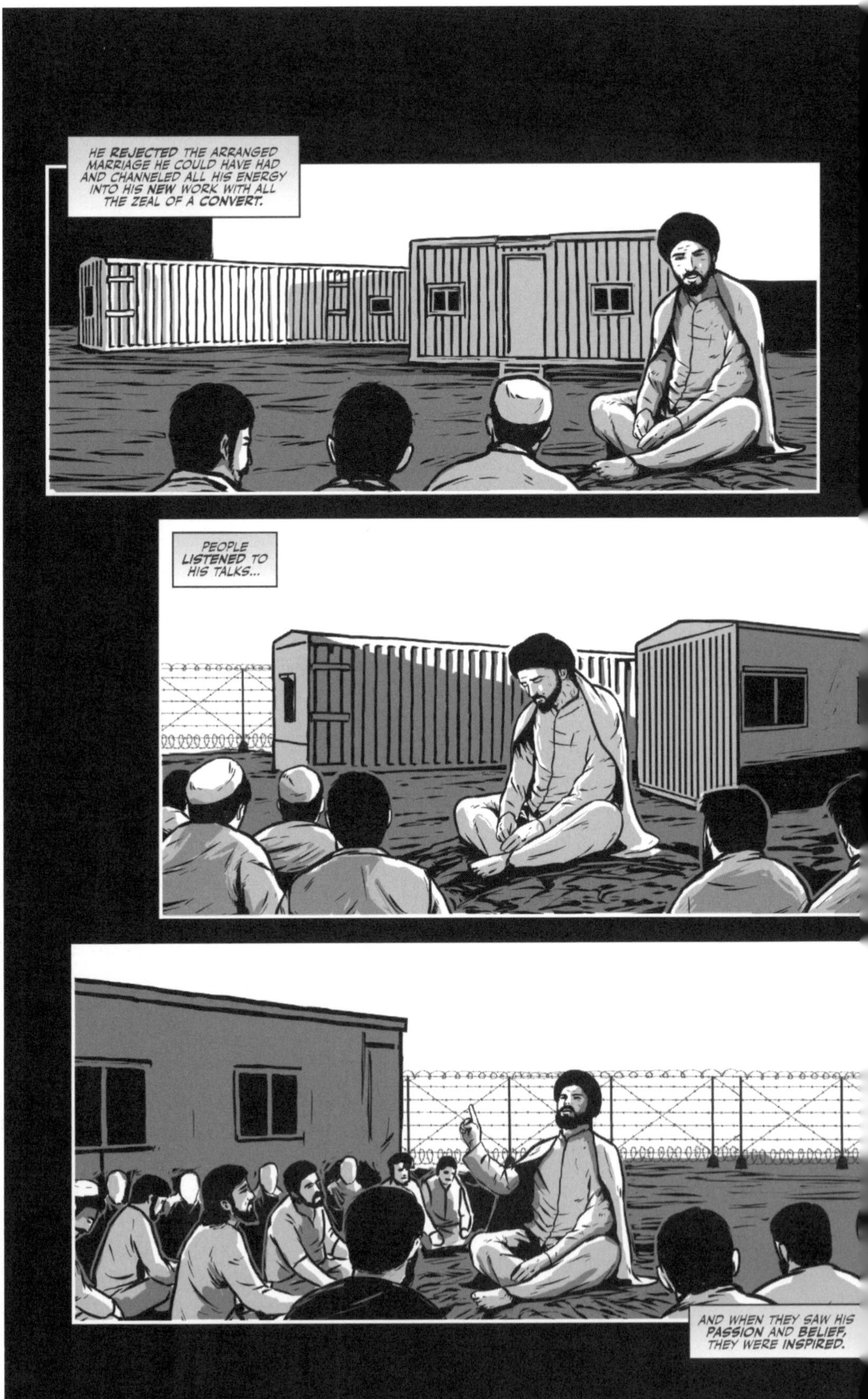
HE REJECTED THE ARRANGED MARRIAGE HE COULD HAVE HAD AND CHANNELED ALL HIS ENERGY INTO HIS NEW WORK WITH ALL THE ZEAL OF A CONVERT.
PEOPLE LISTENED TO HIS TALKS...
AND WHEN THEY SAW HIS PASSION AND BELIEF, THEY WERE INSPIRED.

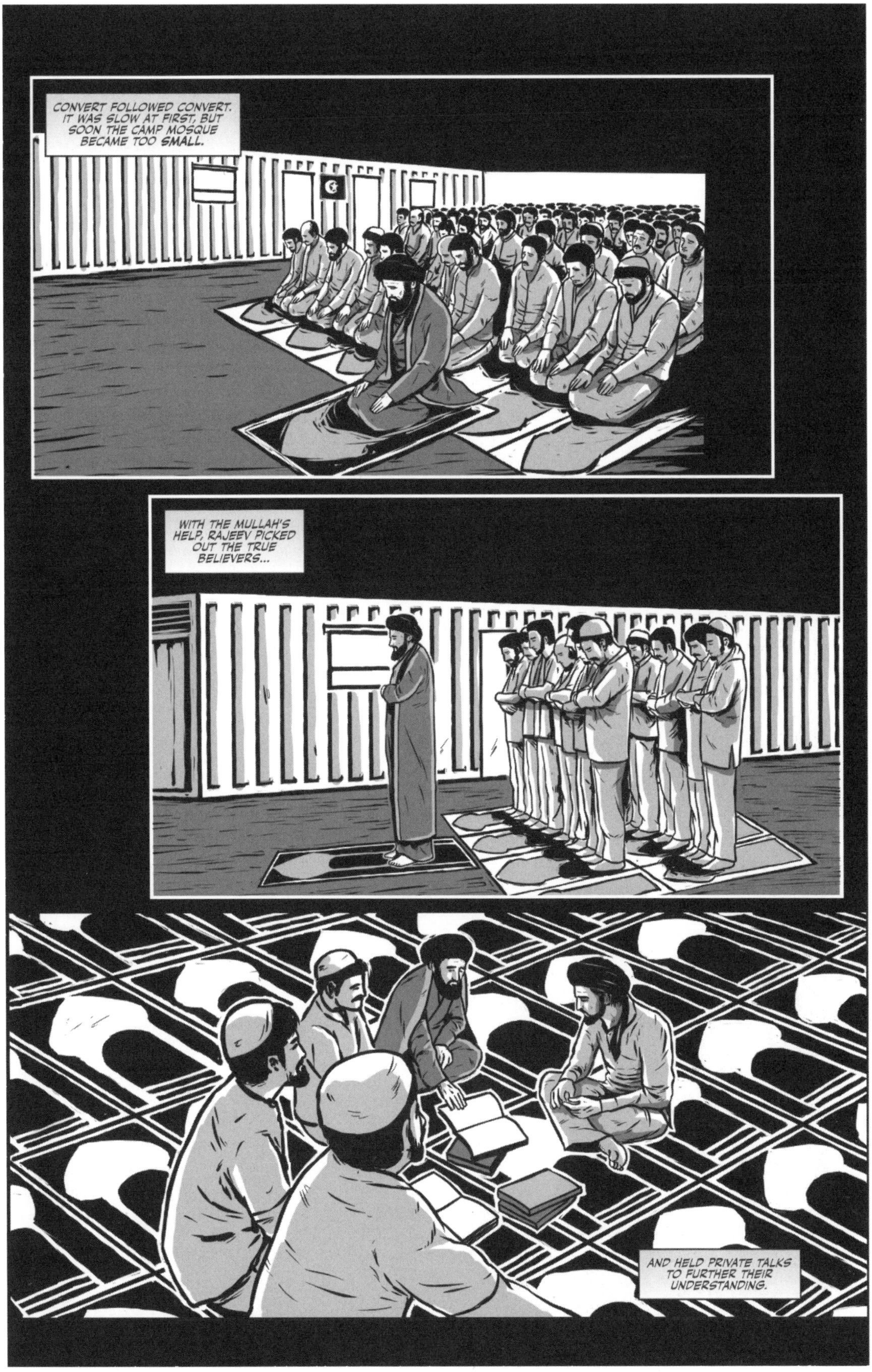
CONVERT FOLLOWED CONVERT. IT WAS SLOW AT FIRST, BUT SOON THE CAMP MOSQUE BECAME TOO SMALL.
WITH THE MULLAH'S HELP, RAJEEV PICKED OUT THE TRUE BELIEVERS...
AND HELD PRIVATE TALKS TO FURTHER THEIR UNDERSTANDING.

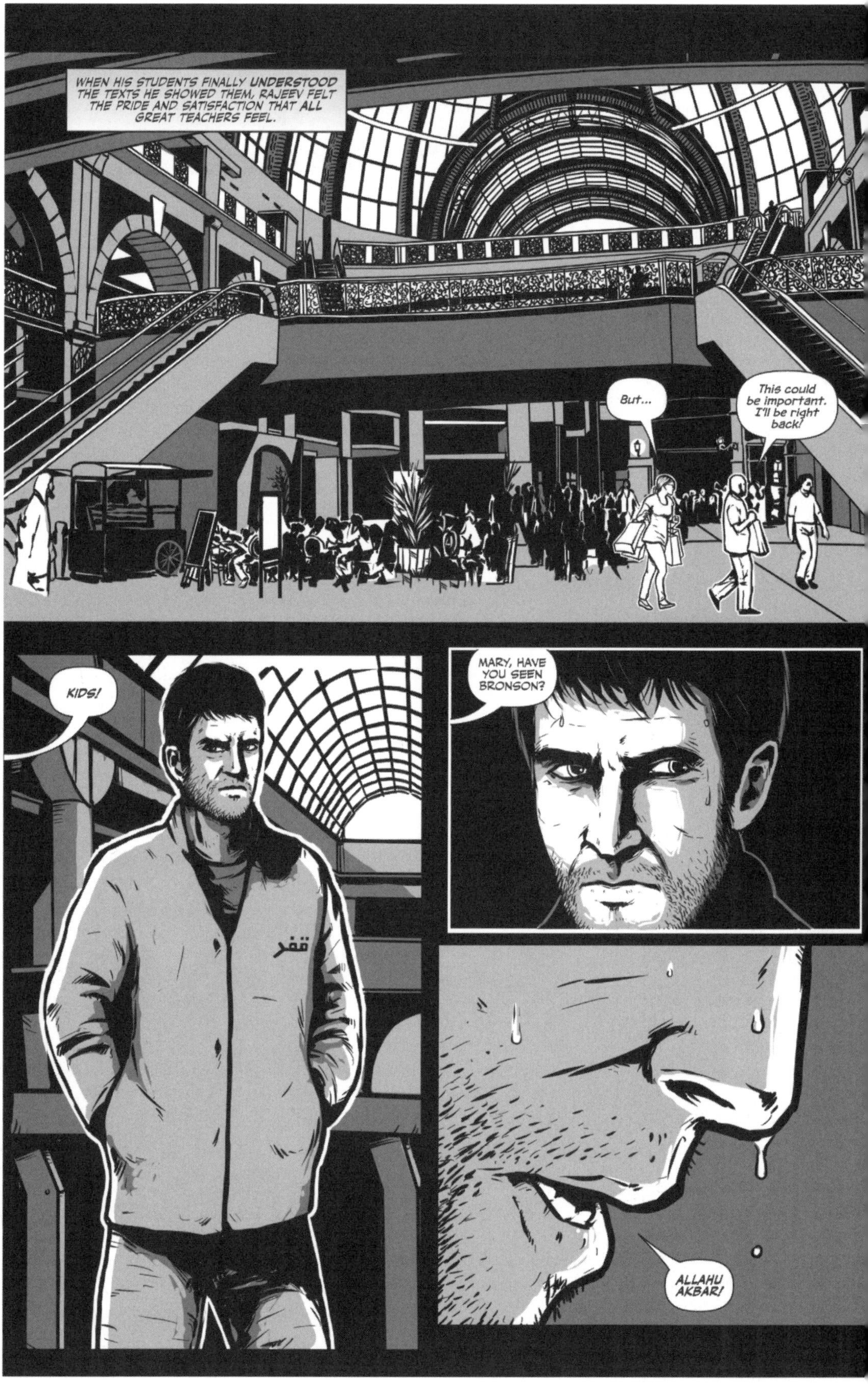
WHEN HIS STUDENTS FINALLY UNDERSTOOD THE TEXTS HE SHOWED THEM, RAJEEV FELT THE PRIDE AND SATISFACTION THAT ALL GREAT TEACHERS FEEL.
But...
This could be important. I'll be right back!
KIDS!
MARY, HAVE YOU SEEN BRONSON?
ALLAHU AKBAR!

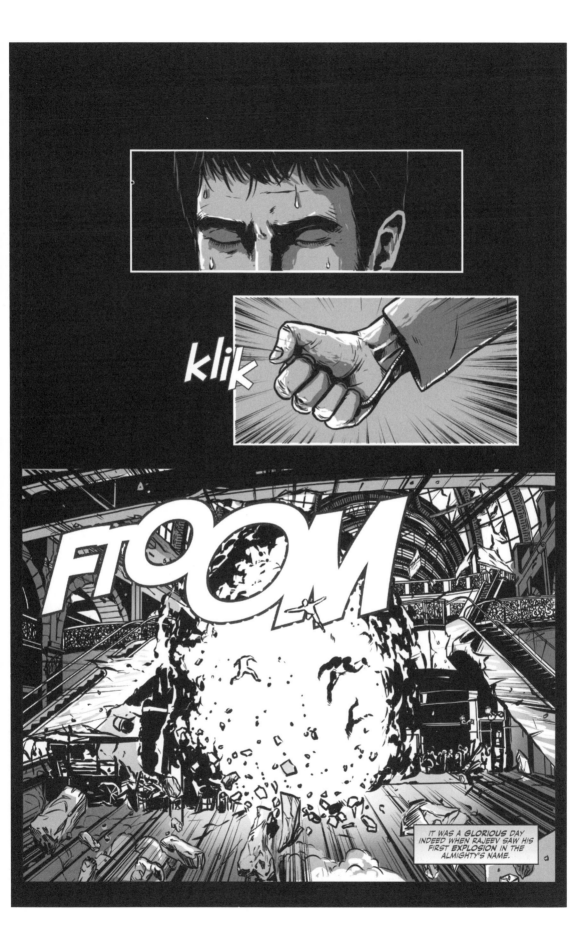

klik

FTOON

IT WAS A GLORIOUS DAY INDEED WHEN RAJEEV SAW HIS FIRST EXPLOSION IN THE ALMIGHTY'S NAME.

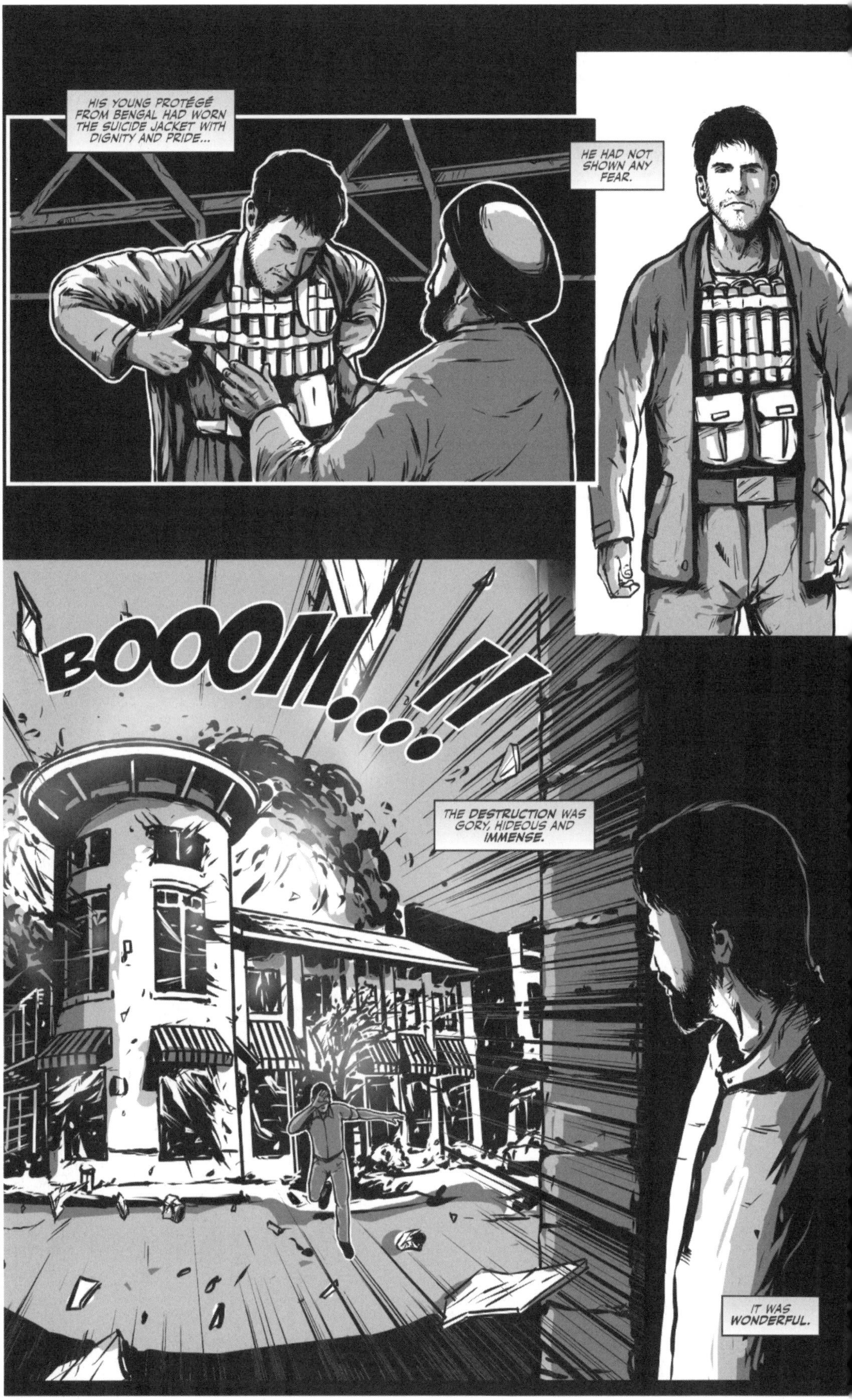
HIS YOUNG PROTÉGÉ FROM BENGAL HAD WORN THE SUICIDE JACKET WITH DIGNITY AND PRIDE...
HE HAD NOT SHOWN ANY FEAR.
BOOOM....!!
THE DESTRUCTION WAS GORY, HIDEOUS AND IMMENSE.
IT WAS WONDERFUL.

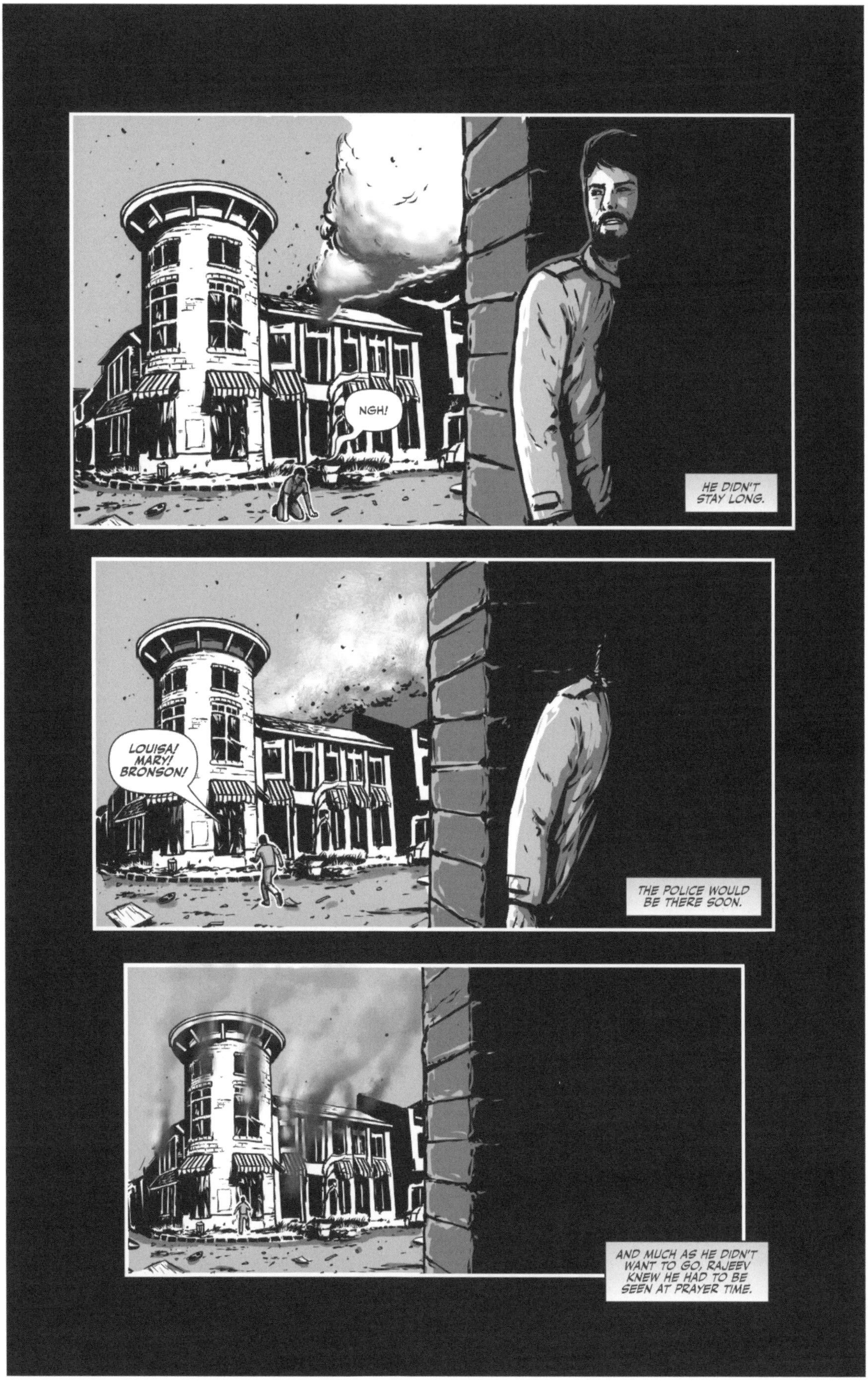
NGH!
HE DIDN'T STAY LONG.
LOUISA! MARY! BRONSON!
THE POLICE WOULD BE THERE SOON.
AND MUCH AS HE DIDN'T WANT TO GO, RAJEEV KNEW HE HAD TO BE SEEN AT PRAYER TIME.

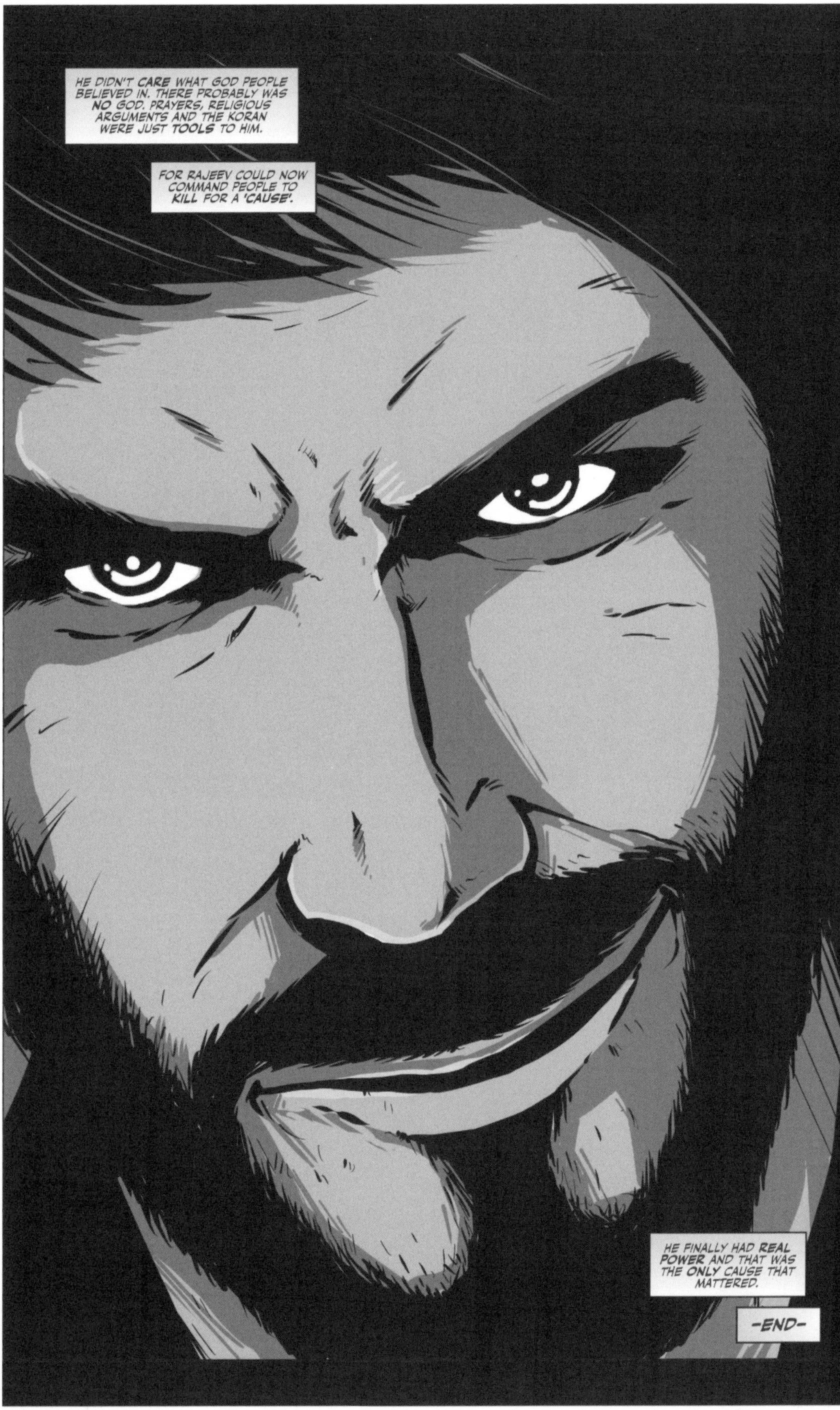

HE DIDN'T CARE WHAT GOD PEOPLE BELIEVED IN. THERE PROBABLY WAS NO GOD. PRAYERS, RELIGIOUS ARGUMENTS AND THE KORAN WERE JUST TOOLS TO HIM.
FOR RAJEEV COULD NOW COMMAND PEOPLE TO KILL FOR A 'CAUSE'.
HE FINALLY HAD REAL POWER AND THAT WAS THE ONLY CAUSE THAT MATTERED.
-END-

Cocaína...

"I'm in favor of legalizing drugs. According to my values system, if people want to kill themselves, they have every right to do so. Most of the harm that comes from drugs is because they are illegal."

-Milton Friedman

Writer/Creator
Neil Gibson

Illustrator
Caspar Wijngaard

www.tpub.co.uk

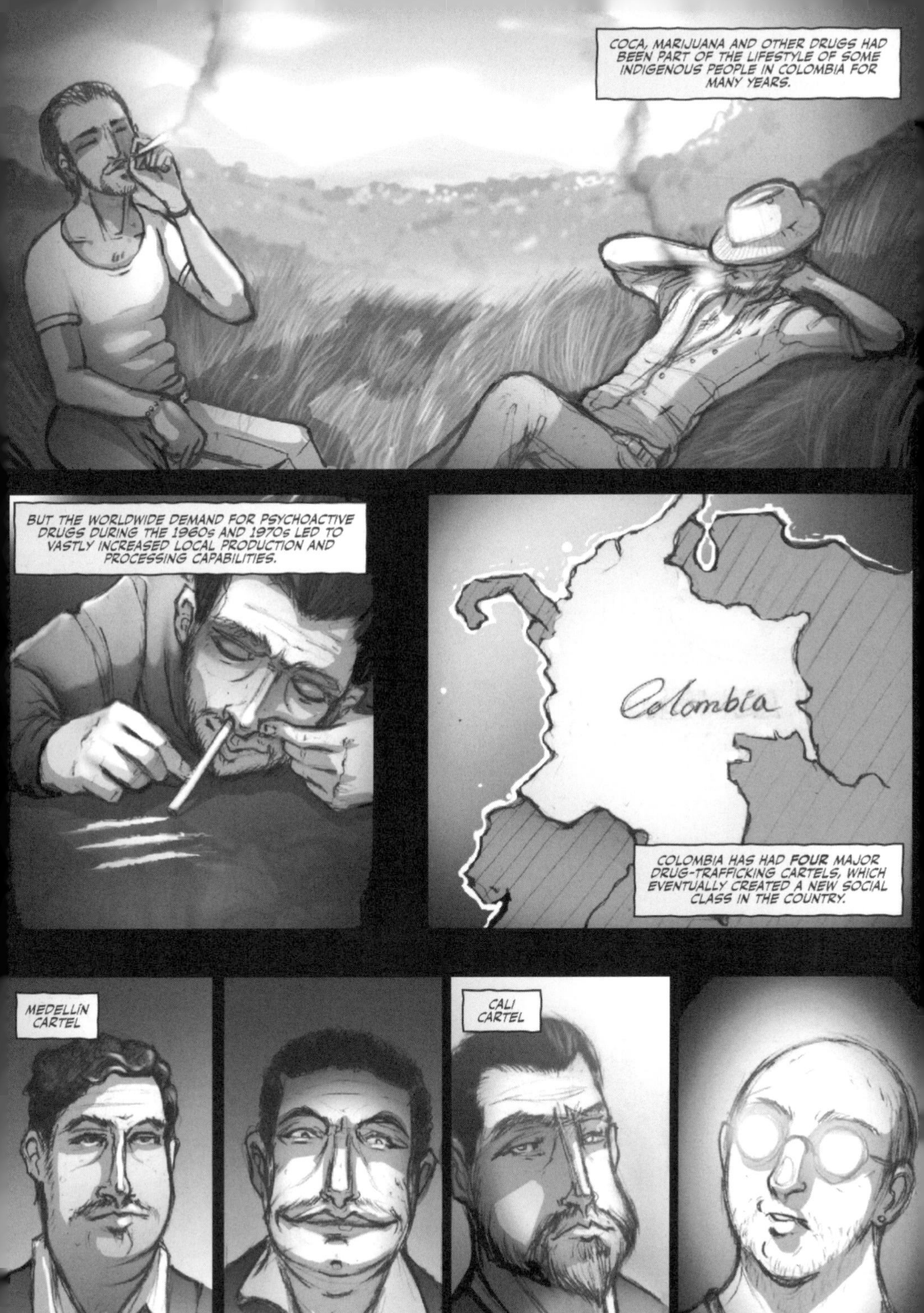
COCA, MARIJUANA AND OTHER DRUGS HAD BEEN PART OF THE LIFESTYLE OF SOME INDIGENOUS PEOPLE IN COLOMBIA FOR MANY YEARS.
BUT THE WORLDWIDE DEMAND FOR PSYCHOACTIVE DRUGS DURING THE 1960s AND 1970s LED TO VASTLY INCREASED LOCAL PRODUCTION AND PROCESSING CAPABILITIES.
Colombia
COLOMBIA HAS HAD **FOUR** MAJOR DRUG-TRAFFICKING CARTELS, WHICH EVENTUALLY CREATED A NEW SOCIAL CLASS IN THE COUNTRY.
MEDELLÍN CARTEL
NORTE DEL VALLE
CALI CARTEL
NORTH COAST CARTEL

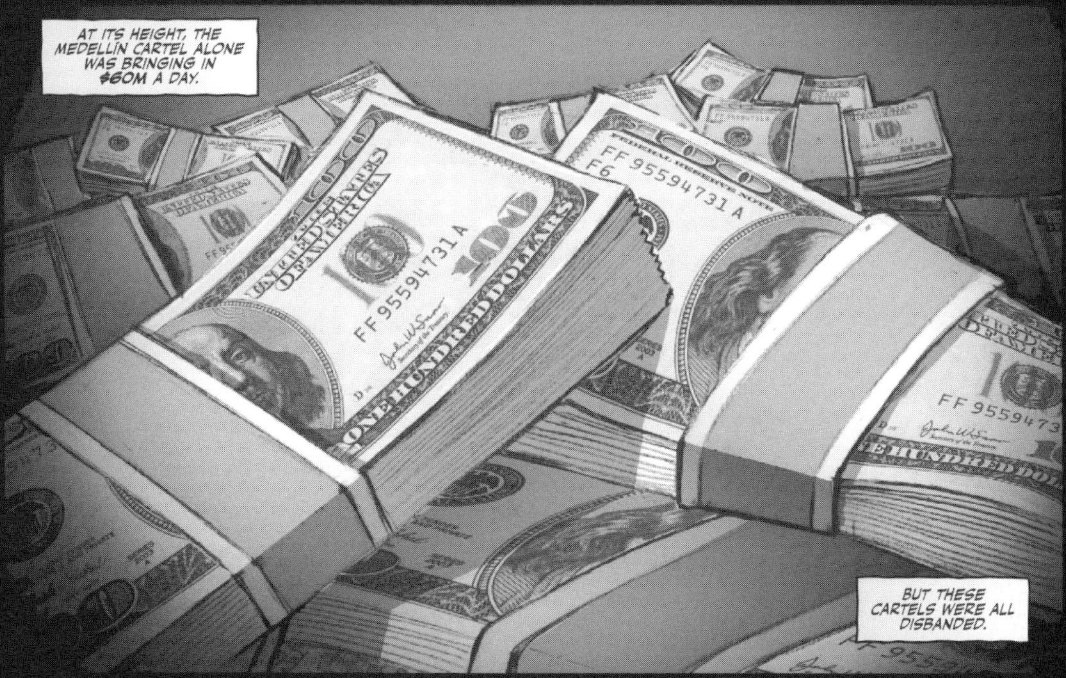
AT ITS HEIGHT, THE MEDELLIN CARTEL ALONE WAS BRINGING IN $60M A DAY.
BUT THESE CARTELS WERE ALL DISBANDED.

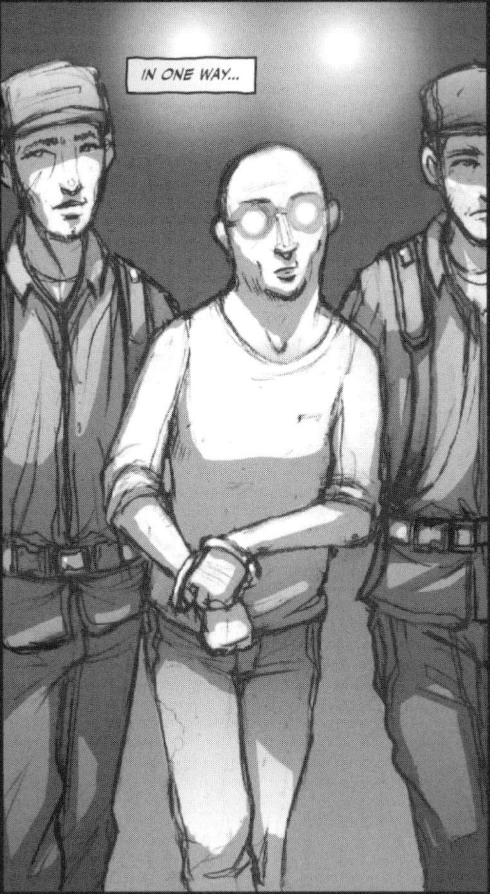
IN ONE WAY...

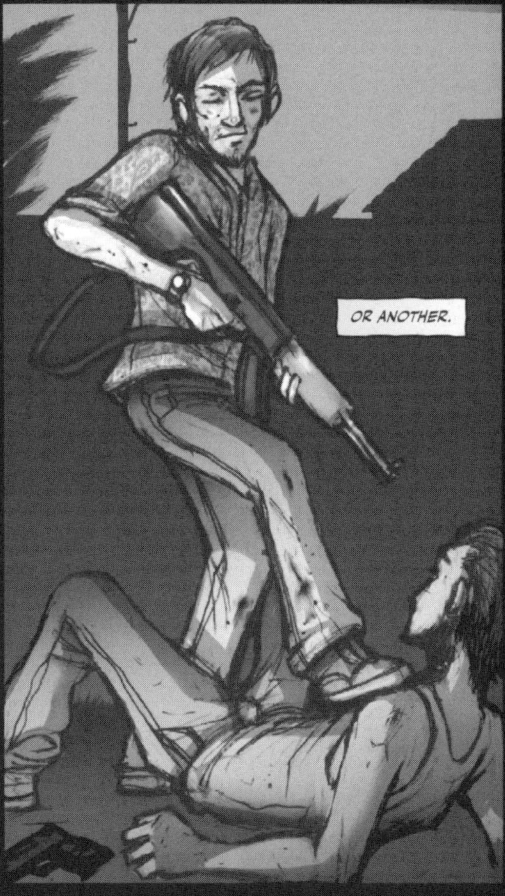
OR ANOTHER.

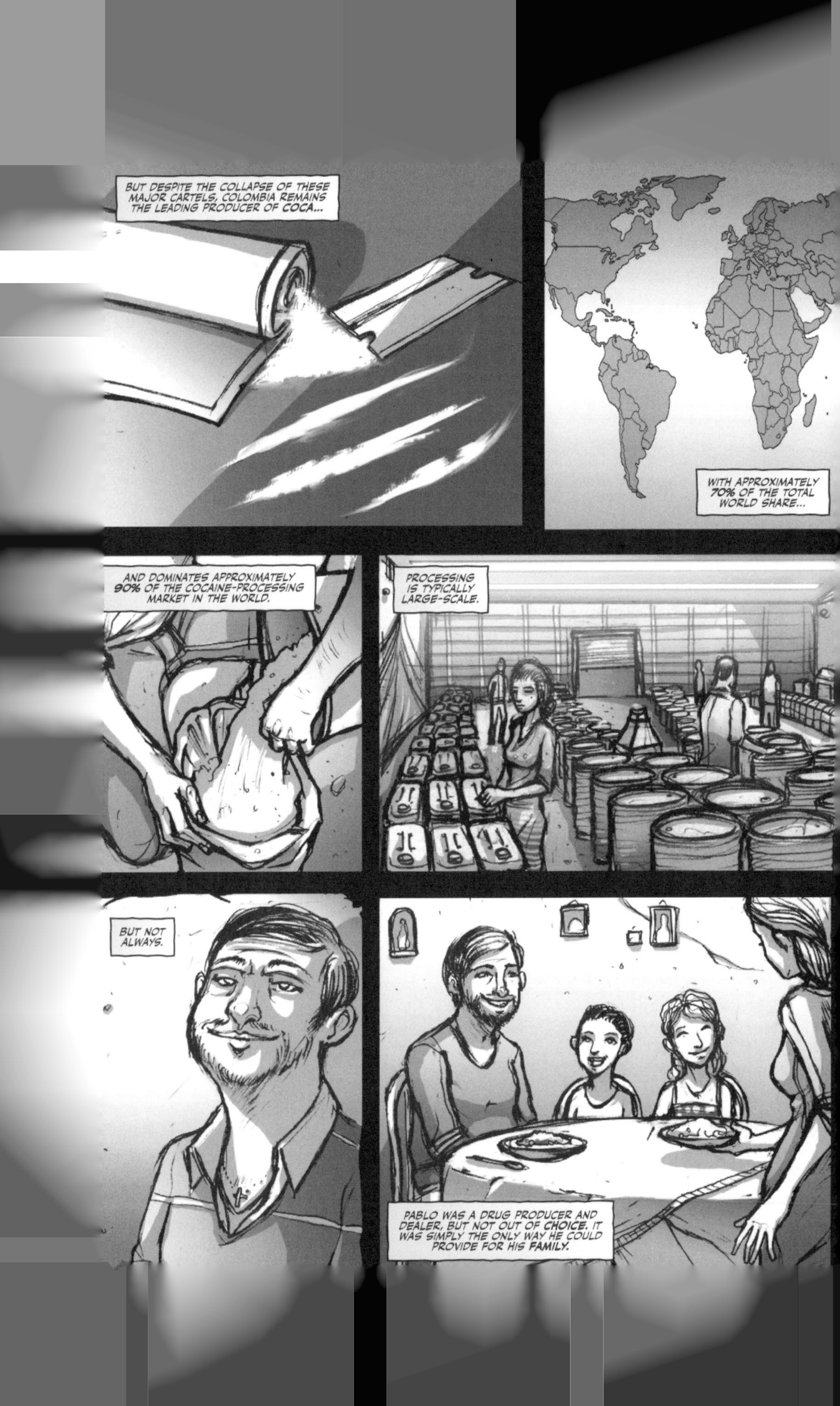
BUT DESPITE THE COLLAPSE OF THESE MAJOR CARTELS, COLOMBIA REMAINS THE LEADING PRODUCER OF COCA...
WITH APPROXIMATELY 70% OF THE TOTAL WORLD SHARE...
AND DOMINATES APPROXIMATELY 90% OF THE COCAINE-PROCESSING MARKET IN THE WORLD.
PROCESSING IS TYPICALLY LARGE-SCALE.
BUT NOT ALWAYS.
PABLO WAS A DRUG PRODUCER AND DEALER, BUT NOT OUT OF CHOICE. IT WAS SIMPLY THE ONLY WAY HE COULD PROVIDE FOR HIS FAMILY.

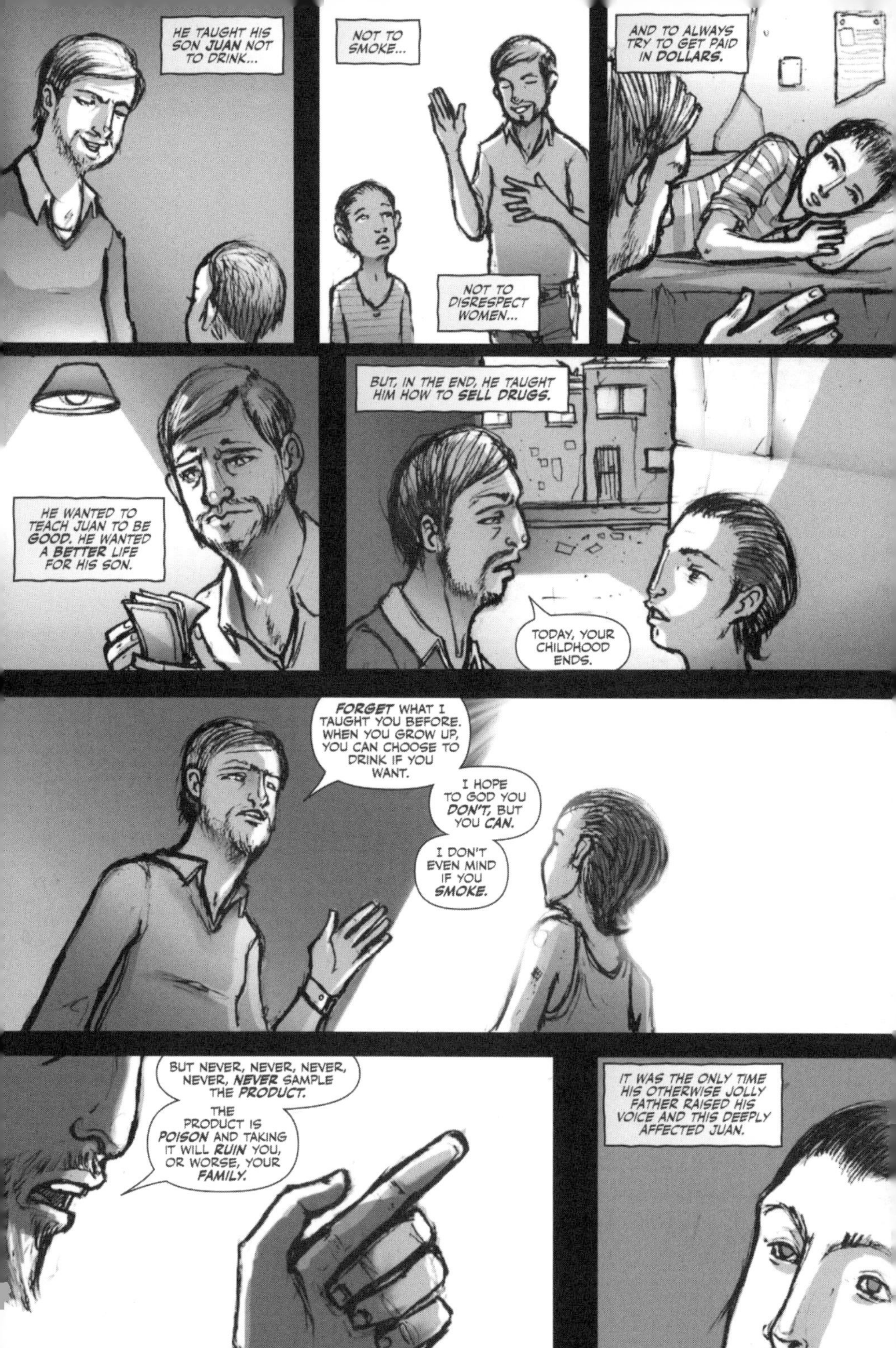

HE TAUGHT HIS SON JUAN NOT TO DRINK...
NOT TO SMOKE...
NOT TO DISRESPECT WOMEN...
AND TO ALWAYS TRY TO GET PAID IN DOLLARS.
HE WANTED TO TEACH JUAN TO BE GOOD. HE WANTED A BETTER LIFE FOR HIS SON.
BUT, IN THE END, HE TAUGHT HIM HOW TO SELL DRUGS.
TODAY, YOUR CHILDHOOD ENDS.
FORGET WHAT I TAUGHT YOU BEFORE. WHEN YOU GROW UP, YOU CAN CHOOSE TO DRINK IF YOU WANT.
I HOPE TO GOD YOU DON'T, BUT YOU CAN.
I DON'T EVEN MIND IF YOU SMOKE.
BUT NEVER, NEVER, NEVER, NEVER, NEVER SAMPLE THE PRODUCT.
THE PRODUCT IS POISON AND TAKING IT WILL RUIN YOU, OR WORSE, YOUR FAMILY.
IT WAS THE ONLY TIME HIS OTHERWISE JOLLY FATHER RAISED HIS VOICE AND THIS DEEPLY AFFECTED JUAN.

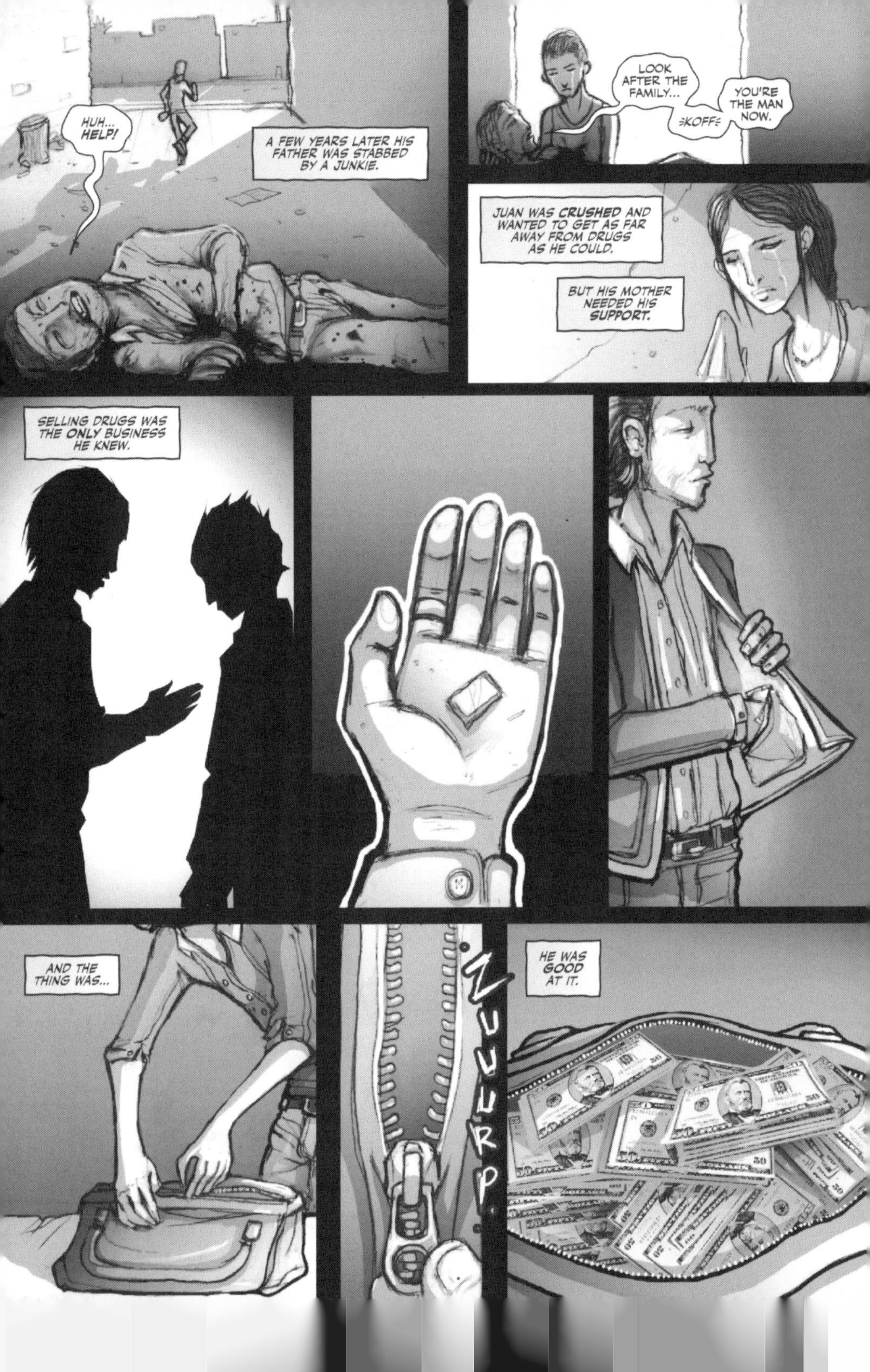
HUH... HELP!
A FEW YEARS LATER HIS FATHER WAS STABBED BY A JUNKIE.
LOOK AFTER THE FAMILY...
KOFF
YOU'RE THE MAN NOW.
JUAN WAS CRUSHED AND WANTED TO GET AS FAR AWAY FROM DRUGS AS HE COULD.
BUT HIS MOTHER NEEDED HIS SUPPORT.
SELLING DRUGS WAS THE ONLY BUSINESS HE KNEW.
AND THE THING WAS...
ZUUURP!
HE WAS GOOD AT IT.

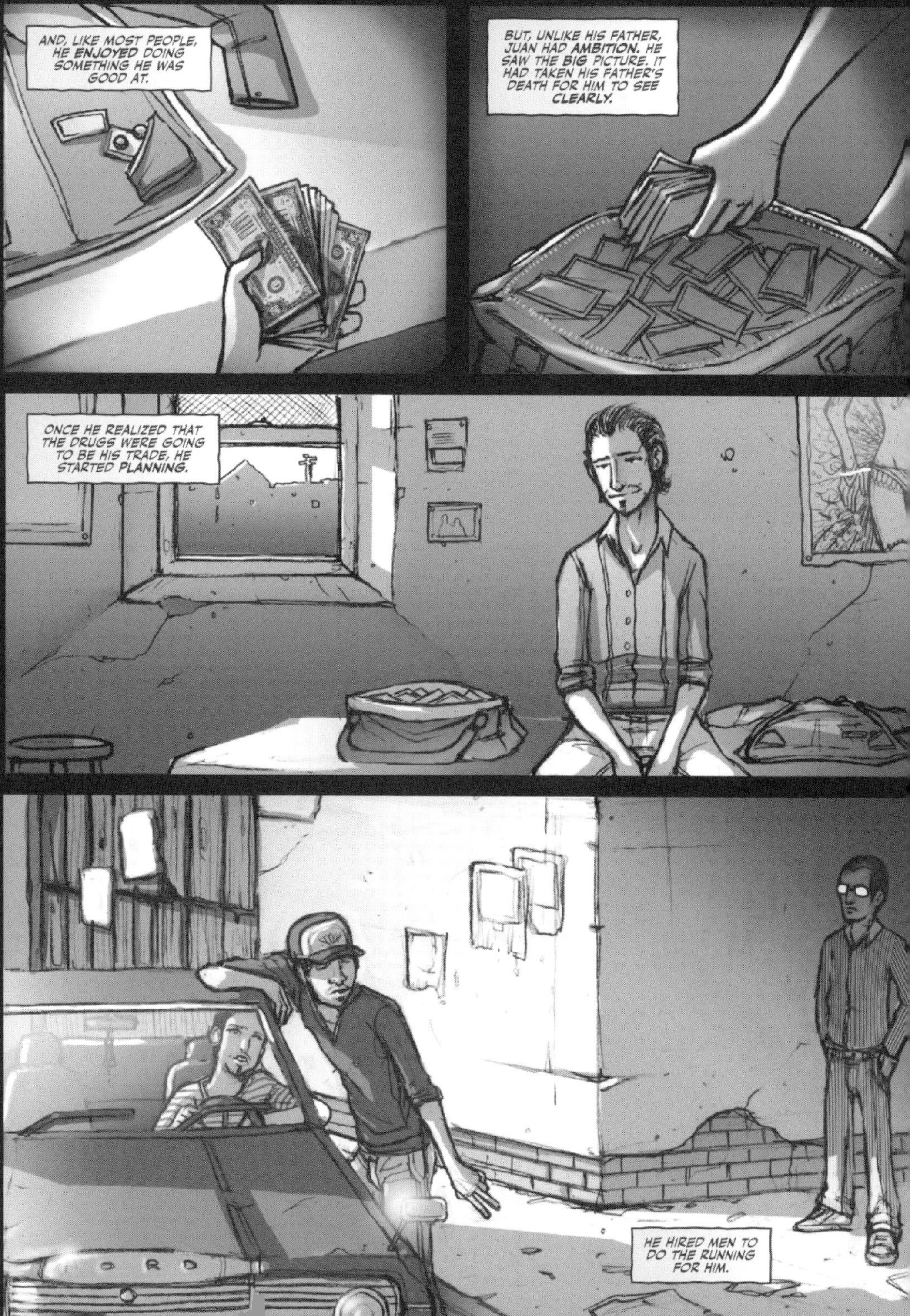
AND, LIKE MOST PEOPLE, HE ENJOYED DOING SOMETHING HE WAS GOOD AT.
BUT, UNLIKE HIS FATHER, JUAN HAD AMBITION. HE SAW THE BIG PICTURE. IT HAD TAKEN HIS FATHER'S DEATH FOR HIM TO SEE CLEARLY.
ONCE HE REALIZED THAT THE DRUGS WERE GOING TO BE HIS TRADE, HE STARTED PLANNING.
FORD
HE HIRED MEN TO DO THE RUNNING FOR HIM.

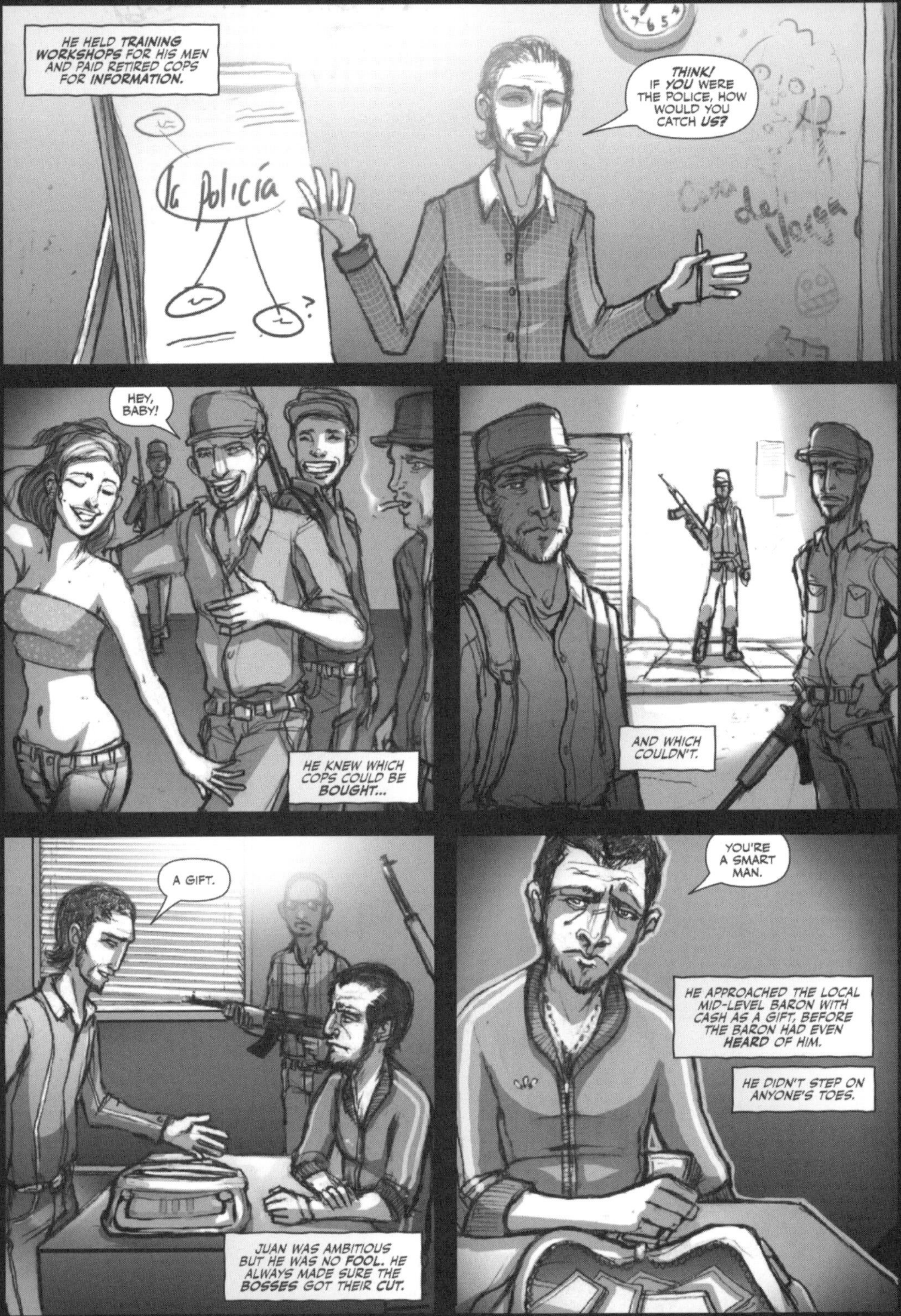

HE HELD TRAINING WORKSHOPS FOR HIS MEN AND PAID RETIRED COPS FOR INFORMATION.
THINK! IF YOU WERE THE POLICE, HOW WOULD YOU CATCH US?
la policía
HEY, BABY!
HE KNEW WHICH COPS COULD BE BOUGHT...
AND WHICH COULDN'T.
A GIFT.
JUAN WAS AMBITIOUS BUT HE WAS NO FOOL. HE ALWAYS MADE SURE THE BOSSES GOT THEIR CUT.
YOU'RE A SMART MAN.
HE APPROACHED THE LOCAL MID-LEVEL BARON WITH CASH AS A GIFT, BEFORE THE BARON HAD EVEN HEARD OF HIM.
HE DIDN'T STEP ON ANYONE'S TOES.

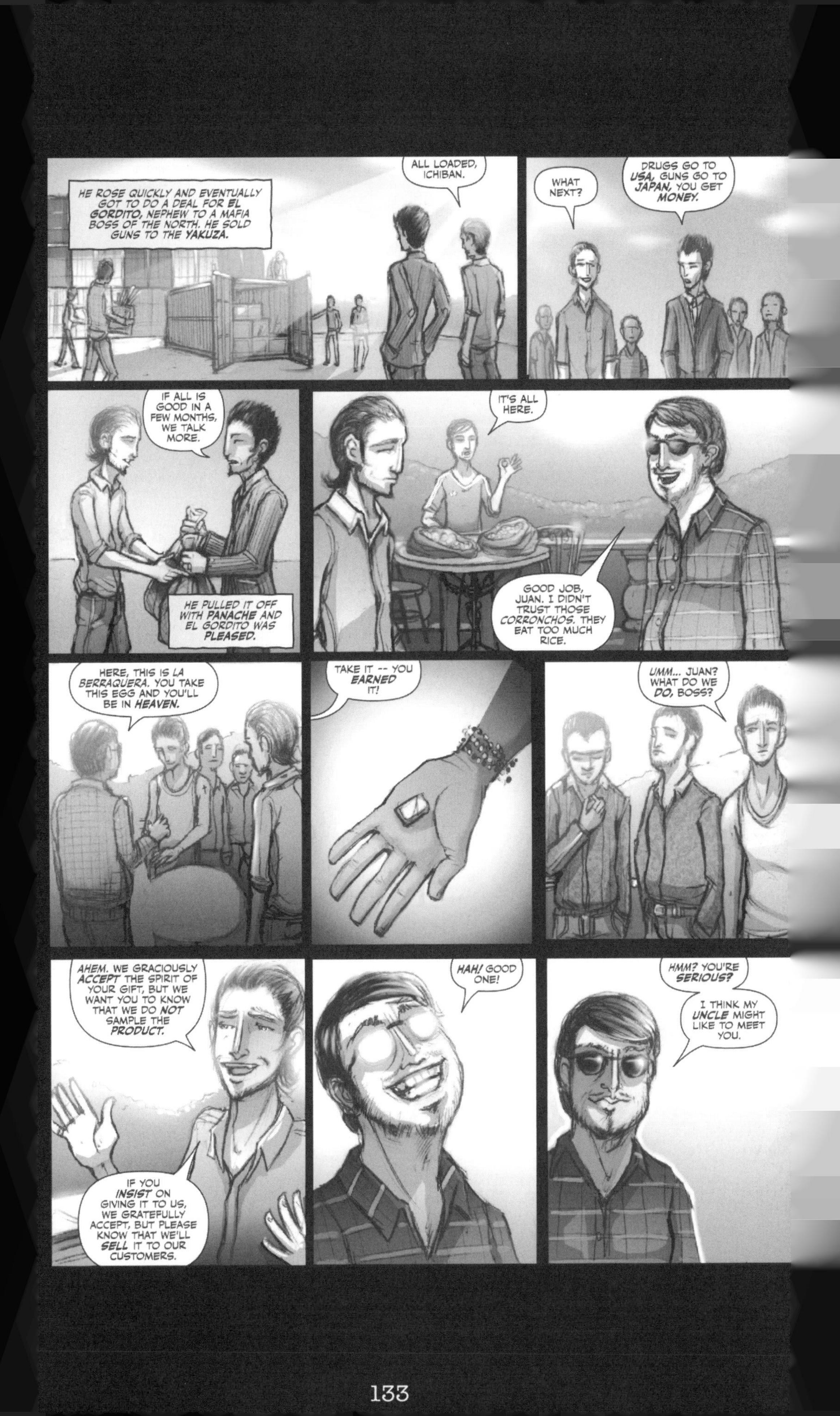
HE ROSE QUICKLY AND EVENTUALLY GOT TO DO A DEAL FOR EL GORDITO, NEPHEW TO A MAFIA BOSS OF THE NORTH. HE SOLD GUNS TO THE YAKUZA.
ALL LOADED, ICHIBAN.
WHAT NEXT?
DRUGS GO TO USA, GUNS GO TO JAPAN, YOU GET MONEY.
IF ALL IS GOOD IN A FEW MONTHS, WE TALK MORE.
HE PULLED IT OFF WITH PANACHE AND EL GORDITO WAS PLEASED.
IT'S ALL HERE.
GOOD JOB, JUAN. I DIDN'T TRUST THOSE CORRONCHOS. THEY EAT TOO MUCH RICE.
HERE, THIS IS LA BERRAQUERA. YOU TAKE THIS EGG AND YOU'LL BE IN HEAVEN.
TAKE IT -- YOU EARNED IT!
UMM... JUAN? WHAT DO WE DO, BOSS?
AHEM. WE GRACIOUSLY ACCEPT THE SPIRIT OF YOUR GIFT, BUT WE WANT YOU TO KNOW THAT WE DO NOT SAMPLE THE PRODUCT.
IF YOU INSIST ON GIVING IT TO US, WE GRATEFULLY ACCEPT, BUT PLEASE KNOW THAT WE'LL SELL IT TO OUR CUSTOMERS.
HAH! GOOD ONE!
HMM? YOU'RE SERIOUS?
I THINK MY UNCLE MIGHT LIKE TO MEET YOU.

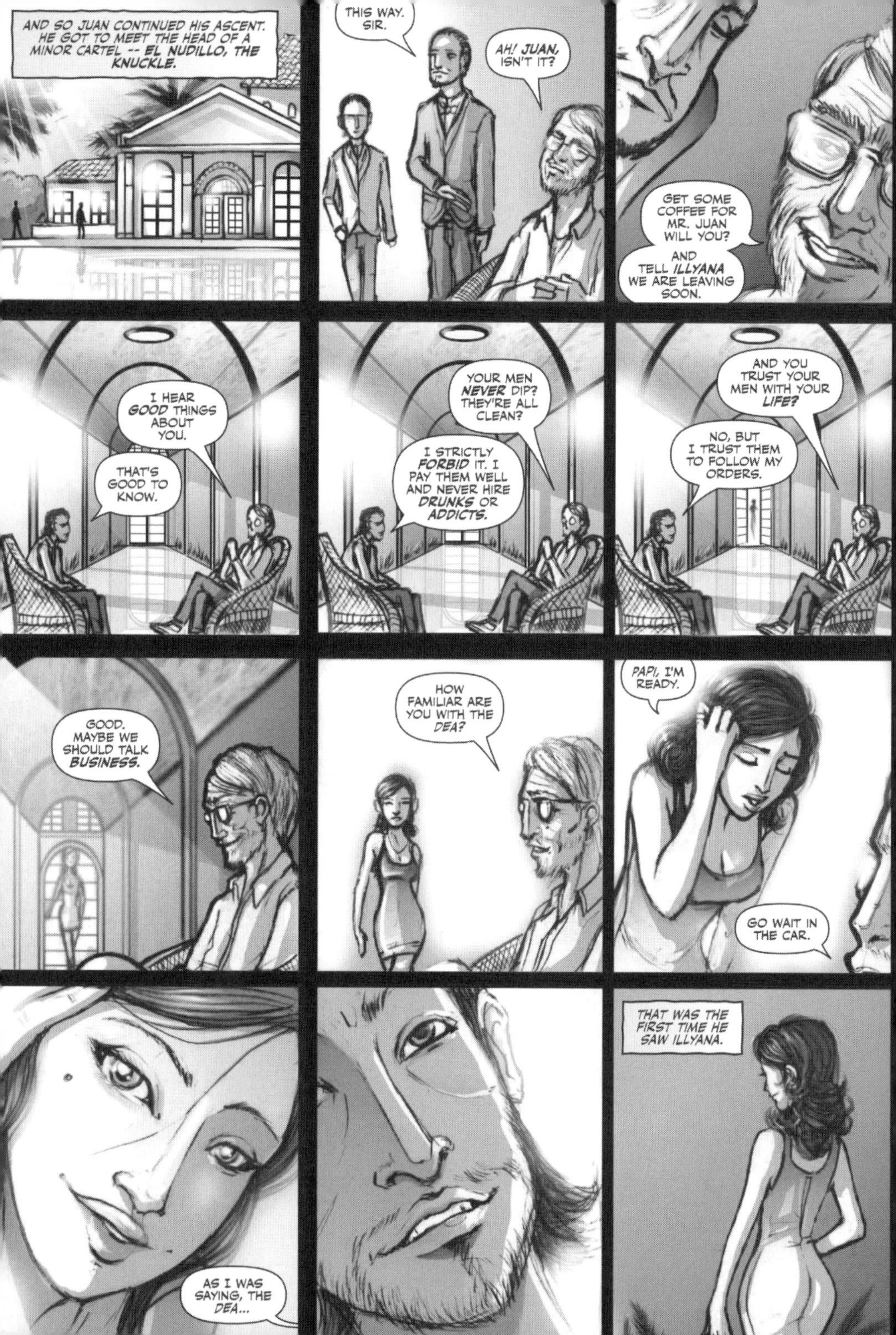
AND SO JUAN CONTINUED HIS ASCENT. HE GOT TO MEET THE HEAD OF A MINOR CARTEL -- EL NUDILLO, THE KNUCKLE.
THIS WAY. SIR.
AH! JUAN, ISN'T IT?
GET SOME COFFEE FOR MR. JUAN WILL YOU?
AND TELL ILLYANA WE ARE LEAVING SOON.
I HEAR GOOD THINGS ABOUT YOU.
THAT'S GOOD TO KNOW.
YOUR MEN NEVER DIP? THEY'RE ALL CLEAN?
I STRICTLY FORBID IT. I PAY THEM WELL AND NEVER HIRE DRUNKS OR ADDICTS.
AND YOU TRUST YOUR MEN WITH YOUR LIFE?
NO, BUT I TRUST THEM TO FOLLOW MY ORDERS.
GOOD. MAYBE WE SHOULD TALK BUSINESS.
HOW FAMILIAR ARE YOU WITH THE DEA?
PAPI, I'M READY.
GO WAIT IN THE CAR.
AS I WAS SAYING, THE DEA...
THAT WAS THE FIRST TIME HE SAW ILLYANA.

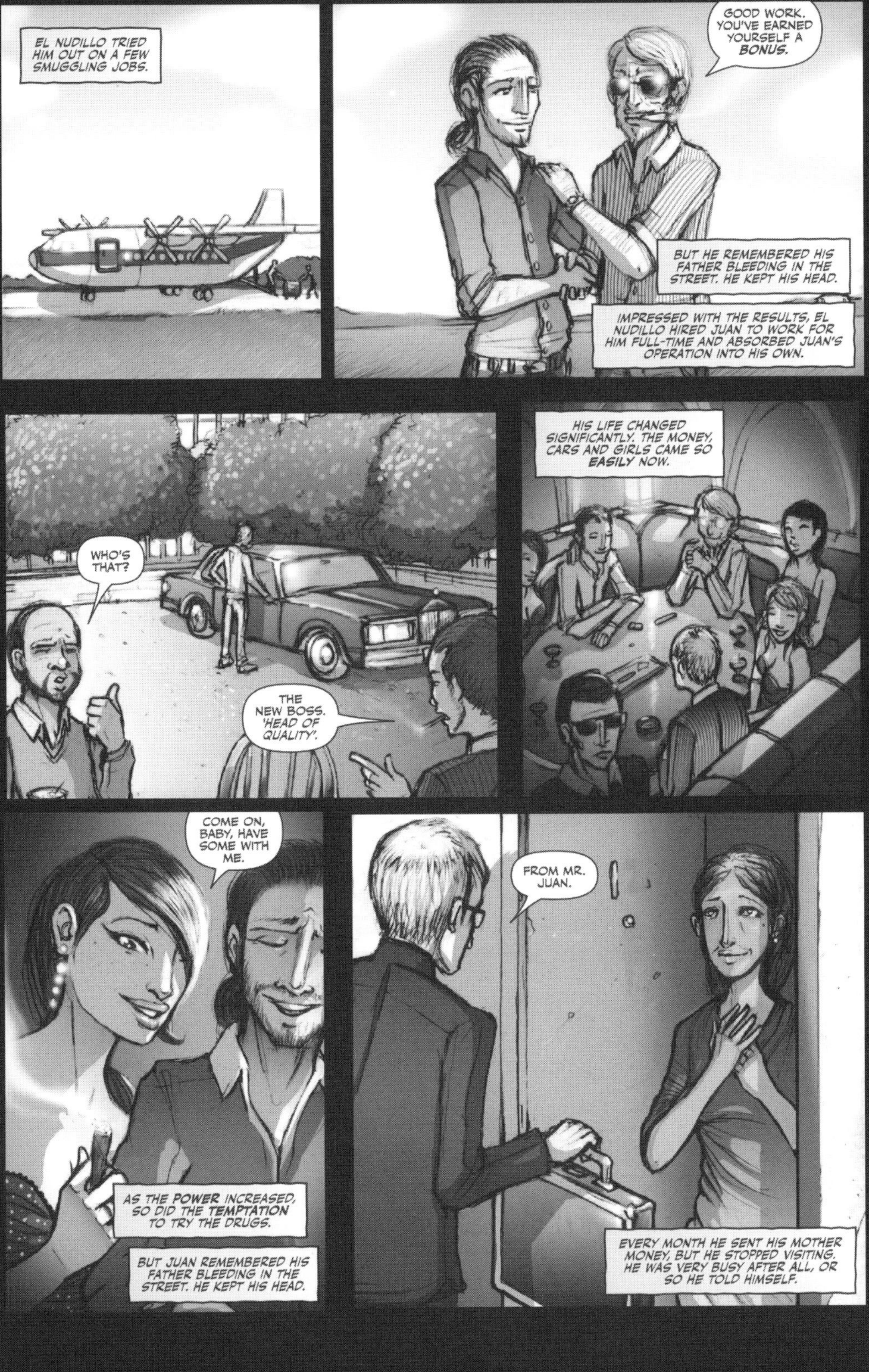
EL NUDILLO TRIED HIM OUT ON A FEW SMUGGLING JOBS.
GOOD WORK. YOU'VE EARNED YOURSELF A BONUS.
BUT HE REMEMBERED HIS FATHER BLEEDING IN THE STREET. HE KEPT HIS HEAD.
IMPRESSED WITH THE RESULTS, EL NUDILLO HIRED JUAN TO WORK FOR HIM FULL-TIME AND ABSORBED JUAN'S OPERATION INTO HIS OWN.
WHO'S THAT?
THE NEW BOSS. 'HEAD OF QUALITY'.
HIS LIFE CHANGED SIGNIFICANTLY. THE MONEY, CARS AND GIRLS CAME SO EASILY NOW.
COME ON, BABY, HAVE SOME WITH ME.
AS THE POWER INCREASED, SO DID THE TEMPTATION TO TRY THE DRUGS.
BUT JUAN REMEMBERED HIS FATHER BLEEDING IN THE STREET. HE KEPT HIS HEAD.
FROM MR. JUAN.
EVERY MONTH HE SENT HIS MOTHER MONEY, BUT HE STOPPED VISITING. HE WAS VERY BUSY AFTER ALL, OR SO HE TOLD HIMSELF.

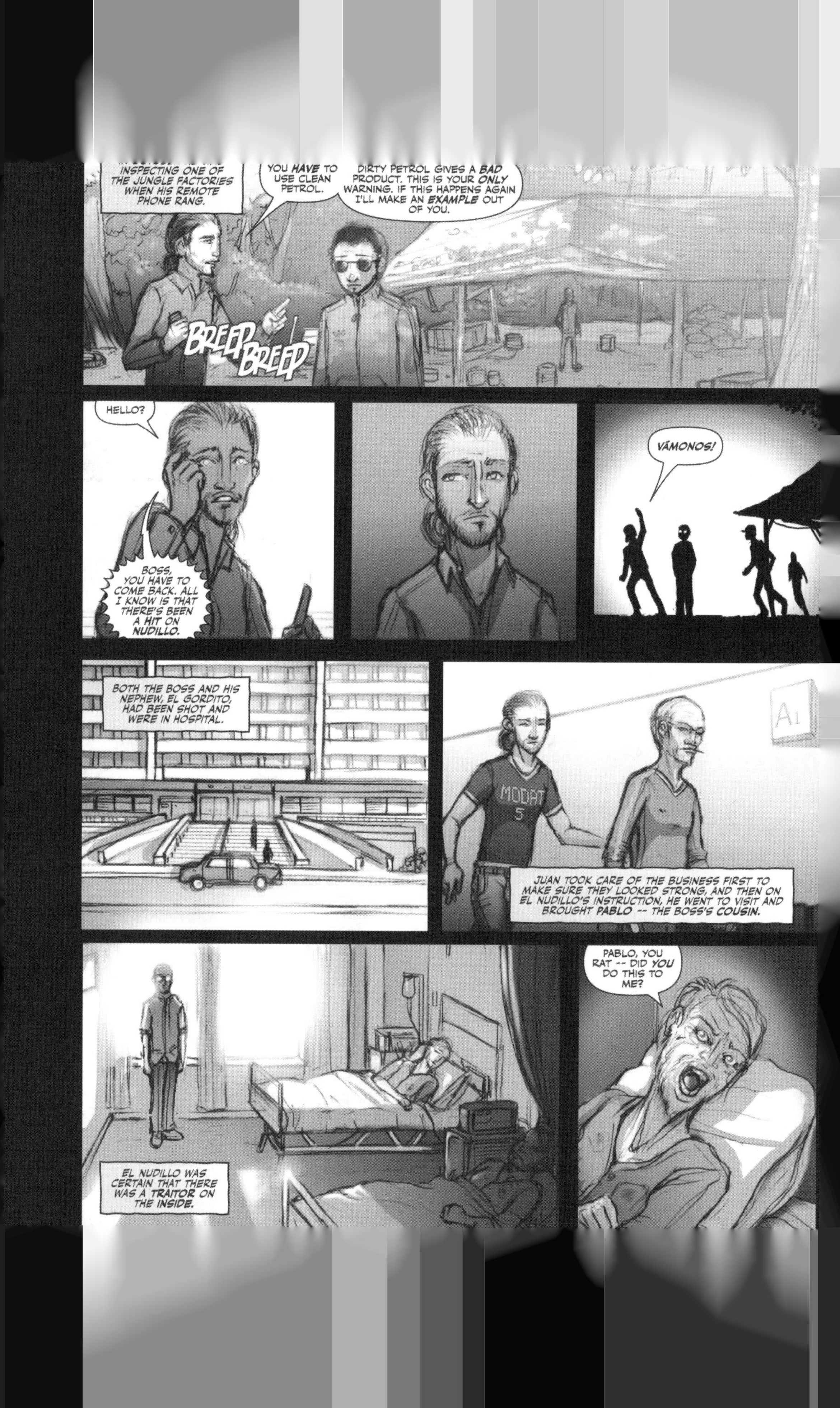
INSPECTING ONE OF THE JUNGLE FACTORIES WHEN HIS REMOTE PHONE RANG.
YOU **HAVE** TO USE CLEAN PETROL.
DIRTY PETROL GIVES A **BAD** PRODUCT. THIS IS YOUR **ONLY** WARNING. IF THIS HAPPENS AGAIN I'LL MAKE AN **EXAMPLE** OUT OF YOU.
BREEP BREEP
HELLO?
BOSS, YOU HAVE TO COME BACK. ALL I KNOW IS THAT THERE'S BEEN A **HIT** ON **NUDILLO.**
VÁMONOS!
BOTH THE BOSS AND HIS NEPHEW, EL GORDITO, HAD BEEN SHOT AND WERE IN HOSPITAL.
A1
MODAT 5
JUAN TOOK CARE OF THE BUSINESS FIRST TO MAKE SURE THEY LOOKED STRONG, AND THEN ON EL NUDILLO'S INSTRUCTION, HE WENT TO VISIT AND BROUGHT **PABLO** -- THE BOSS'S **COUSIN.**
EL NUDILLO WAS CERTAIN THAT THERE WAS A **TRAITOR** ON THE **INSIDE.**
PABLO, YOU RAT -- DID **YOU** DO THIS TO ME?

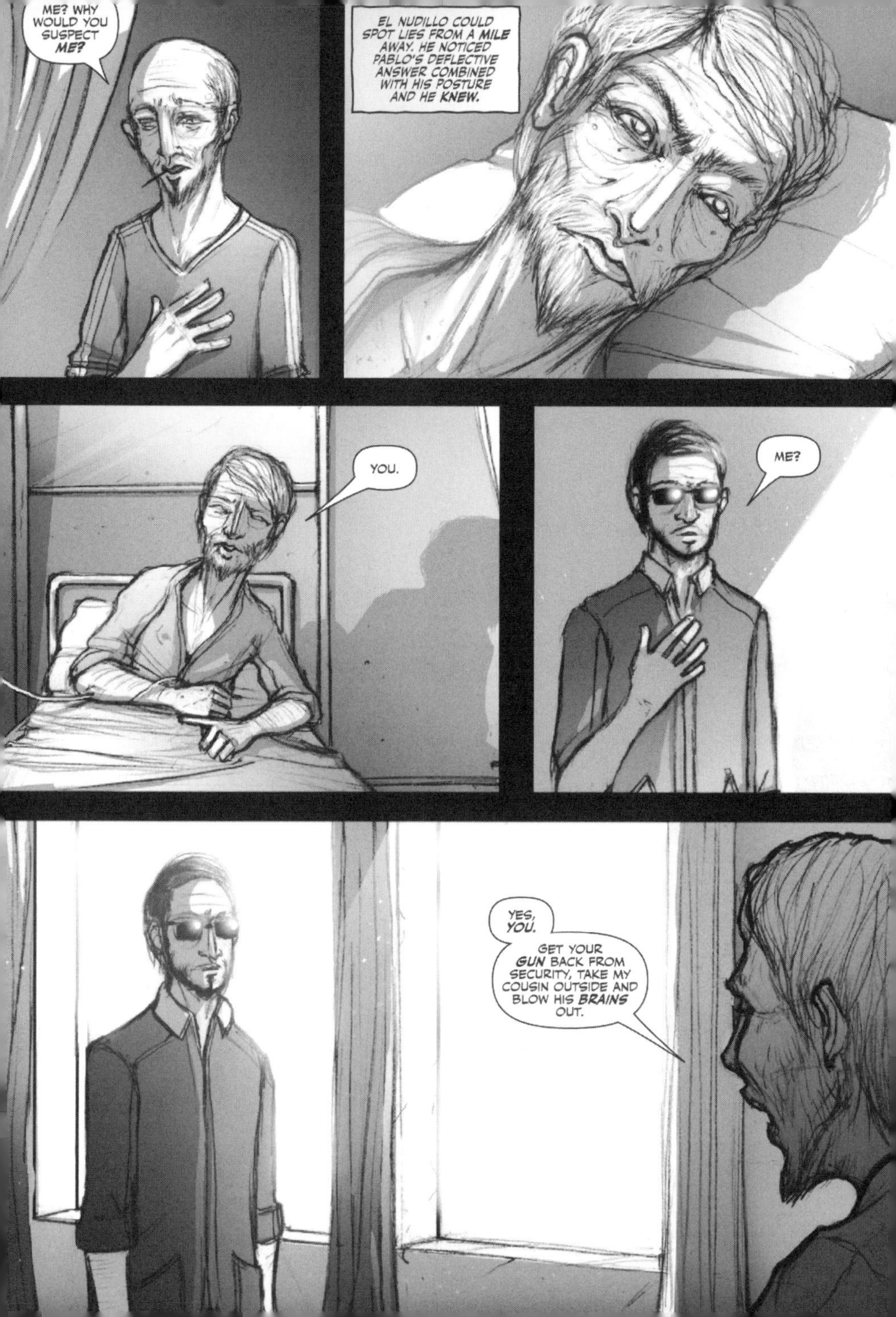

ME? WHY WOULD YOU SUSPECT ME?
EL NUDILLO COULD SPOT LIES FROM A MILE AWAY. HE NOTICED PABLO'S DEFLECTIVE ANSWER COMBINED WITH HIS POSTURE AND HE KNEW.
YOU.
ME?
YES, YOU.
GET YOUR GUN BACK FROM SECURITY, TAKE MY COUSIN OUTSIDE AND BLOW HIS BRAINS OUT.

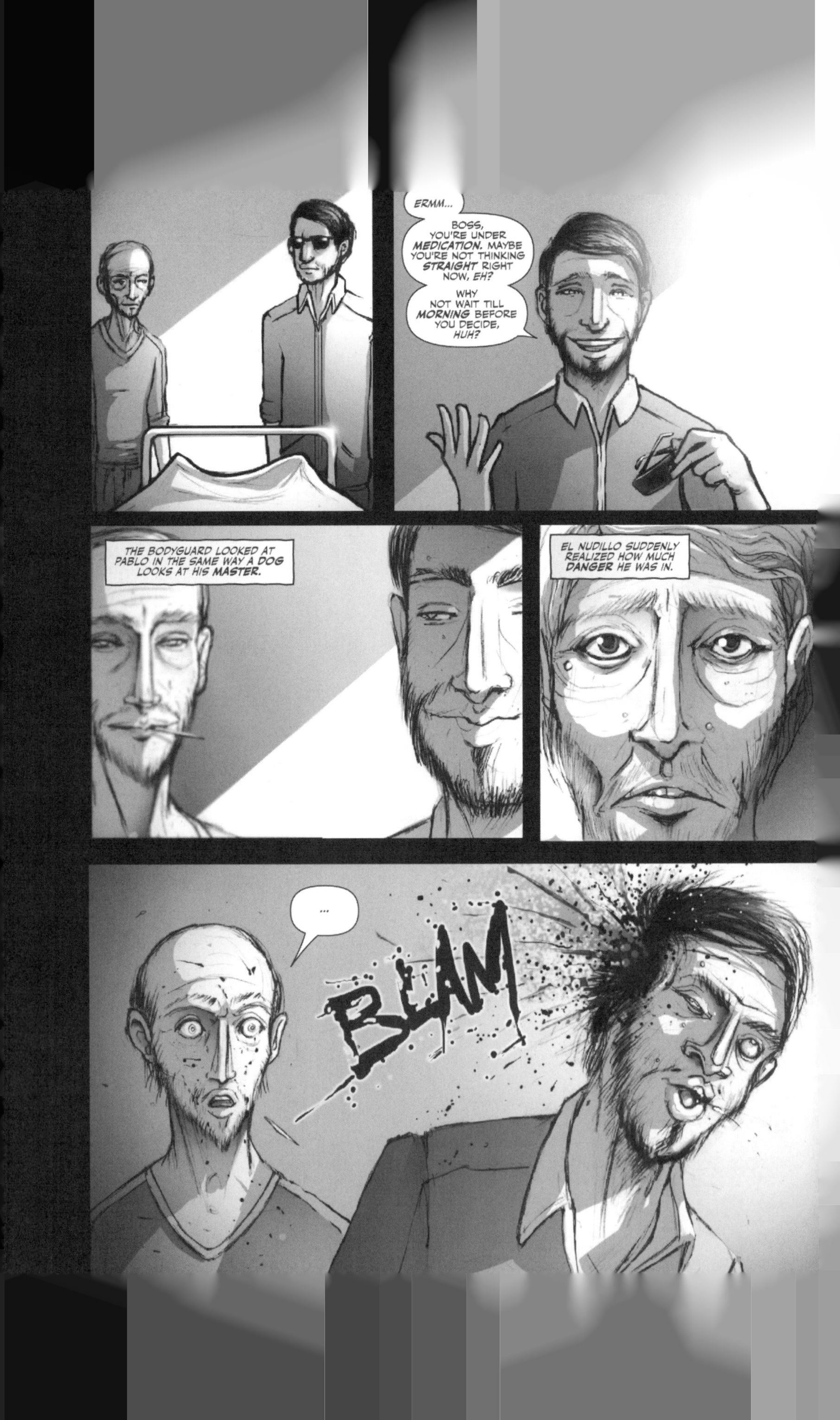
ERMM...
BOSS, YOU'RE UNDER MEDICATION. MAYBE YOU'RE NOT THINKING STRAIGHT RIGHT NOW, EH?
WHY NOT WAIT TILL MORNING BEFORE YOU DECIDE, HUH?
THE BODYGUARD LOOKED AT PABLO IN THE SAME WAY A DOG LOOKS AT HIS MASTER.
EL NUDILLO SUDDENLY REALIZED HOW MUCH DANGER HE WAS IN.
...
BLAM

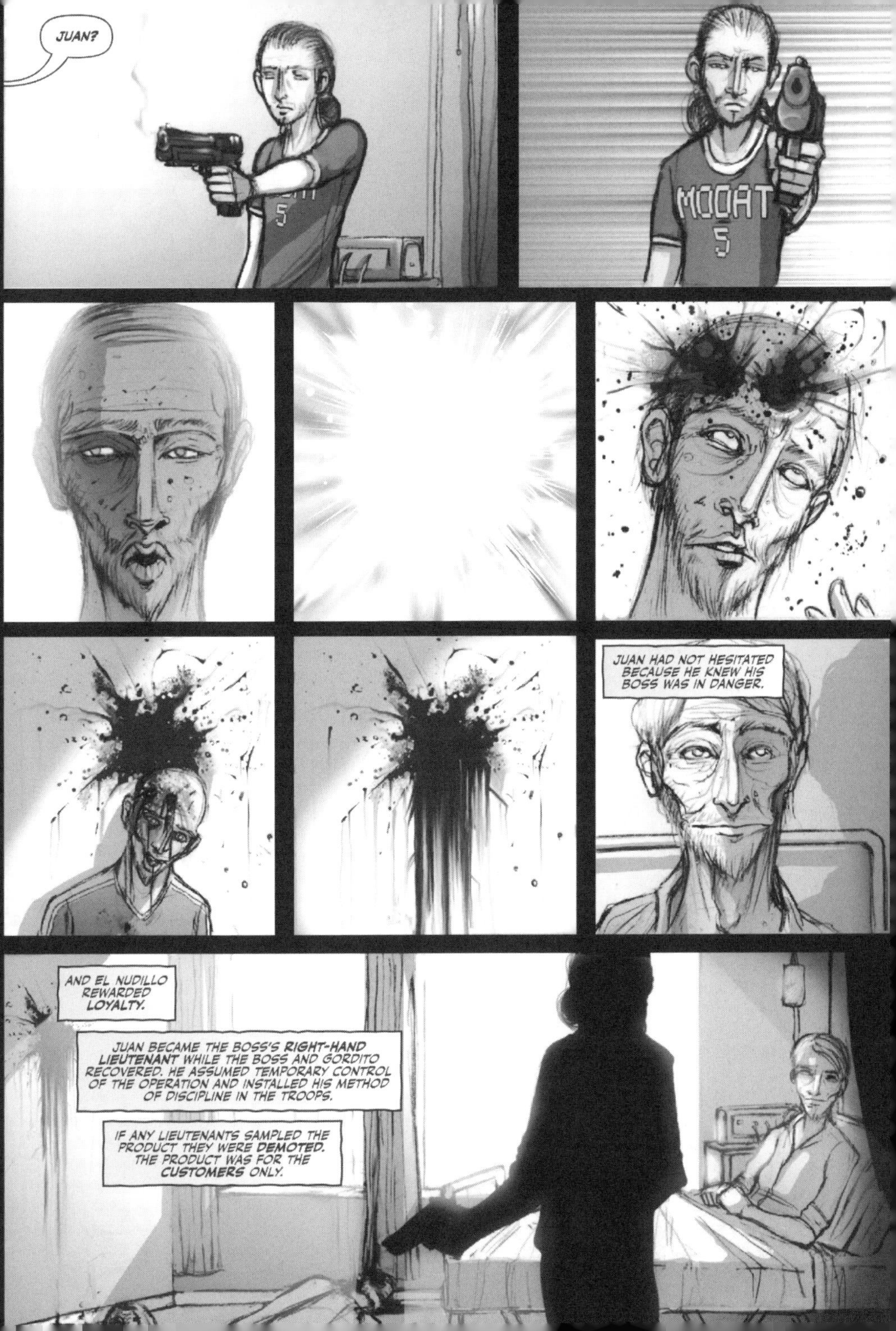
JUAN?
MOOAT
5
JUAN HAD NOT HESITATED BECAUSE HE KNEW HIS BOSS WAS IN DANGER.
AND EL NUDILLO REWARDED **LOYALTY.**
JUAN BECAME THE BOSS'S **RIGHT-HAND LIEUTENANT** WHILE THE BOSS AND GORDITO RECOVERED. HE ASSUMED TEMPORARY CONTROL OF THE OPERATION AND INSTALLED HIS METHOD OF DISCIPLINE IN THE TROOPS.
IF ANY LIEUTENANTS SAMPLED THE PRODUCT THEY WERE **DEMOTED.** THE PRODUCT WAS FOR THE **CUSTOMERS** ONLY.

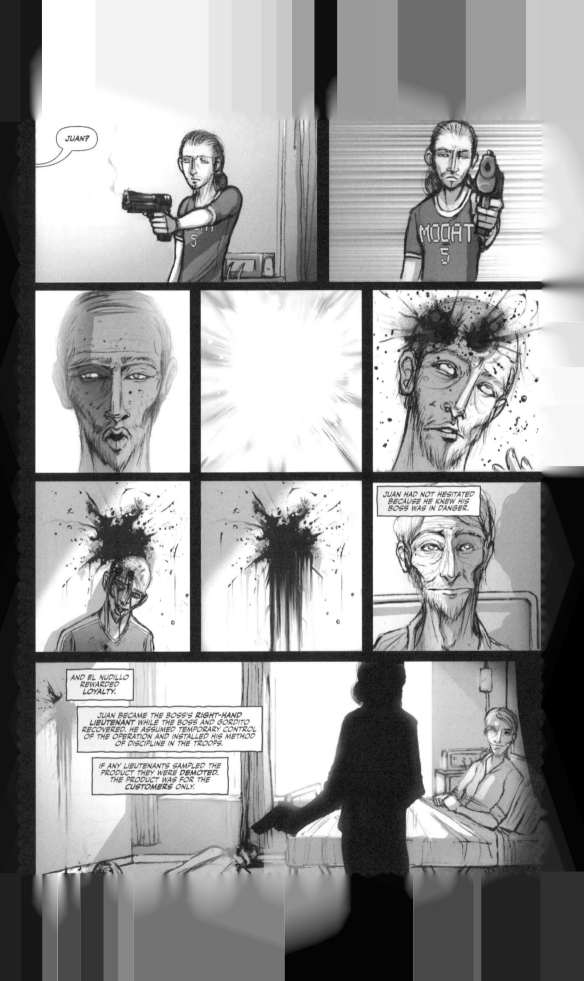

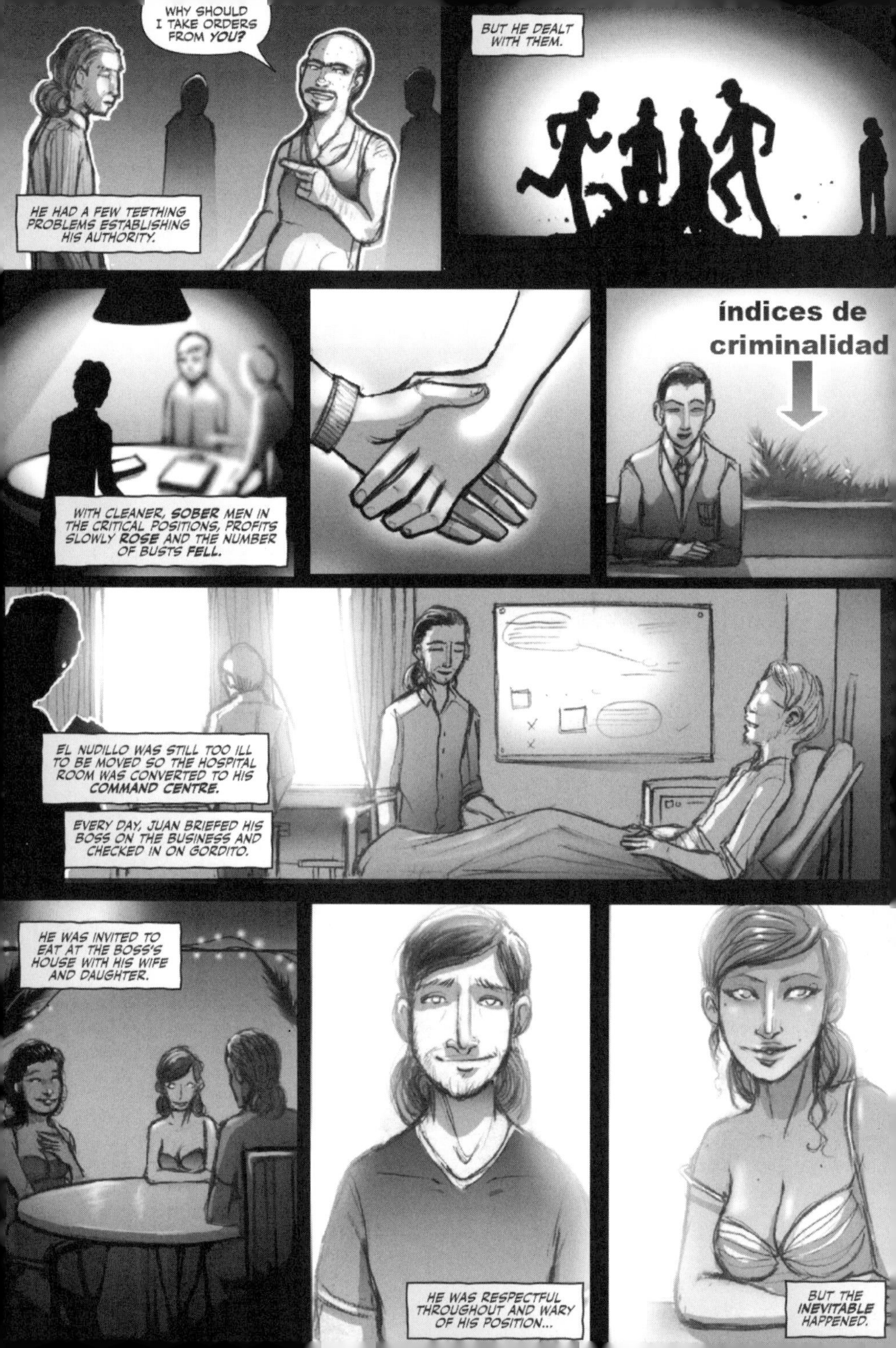
WHY SHOULD I TAKE ORDERS FROM YOU?
HE HAD A FEW TEETHING PROBLEMS ESTABLISHING HIS AUTHORITY.
BUT HE DEALT WITH THEM.
WITH CLEANER, SOBER MEN IN THE CRITICAL POSITIONS, PROFITS SLOWLY ROSE AND THE NUMBER OF BUSTS FELL.
índices de criminalidad
EL NUDILLO WAS STILL TOO ILL TO BE MOVED SO THE HOSPITAL ROOM WAS CONVERTED TO HIS COMMAND CENTRE.
EVERY DAY, JUAN BRIEFED HIS BOSS ON THE BUSINESS AND CHECKED IN ON GORDITO.
HE WAS INVITED TO EAT AT THE BOSS'S HOUSE WITH HIS WIFE AND DAUGHTER.
HE WAS RESPECTFUL THROUGHOUT AND WARY OF HIS POSITION...
BUT THE INEVITABLE HAPPENED.

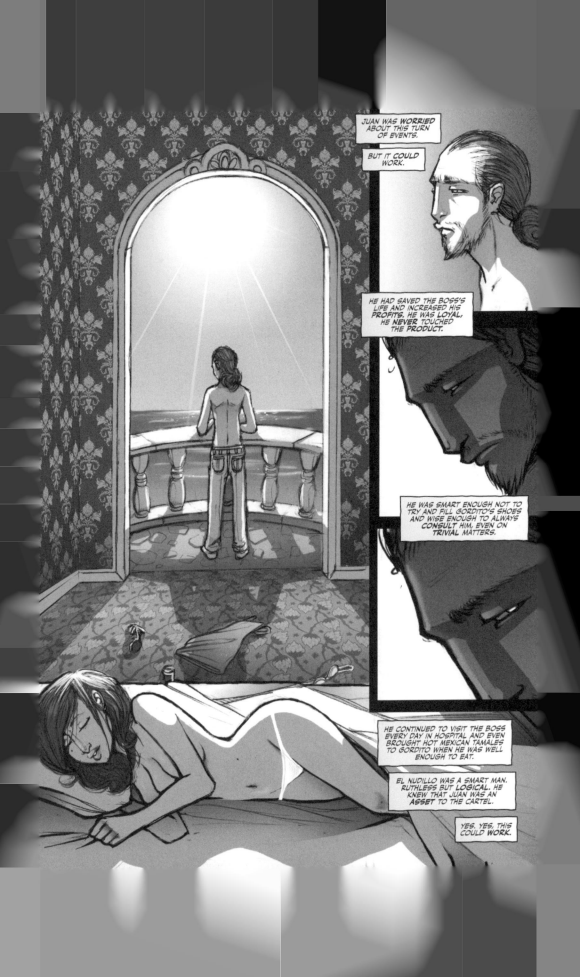

JUAN WAS **WORRIED** ABOUT THIS TURN OF EVENTS.

BUT IT **COULD** WORK.

HE HAD SAVED THE BOSS'S LIFE AND INCREASED HIS **PROFITS.** HE WAS **LOYAL,** HE **NEVER** TOUCHED THE **PRODUCT.**

HE WAS **SMART** ENOUGH NOT TO TRY AND FILL GORDITO'S SHOES AND WISE ENOUGH TO ALWAYS **CONSULT** HIM, EVEN ON TRIVIAL MATTERS.

HE CONTINUED TO VISIT THE BOSS EVERY DAY IN HOSPITAL AND EVEN BROUGHT HOT MEXICAN TAMALES TO GORDITO WHEN HE WAS WELL ENOUGH TO EAT.

EL NUDILLO WAS A SMART MAN. RUTHLESS BUT **LOGICAL.** HE KNEW THAT JUAN WAS AN ASSET TO THE CARTEL.

YES, YES, THIS COULD **WORK.**

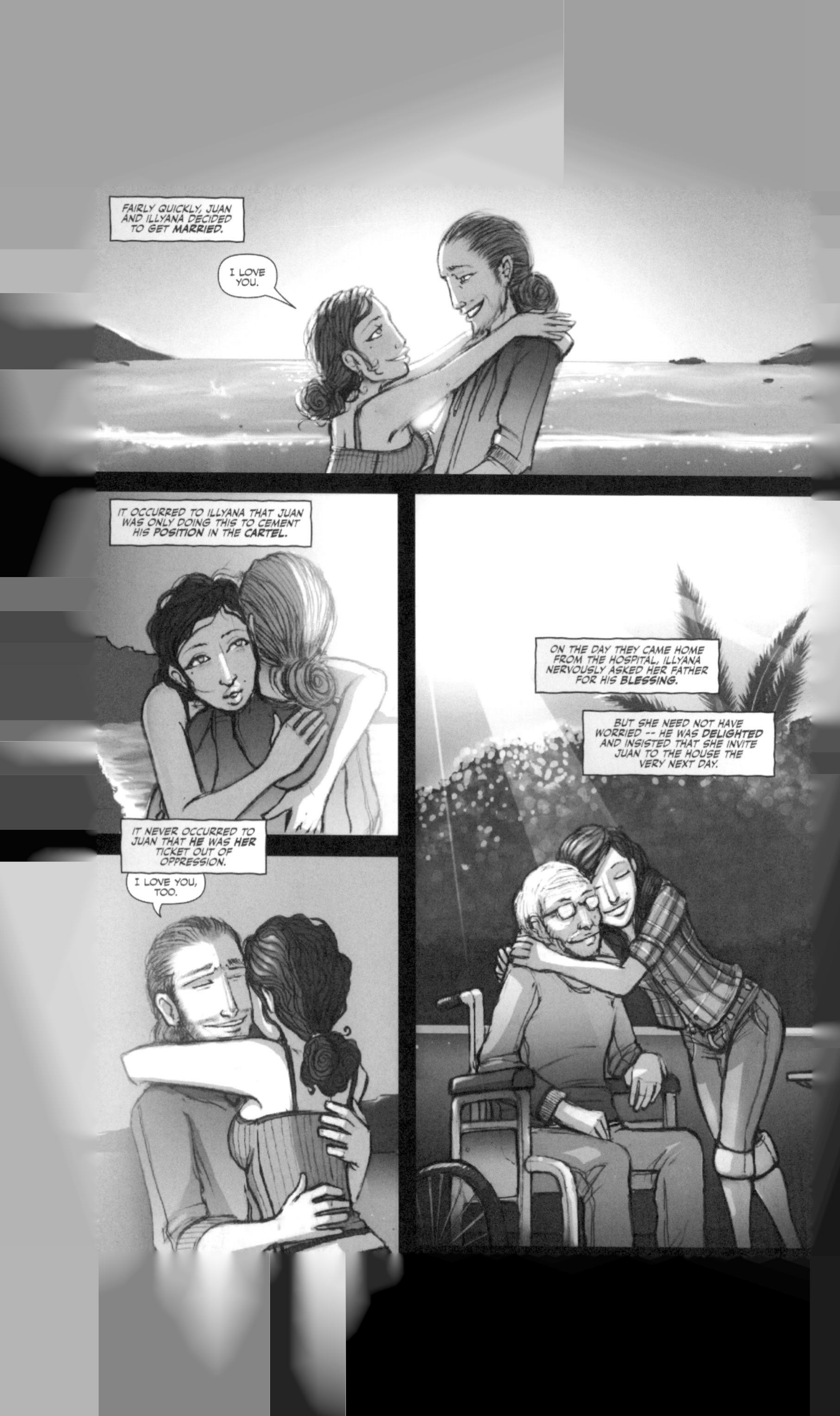
FAIRLY QUICKLY, JUAN AND ILLYANA DECIDED TO GET MARRIED.
I LOVE YOU.
IT OCCURRED TO ILLYANA THAT JUAN WAS ONLY DOING THIS TO CEMENT HIS POSITION IN THE CARTEL.
IT NEVER OCCURRED TO JUAN THAT HE WAS HER TICKET OUT OF OPPRESSION.
I LOVE YOU, TOO.
ON THE DAY THEY CAME HOME FROM THE HOSPITAL, ILLYANA NERVOUSLY ASKED HER FATHER FOR HIS BLESSING.
BUT SHE NEED NOT HAVE WORRIED -- HE WAS DELIGHTED AND INSISTED THAT SHE INVITE JUAN TO THE HOUSE THE VERY NEXT DAY.

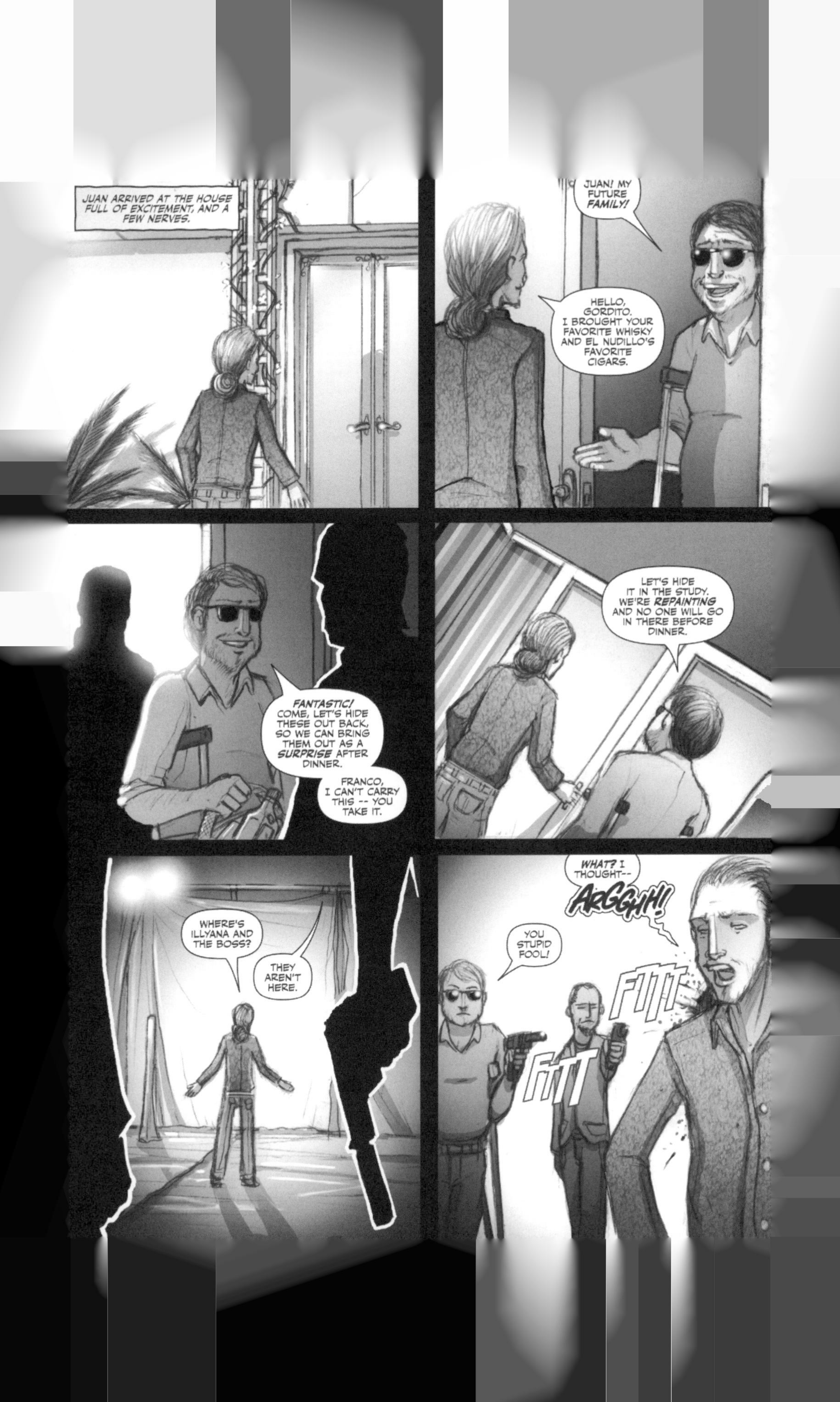
JUAN ARRIVED AT THE HOUSE FULL OF EXCITEMENT, AND A FEW NERVES.
JUAN! MY FUTURE FAMILY!
HELLO, GORDITO. I BROUGHT YOUR FAVORITE WHISKY AND EL NUDILLO'S FAVORITE CIGARS.
FANTASTIC! COME, LET'S HIDE THESE OUT BACK, SO WE CAN BRING THEM OUT AS A SURPRISE AFTER DINNER.
FRANCO, I CAN'T CARRY THIS -- YOU TAKE IT.
LET'S HIDE IT IN THE STUDY. WE'RE REPAINTING AND NO ONE WILL GO IN THERE BEFORE DINNER.
WHERE'S ILLYANA AND THE BOSS?
THEY AREN'T HERE.
WHAT? I THOUGHT--
ARGGHH!
YOU STUPID FOOL!
FTTT
FTTT

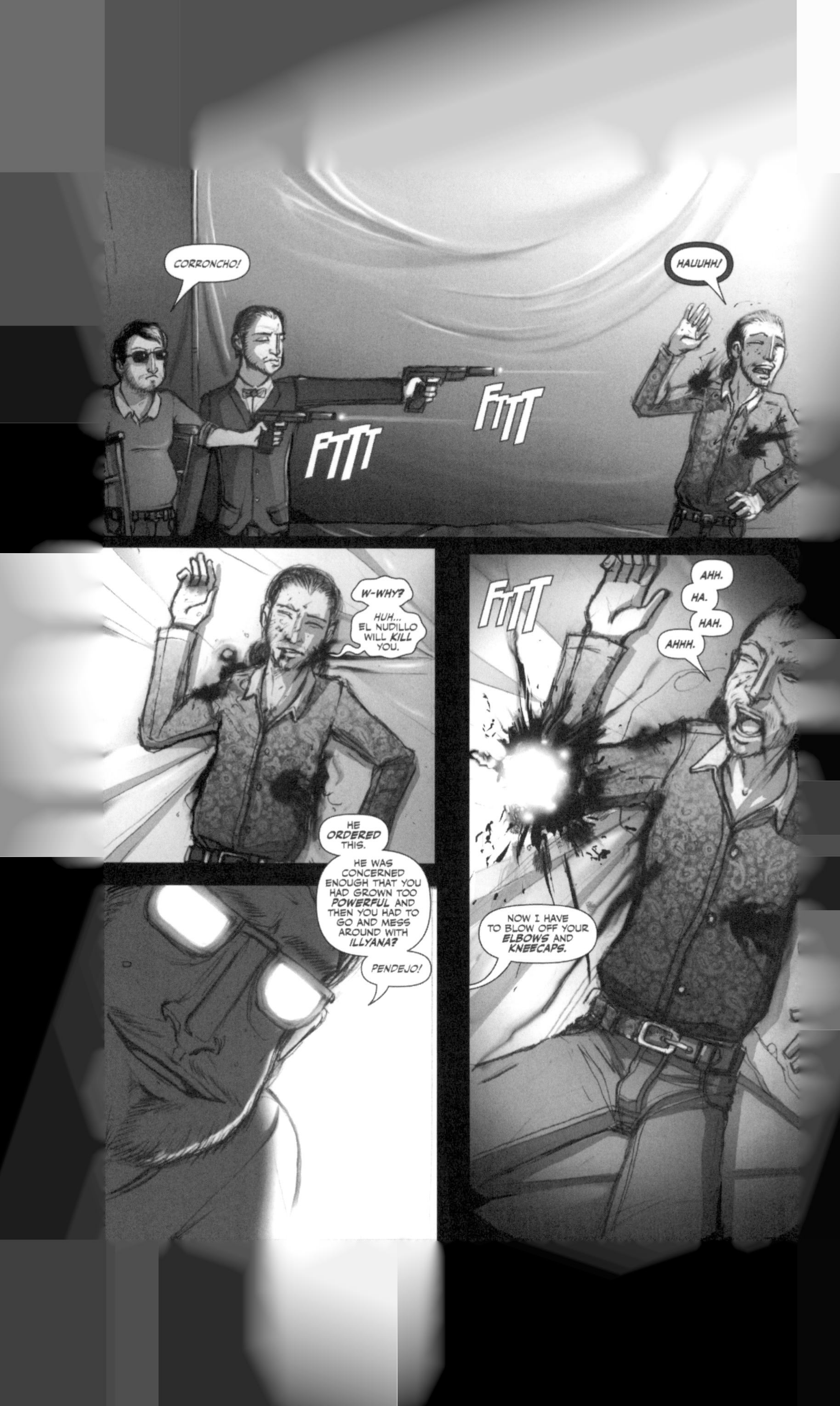
CORRONCHO!
FTTT
FTTT
HAUUHH!
W-WHY?
HUH... EL NUDILLO WILL KILL YOU.
FTTT
AHH.
HA.
HAH.
AHHH.
HE ORDERED THIS.
HE WAS CONCERNED ENOUGH THAT YOU HAD GROWN TOO POWERFUL AND THEN YOU HAD TO GO AND MESS AROUND WITH ILLYANA?
PENDEJO!
NOW I HAVE TO BLOW OFF YOUR ELBOWS AND KNEECAPS.

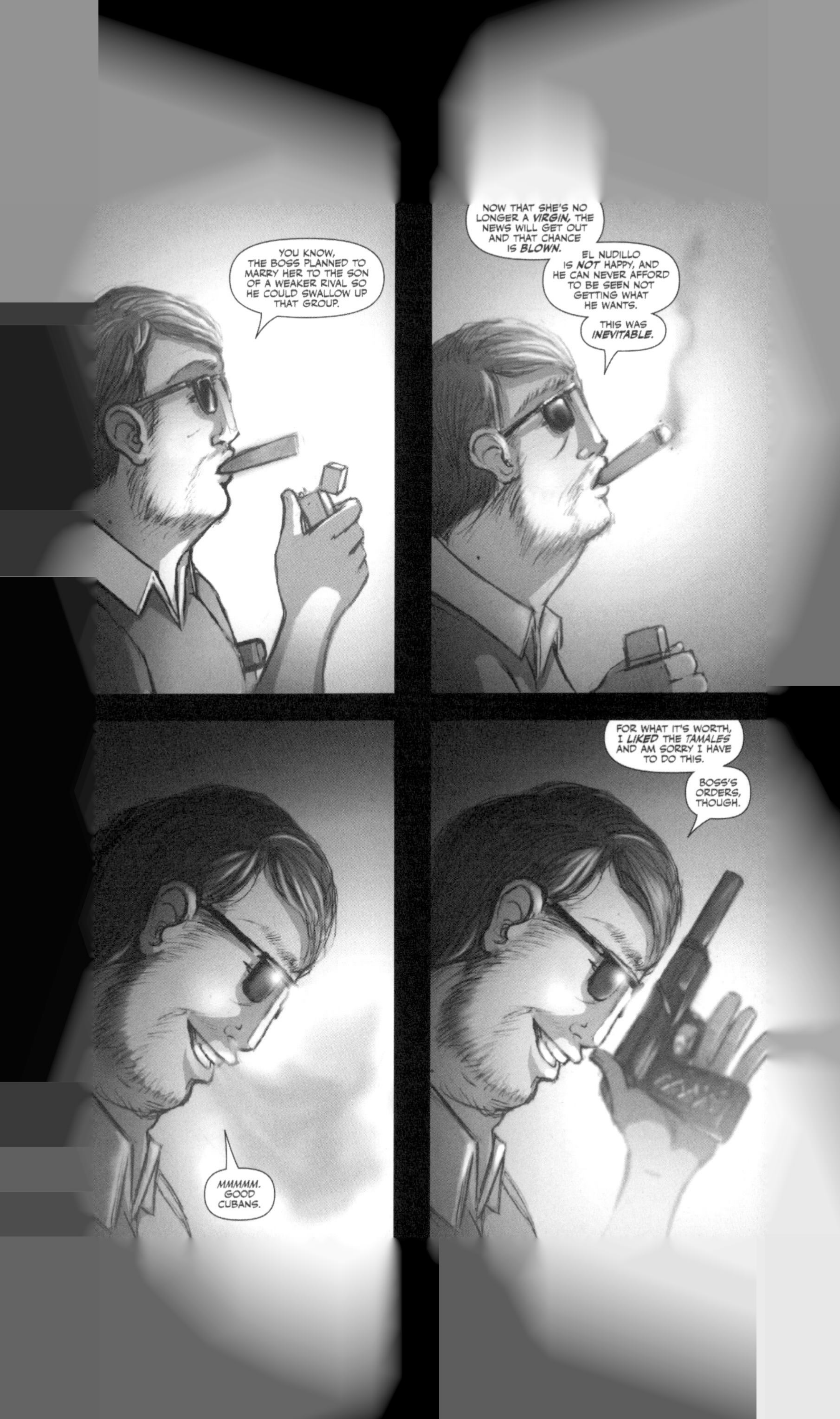
YOU KNOW, THE BOSS PLANNED TO MARRY HER TO THE SON OF A WEAKER RIVAL SO HE COULD SWALLOW UP THAT GROUP.
NOW THAT SHE'S NO LONGER A *VIRGIN*, THE NEWS WILL GET OUT AND THAT CHANCE IS *BLOWN*.
EL NUDILLO IS *NOT* HAPPY, AND HE CAN NEVER AFFORD TO BE SEEN NOT GETTING WHAT HE WANTS.
THIS WAS *INEVITABLE*.
MMMMM. GOOD CUBANS.
FOR WHAT IT'S WORTH, I *LIKED* THE *TAMALES* AND AM SORRY I HAVE TO DO THIS.
BOSS'S ORDERS, THOUGH.

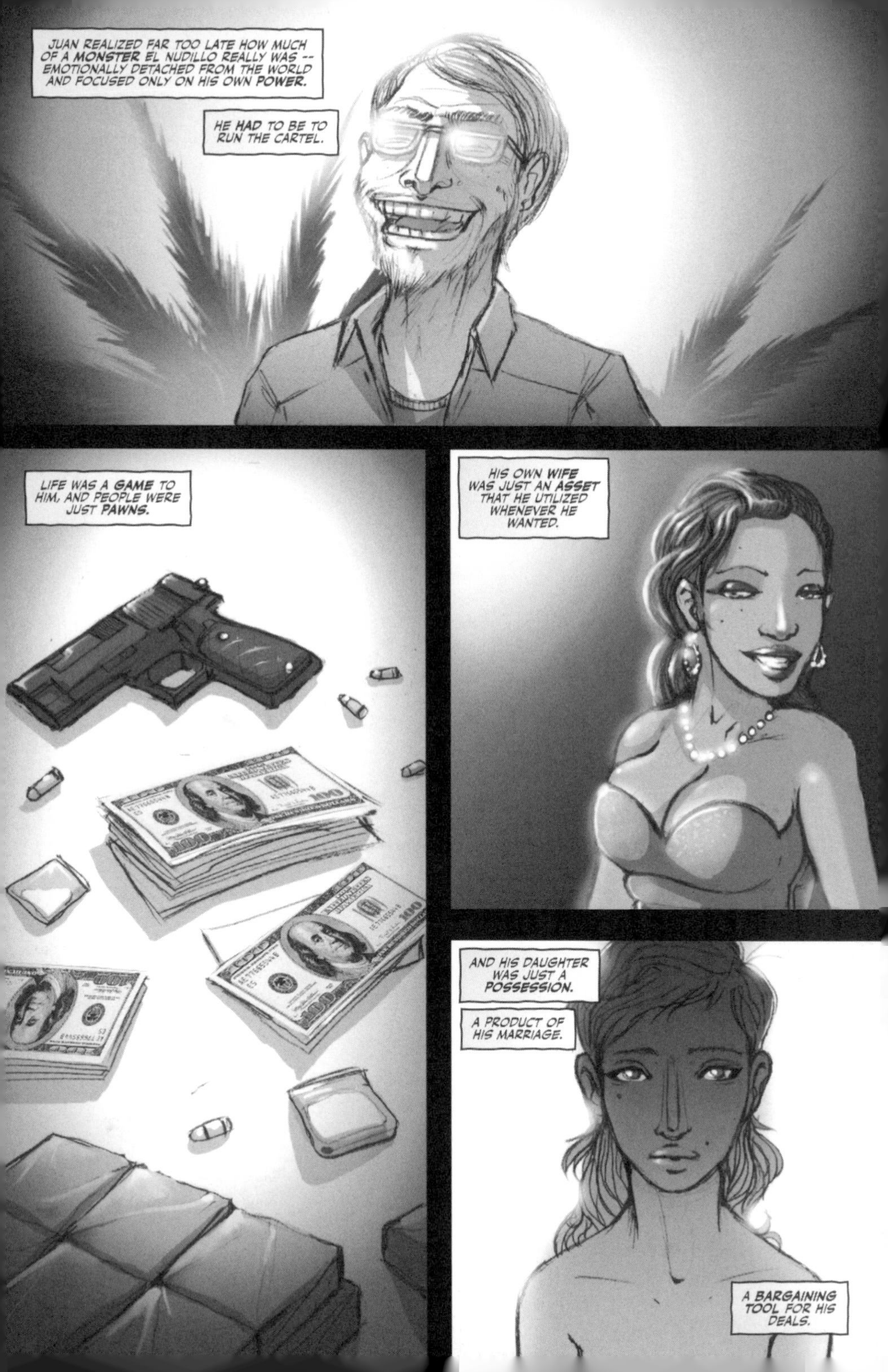
JUAN REALIZED FAR TOO LATE HOW MUCH OF A MONSTER EL NUDILLO REALLY WAS -- EMOTIONALLY DETACHED FROM THE WORLD AND FOCUSED ONLY ON HIS OWN POWER.
HE HAD TO BE TO RUN THE CARTEL.
LIFE WAS A GAME TO HIM, AND PEOPLE WERE JUST PAWNS.
HIS OWN WIFE WAS JUST AN ASSET THAT HE UTILIZED WHENEVER HE WANTED.
AND HIS DAUGHTER WAS JUST A POSSESSION.
A PRODUCT OF HIS MARRIAGE.
A BARGAINING TOOL FOR HIS DEALS.

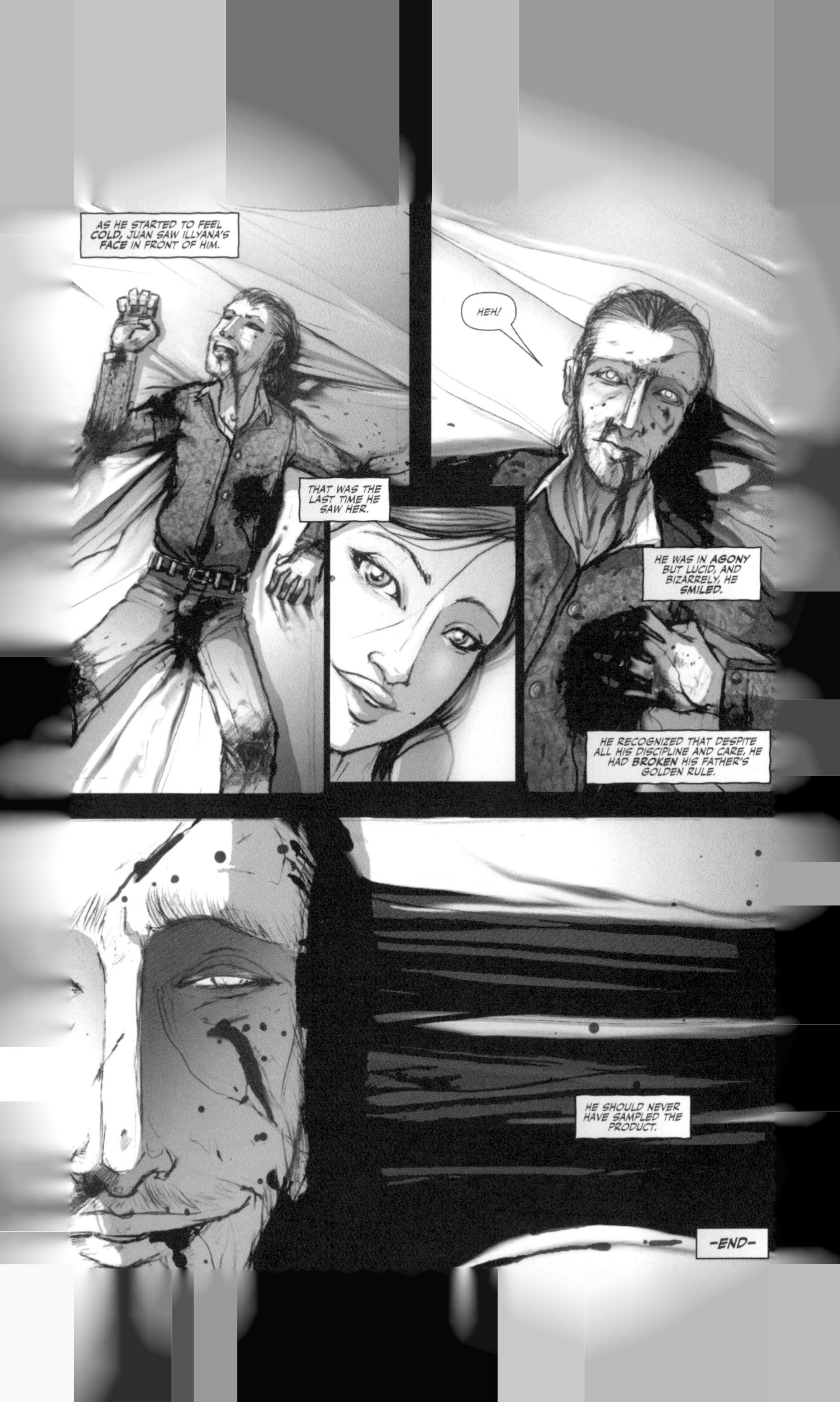

AS HE STARTED TO FEEL COLD, JUAN SAW ILLYANA'S FACE IN FRONT OF HIM.
HEH!
THAT WAS THE LAST TIME HE SAW HER.
HE WAS IN AGONY BUT LUCID, AND BIZARRELY, HE SMILED.
HE RECOGNIZED THAT DESPITE ALL HIS DISCIPLINE AND CARE, HE HAD BROKEN HIS FATHER'S GOLDEN RULE.
HE SHOULD NEVER HAVE SAMPLED THE PRODUCT.
-END-

The Pushman...

"With all of its shame, drudgery, and broken dreams,
it is still a beautiful world.
Be Cheerful.
Strive to be happy."

--Max Ehrmann

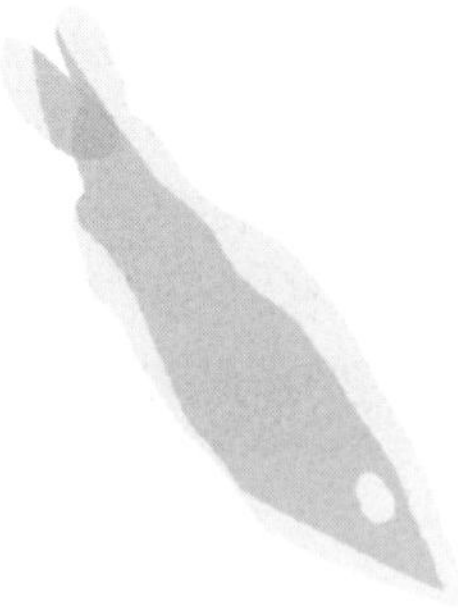

Writer/Creator
Neil Gibson

Illustrator
Jan Wijngaard

www.tpub.co.uk

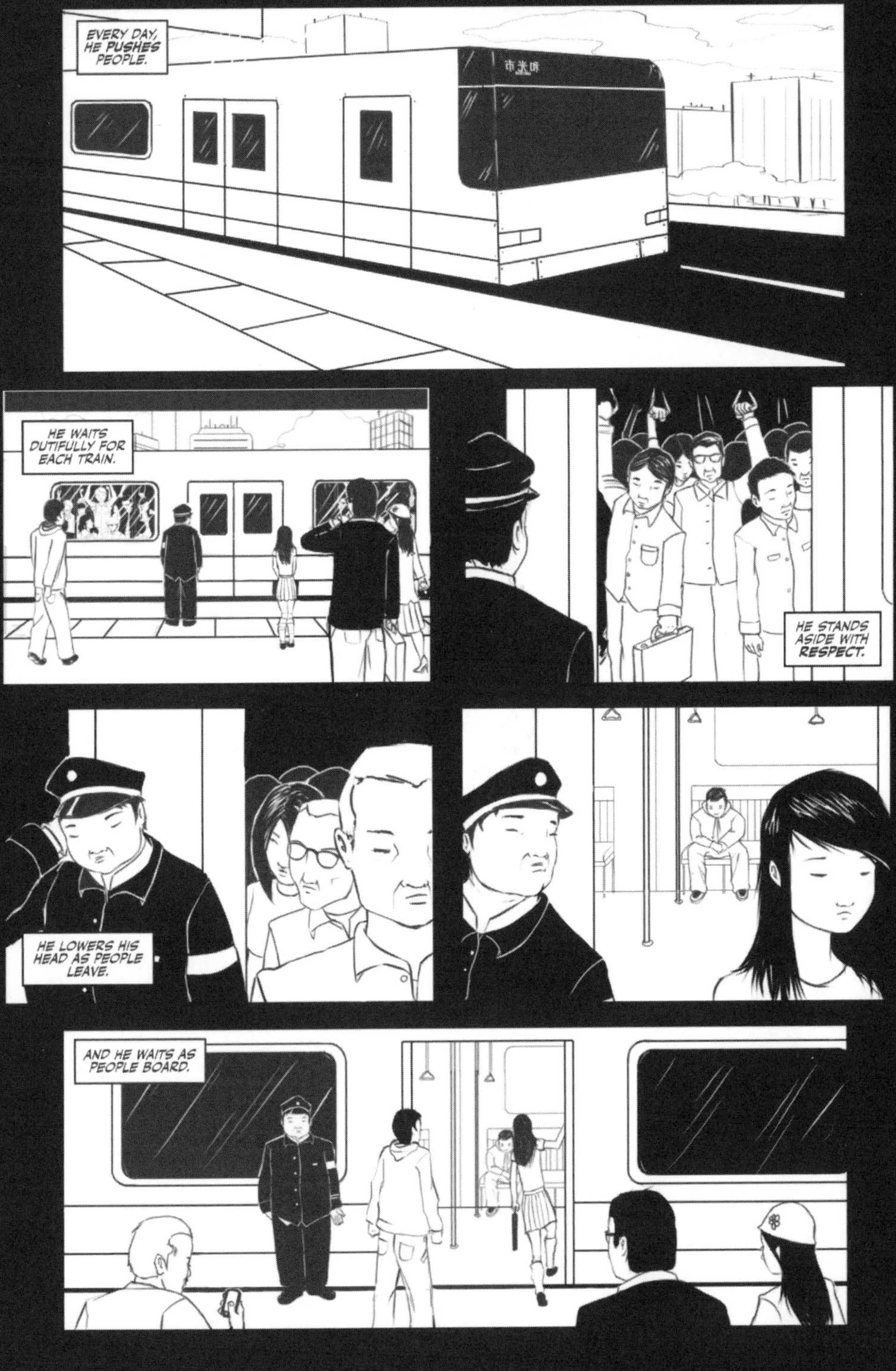
EVERY DAY, HE PUSHES PEOPLE.
HE WAITS DUTIFULLY FOR EACH TRAIN.
HE STANDS ASIDE WITH RESPECT.
HE LOWERS HIS HEAD AS PEOPLE LEAVE.
AND HE WAITS AS PEOPLE BOARD.

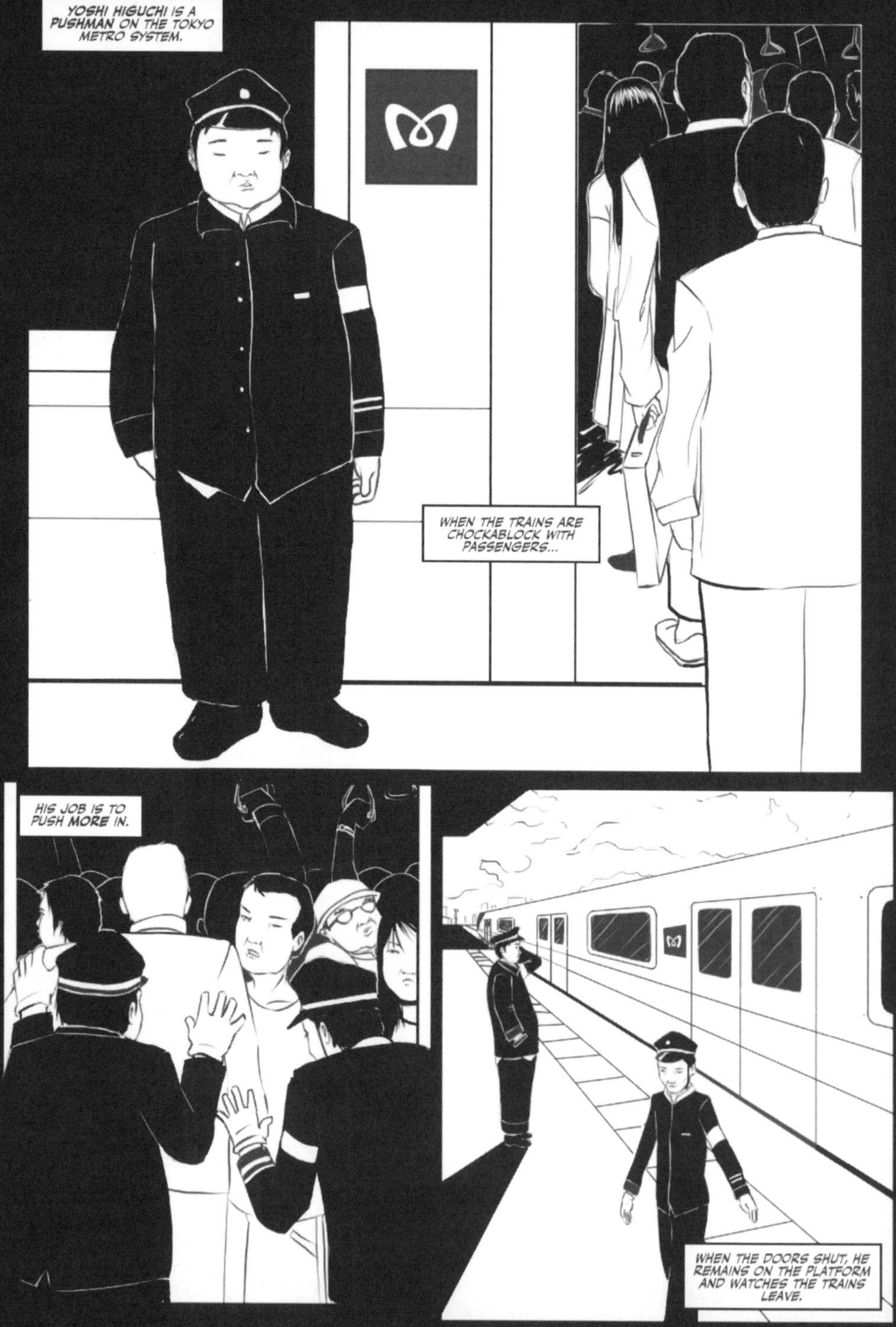
YOSHI HIGUCHI IS A PUSHMAN ON THE TOKYO METRO SYSTEM.
WHEN THE TRAINS ARE CHOCKABLOCK WITH PASSENGERS...
HIS JOB IS TO PUSH MORE IN.
WHEN THE DOORS SHUT, HE REMAINS ON THE PLATFORM AND WATCHES THE TRAINS LEAVE.

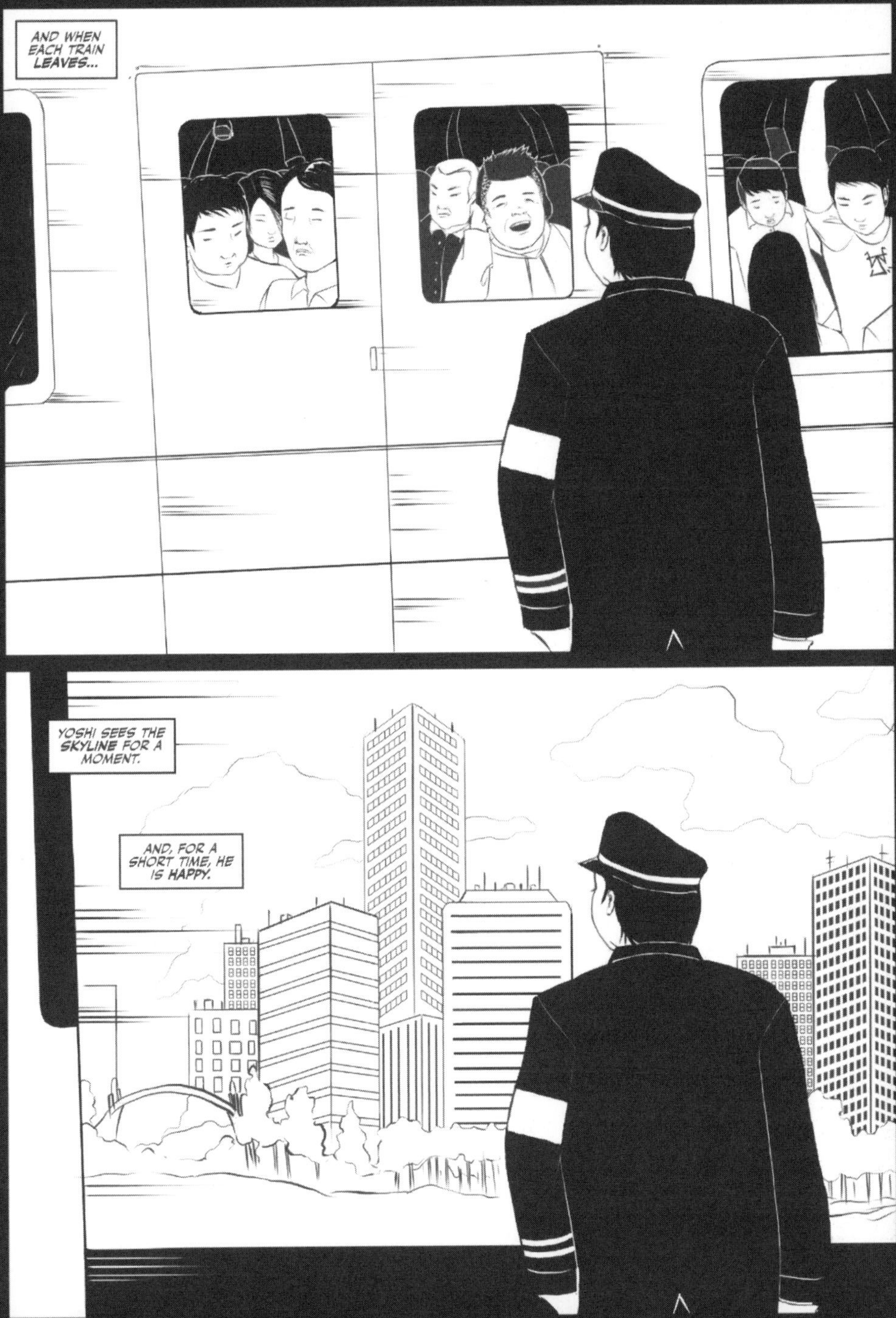
AND WHEN EACH TRAIN LEAVES...
YOSHI SEES THE SKYLINE FOR A MOMENT.
AND, FOR A SHORT TIME, HE IS HAPPY.

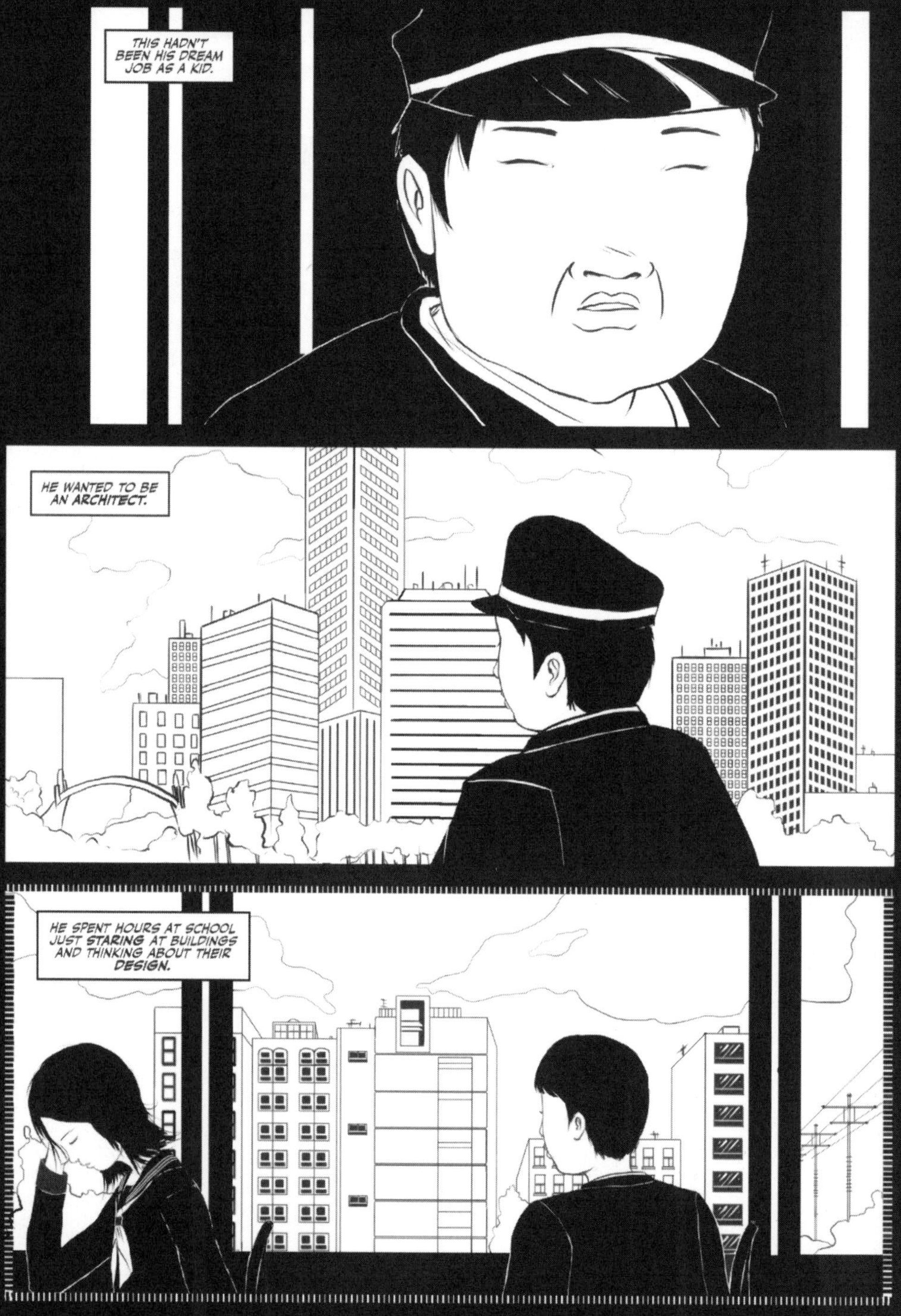
THIS HADN'T BEEN HIS DREAM JOB AS A KID.
HE WANTED TO BE AN ARCHITECT.
HE SPENT HOURS AT SCHOOL JUST STARING AT BUILDINGS AND THINKING ABOUT THEIR DESIGN.

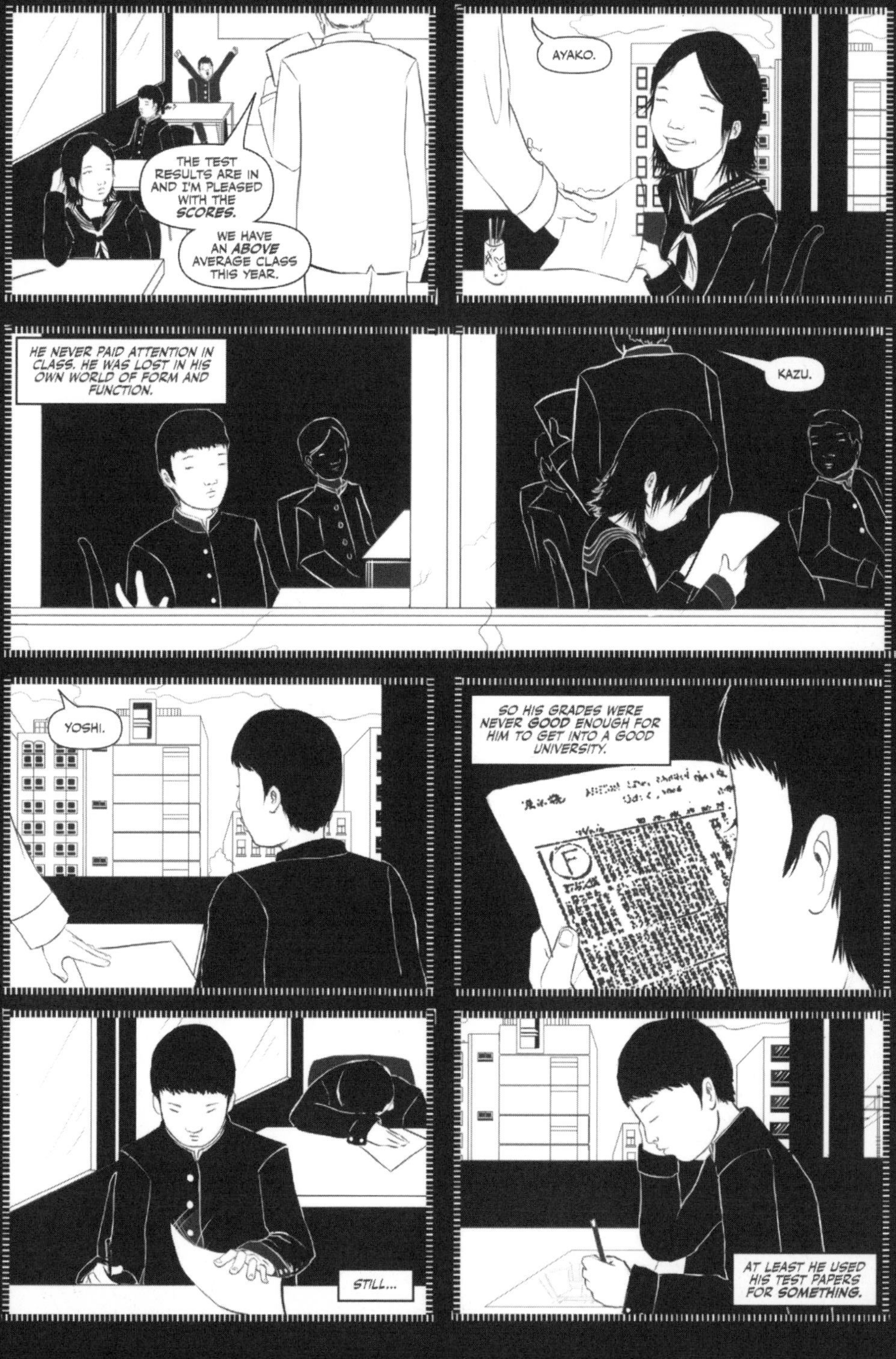
THE TEST RESULTS ARE IN AND I'M PLEASED WITH THE SCORES.
WE HAVE AN ABOVE AVERAGE CLASS THIS YEAR.
AYAKO.
HE NEVER PAID ATTENTION IN CLASS. HE WAS LOST IN HIS OWN WORLD OF FORM AND FUNCTION.
KAZU.
YOSHI.
SO HIS GRADES WERE NEVER GOOD ENOUGH FOR HIM TO GET INTO A GOOD UNIVERSITY.
F
STILL...
AT LEAST HE USED HIS TEST PAPERS FOR SOMETHING.

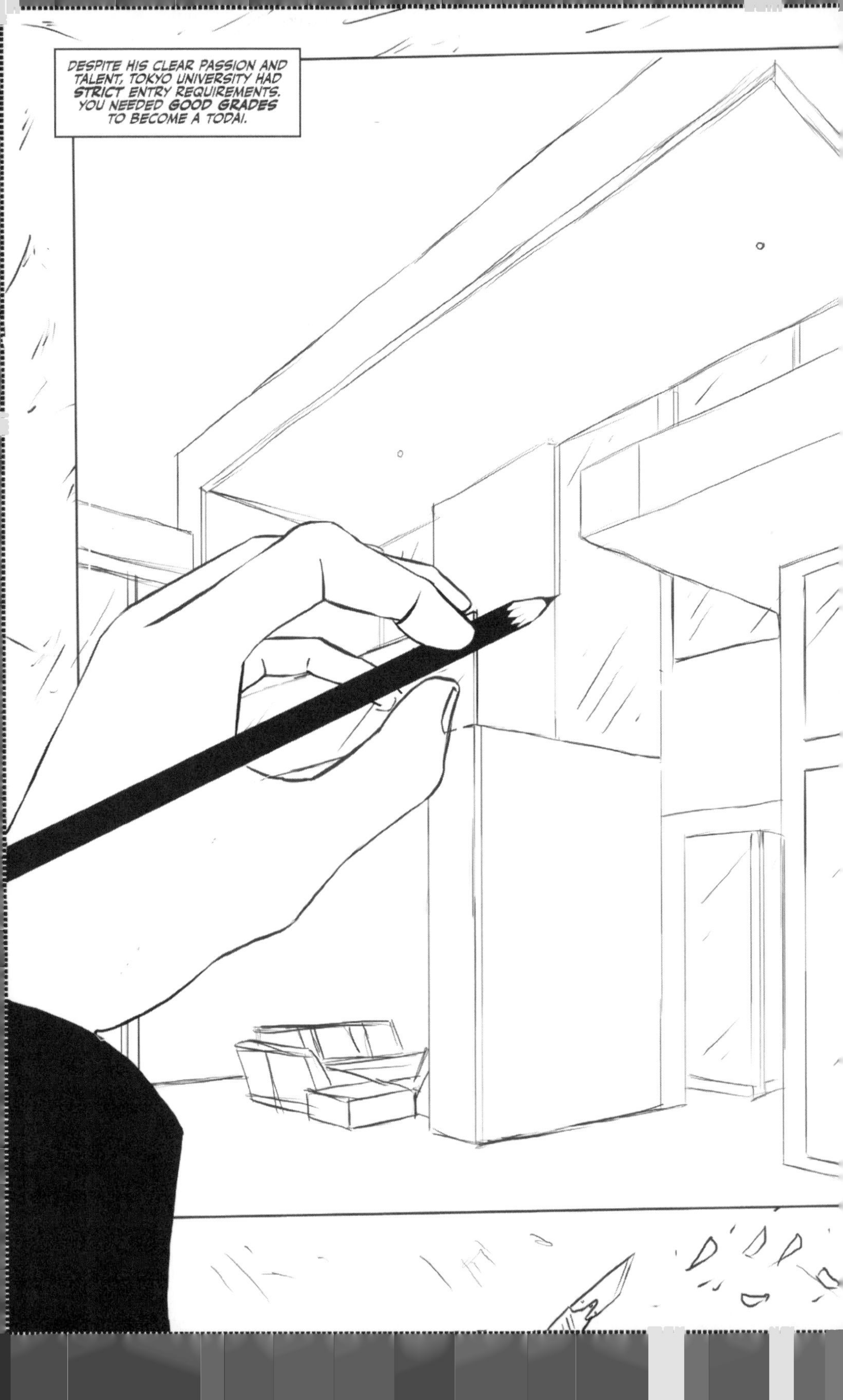
DESPITE HIS CLEAR PASSION AND TALENT, TOKYO UNIVERSITY HAD STRICT ENTRY REQUIREMENTS. YOU NEEDED GOOD GRADES TO BECOME A TODAI.

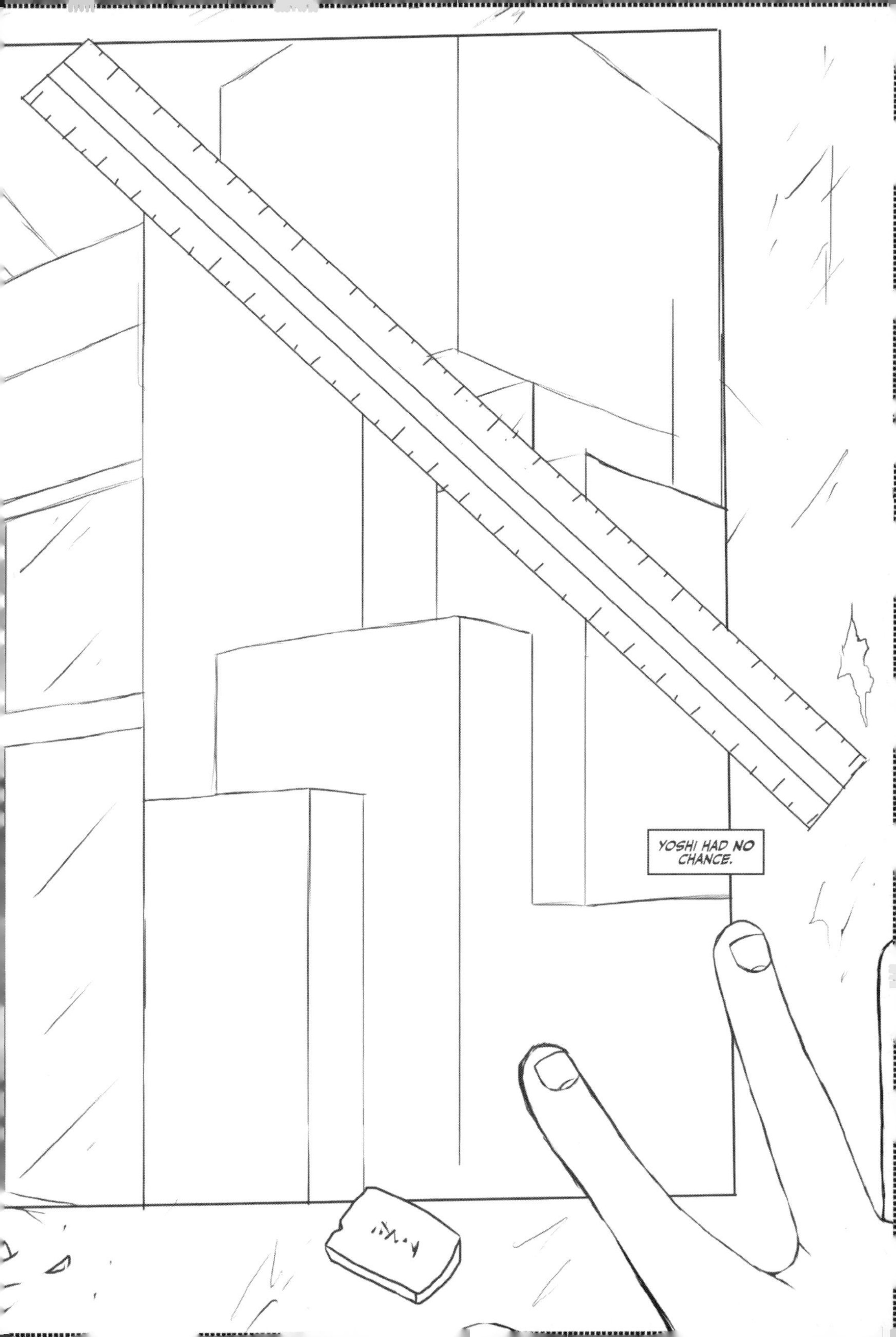
YOSHI HAD NO CHANCE.

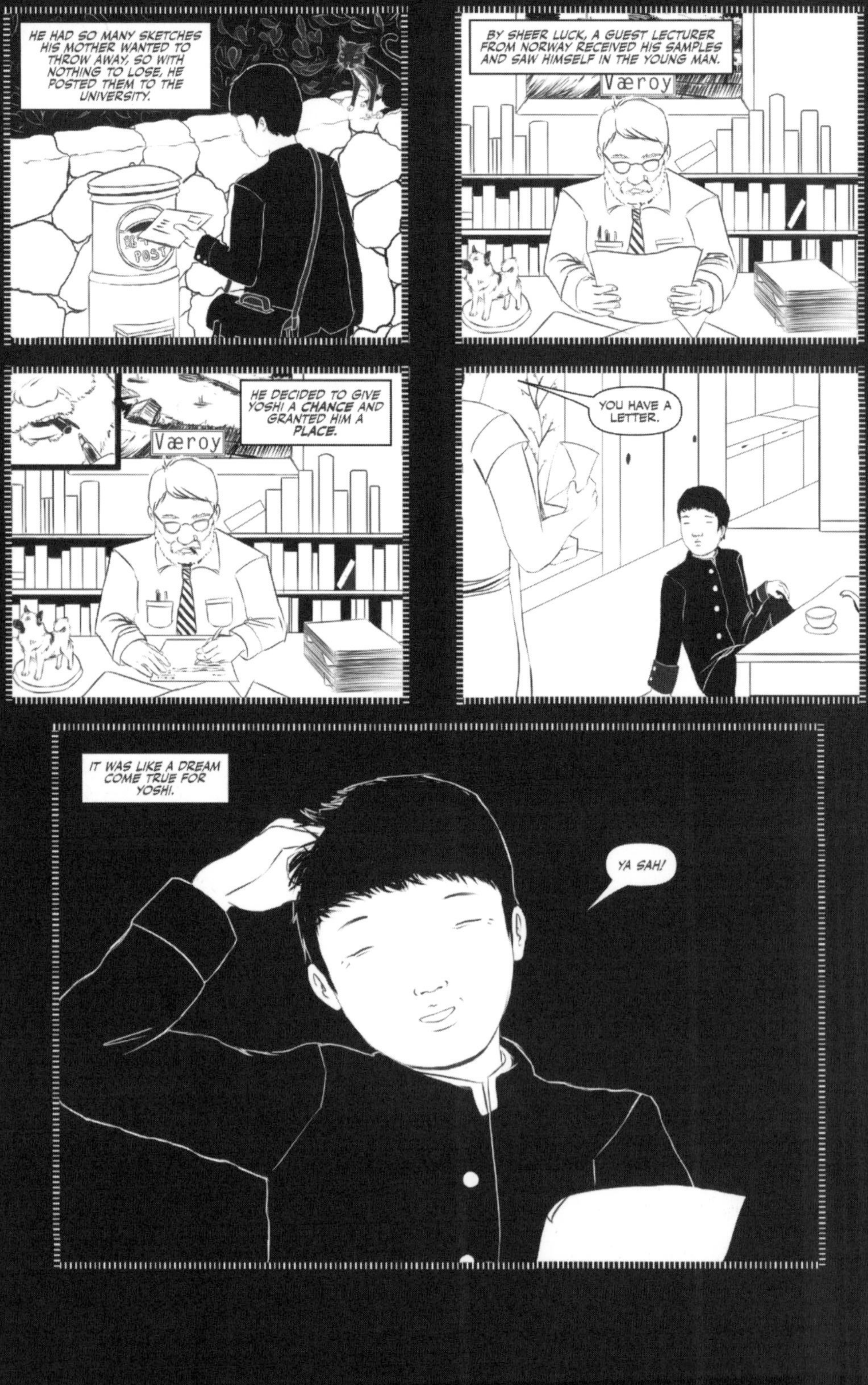
HE HAD SO MANY SKETCHES HIS MOTHER WANTED TO THROW AWAY, SO WITH NOTHING TO LOSE, HE POSTED THEM TO THE UNIVERSITY.
POST
BY SHEER LUCK, A GUEST LECTURER FROM NORWAY RECEIVED HIS SAMPLES AND SAW HIMSELF IN THE YOUNG MAN.
Værøy
Værøy
HE DECIDED TO GIVE YOSHI A CHANCE AND GRANTED HIM A PLACE.
YOU HAVE A LETTER.
IT WAS LIKE A DREAM COME TRUE FOR YOSHI.
YA SAH!

BUT DREAMS OFTEN FADE...
HIS FATHER GOT SICK AT THE START OF HIS FIRST TERM, CUTTING THE FAMILY INCOME.
YOSHI HAD NO CHOICE BUT TO DROP OUT AND FIND A JOB.
NOW, EVERY DAY...
HE PUSHES PEOPLE.

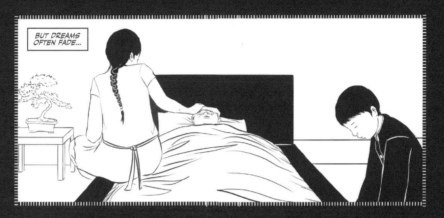

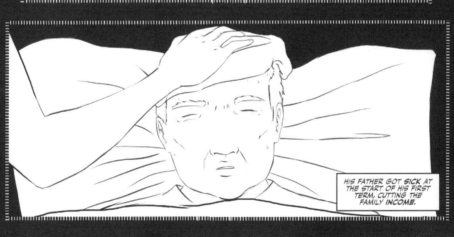

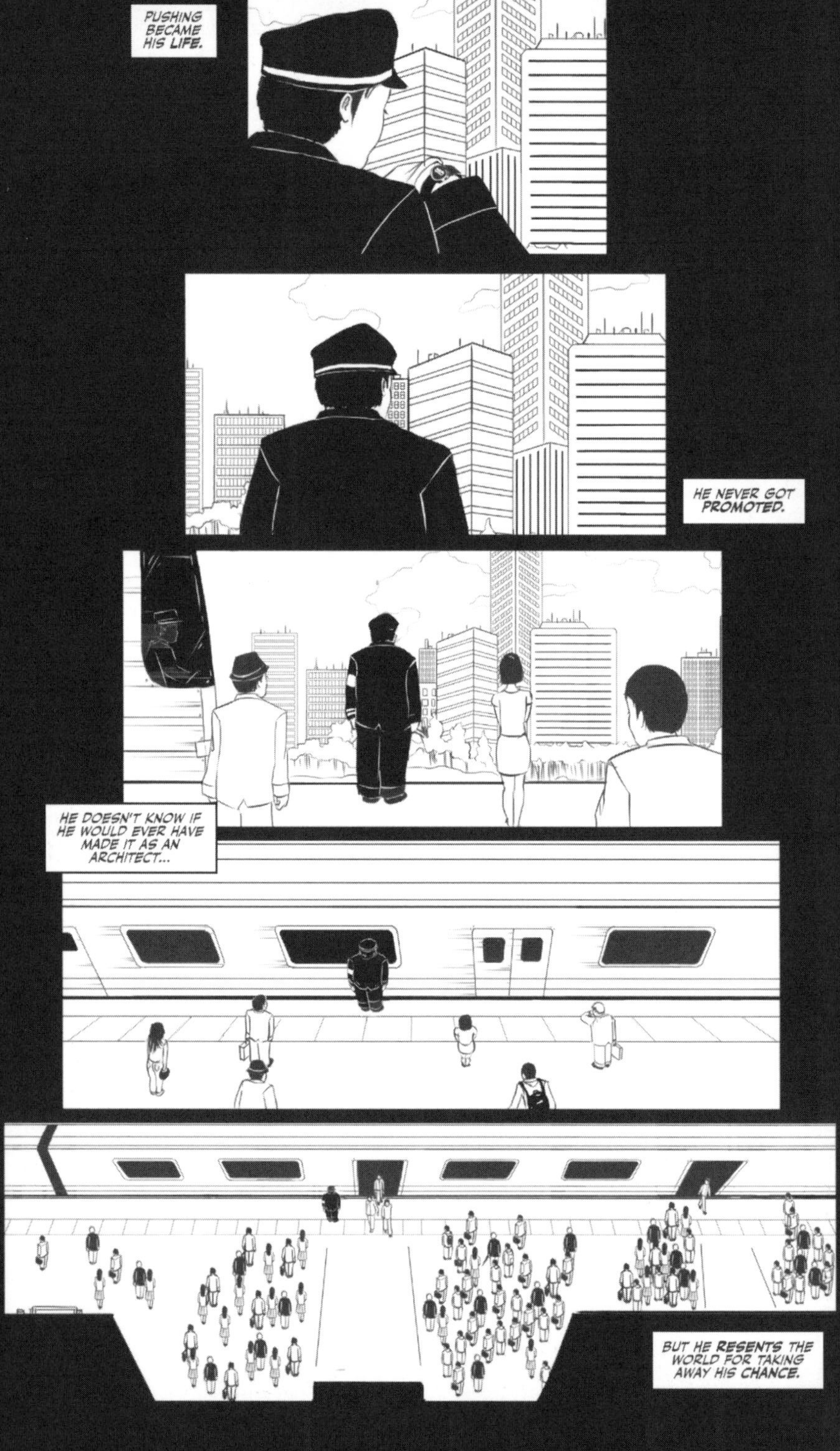
PUSHING BECAME HIS LIFE.
HE NEVER GOT PROMOTED.
HE DOESN'T KNOW IF HE WOULD EVER HAVE MADE IT AS AN ARCHITECT...
BUT HE RESENTS THE WORLD FOR TAKING AWAY HIS CHANCE.

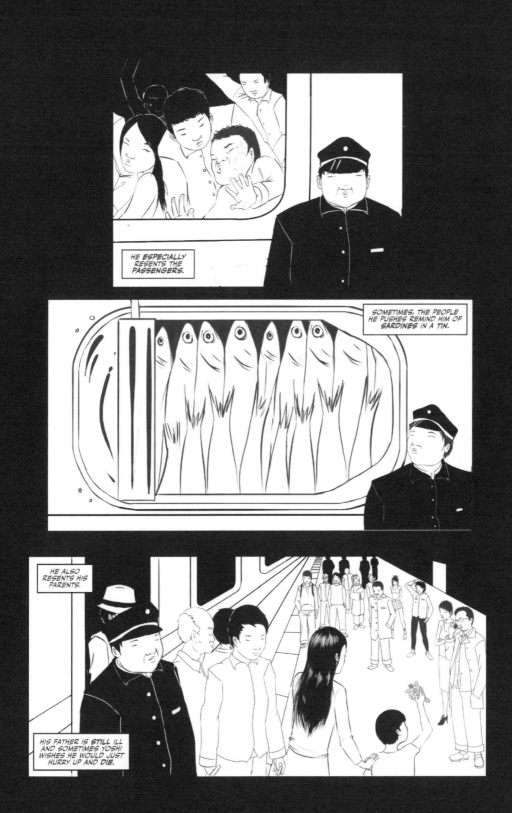

HE ESPECIALLY RESENTS THE PASSENGERS.

SOMETIMES, THE PEOPLE HE PUSHES REMIND HIM OF SARDINES IN A TIN.

HE ALSO RESENTS HIS PARENTS.

HIS FATHER IS STILL ILL AND SOMETIMES YOSHI WISHES HE WOULD JUST HURRY UP AND DIE.

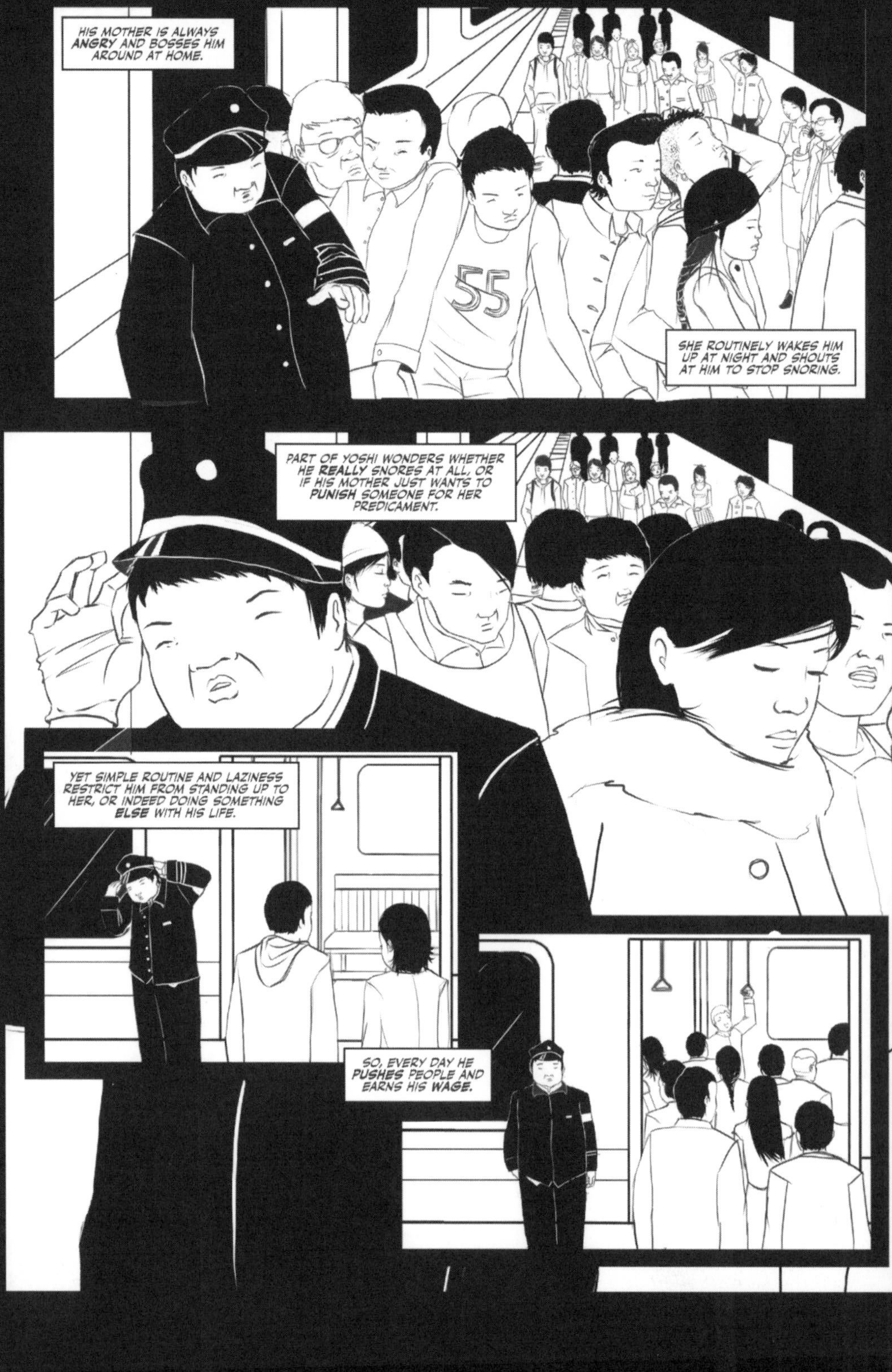
HIS MOTHER IS ALWAYS ANGRY AND BOSSES HIM AROUND AT HOME.
55
SHE ROUTINELY WAKES HIM UP AT NIGHT AND SHOUTS AT HIM TO STOP SNORING.
PART OF YOSHI WONDERS WHETHER HE REALLY SNORES AT ALL, OR IF HIS MOTHER JUST WANTS TO PUNISH SOMEONE FOR HER PREDICAMENT.
YET SIMPLE ROUTINE AND LAZINESS RESTRICT HIM FROM STANDING UP TO HER, OR INDEED DOING SOMETHING ELSE WITH HIS LIFE.
SO, EVERY DAY HE PUSHES PEOPLE AND EARNS HIS WAGE.

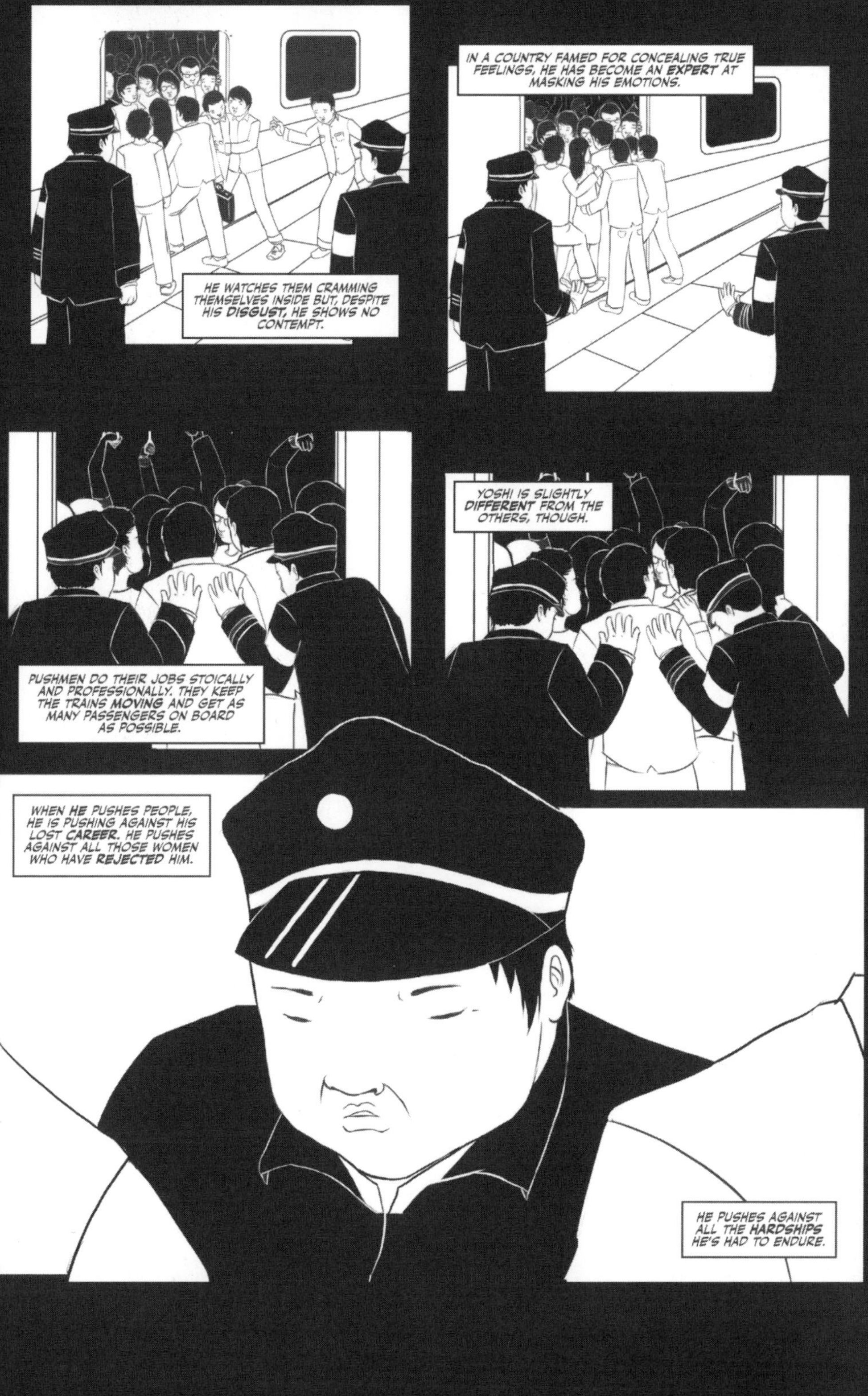
HE WATCHES THEM CRAMMING THEMSELVES INSIDE BUT, DESPITE HIS DISGUST, HE SHOWS NO CONTEMPT.
IN A COUNTRY FAMED FOR CONCEALING TRUE FEELINGS, HE HAS BECOME AN EXPERT AT MASKING HIS EMOTIONS.
PUSHMEN DO THEIR JOBS STOICALLY AND PROFESSIONALLY. THEY KEEP THE TRAINS MOVING AND GET AS MANY PASSENGERS ON BOARD AS POSSIBLE.
YOSHI IS SLIGHTLY DIFFERENT FROM THE OTHERS, THOUGH.
WHEN HE PUSHES PEOPLE, HE IS PUSHING AGAINST HIS LOST CAREER. HE PUSHES AGAINST ALL THOSE WOMEN WHO HAVE REJECTED HIM.
HE PUSHES AGAINST ALL THE HARDSHIPS HE'S HAD TO ENDURE.

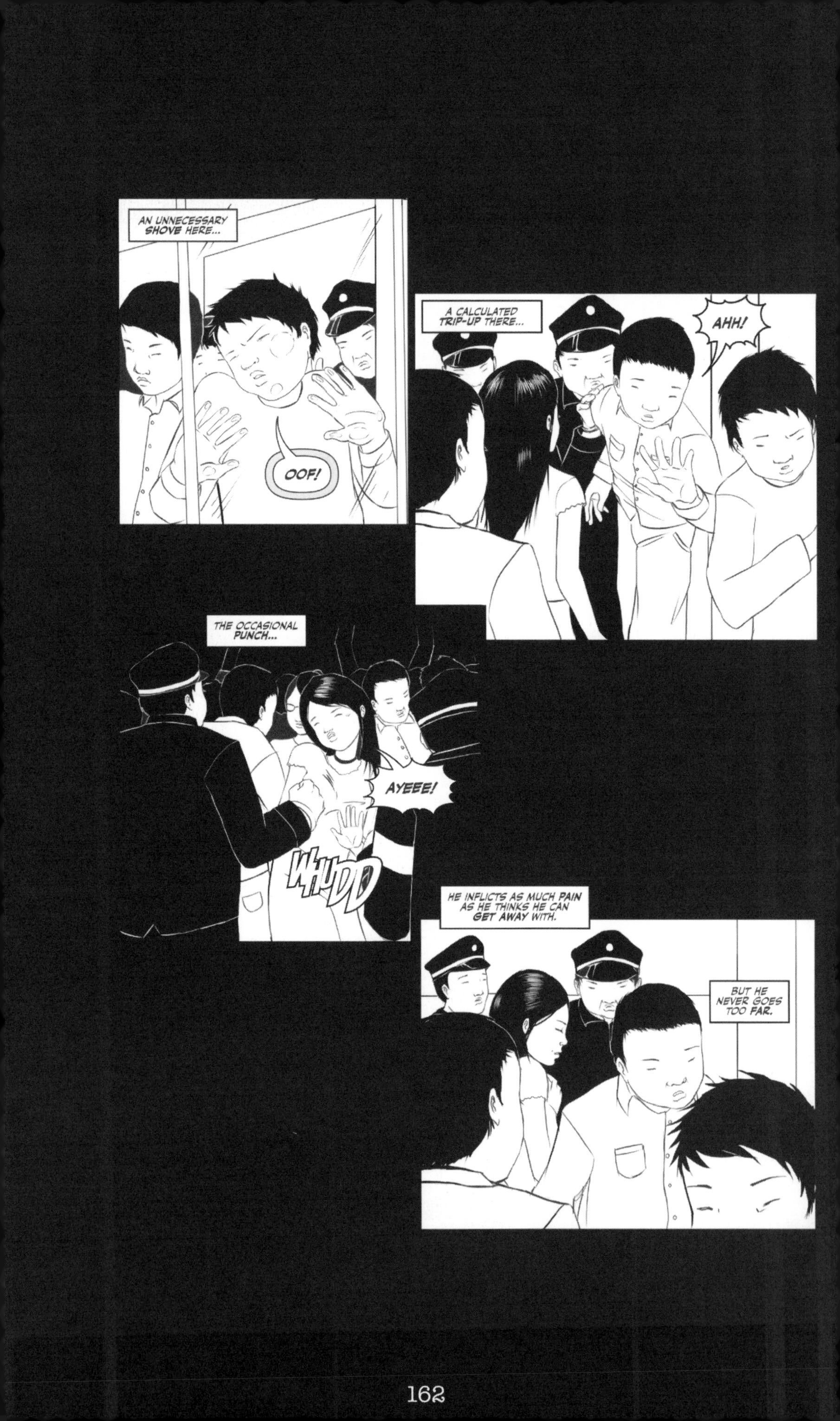
AN UNNECESSARY SHOVE HERE...
OOF!
A CALCULATED TRIP-UP THERE...
AHH!
THE OCCASIONAL PUNCH...
AYEEE!
WHUDD
HE INFLICTS AS MUCH PAIN AS HE THINKS HE CAN GET AWAY WITH.
BUT HE NEVER GOES TOO FAR.

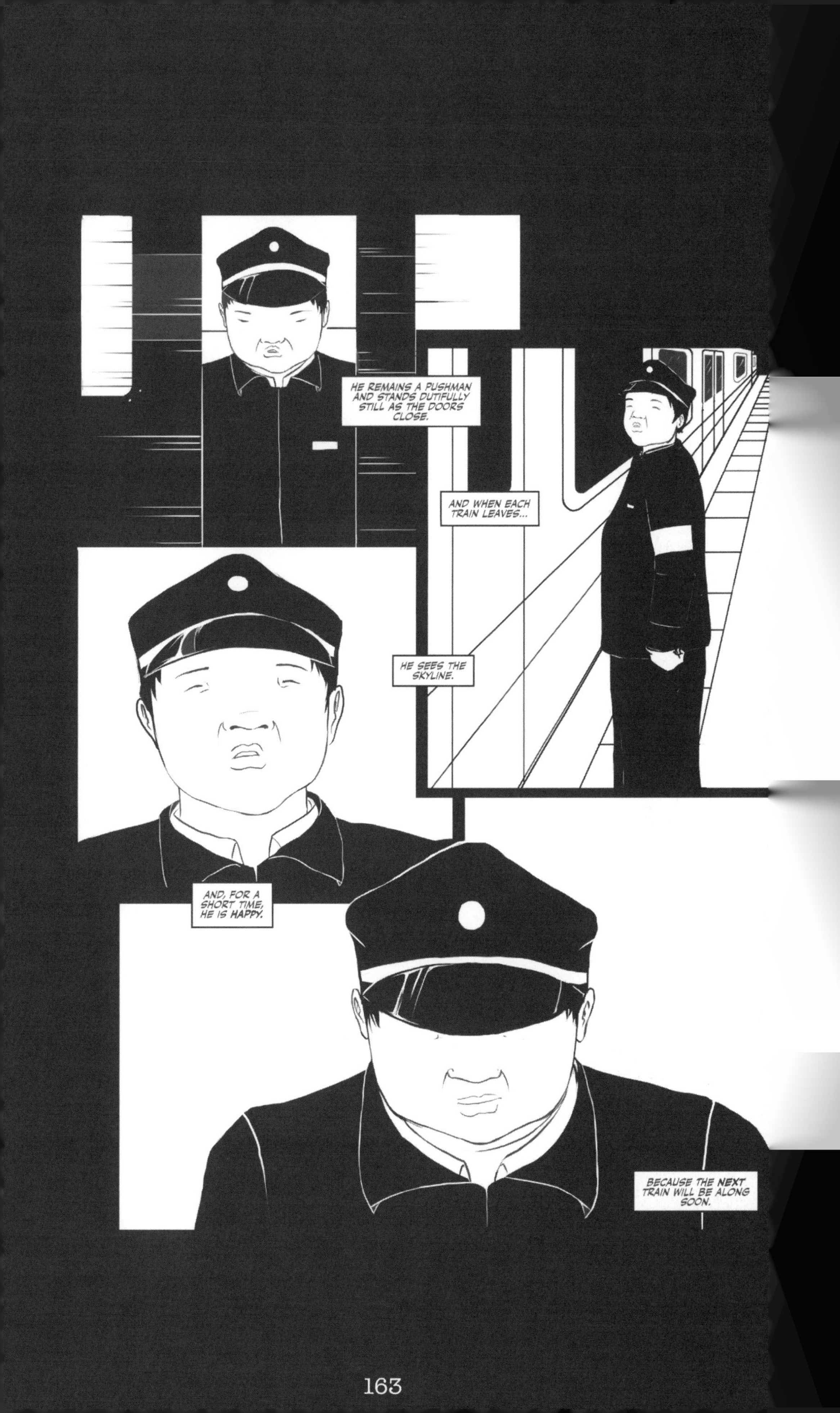
HE REMAINS A PUSHMAN AND STANDS DUTIFULLY STILL AS THE DOORS CLOSE.
AND WHEN EACH TRAIN LEAVES...
HE SEES THE SKYLINE.
AND, FOR A SHORT TIME, HE IS HAPPY.
BECAUSE THE NEXT TRAIN WILL BE ALONG SOON.

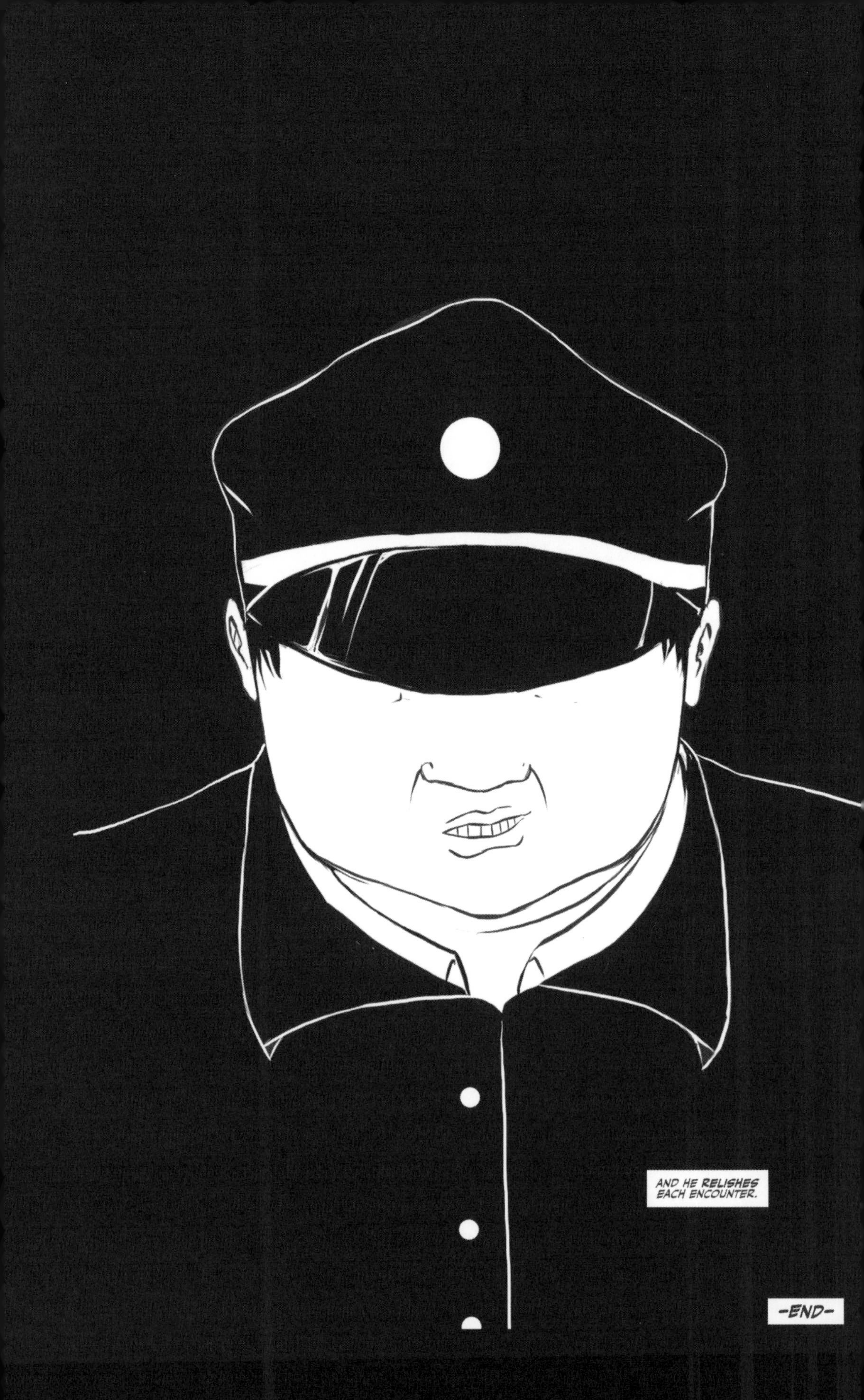
AND HE RELISHES
EACH ENCOUNTER.
-END-

Münchausen's Little Proxy...

"It's like I have a loaded gun in my mouth, and i like the taste of metal."

--Robert Downey Jr., on his addiction

Writer/Creator
Neil Gibson

Illustrator
Jan Wijngaard

www.tpub.co.uk

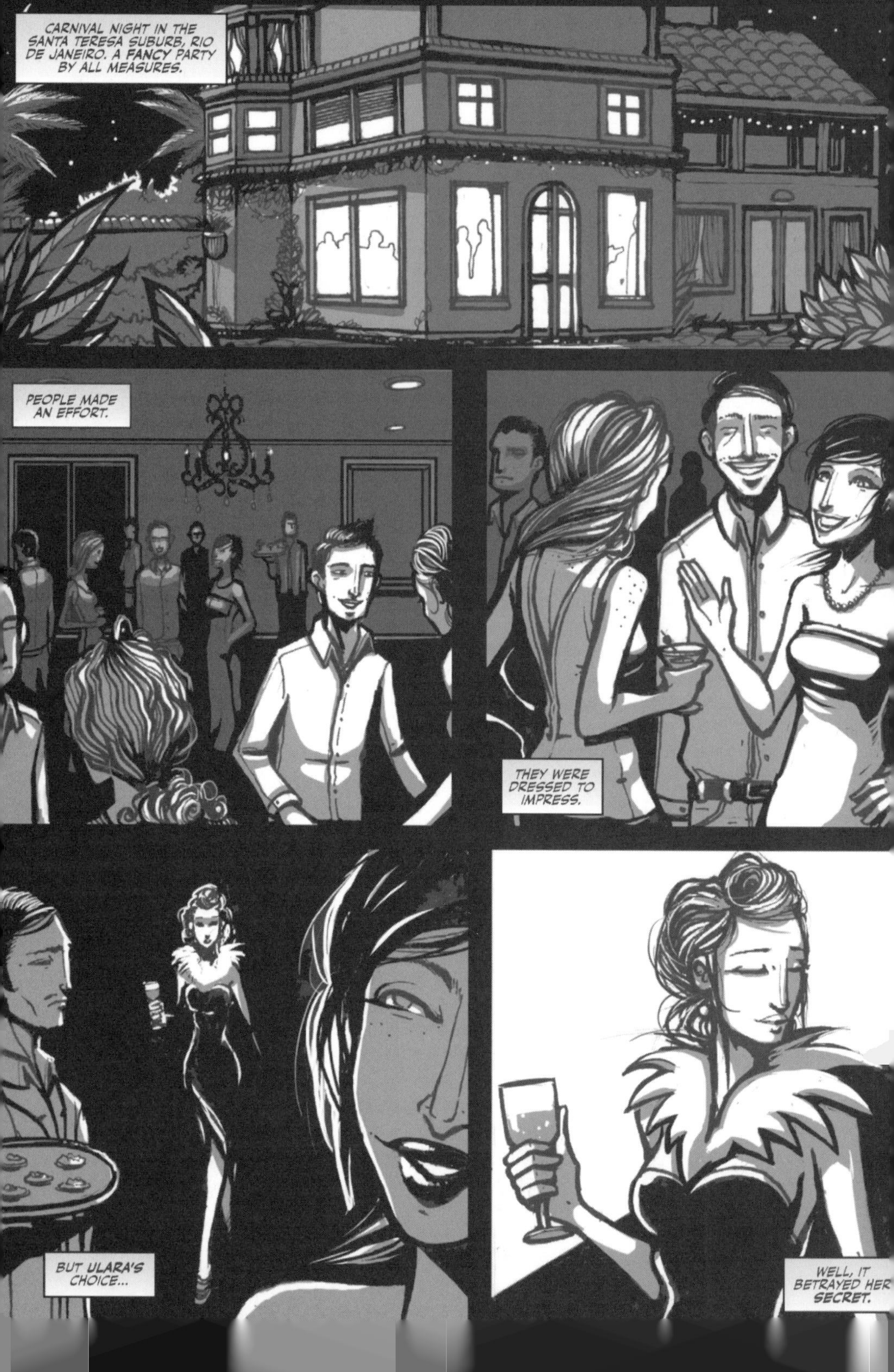
CARNIVAL NIGHT IN THE SANTA TERESA SUBURB, RIO DE JANEIRO. A FANCY PARTY BY ALL MEASURES.
PEOPLE MADE AN EFFORT.
THEY WERE DRESSED TO IMPRESS.
BUT ULARA'S CHOICE...
WELL, IT BETRAYED HER SECRET.

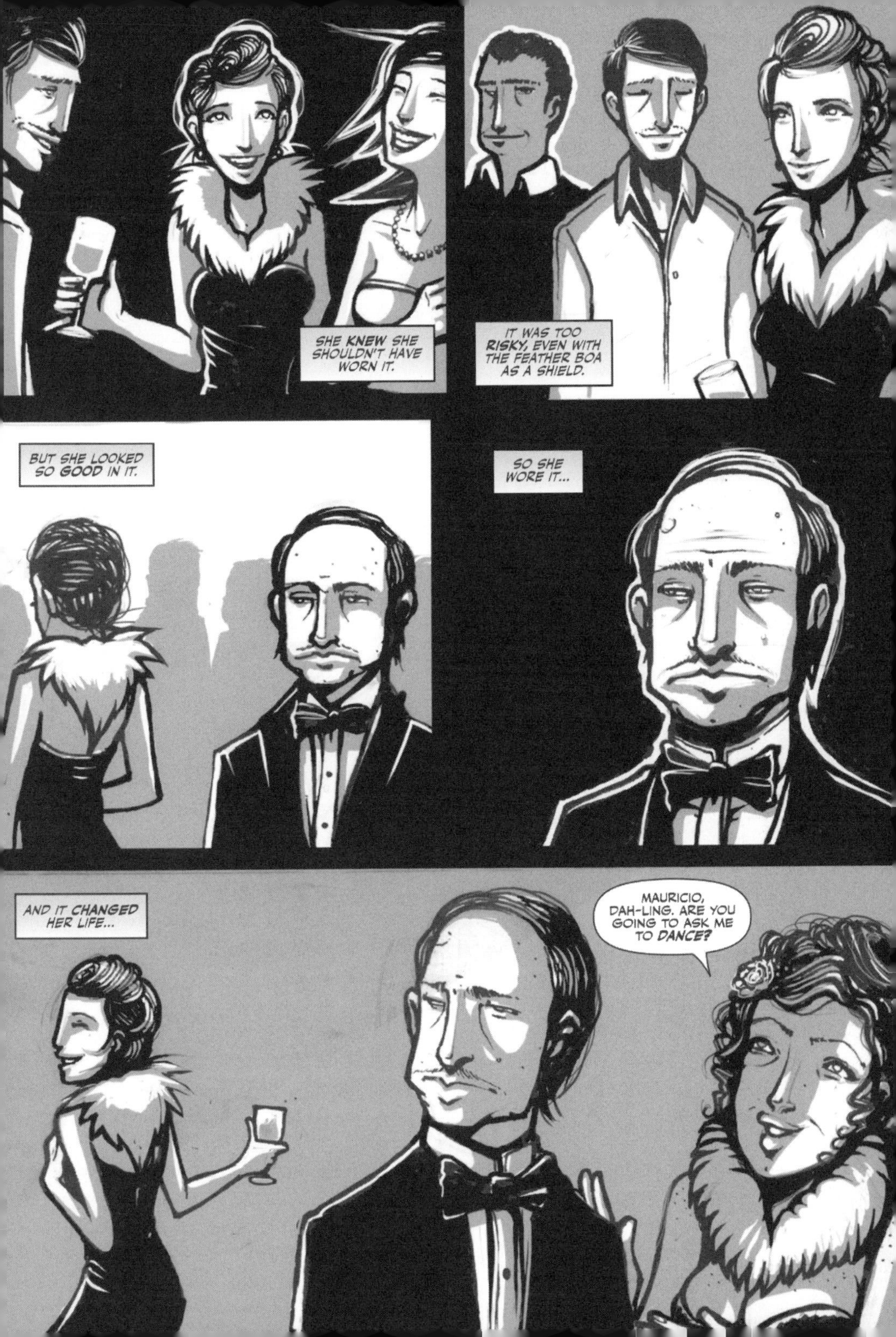
SHE KNEW SHE SHOULDN'T HAVE WORN IT.
IT WAS TOO RISKY, EVEN WITH THE FEATHER BOA AS A SHIELD.
BUT SHE LOOKED SO GOOD IN IT.
SO SHE WORE IT...
AND IT CHANGED HER LIFE...
MAURICIO, DAH-LING. ARE YOU GOING TO ASK ME TO DANCE?

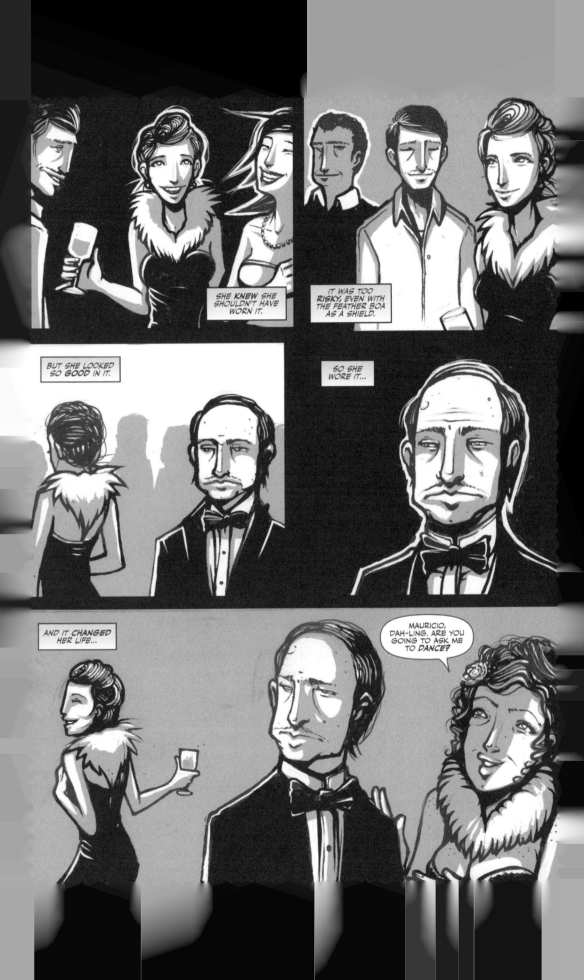

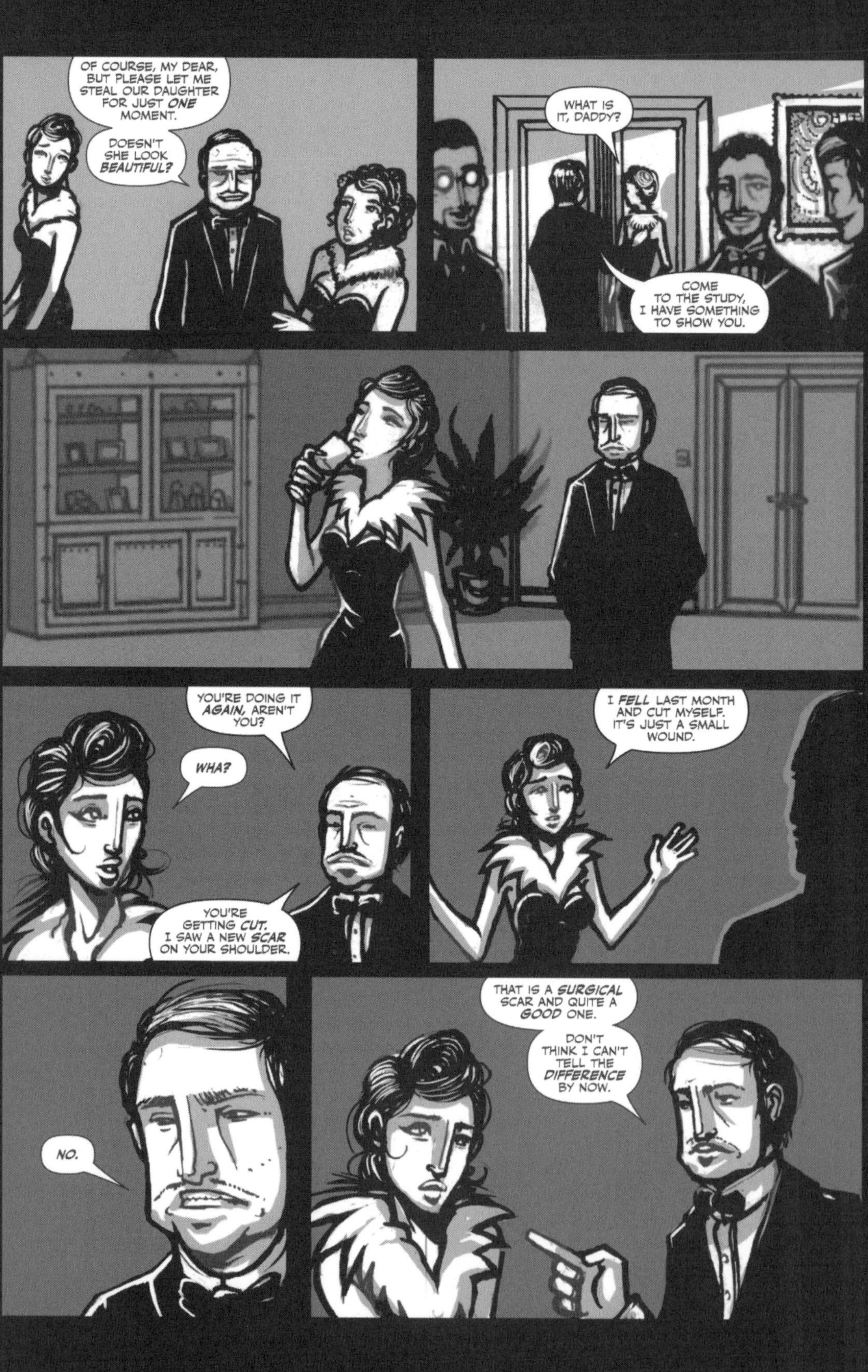
OF COURSE, MY DEAR, BUT PLEASE LET ME STEAL OUR DAUGHTER FOR JUST ONE MOMENT.
DOESN'T SHE LOOK BEAUTIFUL?
WHAT IS IT, DADDY?
COME TO THE STUDY, I HAVE SOMETHING TO SHOW YOU.
YOU'RE DOING IT AGAIN, AREN'T YOU?
WHA?
YOU'RE GETTING CUT. I SAW A NEW SCAR ON YOUR SHOULDER.
I FELL LAST MONTH AND CUT MYSELF. IT'S JUST A SMALL WOUND.
NO.
THAT IS A SURGICAL SCAR AND QUITE A GOOD ONE.
DON'T THINK I CAN'T TELL THE DIFFERENCE BY NOW.

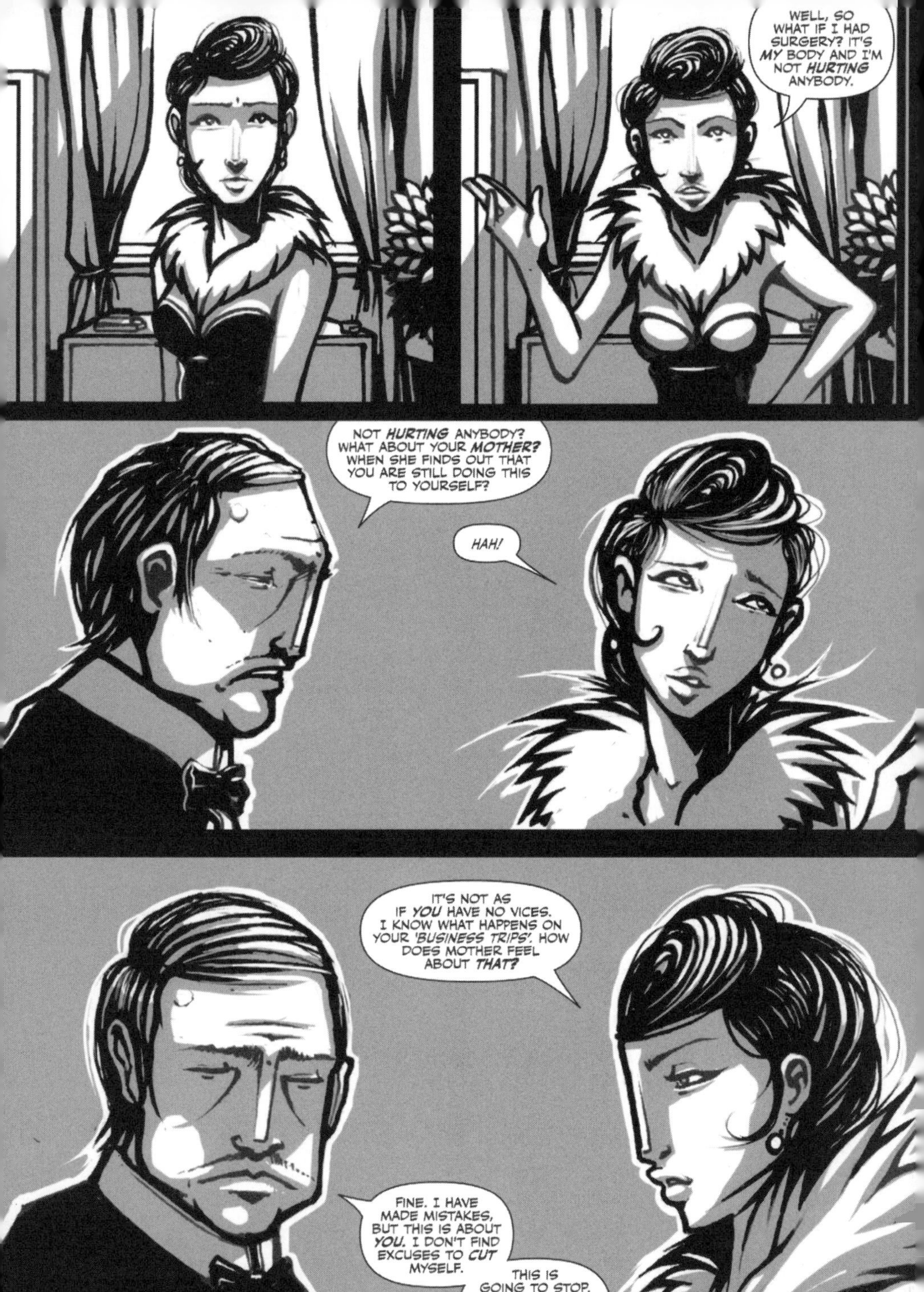

WELL, SO WHAT IF I HAD SURGERY? IT'S MY BODY AND I'M NOT HURTING ANYBODY.
NOT HURTING ANYBODY? WHAT ABOUT YOUR MOTHER? WHEN SHE FINDS OUT THAT YOU ARE STILL DOING THIS TO YOURSELF?
HAH!
IT'S NOT AS IF YOU HAVE NO VICES. I KNOW WHAT HAPPENS ON YOUR 'BUSINESS TRIPS'. HOW DOES MOTHER FEEL ABOUT THAT?
FINE. I HAVE MADE MISTAKES, BUT THIS IS ABOUT YOU. I DON'T FIND EXCUSES TO CUT MYSELF.
THIS IS GOING TO STOP. YOU ARE SICK AND NEED HELP. I WILL TOLERATE THIS NO LONGER.

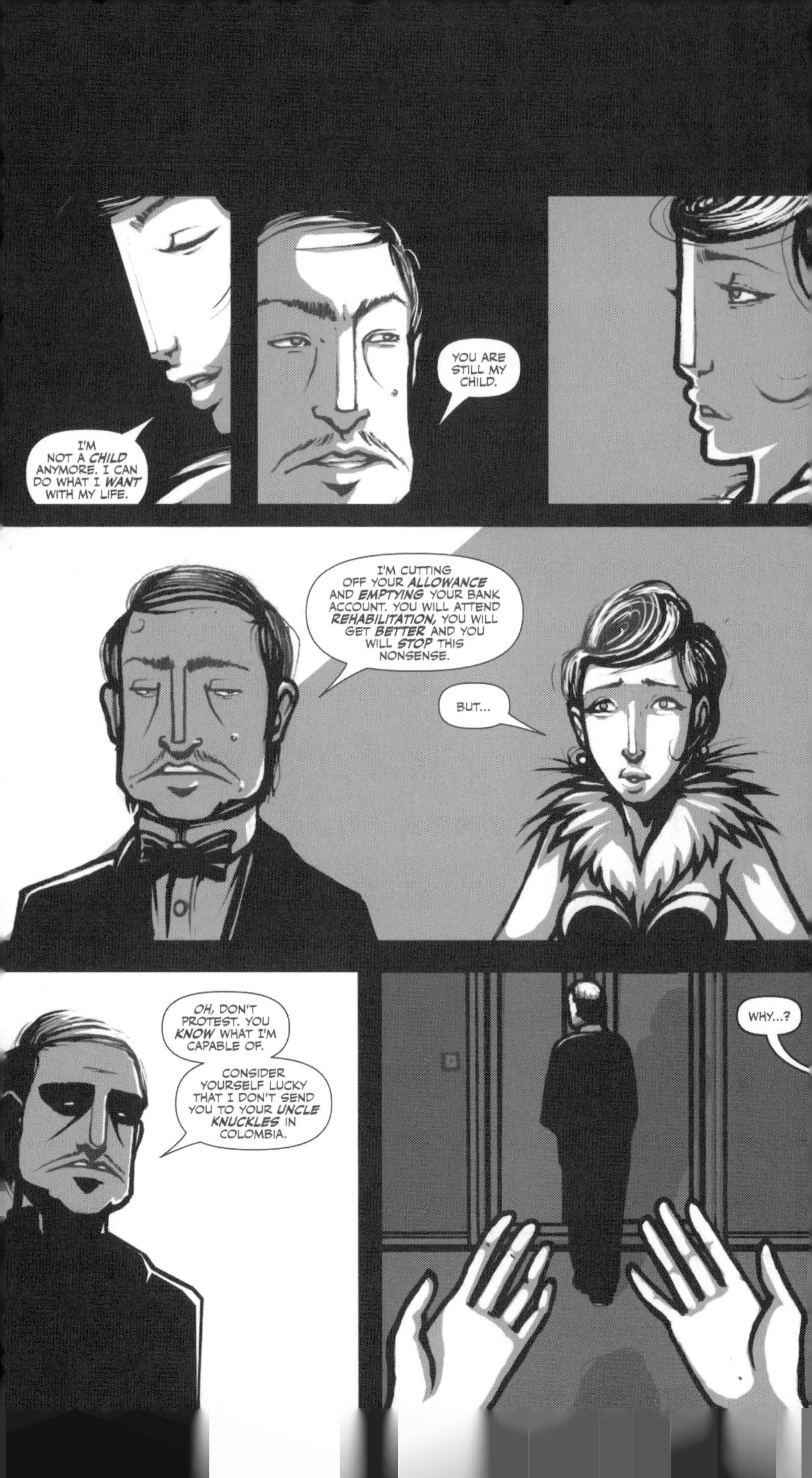
I'M NOT A CHILD ANYMORE. I CAN DO WHAT I WANT WITH MY LIFE.
YOU ARE STILL MY CHILD.
I'M CUTTING OFF YOUR ALLOWANCE AND EMPTYING YOUR BANK ACCOUNT. YOU WILL ATTEND REHABILITATION, YOU WILL GET BETTER AND YOU WILL STOP THIS NONSENSE.
BUT...
OH, DON'T PROTEST. YOU KNOW WHAT I'M CAPABLE OF.
CONSIDER YOURSELF LUCKY THAT I DON'T SEND YOU TO YOUR UNCLE KNUCKLES IN COLOMBIA.
WHY...?

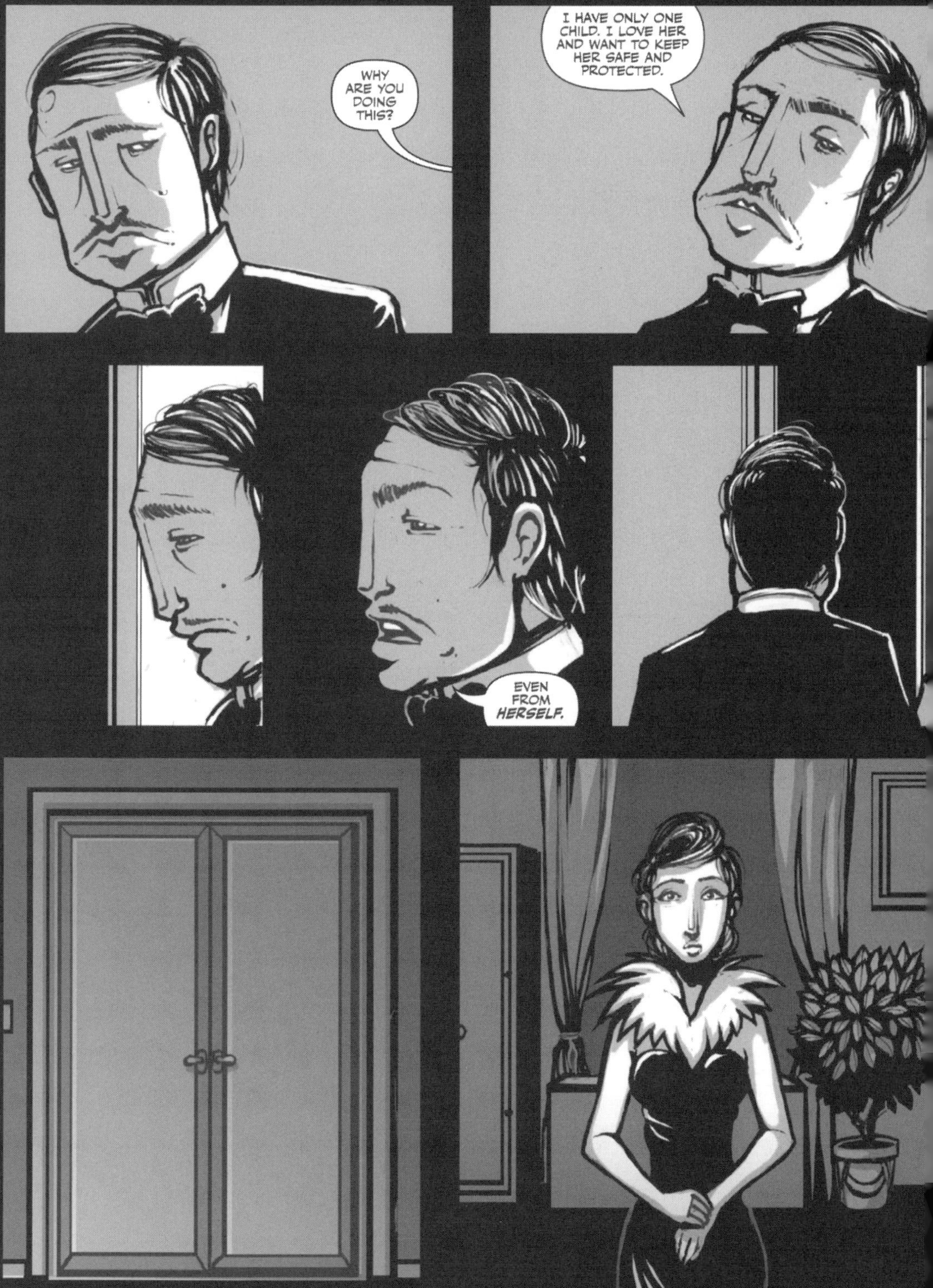
WHY ARE YOU DOING THIS?
I HAVE ONLY ONE CHILD. I LOVE HER AND WANT TO KEEP HER SAFE AND PROTECTED.
EVEN FROM *HERSELF*.

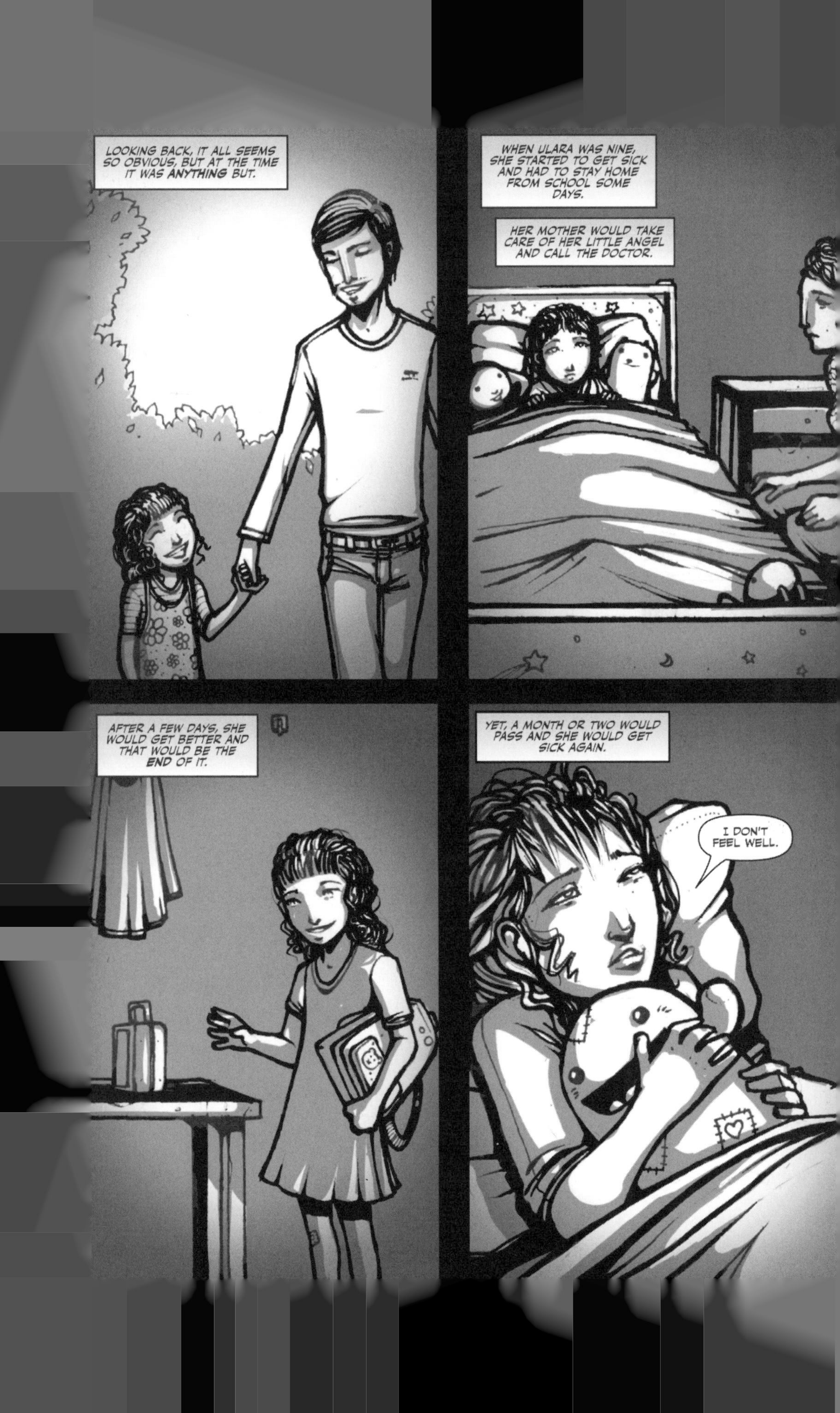
LOOKING BACK, IT ALL SEEMS SO OBVIOUS, BUT AT THE TIME IT WAS **ANYTHING** BUT.
WHEN ULARA WAS NINE, SHE STARTED TO GET SICK AND HAD TO STAY HOME FROM SCHOOL SOME DAYS.
HER MOTHER WOULD TAKE CARE OF HER LITTLE ANGEL AND CALL THE DOCTOR.
AFTER A FEW DAYS, SHE WOULD GET BETTER AND THAT WOULD BE THE **END** OF IT.
YET, A MONTH OR TWO WOULD PASS AND SHE WOULD GET SICK AGAIN.
I DON'T FEEL WELL.

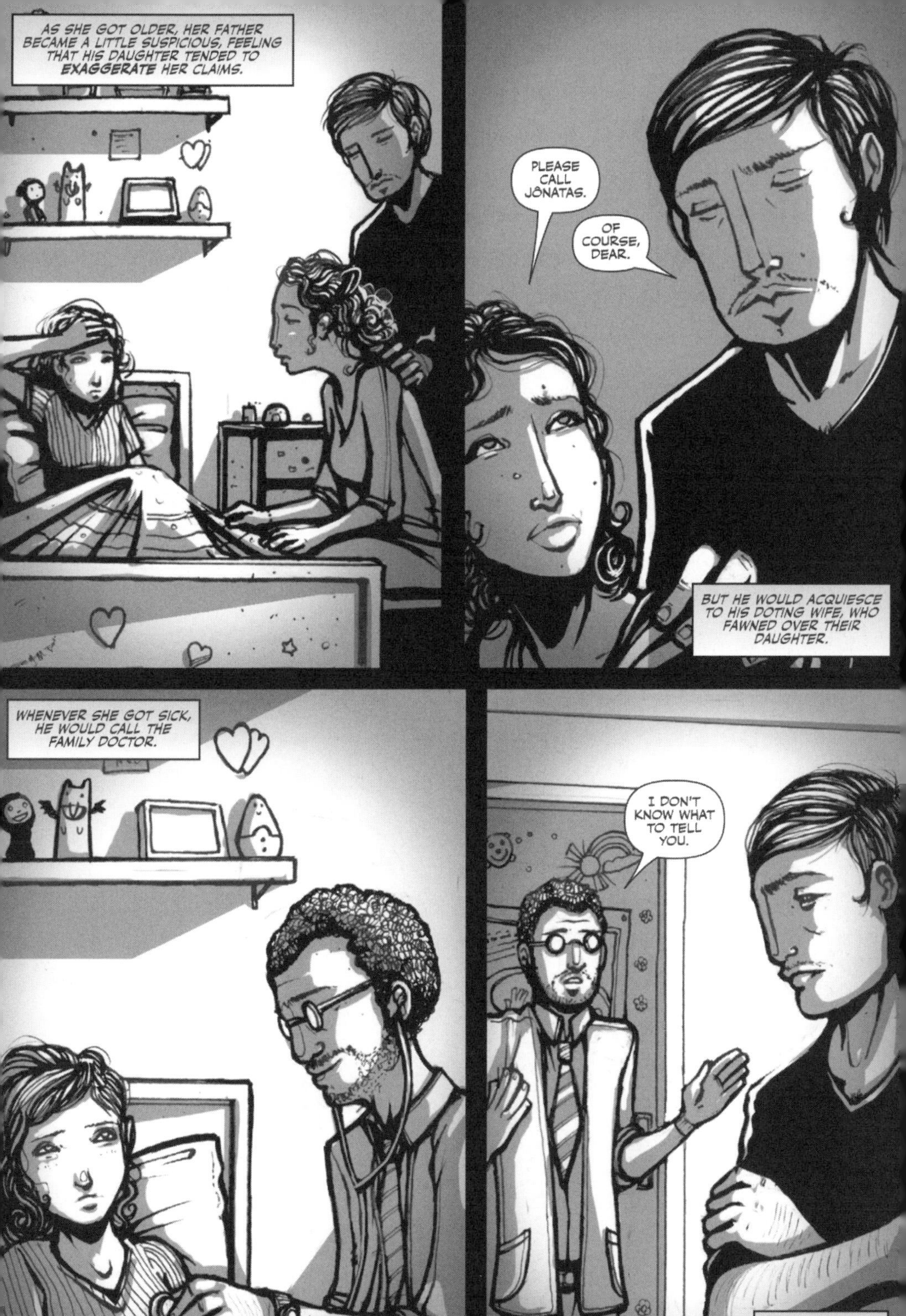
AS SHE GOT OLDER, HER FATHER BECAME A LITTLE SUSPICIOUS, FEELING THAT HIS DAUGHTER TENDED TO EXAGGERATE HER CLAIMS.
PLEASE CALL JÔNATAS.
OF COURSE, DEAR.
BUT HE WOULD ACQUIESCE TO HIS DOTING WIFE, WHO FAWNED OVER THEIR DAUGHTER.
WHENEVER SHE GOT SICK, HE WOULD CALL THE FAMILY DOCTOR.
I DON'T KNOW WHAT TO TELL YOU.
BUT THE DOCTOR NEVER FOUND ANYTHING.

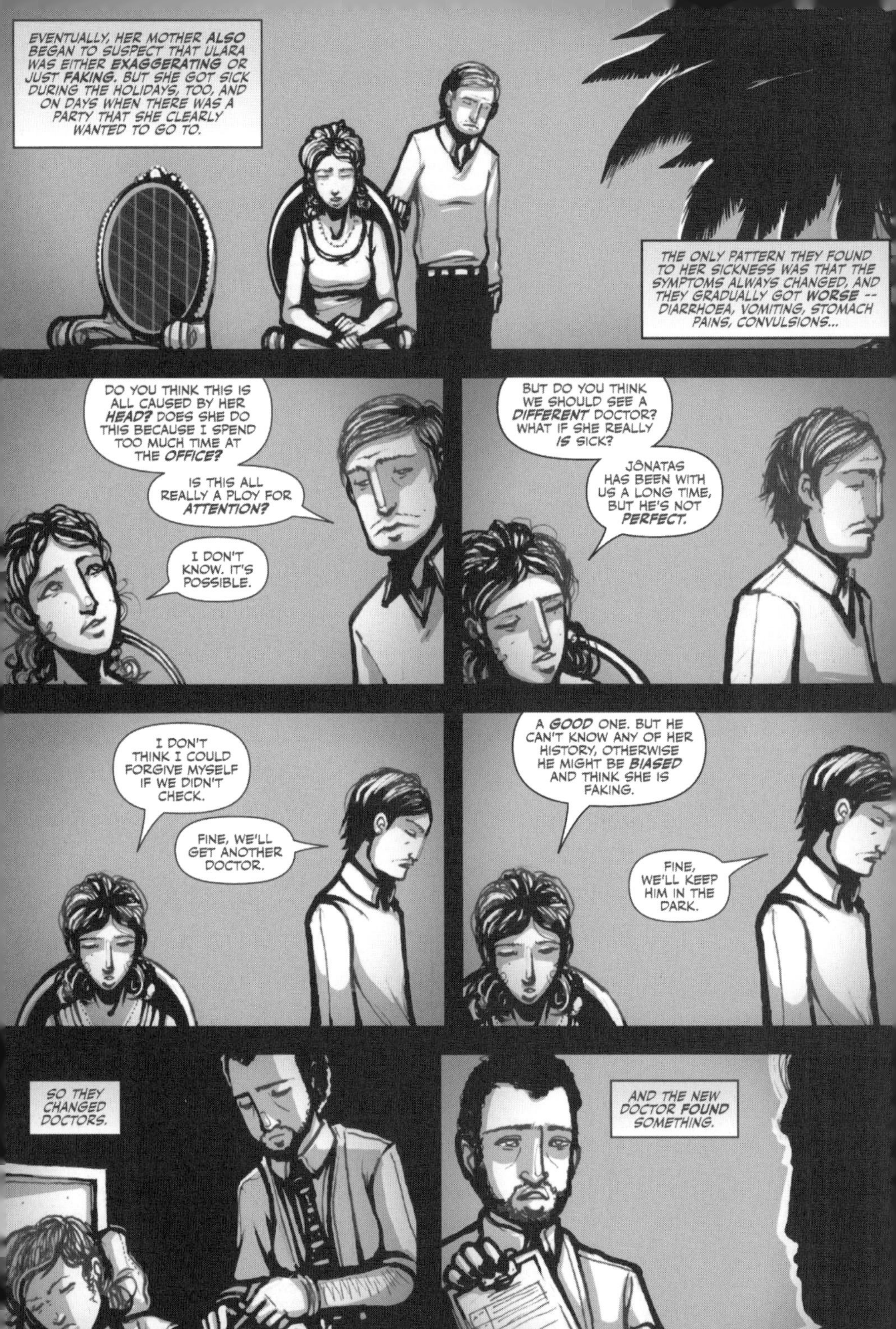
EVENTUALLY, HER MOTHER ALSO BEGAN TO SUSPECT THAT ULARA WAS EITHER EXAGGERATING OR JUST FAKING. BUT SHE GOT SICK DURING THE HOLIDAYS, TOO, AND ON DAYS WHEN THERE WAS A PARTY THAT SHE CLEARLY WANTED TO GO TO.
THE ONLY PATTERN THEY FOUND TO HER SICKNESS WAS THAT THE SYMPTOMS ALWAYS CHANGED, AND THEY GRADUALLY GOT WORSE -- DIARRHOEA, VOMITING, STOMACH PAINS, CONVULSIONS...
DO YOU THINK THIS IS ALL CAUSED BY HER HEAD? DOES SHE DO THIS BECAUSE I SPEND TOO MUCH TIME AT THE OFFICE?
IS THIS ALL REALLY A PLOY FOR ATTENTION?
I DON'T KNOW. IT'S POSSIBLE.
BUT DO YOU THINK WE SHOULD SEE A DIFFERENT DOCTOR? WHAT IF SHE REALLY IS SICK?
JÔNATAS HAS BEEN WITH US A LONG TIME, BUT HE'S NOT PERFECT.
I DON'T THINK I COULD FORGIVE MYSELF IF WE DIDN'T CHECK.
FINE, WE'LL GET ANOTHER DOCTOR.
A GOOD ONE. BUT HE CAN'T KNOW ANY OF HER HISTORY, OTHERWISE HE MIGHT BE BIASED AND THINK SHE IS FAKING.
FINE, WE'LL KEEP HIM IN THE DARK.
SO THEY CHANGED DOCTORS.
AND THE NEW DOCTOR FOUND SOMETHING.

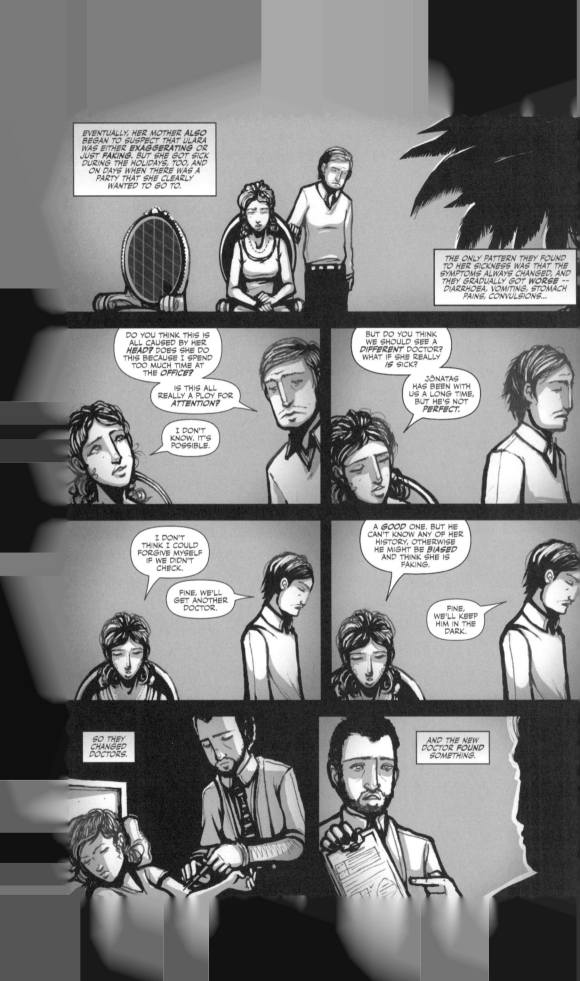

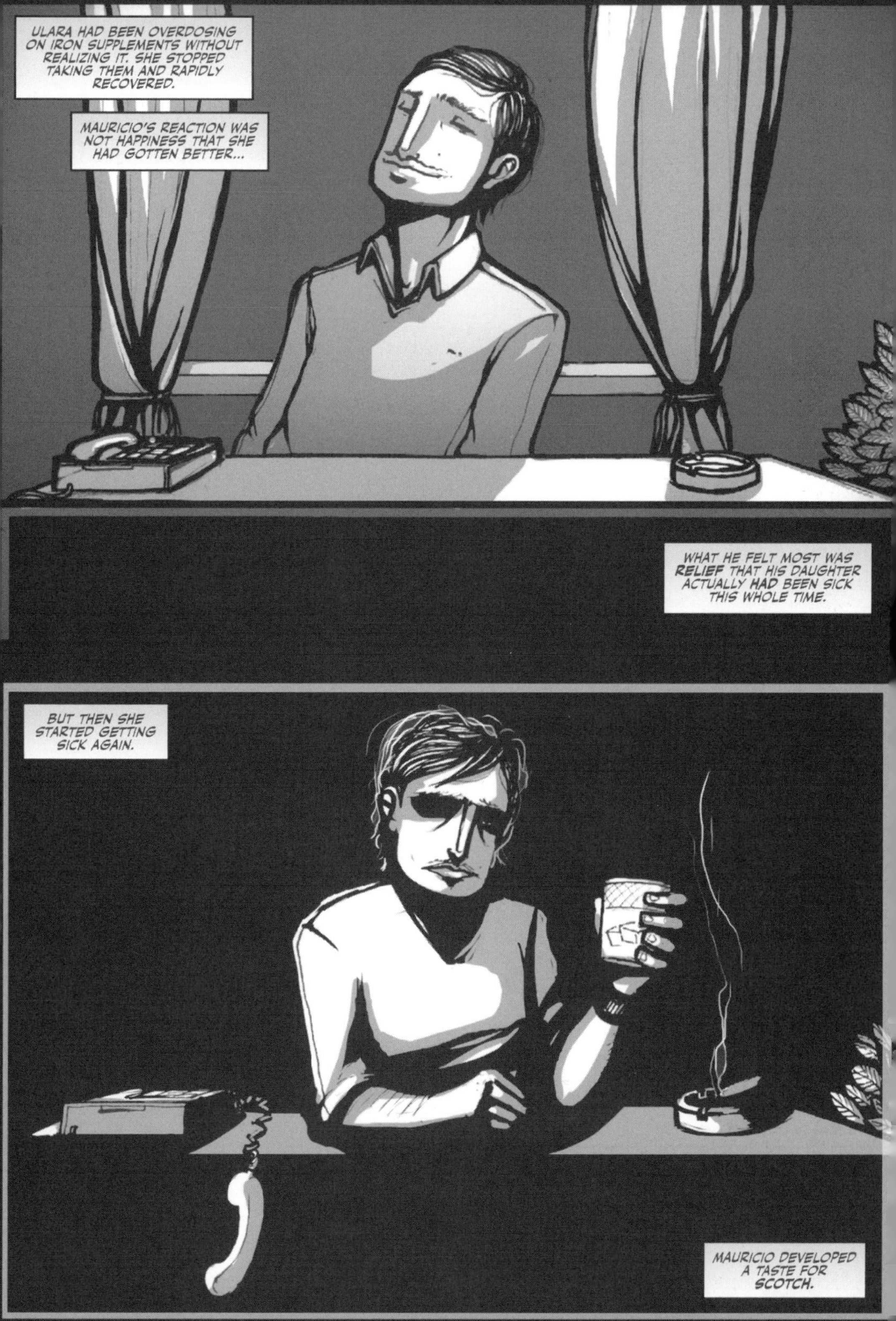
ULARA HAD BEEN OVERDOSING ON IRON SUPPLEMENTS WITHOUT REALIZING IT. SHE STOPPED TAKING THEM AND RAPIDLY RECOVERED.
MAURICIO'S REACTION WAS NOT HAPPINESS THAT SHE HAD GOTTEN BETTER...
WHAT HE FELT MOST WAS RELIEF THAT HIS DAUGHTER ACTUALLY HAD BEEN SICK THIS WHOLE TIME.
BUT THEN SHE STARTED GETTING SICK AGAIN.
MAURICIO DEVELOPED A TASTE FOR SCOTCH.

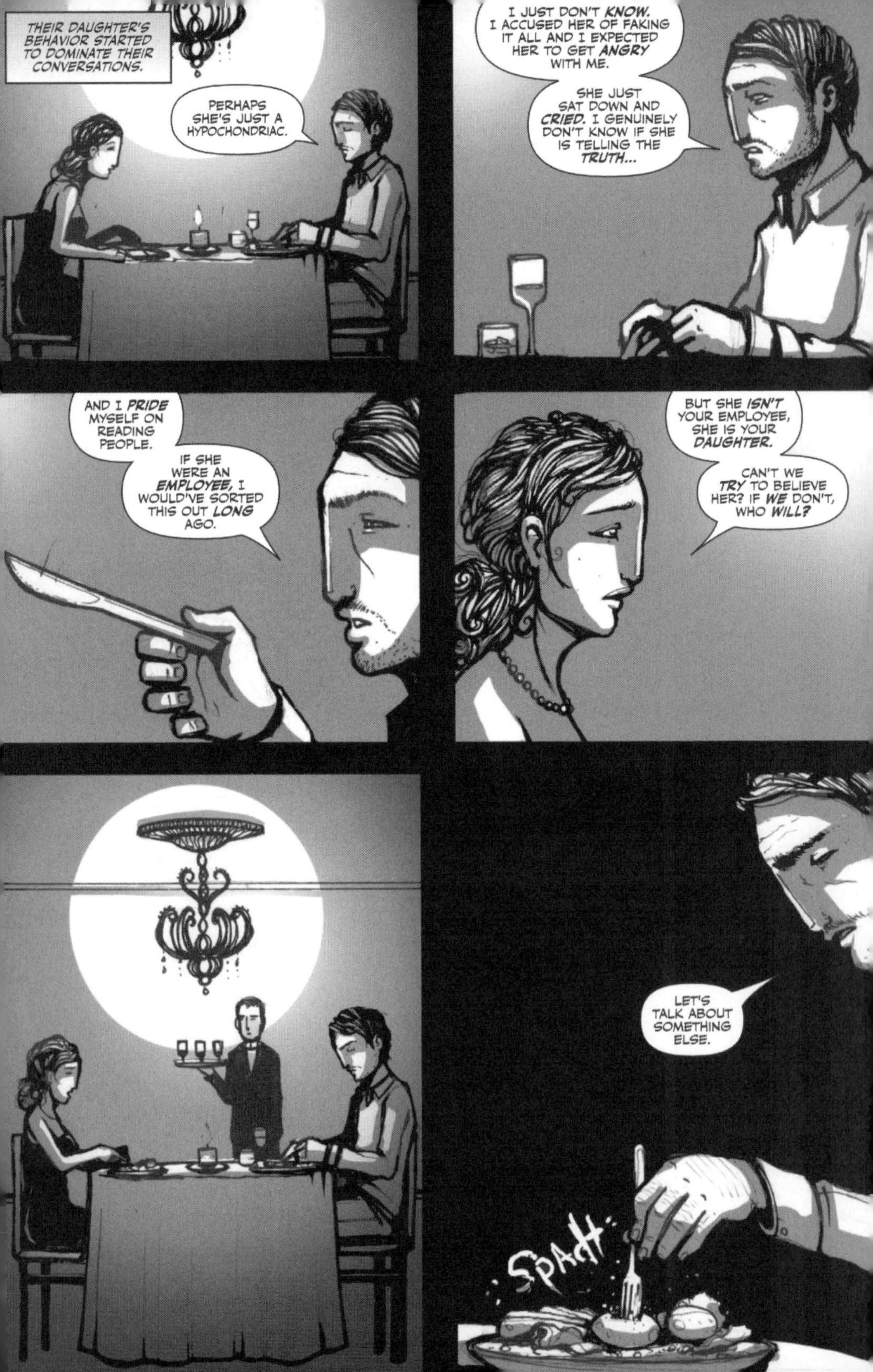
THEIR DAUGHTER'S BEHAVIOR STARTED TO DOMINATE THEIR CONVERSATIONS.
PERHAPS SHE'S JUST A HYPOCHONDRIAC.
I JUST DON'T KNOW. I ACCUSED HER OF FAKING IT ALL AND I EXPECTED HER TO GET ANGRY WITH ME.
SHE JUST SAT DOWN AND CRIED. I GENUINELY DON'T KNOW IF SHE IS TELLING THE TRUTH...
AND I PRIDE MYSELF ON READING PEOPLE.
IF SHE WERE AN EMPLOYEE, I WOULD'VE SORTED THIS OUT LONG AGO.
BUT SHE ISN'T YOUR EMPLOYEE, SHE IS YOUR DAUGHTER.
CAN'T WE TRY TO BELIEVE HER? IF WE DON'T, WHO WILL?
LET'S TALK ABOUT SOMETHING ELSE.
SPAH

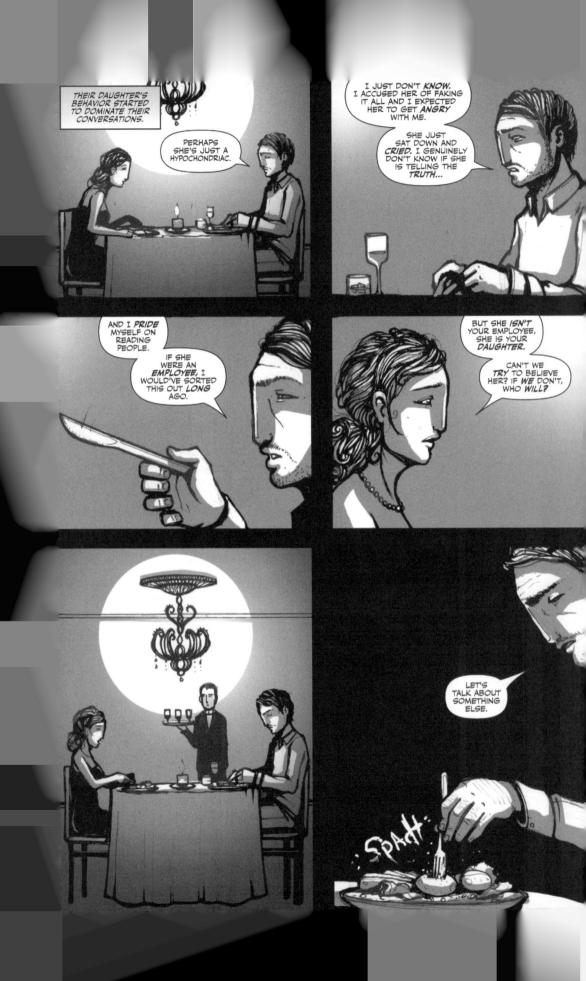

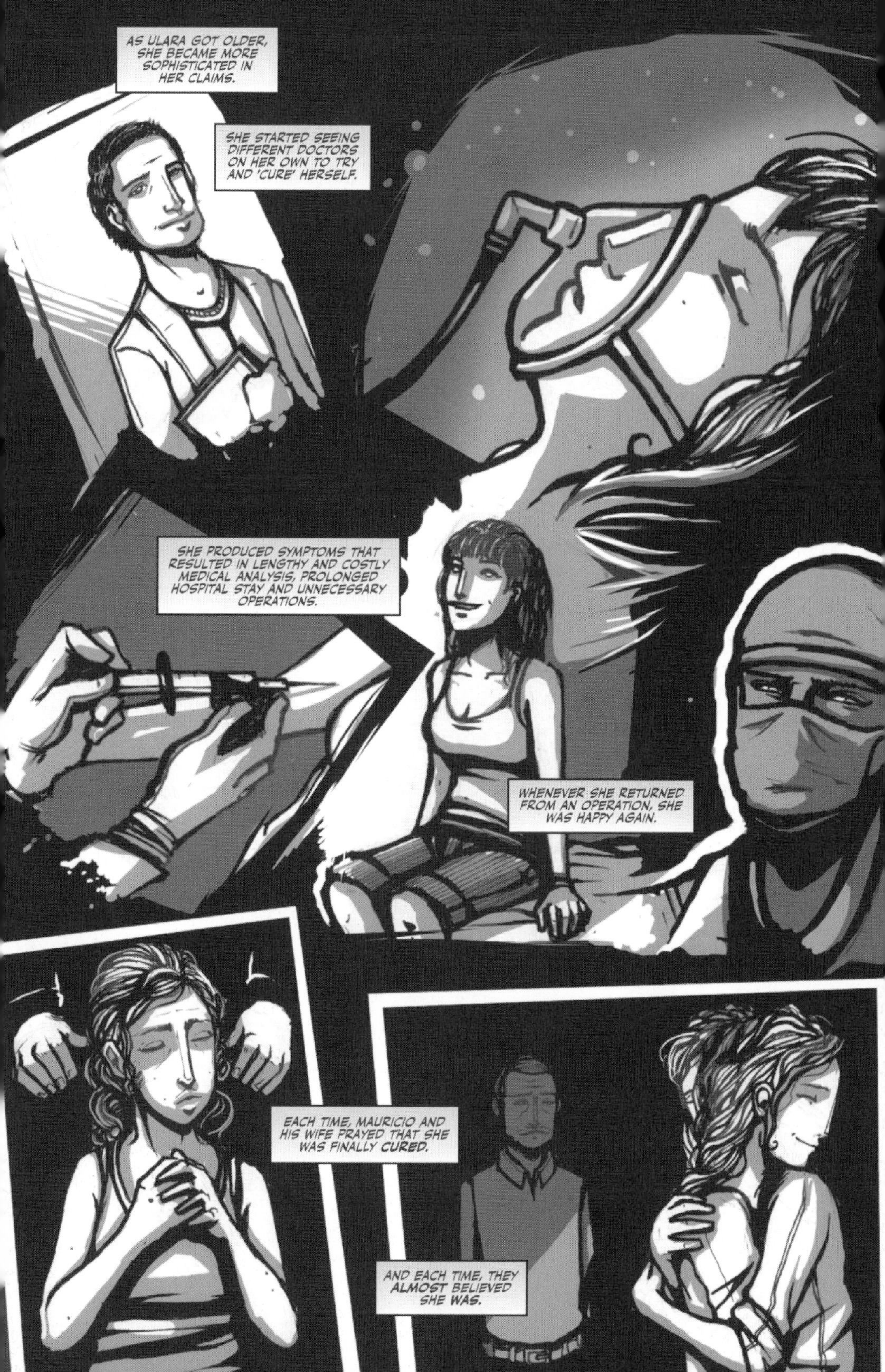
AS ULARA GOT OLDER, SHE BECAME MORE SOPHISTICATED IN HER CLAIMS.
SHE STARTED SEEING DIFFERENT DOCTORS ON HER OWN TO TRY AND 'CURE' HERSELF.
SHE PRODUCED SYMPTOMS THAT RESULTED IN LENGTHY AND COSTLY MEDICAL ANALYSIS, PROLONGED HOSPITAL STAY AND UNNECESSARY OPERATIONS.
WHENEVER SHE RETURNED FROM AN OPERATION, SHE WAS HAPPY AGAIN.
EACH TIME, MAURICIO AND HIS WIFE PRAYED THAT SHE WAS FINALLY **CURED**.
AND EACH TIME, THEY **ALMOST** BELIEVED SHE **WAS**.

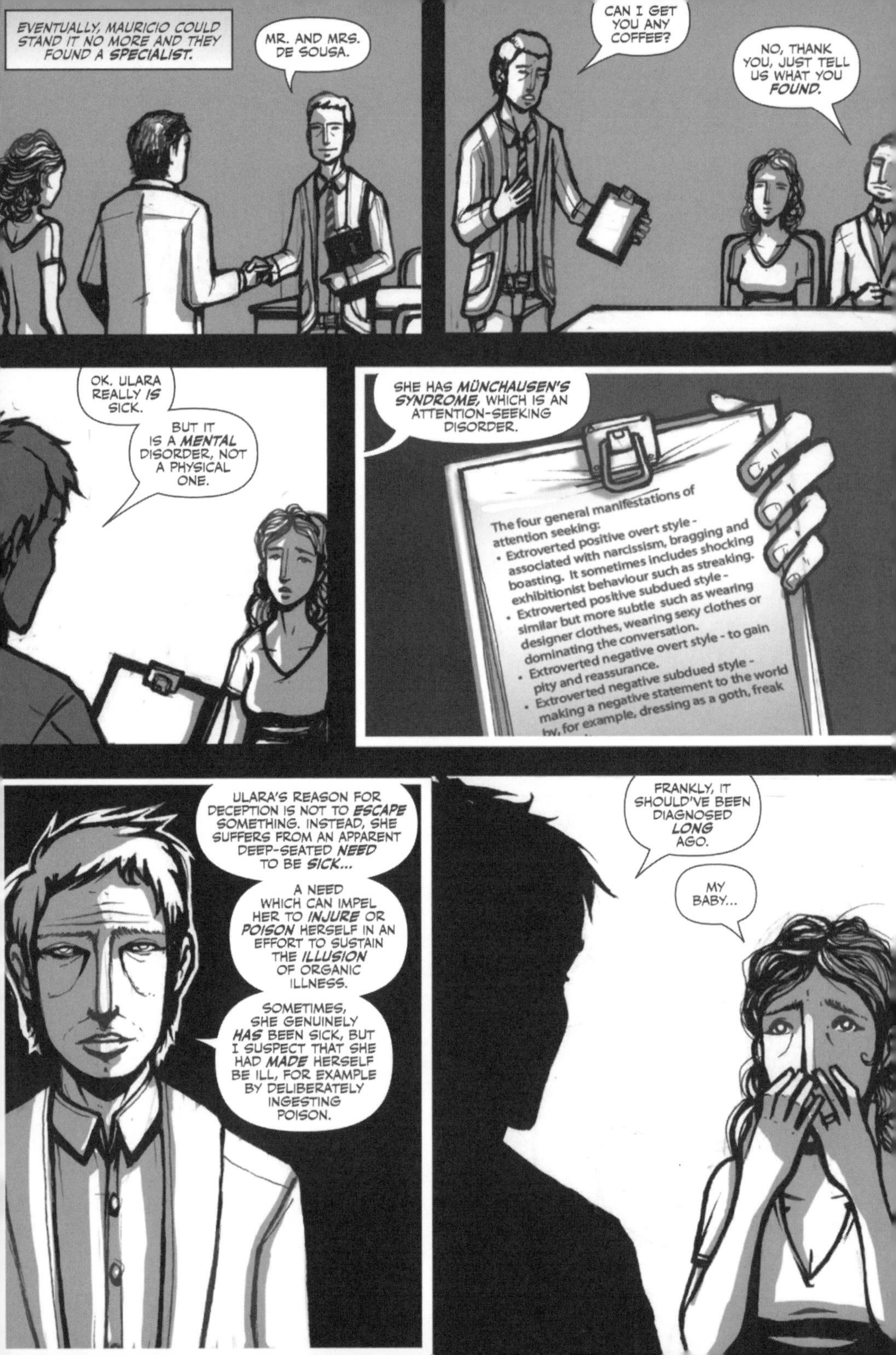
EVENTUALLY, MAURICIO COULD STAND IT NO MORE AND THEY FOUND A SPECIALIST.
MR. AND MRS. DE SOUSA.
CAN I GET YOU ANY COFFEE?
NO, THANK YOU, JUST TELL US WHAT YOU FOUND.
OK. ULARA REALLY IS SICK.
BUT IT IS A MENTAL DISORDER, NOT A PHYSICAL ONE.
SHE HAS MÜNCHAUSEN'S SYNDROME, WHICH IS AN ATTENTION-SEEKING DISORDER.
The four general manifestations of attention seeking:
• Extroverted positive overt style - associated with narcissism, bragging and boasting. It sometimes includes shocking exhibitionist behaviour such as streaking.
• Extroverted positive subdued style - similar but more subtle such as wearing designer clothes, wearing sexy clothes or dominating the conversation.
• Extroverted negative overt style - to gain pity and reassurance.
• Extroverted negative subdued style - making a negative statement to the world by, for example, dressing as a goth, freak
ULARA'S REASON FOR DECEPTION IS NOT TO ESCAPE SOMETHING. INSTEAD, SHE SUFFERS FROM AN APPARENT DEEP-SEATED NEED TO BE SICK...
A NEED WHICH CAN IMPEL HER TO INJURE OR POISON HERSELF IN AN EFFORT TO SUSTAIN THE ILLUSION OF ORGANIC ILLNESS.
SOMETIMES, SHE GENUINELY HAS BEEN SICK, BUT I SUSPECT THAT SHE HAD MADE HERSELF BE ILL, FOR EXAMPLE BY DELIBERATELY INGESTING POISON.
FRANKLY, IT SHOULD'VE BEEN DIAGNOSED LONG AGO.
MY BABY...

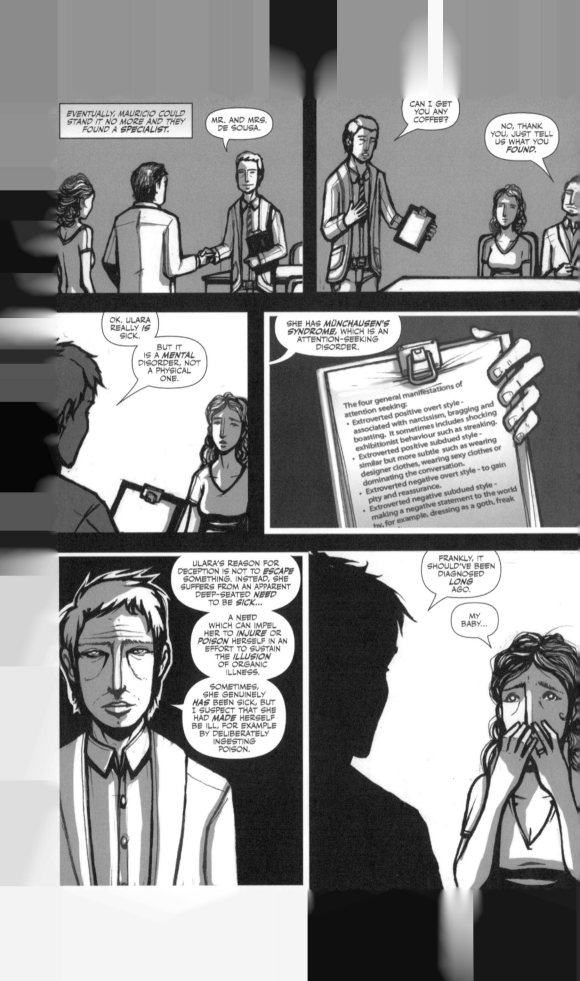

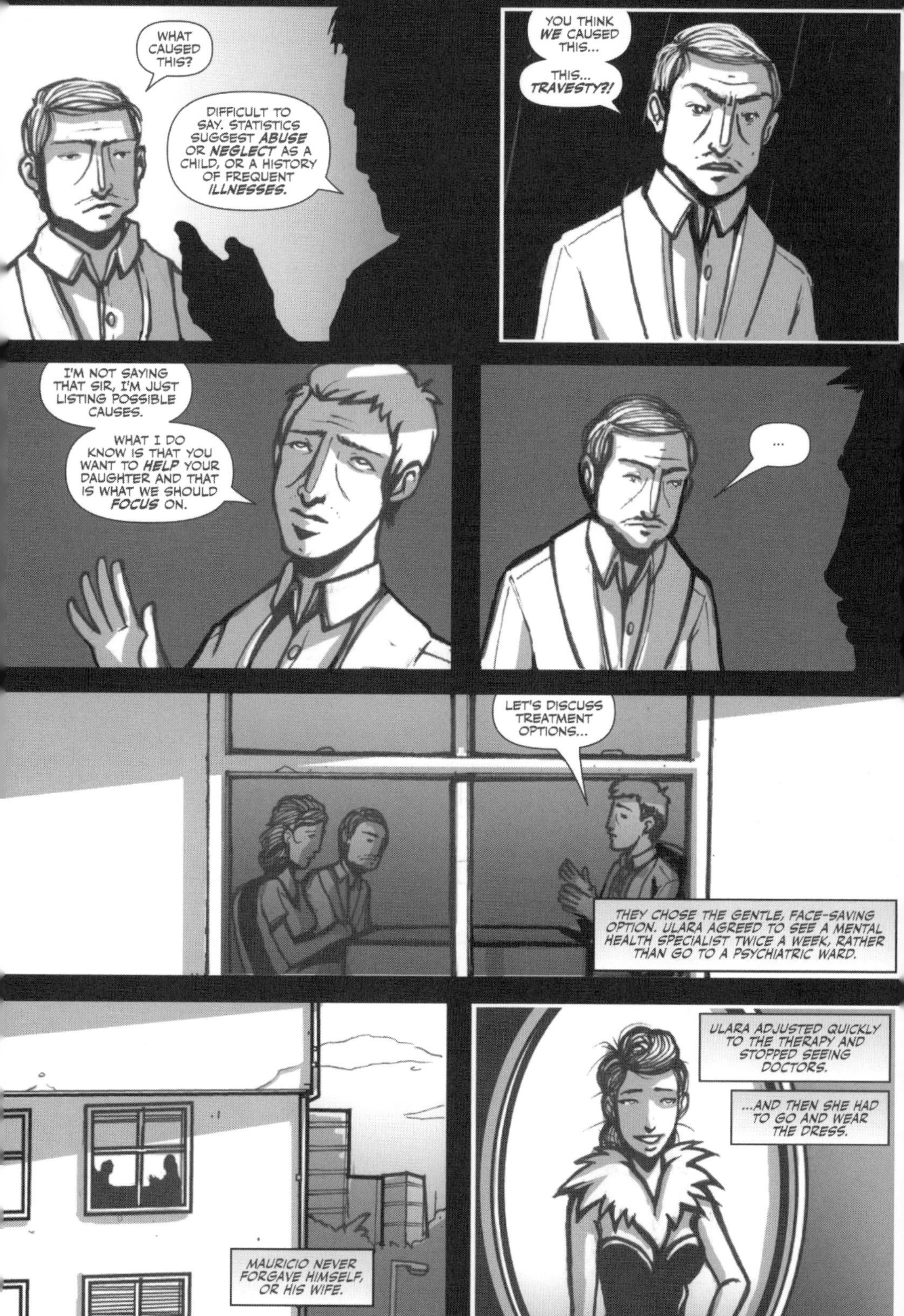
WHAT CAUSED THIS?
DIFFICULT TO SAY. STATISTICS SUGGEST ABUSE OR NEGLECT AS A CHILD, OR A HISTORY OF FREQUENT ILLNESSES.
YOU THINK WE CAUSED THIS...
THIS... TRAVESTY?!
I'M NOT SAYING THAT SIR, I'M JUST LISTING POSSIBLE CAUSES.
WHAT I DO KNOW IS THAT YOU WANT TO HELP YOUR DAUGHTER AND THAT IS WHAT WE SHOULD FOCUS ON.
...
LET'S DISCUSS TREATMENT OPTIONS...
THEY CHOSE THE GENTLE, FACE-SAVING OPTION. ULARA AGREED TO SEE A MENTAL HEALTH SPECIALIST TWICE A WEEK, RATHER THAN GO TO A PSYCHIATRIC WARD.
MAURICIO NEVER FORGAVE HIMSELF, OR HIS WIFE.
HE STARTED TAKING LONGER BUSINESS TRIPS.
ULARA ADJUSTED QUICKLY TO THE THERAPY AND STOPPED SEEING DOCTORS.
...AND THEN SHE HAD TO GO AND WEAR THE DRESS.

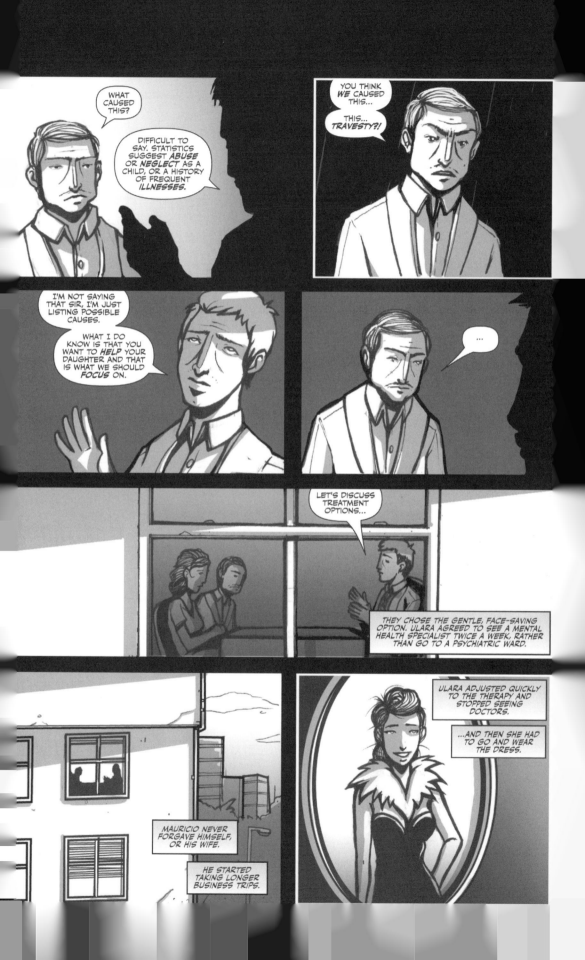

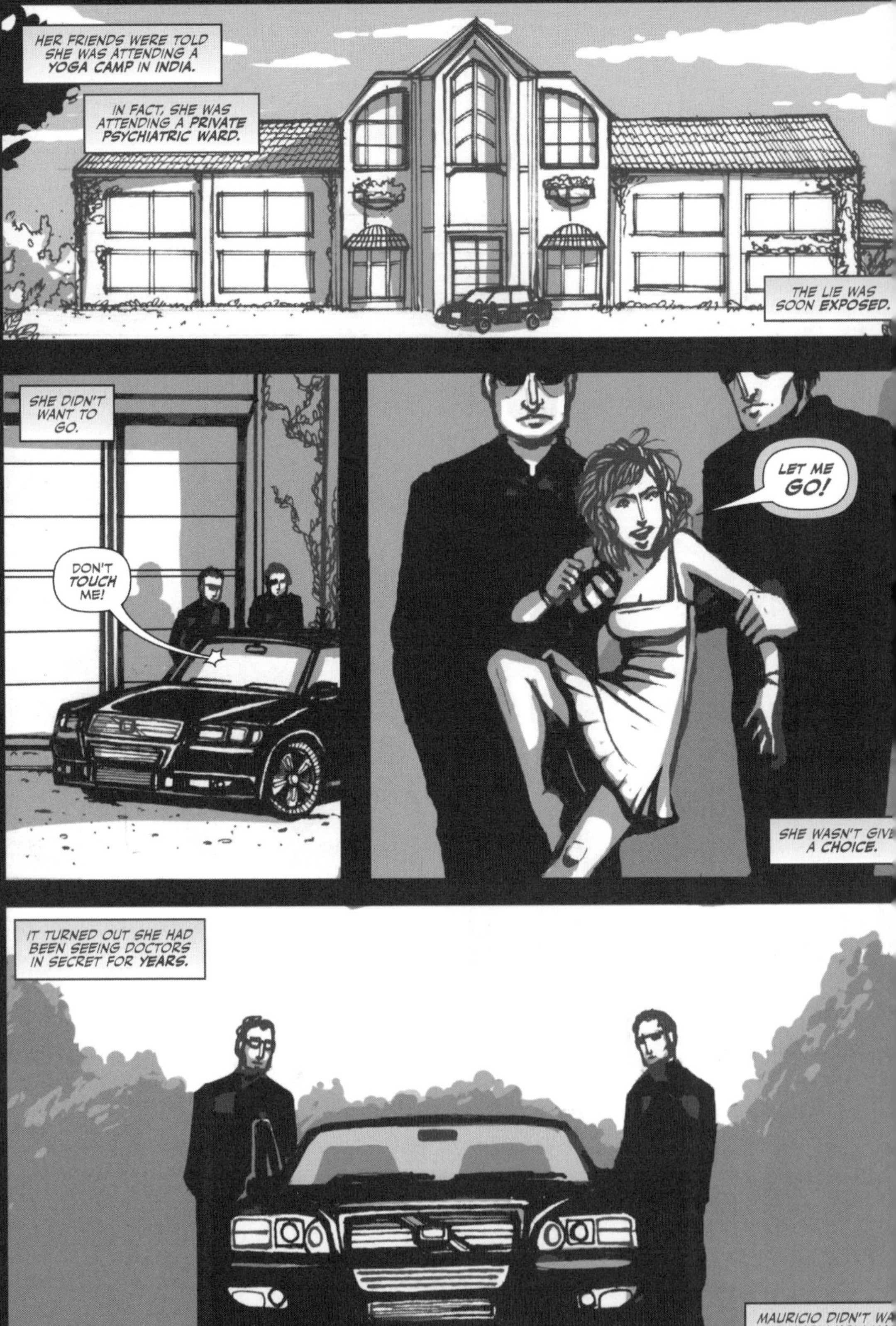
HER FRIENDS WERE TOLD SHE WAS ATTENDING A YOGA CAMP IN INDIA.
IN FACT, SHE WAS ATTENDING A PRIVATE PSYCHIATRIC WARD.
THE LIE WAS SOON EXPOSED.
SHE DIDN'T WANT TO GO.
DON'T TOUCH ME!
LET ME GO!
SHE WASN'T GIVE A CHOICE.
IT TURNED OUT SHE HAD BEEN SEEING DOCTORS IN SECRET FOR YEARS.
MAURICIO DIDN'T WA TO KNOW HOW MA SURGERIES SHE HA ORGANISED. HE JUST WANTED IT FIXED.

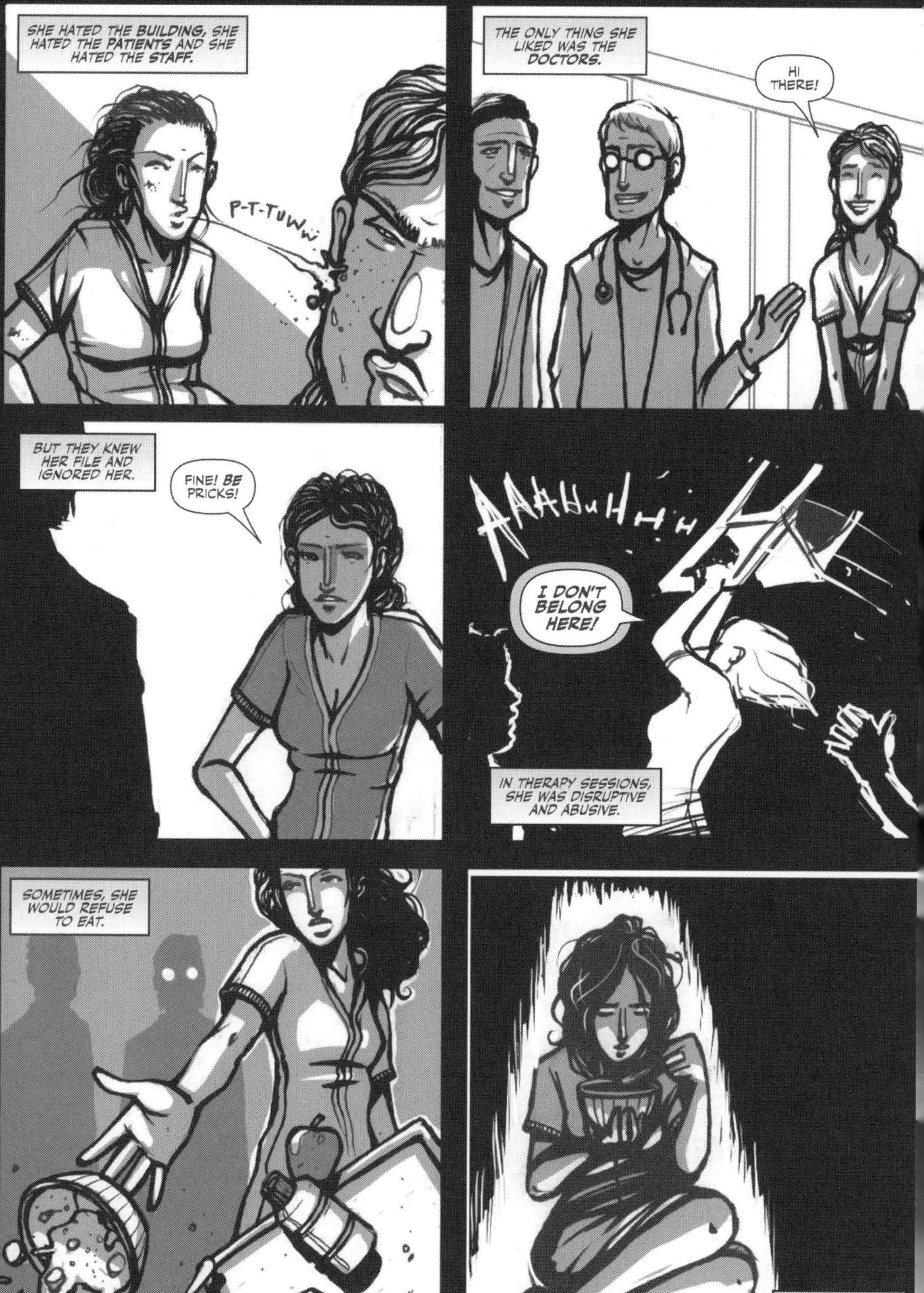
SHE HATED THE BUILDING, SHE HATED THE PATIENTS AND SHE HATED THE STAFF.
P-T-TUWW
THE ONLY THING SHE LIKED WAS THE DOCTORS.
HI THERE!
BUT THEY KNEW HER FILE AND IGNORED HER.
FINE! BE PRICKS!
AAAHUHHHH
I DON'T BELONG HERE!
IN THERAPY SESSIONS, SHE WAS DISRUPTIVE AND ABUSIVE.
SOMETIMES, SHE WOULD REFUSE TO EAT.
BUT MONTHS PASSED AND HER WILL BEGAN TO BREAK.

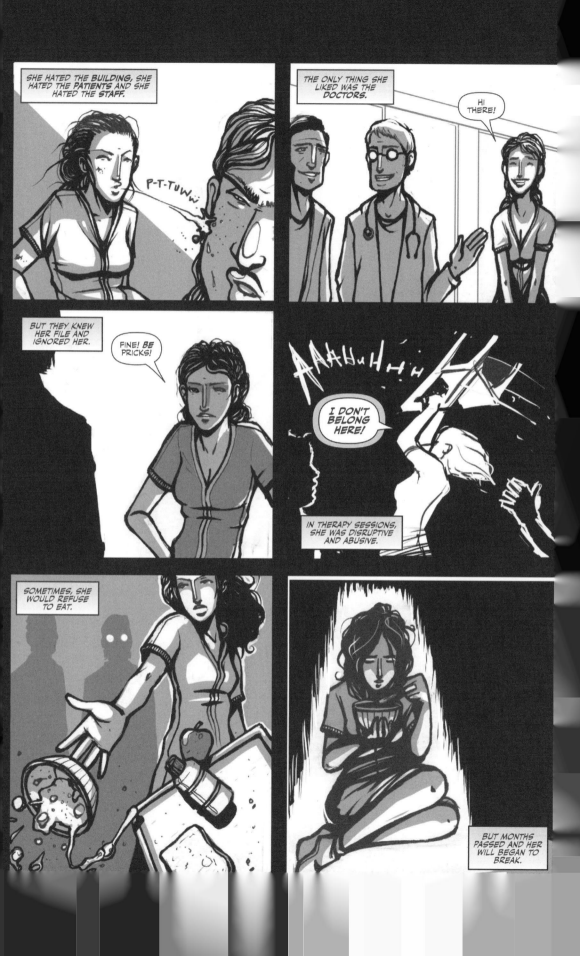

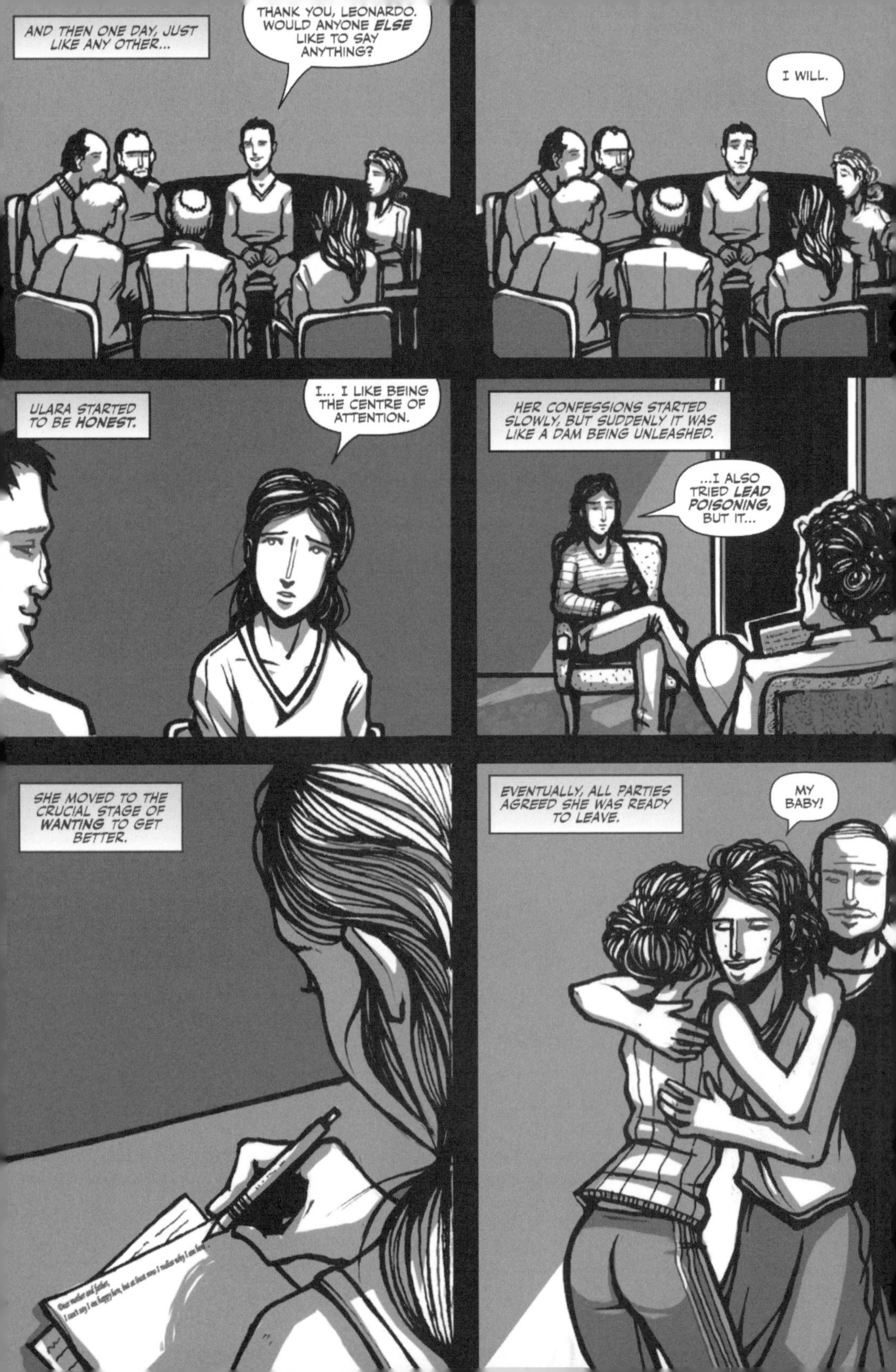
AND THEN ONE DAY, JUST LIKE ANY OTHER...
THANK YOU, LEONARDO. WOULD ANYONE ELSE LIKE TO SAY ANYTHING?
I WILL.
ULARA STARTED TO BE HONEST.
I... I LIKE BEING THE CENTRE OF ATTENTION.
HER CONFESSIONS STARTED SLOWLY, BUT SUDDENLY IT WAS LIKE A DAM BEING UNLEASHED.
...I ALSO TRIED LEAD POISONING, BUT IT...
SHE MOVED TO THE CRUCIAL STAGE OF WANTING TO GET BETTER.
Dear mother and father,
EVENTUALLY, ALL PARTIES AGREED SHE WAS READY TO LEAVE.
MY BABY!

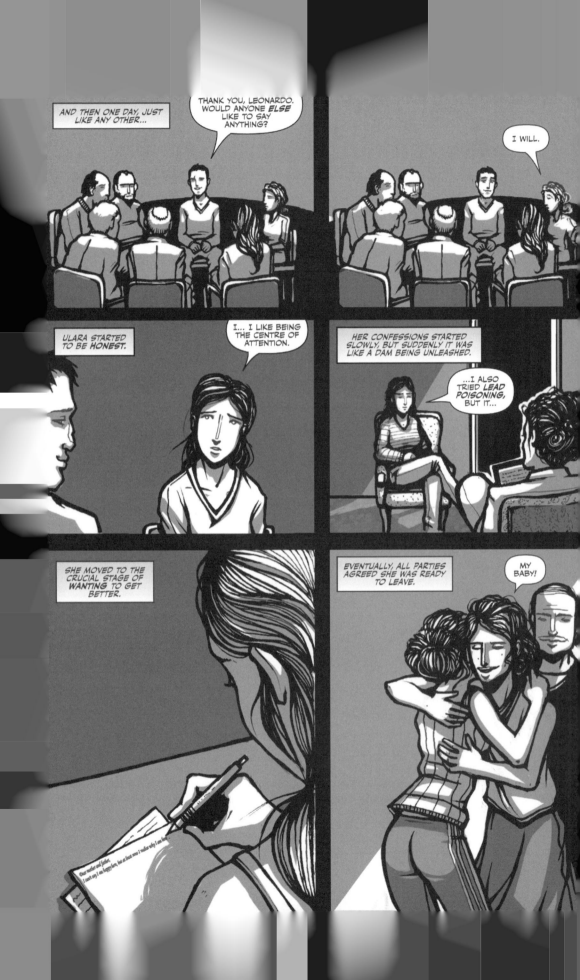

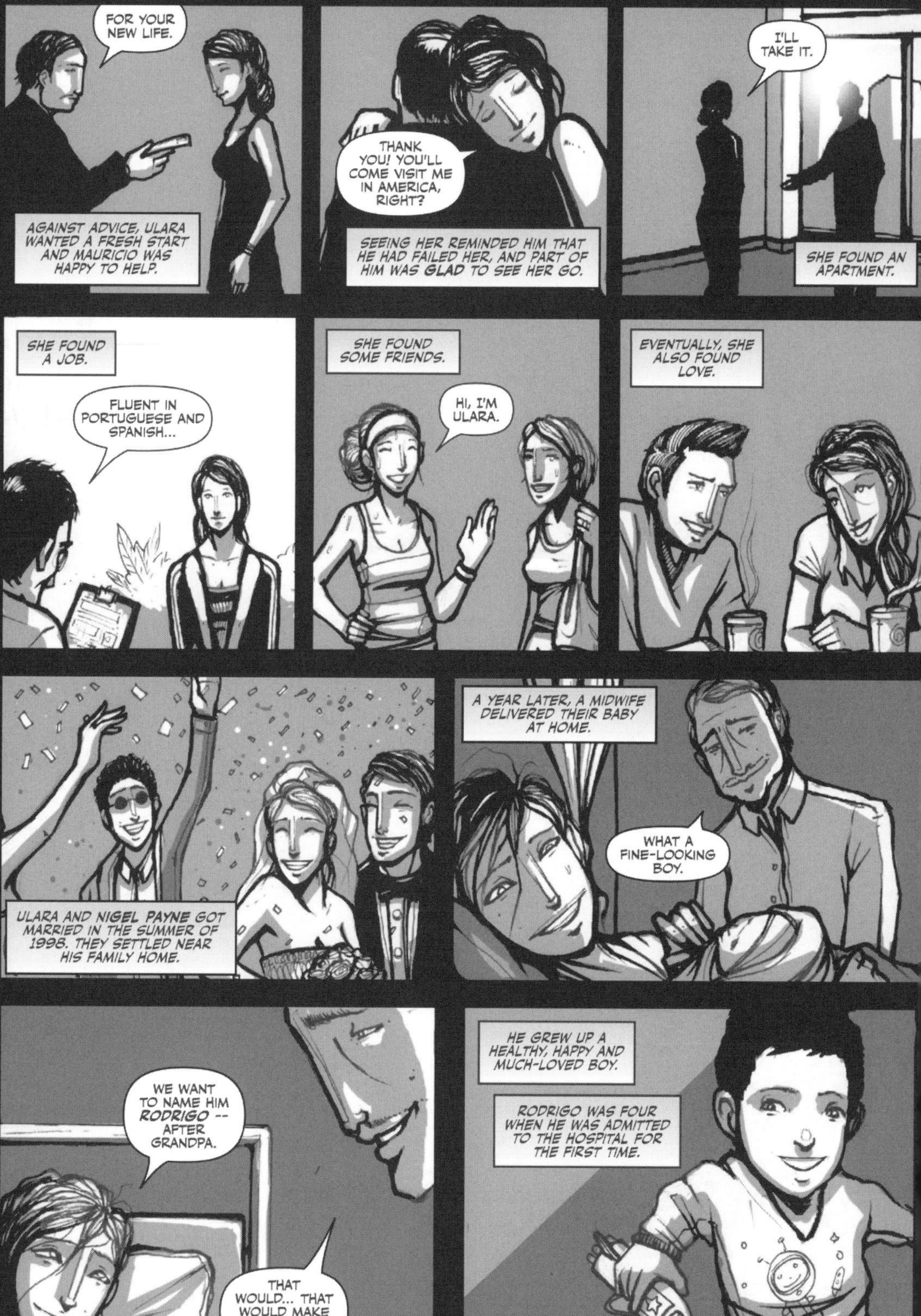

FOR YOUR NEW LIFE.
AGAINST ADVICE, ULARA WANTED A FRESH START AND MAURICIO WAS HAPPY TO HELP.
THANK YOU! YOU'LL COME VISIT ME IN AMERICA, RIGHT?
SEEING HER REMINDED HIM THAT HE HAD FAILED HER, AND PART OF HIM WAS GLAD TO SEE HER GO.
I'LL TAKE IT.
SHE FOUND AN APARTMENT.
SHE FOUND A JOB.
FLUENT IN PORTUGUESE AND SPANISH...
SHE FOUND SOME FRIENDS.
HI, I'M ULARA.
EVENTUALLY, SHE ALSO FOUND LOVE.
ULARA AND NIGEL PAYNE GOT MARRIED IN THE SUMMER OF 1998. THEY SETTLED NEAR HIS FAMILY HOME.
A YEAR LATER, A MIDWIFE DELIVERED THEIR BABY AT HOME.
WHAT A FINE-LOOKING BOY.
WE WANT TO NAME HIM RODRIGO -- AFTER GRANDPA.
THAT WOULD... THAT WOULD MAKE ME VERY HAPPY.
HE GREW UP A HEALTHY, HAPPY AND MUCH-LOVED BOY.
RODRIGO WAS FOUR WHEN HE WAS ADMITTED TO THE HOSPITAL FOR THE FIRST TIME.

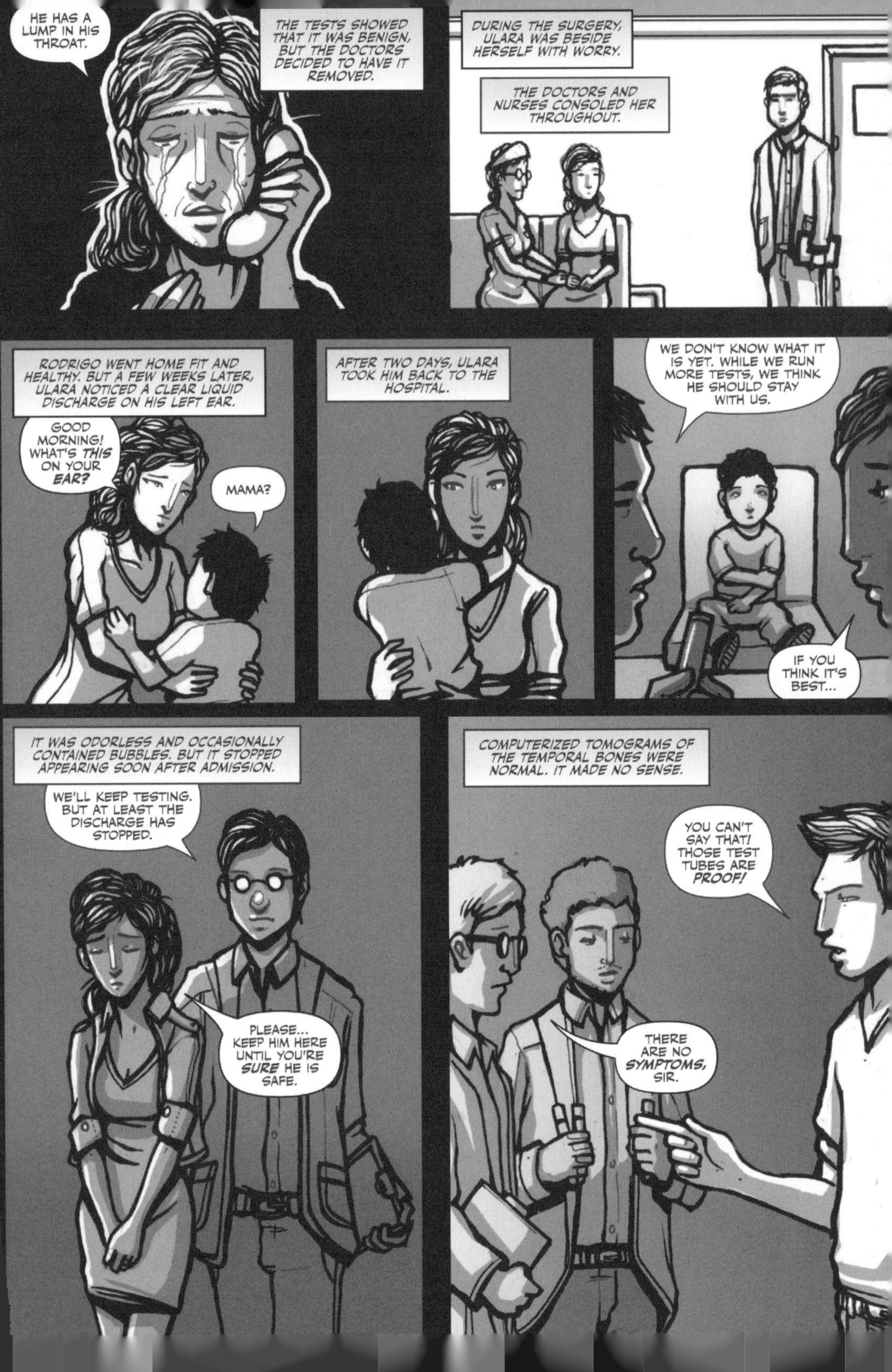
HE HAS A LUMP IN HIS THROAT.
THE TESTS SHOWED THAT IT WAS BENIGN, BUT THE DOCTORS DECIDED TO HAVE IT REMOVED.
DURING THE SURGERY, ULARA WAS BESIDE HERSELF WITH WORRY.
THE DOCTORS AND NURSES CONSOLED HER THROUGHOUT.
RODRIGO WENT HOME FIT AND HEALTHY. BUT A FEW WEEKS LATER, ULARA NOTICED A CLEAR LIQUID DISCHARGE ON HIS LEFT EAR.
GOOD MORNING! WHAT'S THIS ON YOUR EAR?
MAMA?
AFTER TWO DAYS, ULARA TOOK HIM BACK TO THE HOSPITAL.
WE DON'T KNOW WHAT IT IS YET. WHILE WE RUN MORE TESTS, WE THINK HE SHOULD STAY WITH US.
IF YOU THINK IT'S BEST...
IT WAS ODORLESS AND OCCASIONALLY CONTAINED BUBBLES. BUT IT STOPPED APPEARING SOON AFTER ADMISSION.
WE'LL KEEP TESTING. BUT AT LEAST THE DISCHARGE HAS STOPPED.
PLEASE... KEEP HIM HERE UNTIL YOU'RE SURE HE IS SAFE.
COMPUTERIZED TOMOGRAMS OF THE TEMPORAL BONES WERE NORMAL. IT MADE NO SENSE.
YOU CAN'T SAY THAT! THOSE TEST TUBES ARE PROOF!
THERE ARE NO SYMPTOMS, SIR.

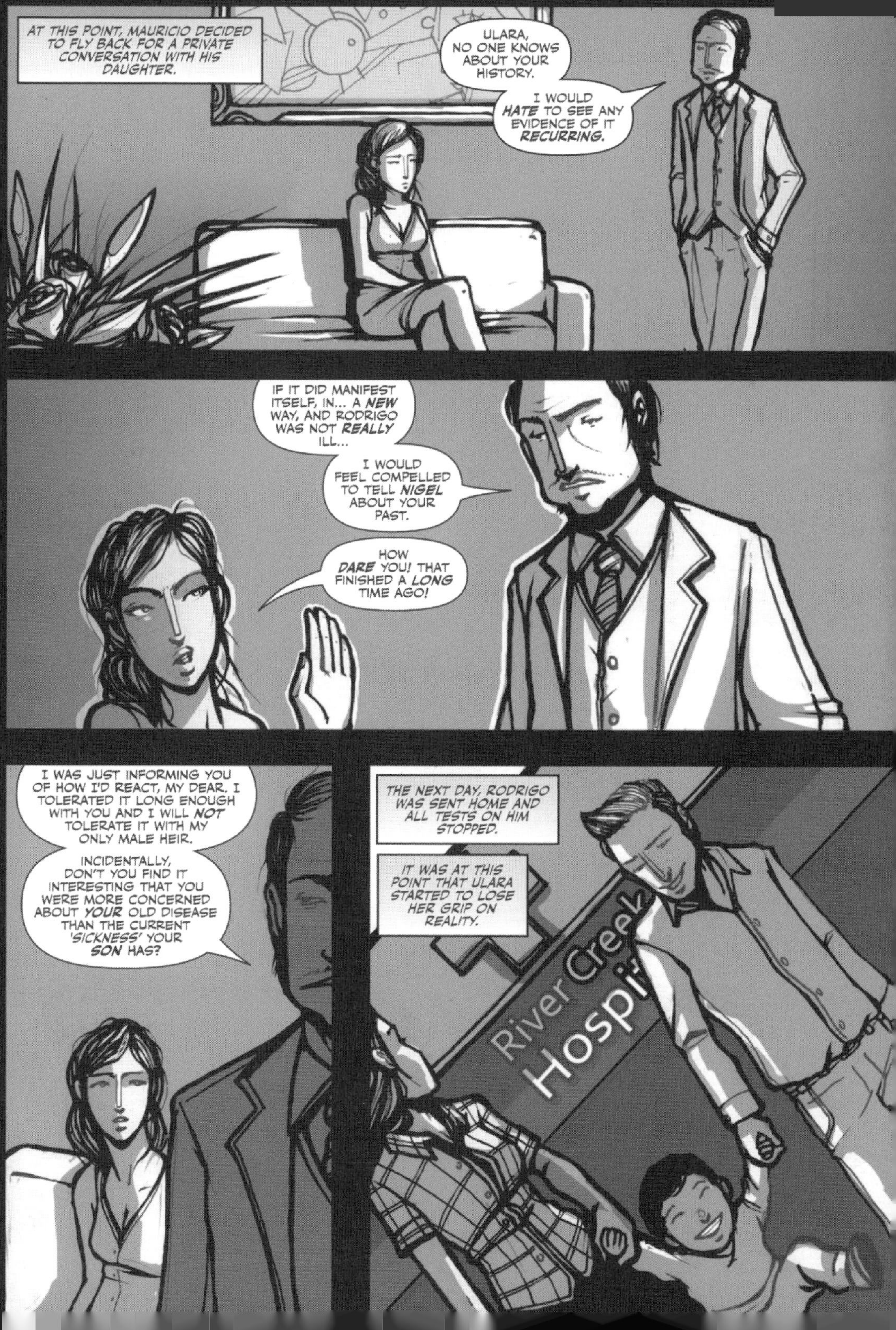
AT THIS POINT, MAURICIO DECIDED TO FLY BACK FOR A PRIVATE CONVERSATION WITH HIS DAUGHTER.
ULARA, NO ONE KNOWS ABOUT YOUR HISTORY.
I WOULD *HATE* TO SEE ANY EVIDENCE OF IT *RECURRING.*
IF IT DID MANIFEST ITSELF, IN... A *NEW* WAY, AND RODRIGO WAS NOT *REALLY* ILL...
I WOULD FEEL COMPELLED TO TELL *NIGEL* ABOUT YOUR PAST.
HOW *DARE* YOU! THAT FINISHED A *LONG* TIME AGO!
I WAS JUST INFORMING YOU OF HOW I'D REACT, MY DEAR. I TOLERATED IT LONG ENOUGH WITH YOU AND I WILL *NOT* TOLERATE IT WITH MY ONLY MALE HEIR.
INCIDENTALLY, DON'T YOU FIND IT INTERESTING THAT YOU WERE MORE CONCERNED ABOUT *YOUR* OLD DISEASE THAN THE CURRENT *'SICKNESS'* YOUR *SON* HAS?
THE NEXT DAY, RODRIGO WAS SENT HOME AND ALL TESTS ON HIM STOPPED.
IT WAS AT THIS POINT THAT ULARA STARTED TO LOSE HER GRIP ON REALITY.
River Creek
Hospi

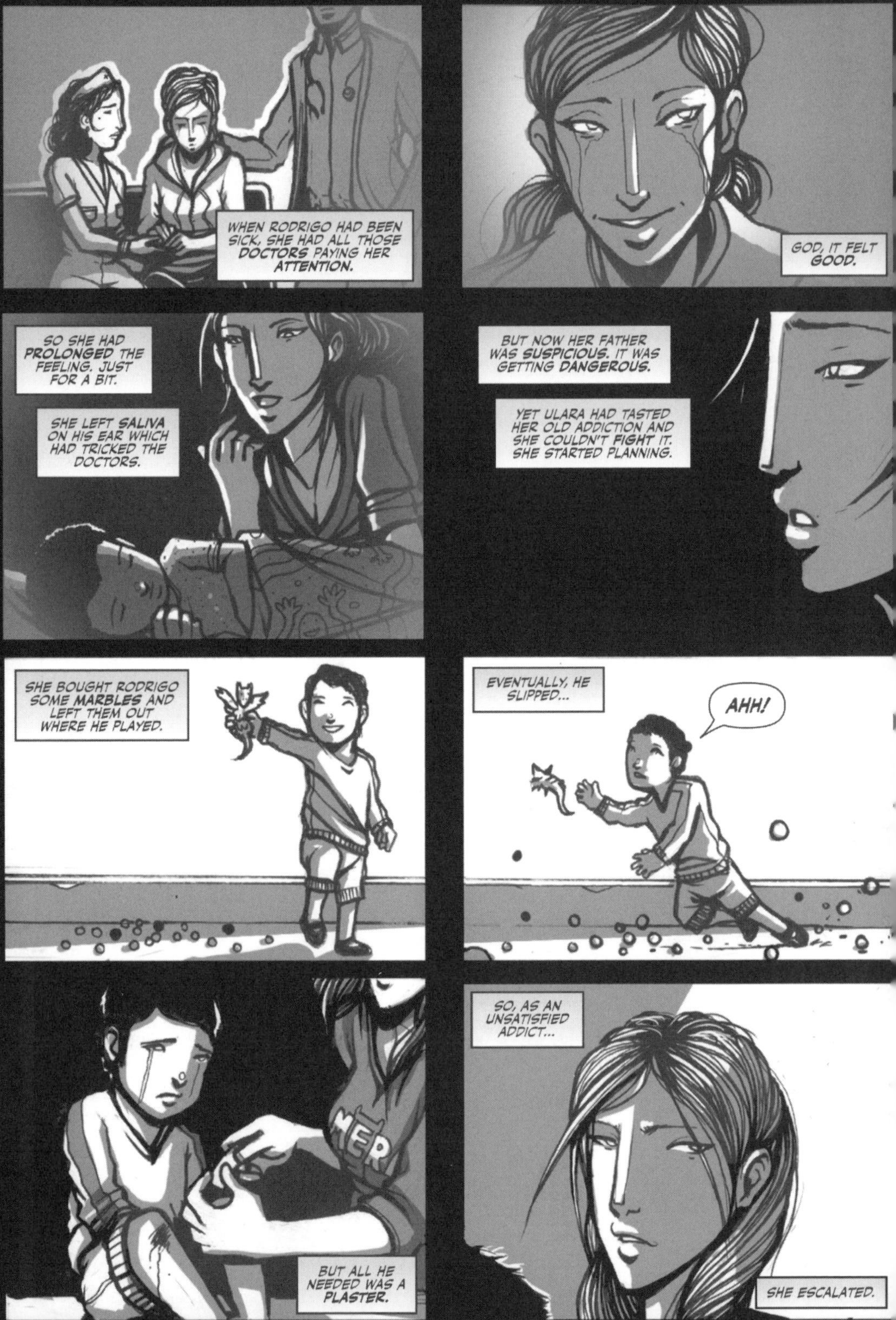
WHEN RODRIGO HAD BEEN SICK, SHE HAD ALL THOSE DOCTORS PAYING HER ATTENTION.
GOD, IT FELT GOOD.
SO SHE HAD PROLONGED THE FEELING. JUST FOR A BIT.
SHE LEFT SALIVA ON HIS EAR WHICH HAD TRICKED THE DOCTORS.
BUT NOW HER FATHER WAS SUSPICIOUS. IT WAS GETTING DANGEROUS.
YET ULARA HAD TASTED HER OLD ADDICTION AND SHE COULDN'T FIGHT IT. SHE STARTED PLANNING.
SHE BOUGHT RODRIGO SOME MARBLES AND LEFT THEM OUT WHERE HE PLAYED.
EVENTUALLY, HE SLIPPED...
AHH!
MER
BUT ALL HE NEEDED WAS A PLASTER.
SO, AS AN UNSATISFIED ADDICT...
SHE ESCALATED.

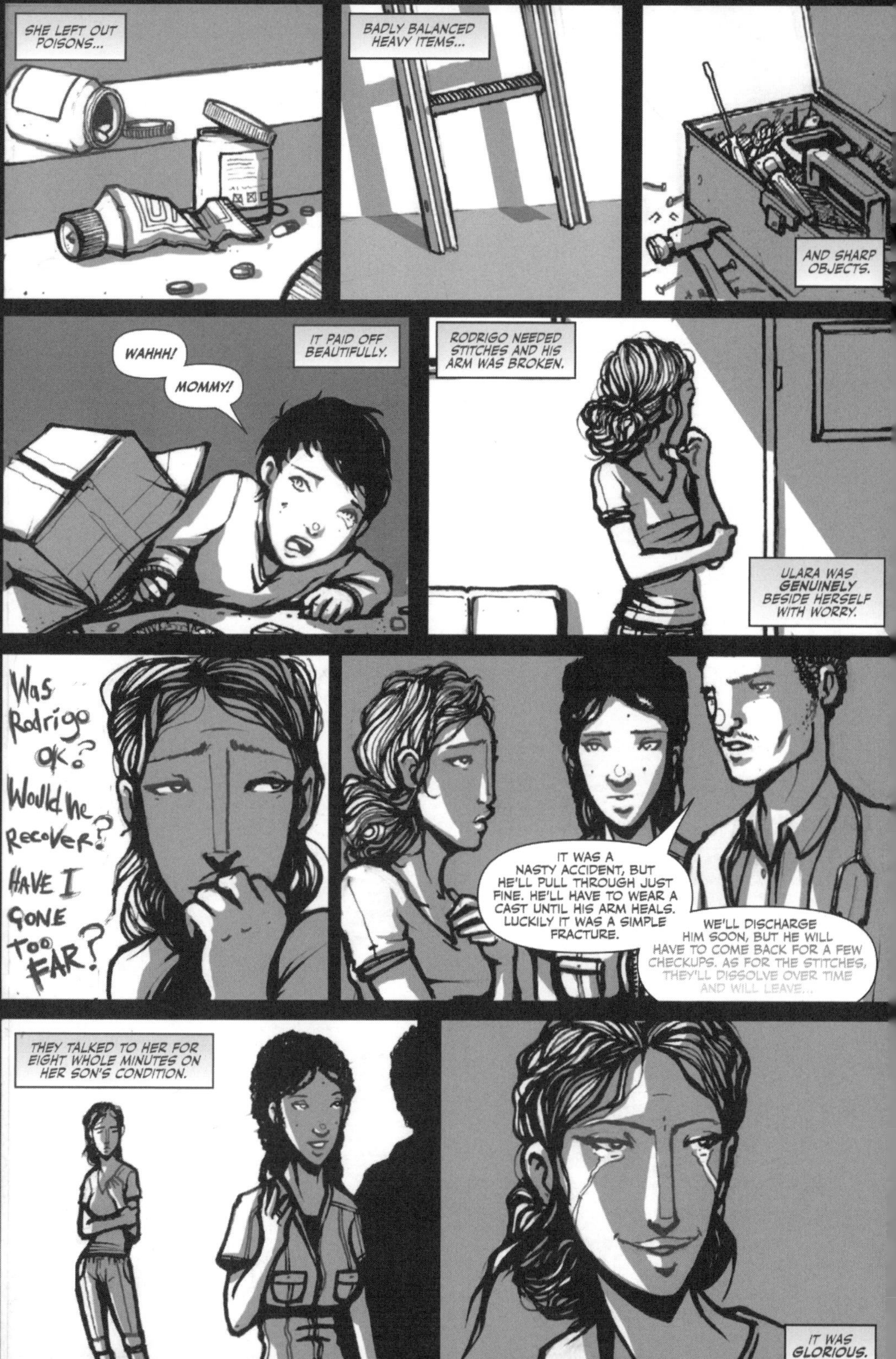
SHE LEFT OUT POISONS...
BADLY BALANCED HEAVY ITEMS...
AND SHARP OBJECTS.
IT PAID OFF BEAUTIFULLY.
WAHHH!
MOMMY!
RODRIGO NEEDED STITCHES AND HIS ARM WAS BROKEN.
ULARA WAS GENUINELY BESIDE HERSELF WITH WORRY.
Was Rodrigo ok? Would he recover? HAVE I GONE TOO FAR?
IT WAS A NASTY ACCIDENT, BUT HE'LL PULL THROUGH JUST FINE. HE'LL HAVE TO WEAR A CAST UNTIL HIS ARM HEALS. LUCKILY IT WAS A SIMPLE FRACTURE.
WE'LL DISCHARGE HIM SOON, BUT HE WILL HAVE TO COME BACK FOR A FEW CHECKUPS. AS FOR THE STITCHES, THEY'LL DISSOLVE OVER TIME AND WILL LEAVE...
THEY TALKED TO HER FOR EIGHT WHOLE MINUTES ON HER SON'S CONDITION.
IT WAS GLORIOUS.

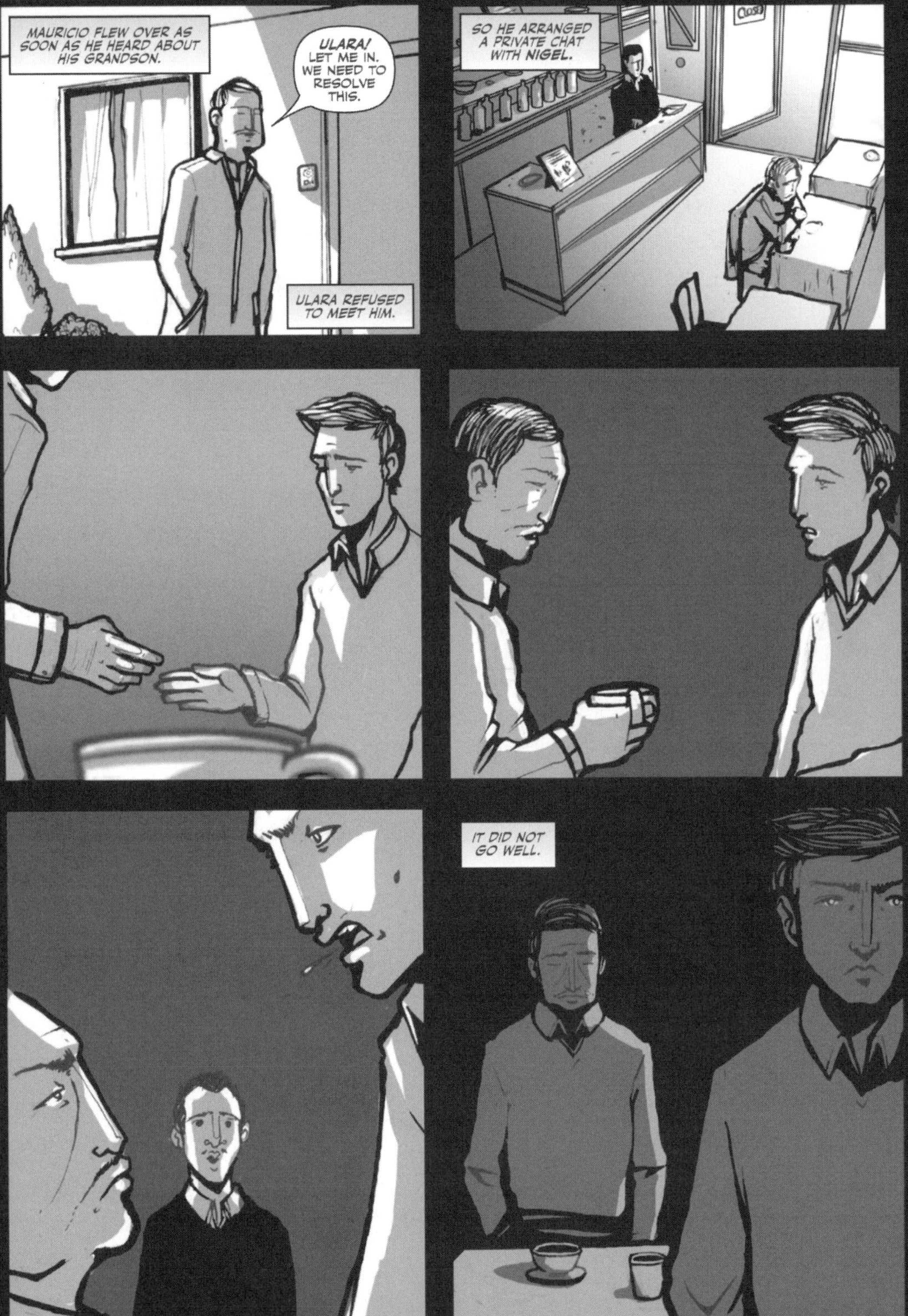
MAURICIO FLEW OVER AS SOON AS HE HEARD ABOUT HIS GRANDSON.
ULARA! LET ME IN. WE NEED TO RESOLVE THIS.
ULARA REFUSED TO MEET HIM.
SO HE ARRANGED A PRIVATE CHAT WITH NIGEL.
IT DID NOT GO WELL.

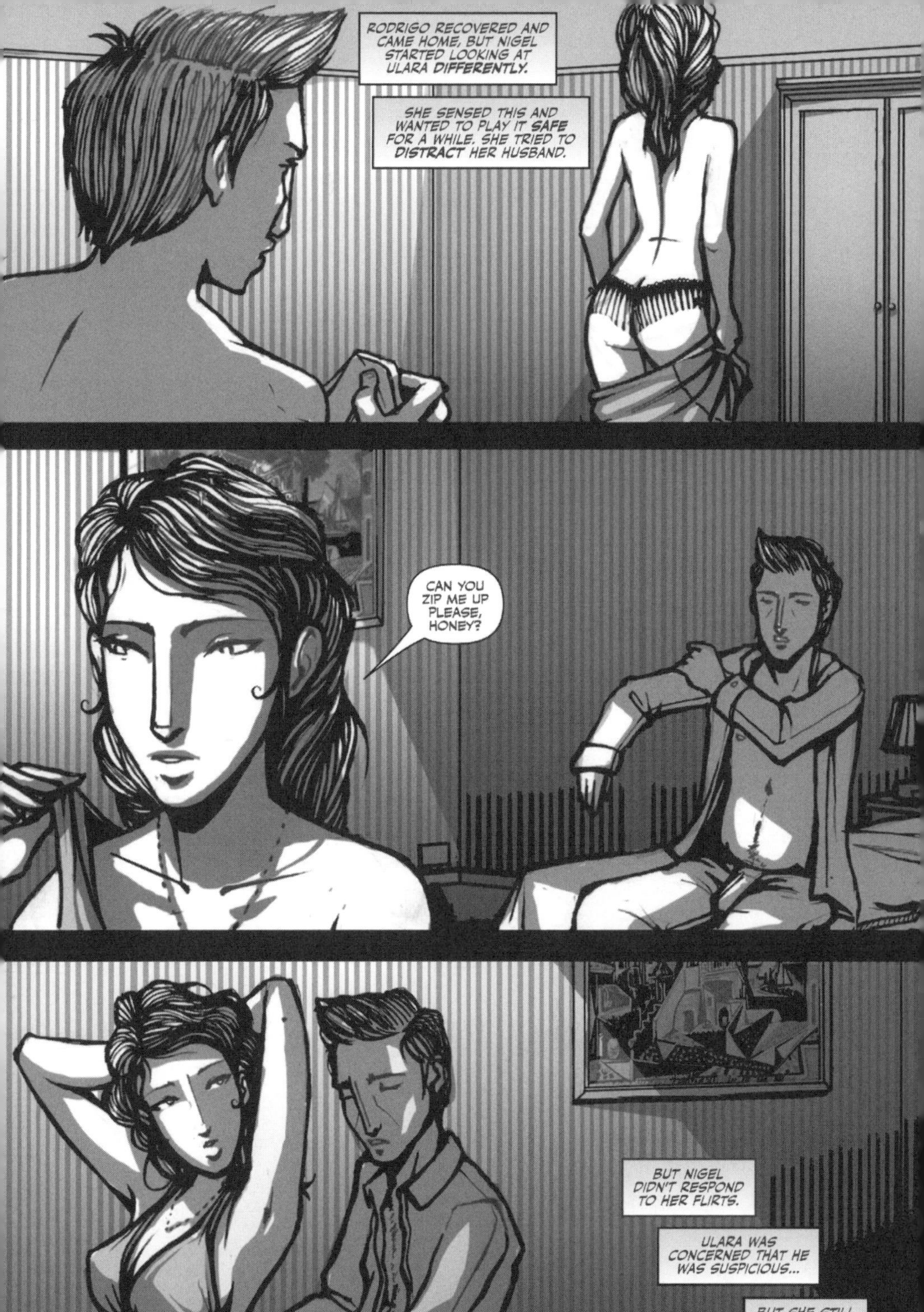
RODRIGO RECOVERED AND CAME HOME, BUT NIGEL STARTED LOOKING AT ULARA **DIFFERENTLY.**
SHE SENSED THIS AND WANTED TO PLAY IT **SAFE** FOR A WHILE. SHE TRIED TO **DISTRACT** HER HUSBAND.
CAN YOU ZIP ME UP PLEASE, HONEY?
BUT NIGEL DIDN'T RESPOND TO HER FLIRTS.
ULARA WAS CONCERNED THAT HE WAS SUSPICIOUS...
BUT SHE STILL NEEDED HER NEXT FIX.

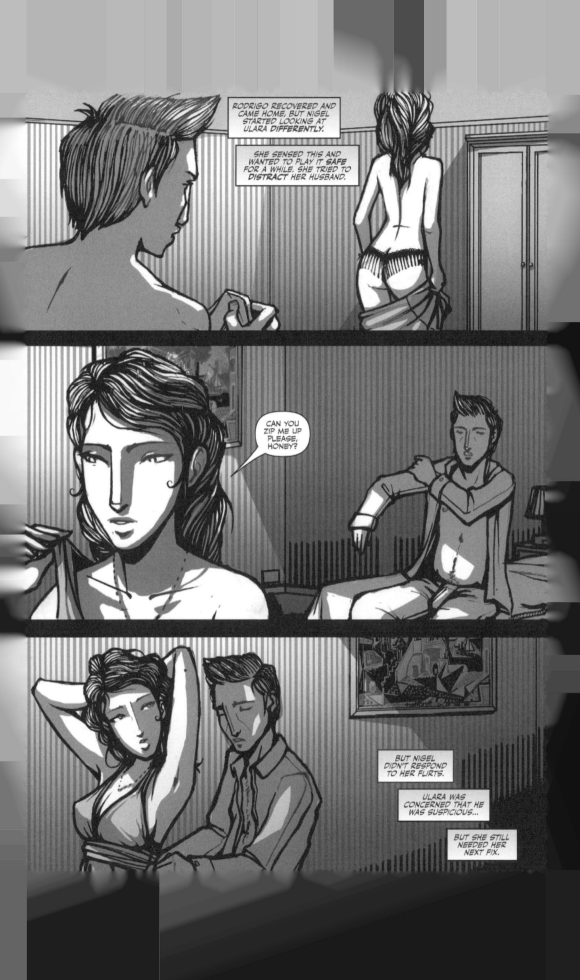

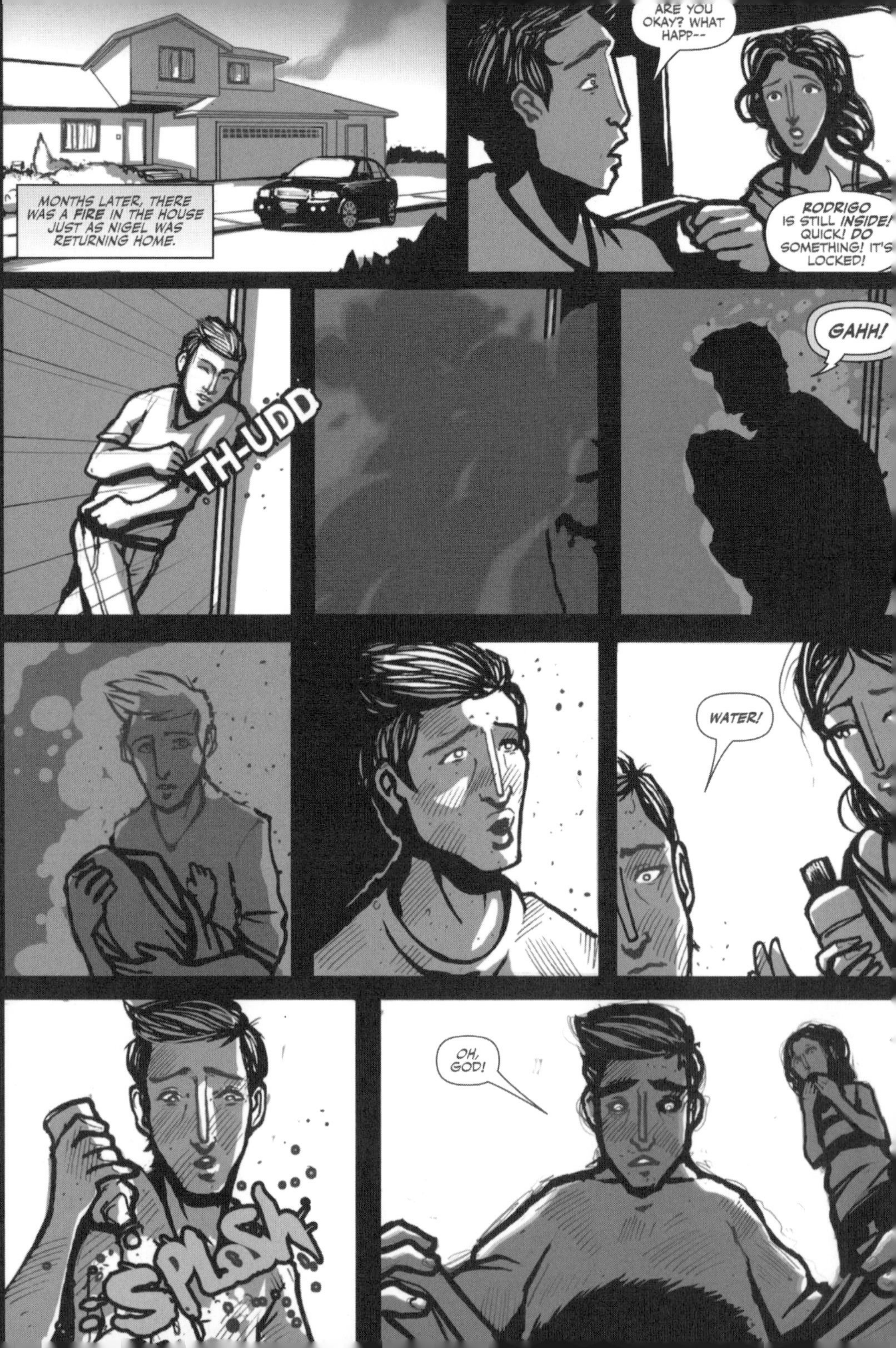
MONTHS LATER, THERE WAS A FIRE IN THE HOUSE JUST AS NIGEL WAS RETURNING HOME.
ARE YOU OKAY? WHAT HAPP--
RODRIGO IS STILL INSIDE! QUICK! DO SOMETHING! IT'S LOCKED!
TH-UDD
GAHH!
WATER!
SPLOSH
OH, GOD!

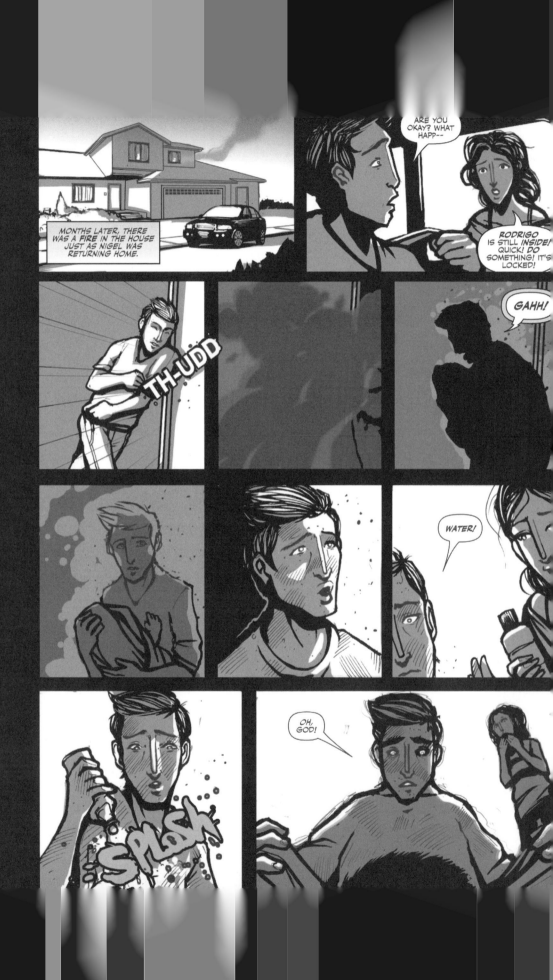

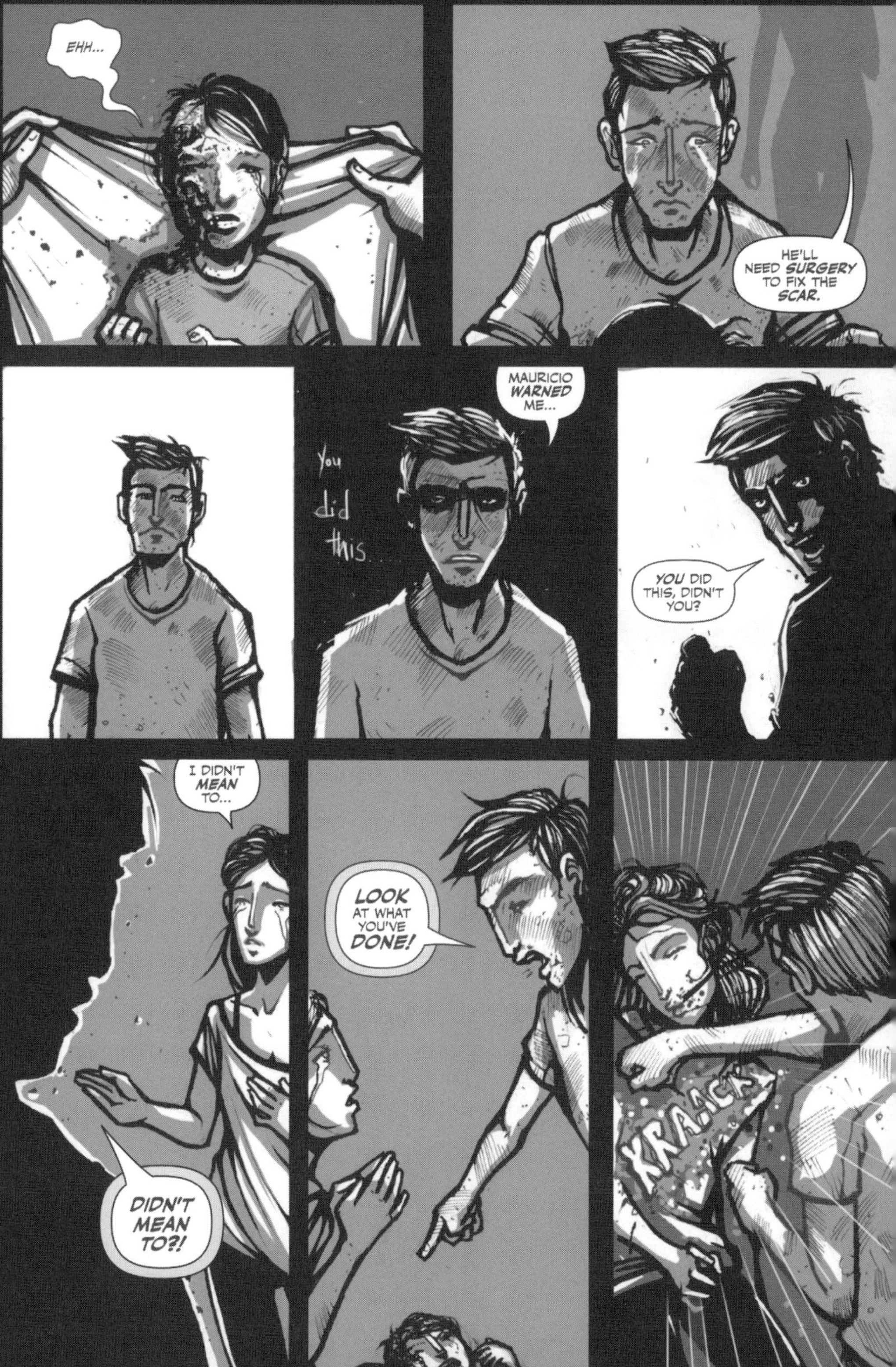
EHH...
HE'LL NEED SURGERY TO FIX THE SCAR.
MAURICIO WARNED ME...
You did this...
YOU DID THIS, DIDN'T YOU?
I DIDN'T MEAN TO...
DIDN'T MEAN TO?!
LOOK AT WHAT YOU'VE DONE!
KRAACK

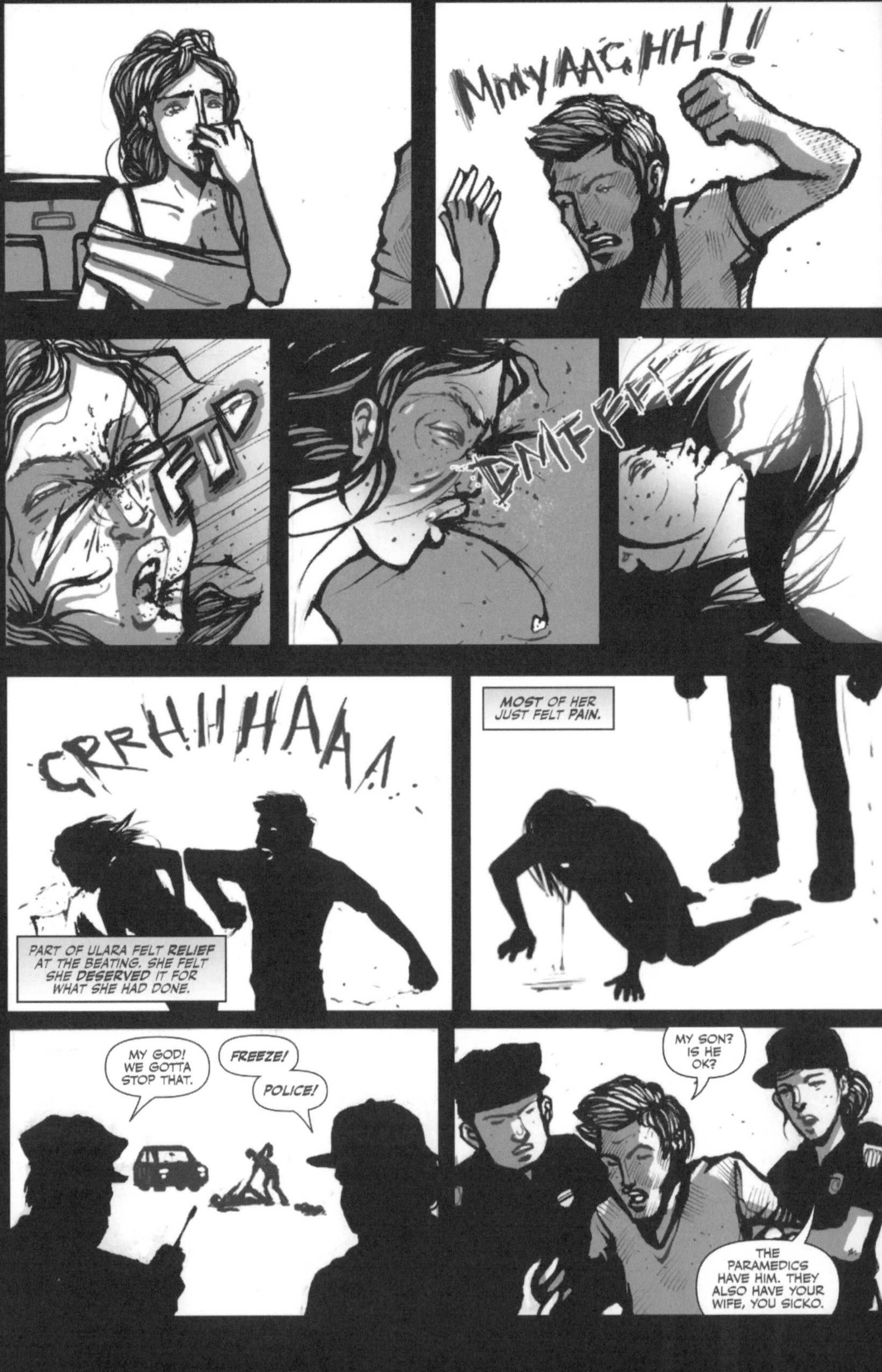
MMYAACHH!!
FUD
DMFFFF
CRRHHHAAA
PART OF ULARA FELT RELIEF AT THE BEATING. SHE FELT SHE DESERVED IT FOR WHAT SHE HAD DONE.
MOST OF HER JUST FELT PAIN.
MY GOD! WE GOTTA STOP THAT.
FREEZE!
POLICE!
MY SON? IS HE OK?
THE PARAMEDICS HAVE HIM. THEY ALSO HAVE YOUR WIFE, YOU SICKO.

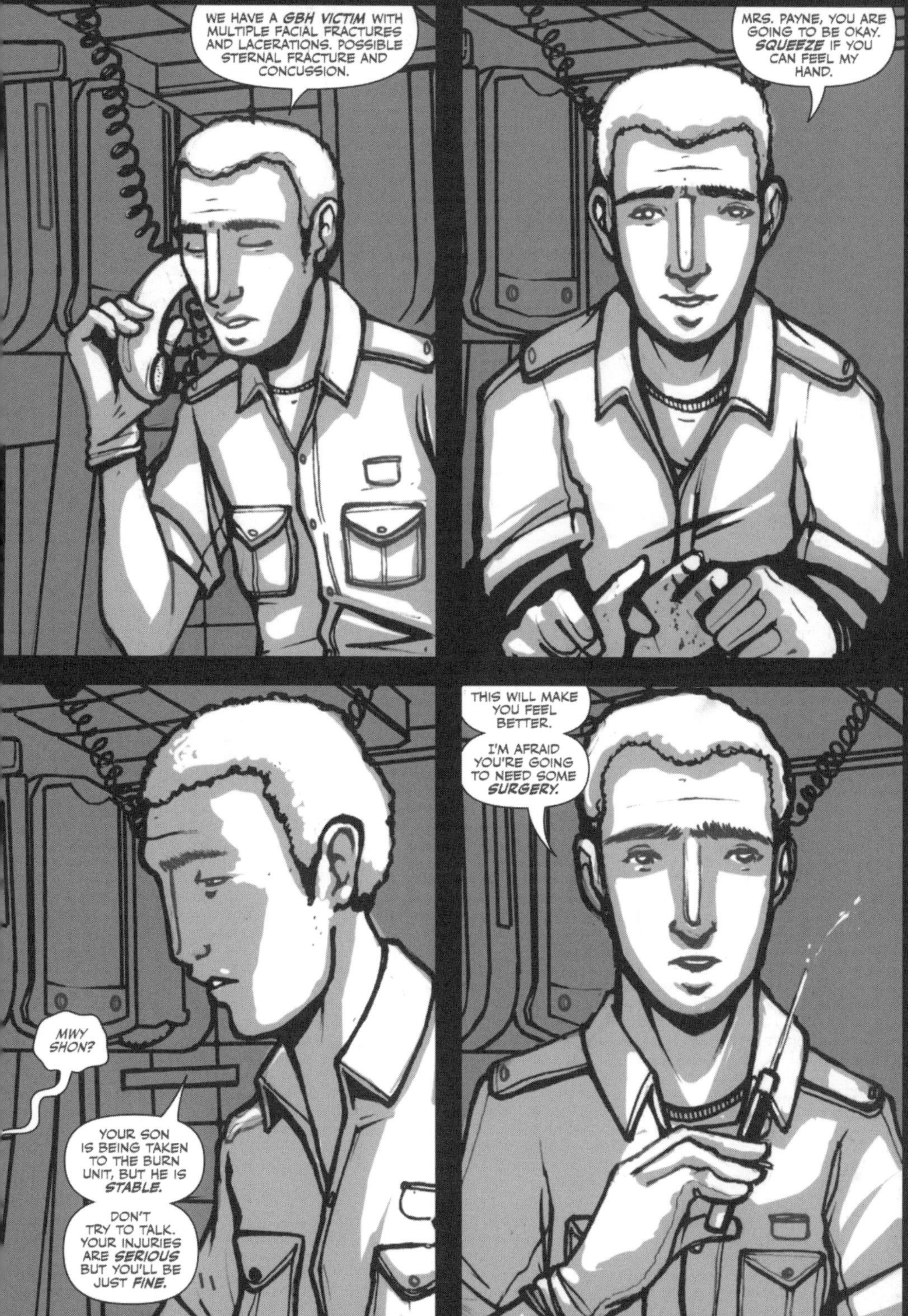
WE HAVE A GBH VICTIM WITH MULTIPLE FACIAL FRACTURES AND LACERATIONS. POSSIBLE STERNAL FRACTURE AND CONCUSSION.
MRS. PAYNE, YOU ARE GOING TO BE OKAY. SQUEEZE IF YOU CAN FEEL MY HAND.
MWY SHON?
YOUR SON IS BEING TAKEN TO THE BURN UNIT, BUT HE IS STABLE.
DON'T TRY TO TALK. YOUR INJURIES ARE SERIOUS BUT YOU'LL BE JUST FINE.
THIS WILL MAKE YOU FEEL BETTER.
I'M AFRAID YOU'RE GOING TO NEED SOME SURGERY.

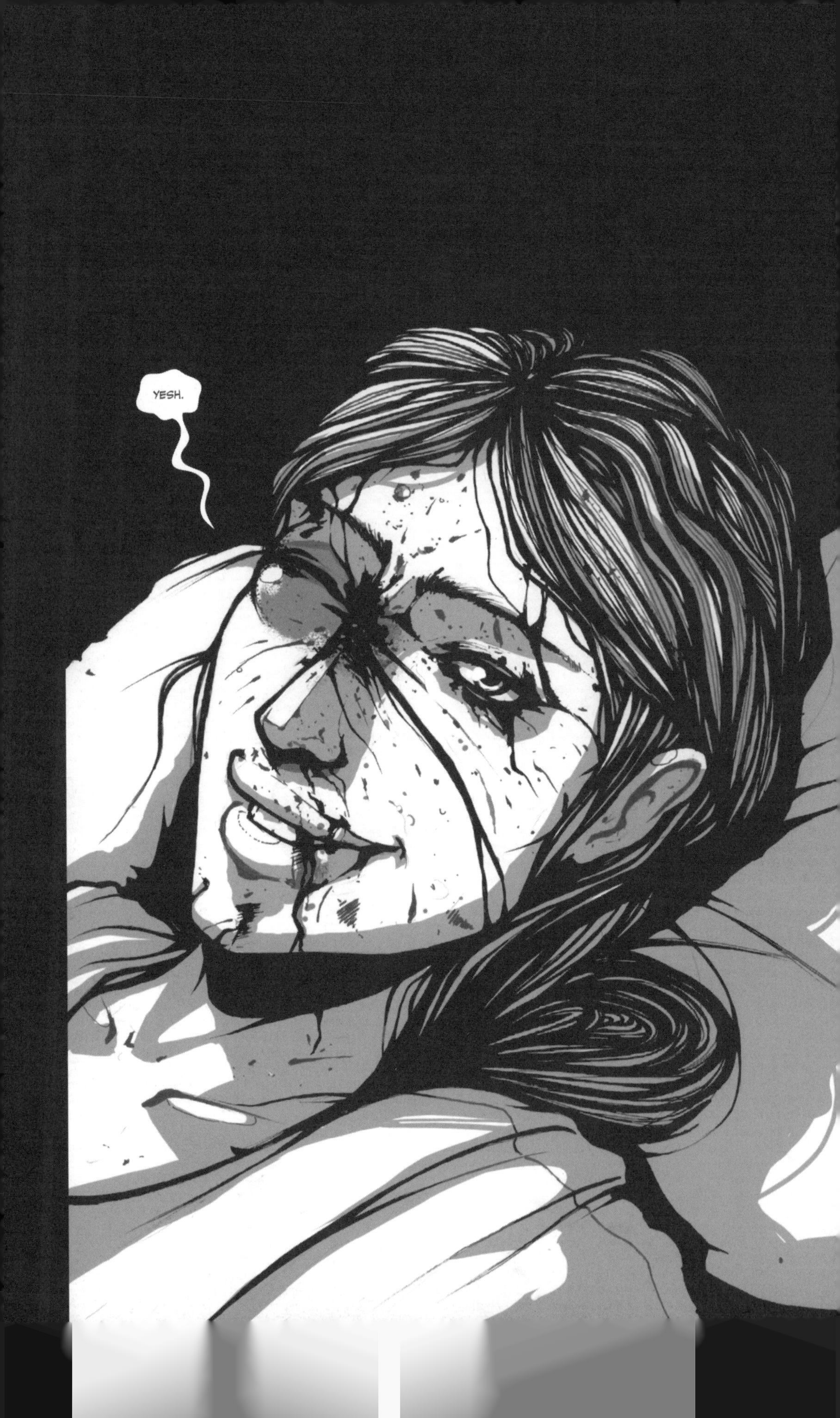
YESH.

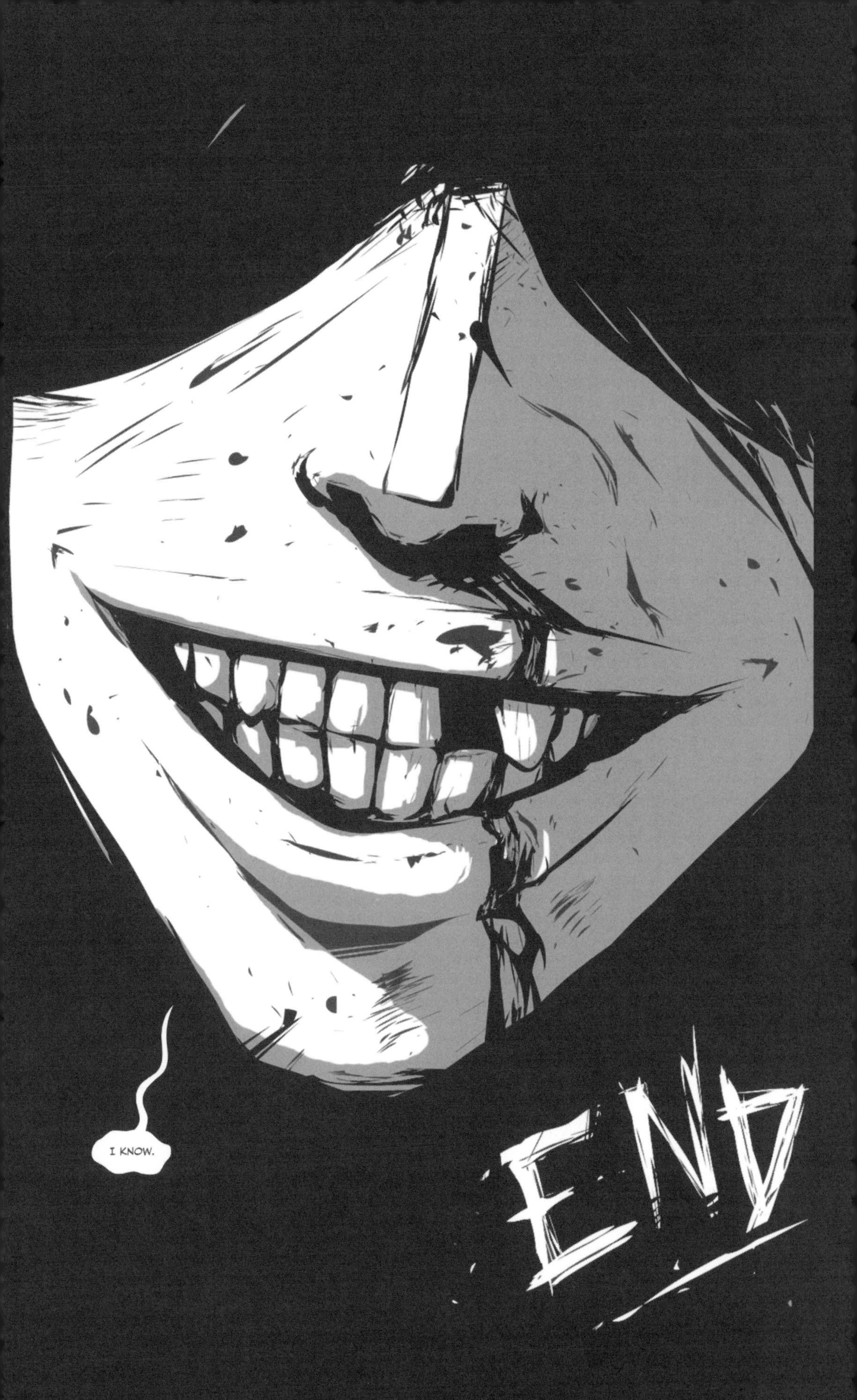
I KNOW.
END

The Last Laugh...

"Nothing shows a man's character more than what he laughs at."

--Johan Wolfgang Von Goethe

Writer/Creator
Neil Gibson

Illustrator
Dan West

www.tpub.co.uk

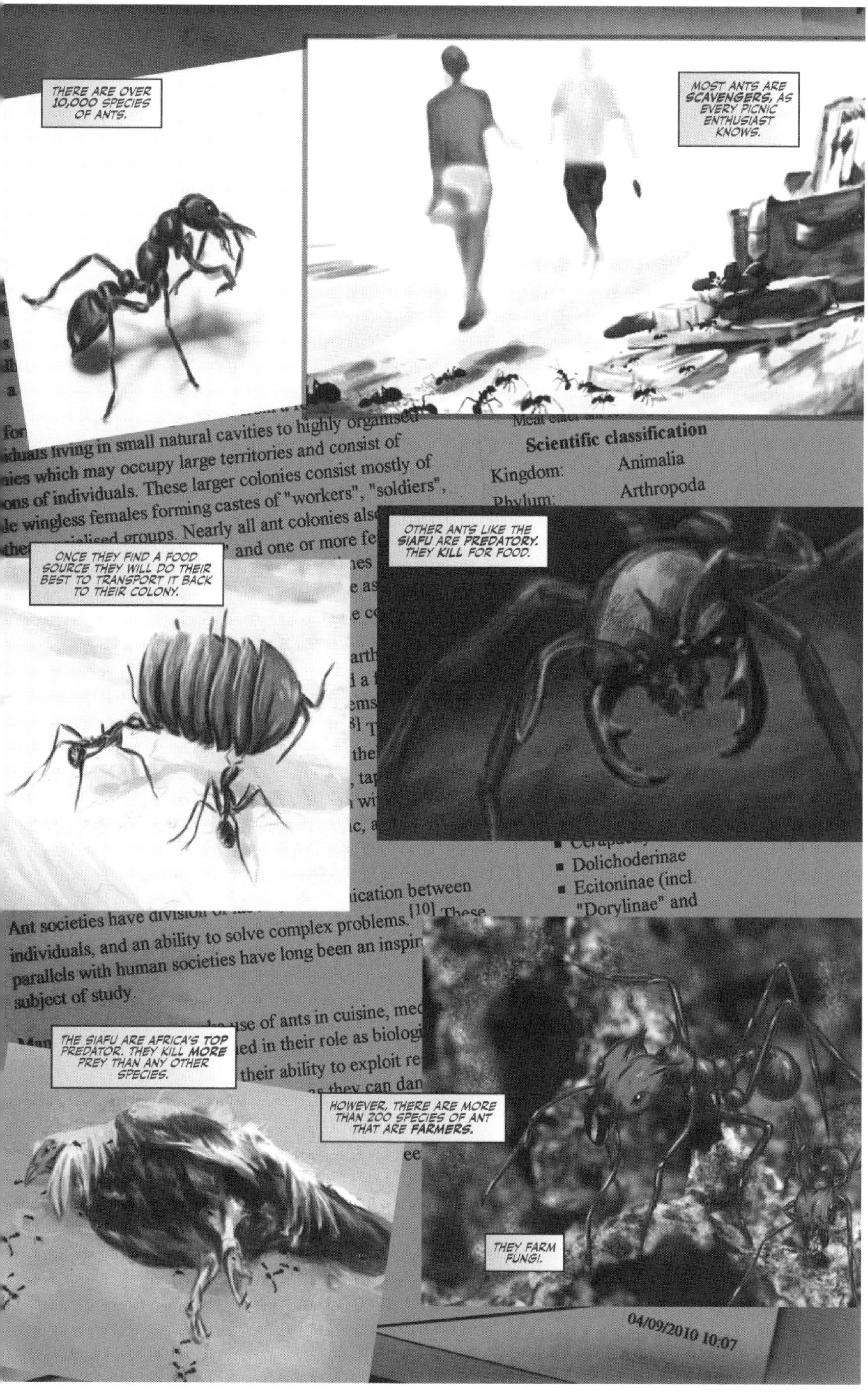
THERE ARE OVER 10,000 SPECIES OF ANTS.
MOST ANTS ARE SCAVENGERS, AS EVERY PICNIC ENTHUSIAST KNOWS.
ONCE THEY FIND A FOOD SOURCE THEY WILL DO THEIR BEST TO TRANSPORT IT BACK TO THEIR COLONY.
OTHER ANTS LIKE THE SIAFU ARE PREDATORY. THEY KILL FOR FOOD.
THE SIAFU ARE AFRICA'S TOP PREDATOR. THEY KILL MORE PREY THAN ANY OTHER SPECIES.
HOWEVER, THERE ARE MORE THAN 200 SPECIES OF ANT THAT ARE FARMERS.
THEY FARM FUNGI.
04/09/2010 10:07

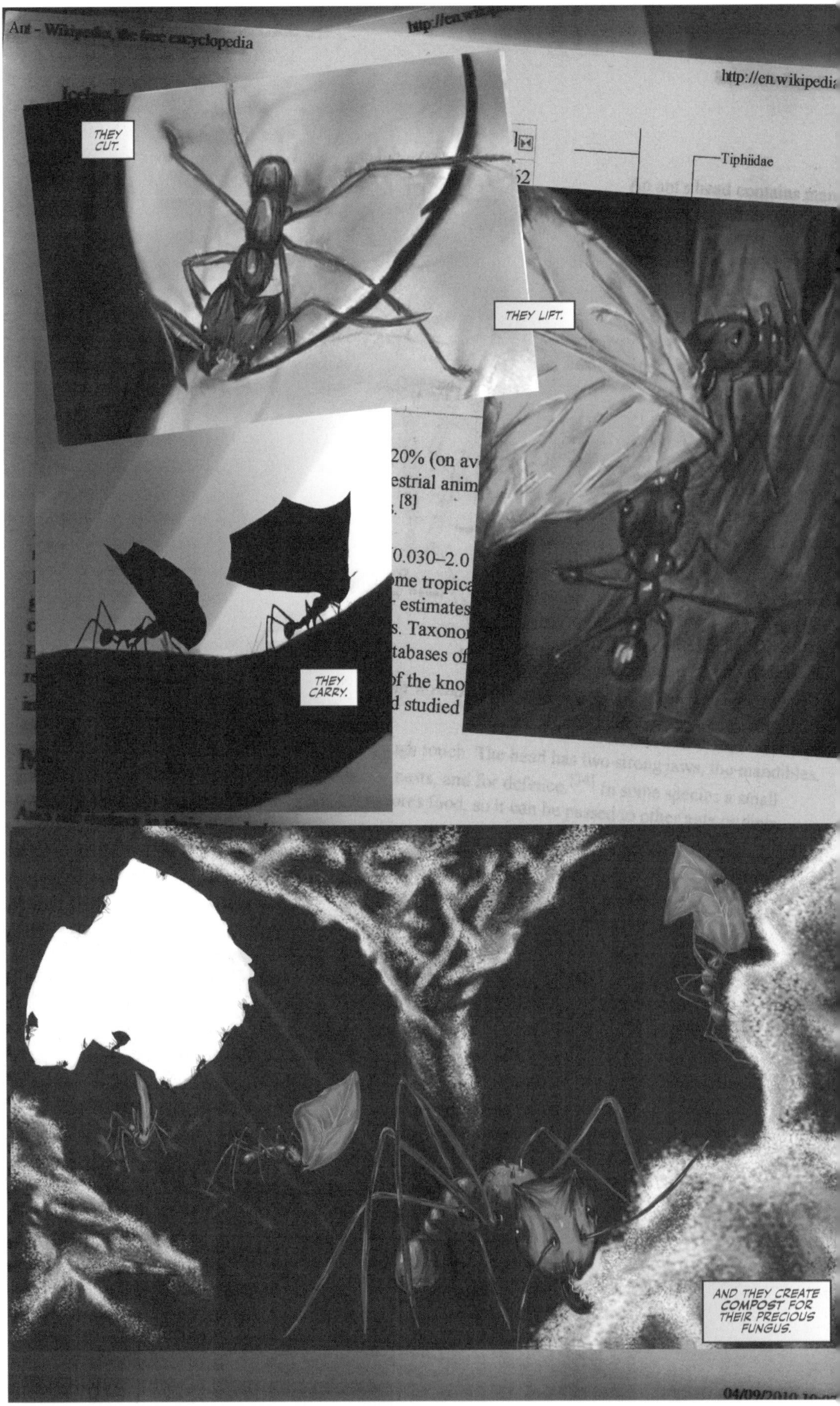
THEY CUT.
THEY LIFT.
THEY CARRY.
AND THEY CREATE COMPOST FOR THEIR PRECIOUS FUNGUS.

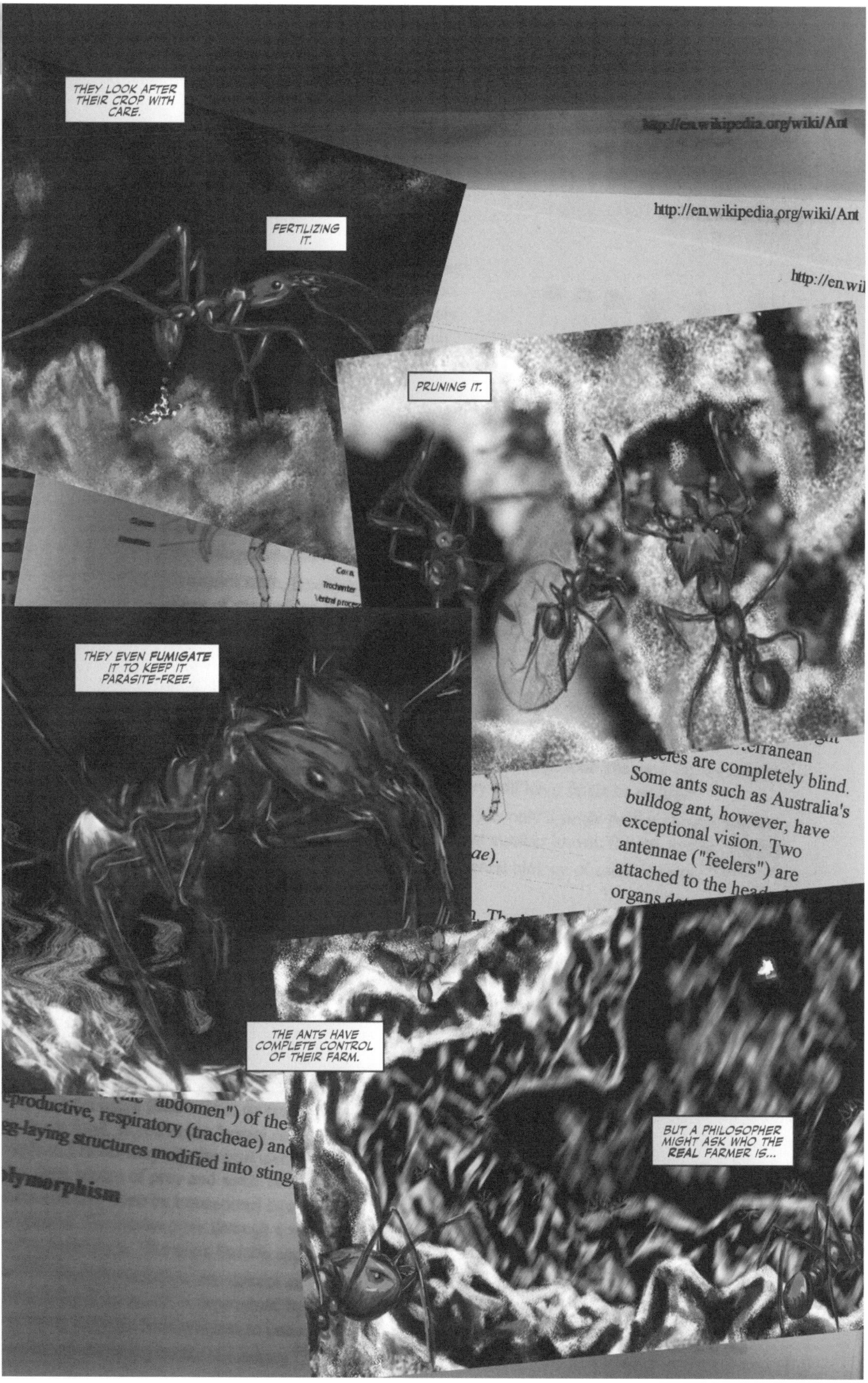
THEY LOOK AFTER THEIR CROP WITH CARE.
http://en.wikipedia.org/wiki/Ant
http://en.wikipedia.org/wiki/Ant
FERTILIZING IT.
PRUNING IT.
THEY EVEN FUMIGATE IT TO KEEP IT PARASITE-FREE.
species are completely blind. Some ants such as Australia's bulldog ant, however, have exceptional vision. Two antennae ("feelers") are attached to the head
THE ANTS HAVE COMPLETE CONTROL OF THEIR FARM.
eproductive, respiratory (tracheae) and
gg-laying structures modified into sting
lymorphism
BUT A PHILOSOPHER MIGHT ASK WHO THE REAL FARMER IS...

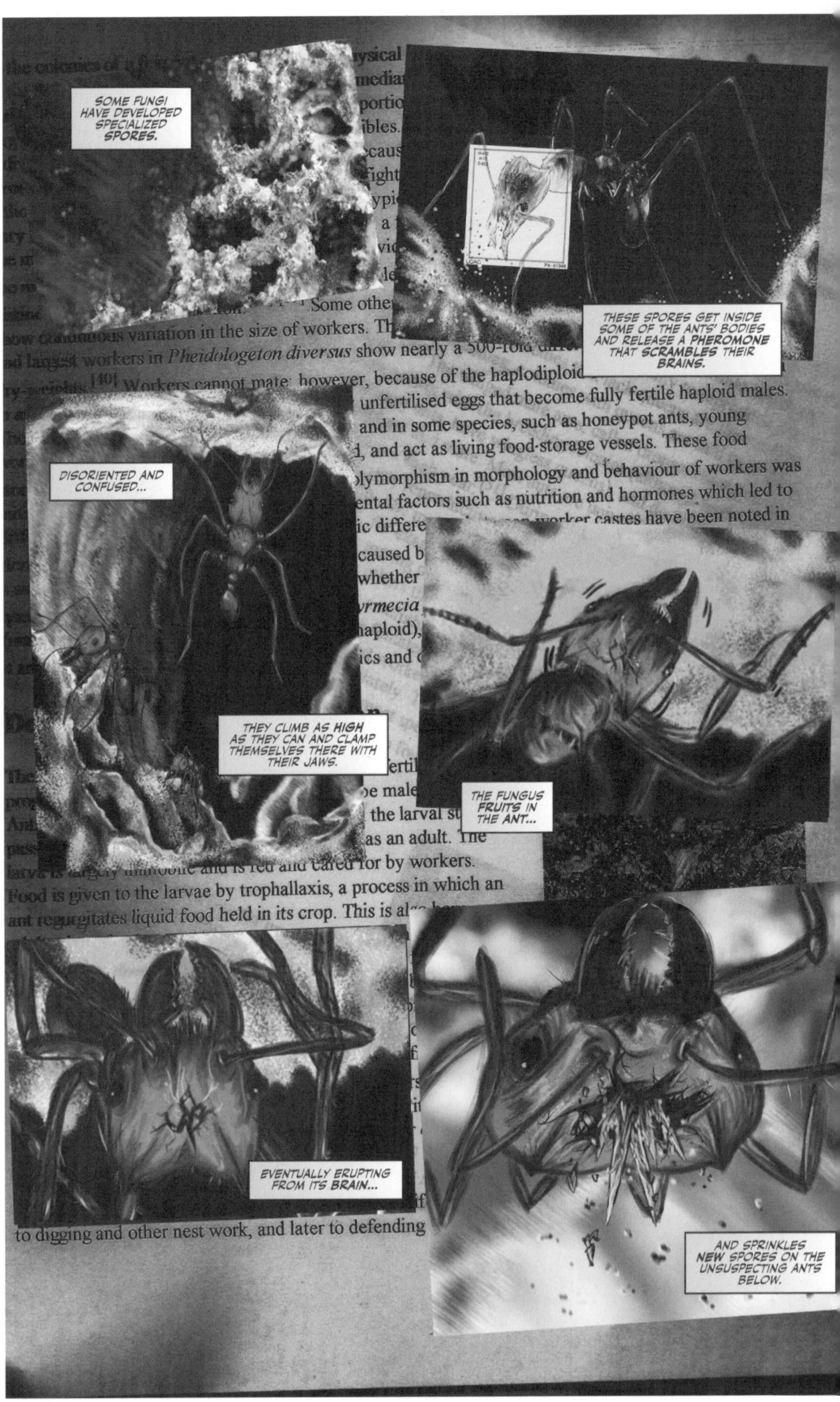
SOME FUNGI HAVE DEVELOPED SPECIALIZED SPORES.
THESE SPORES GET INSIDE SOME OF THE ANTS' BODIES AND RELEASE A PHEROMONE THAT SCRAMBLES THEIR BRAINS.
DISORIENTED AND CONFUSED...
THEY CLIMB AS HIGH AS THEY CAN AND CLAMP THEMSELVES THERE WITH THEIR JAWS.
THE FUNGUS FRUITS IN THE ANT...
EVENTUALLY ERUPTING FROM ITS BRAIN...
AND SPRINKLES NEW SPORES ON THE UNSUSPECTING ANTS BELOW.

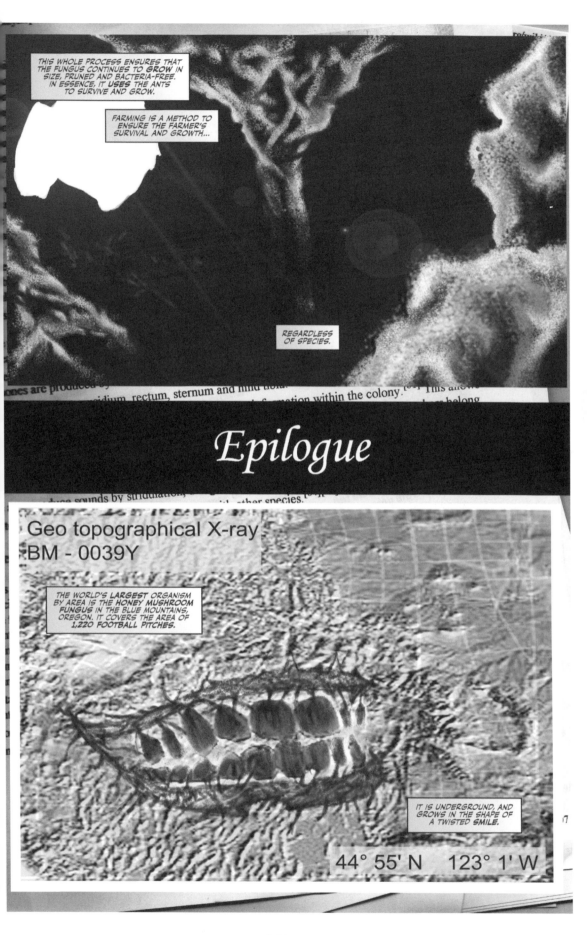

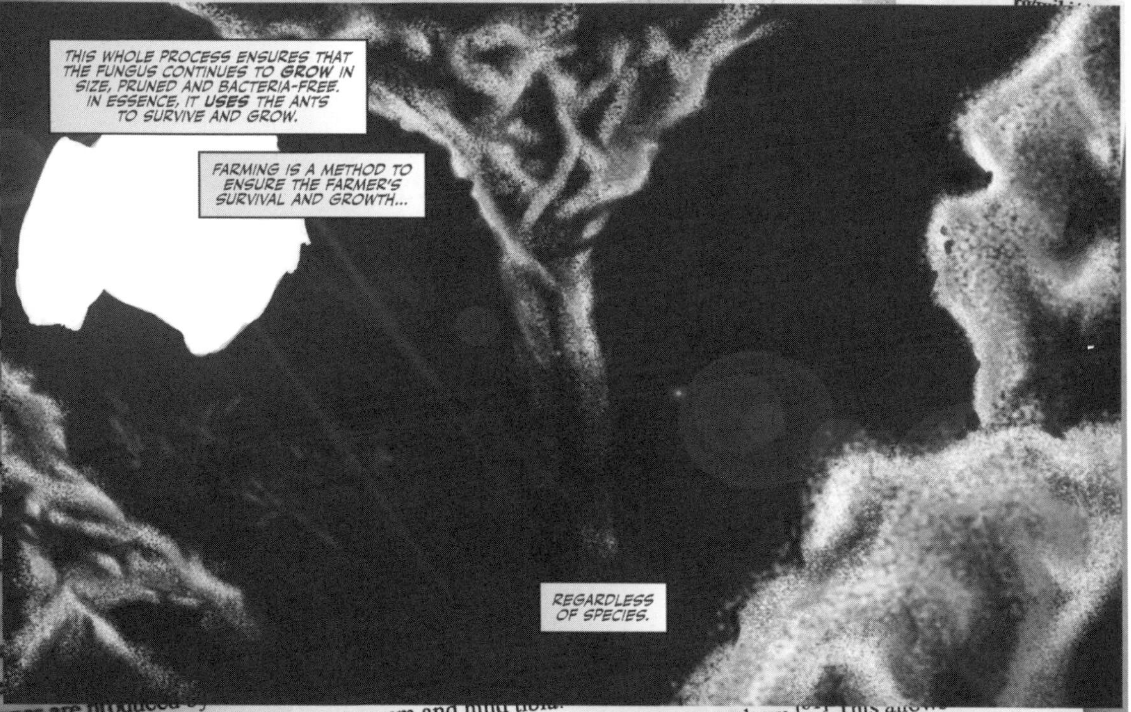
THIS WHOLE PROCESS ENSURES THAT THE FUNGUS CONTINUES TO GROW IN SIZE, PRUNED AND BACTERIA-FREE. IN ESSENCE, IT USES THE ANTS TO SURVIVE AND GROW.
FARMING IS A METHOD TO ENSURE THE FARMER'S SURVIVAL AND GROWTH...
REGARDLESS OF SPECIES.

Epilogue

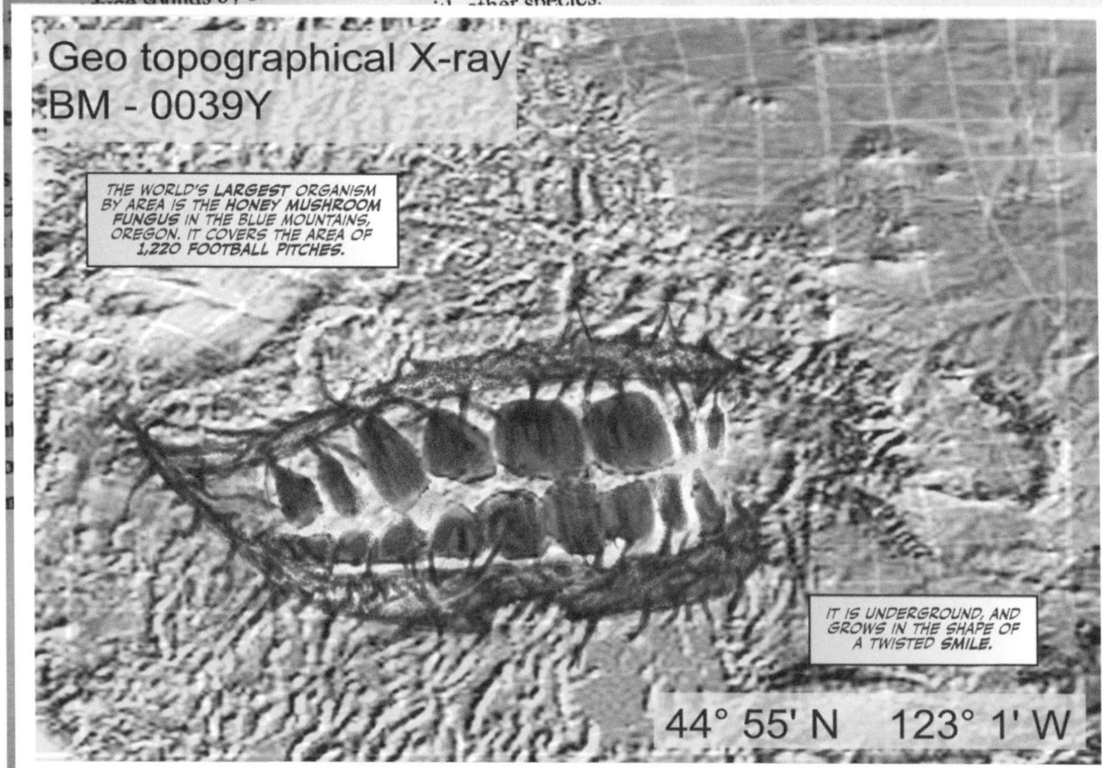
Geo topographical X-ray
BM - 0039Y
THE WORLD'S LARGEST ORGANISM BY AREA IS THE HONEY MUSHROOM FUNGUS IN THE BLUE MOUNTAINS, OREGON. IT COVERS THE AREA OF 1,220 FOOTBALL PITCHES.
IT IS UNDERGROUND, AND GROWS IN THE SHAPE OF A TWISTED SMILE.
44° 55' N 123° 1' W

Thanks for reading the first volume of Twisted Dark. We hope you enjoyed it.

To see more from the TPub team, head over to our website where you can read some free samples and hear about all the other great titles we have on offer.

If you are cool and trendy, you already like us on Facebook and follow us on Twitter, getting to see al kinds of bonus material. If you really want us to like you, feel free to tweet about us, using #tpublicationss.

When you promote us, not olny will we be able to keep making comics for you, but also fewer people will confuse Neil Gibson with Mel Gibson–that's a win-win!

www.tpub.co.uk
www.facebook.com/tpublications
@TPublications

Continue the journey into Neil's twisted universe...

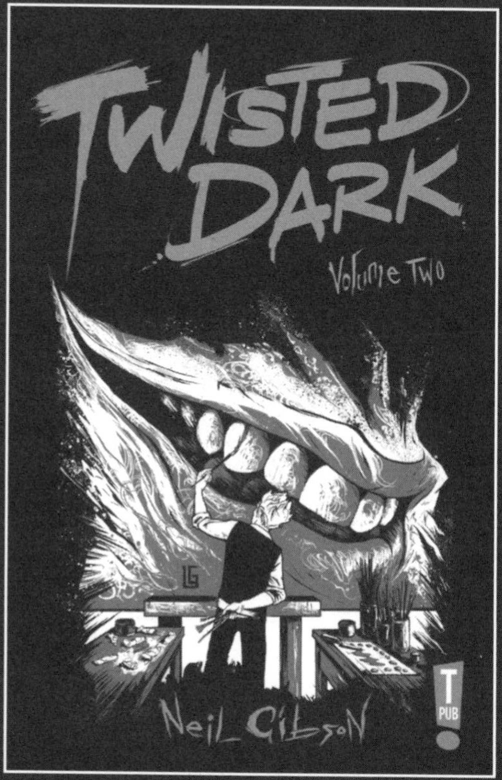
TWISTED DARK
Volume Two
Neil Gibson
T PUB

Twisted Dark Volume two
available November 2014

Other Titles from T Pub

Volume 1

Volume 2

Volume 3

Volume 4

Volume 5

Volume 6

Twisted Light

The World of
Chub Chub

Tortured Life

Tabatha

More titles
coming soon...